OFFICE PRACTICE
Made Simple

The Made Simple series
has been created
primarily for self-education
but can equally well
be used as
an aid to group study.
However complex the subject,
the reader is taken
step by step,
clearly and methodically,
through the course. Each volume
has been prepared by experts,
taking account of
modern educational requirements,
to ensure the most
effective way of
acquiring knowledge.

In the same series

OFFICE PRACTICE Made Simple

Geoffrey Whitehead, BSc (Econ)

MADE SIMPLE
BOOKS

HEINEMANN : London

© Geoffrey Whitehead, 1973

Made and printed in Great Britain
by Richard Clay Ltd, Bungay, Suffolk
Filmset by Northumberland Press Ltd, Gateshead, Tyne and Wear
for the publishers William Heinemann Ltd,
10 Upper Grosvenor Street, London W1X 9PA

First edition 1973
Reprinted 1974
Second edition 1976
Third (enlarged) edition 1977
Fourth (enlarged) edition 1979
Reprinted (with revisions) 1981
Fifth edition 1982
Reprinted 1987

ISBN 0 434 98458 2

Preface

This book explains and illustrates the principles of office organisation. It is designed as basic reading material for all those who propose to take up a career involving clerical duties, office management or as self-employed persons in small businesses. It will be found equally helpful to school or college students preparing for examinations in the field of Office Practice or Clerical Duties; to experienced personnel considering promotion prospects; to office managers reviewing organisation and to small businessmen considering the next stage in the expansion of their enterprises.

The book is particularly directed at students preparing for the examinations of public bodies in Office Practice and Clerical Duties. It will appeal to pupils in schools taking the Certificate of Secondary Education; to college students on the Scotbec Certificate of Office Studies course and those taking Office Practice based on the syllabuses of the recognised commercial education bodies, such as the Royal Society of Arts and the London Chamber of Commerce and Industry. It covers all the Office Practice requirements of the BEC General Course 'The World at Work'.

Many features have been included which will be of great assistance to teachers, in particular the large number of diagrams and illustrations, including a large number of photographs. The 'Rapid Revision' pages, which have proved so useful to students in my other *Made Simple* titles, will be found here also: they form both a summary and a self-teaching and self-testing device of the subject matter in each chapter. Teachers will discover too, that the many exercises cover the full range of the syllabuses mentioned, and provide numerous opportunities for them to amplify and expand the text in the light of their experience.

The field of Office Practice is enormous, and it is impossible to include in a single volume illustrations of every device designed to promote office efficiency. I have tried, therefore, to provide a balanced selection of equipment from the wealth of material available, and urge those seeking a completely comprehensive display to visit the trade exhibitions, such as the International Business Show held in Birmingham.

Over the years since this book first appeared I have had to acknowledge the help of many organisations and individuals. With changes occurring so frequently in machines and documents the list has become so long that lack of space prohibits detailed mention of individuals. The organisations who have supplied photographs, diagrams, etc., are acknowledged in the book where the illustrations appear. To those individuals who have kindly assisted may I express my sincere thanks.

G.W.

Preface to the Fifth Edition

The need to re-set this book completely has provided an opportunity to revise the text extensively, and to include some of the developments resulting from microchip technology in the telecommunication, type-writing, word-processing and accounting fields. Refinements in export documentation have also been covered. I am indebted to firms and individuals for their cooperation in providing illustrations and factual information incorporated in the text.

Geoffrey Whitehead
February, 1982

Other Made Simple books by the same author
Book-keeping
Business and Administrative Organisation
Business Economics (with Ken Hoyle)
Business Statistics and Accounting (with Ken Hoyle)
Commerce
Economics
Money and Banking (with Ken Hoyle)
Secretarial Practice
Transport and Distribution (with Don Benson)

From Croner Publications Ltd, New Malden, Surrey
Elements of Overseas Trade

From George Vyner Ltd, Mytholmbridge Mills, Huddersfield
Simplified Book-keeping for Small Businesses
The Simplex Club Accounts Book
The Teachers' Series of Record Books (for Lesson Preparation, etc.)
Working for Yourself is *also* a Career
Choosing Options for your Future in the World of Work

From Shaw & Sons Ltd, Lower Sydenham
Test Yourself on the Highway Code
Ridley's Law of Carriage of Goods by Land, Sea and Air (Editor)

Contents

1

THE WORLD OF WORK

1.1 The Nature of the Working World

We live in a world where everyone 'wants' things. Babies cry for milk, warmth and protection. Teenagers demand trendy clothes, the latest 'hit' records, driving licences and interesting textbooks. Old-age pensioners 'want' tasty food, television sets, geriatric wards and pain-killing drugs. It is the working world that supplies these things, satisfying the wants of millions of people by the production of goods and services. An endless flood of cornflakes, biscuits, loaves of bread, clothing, footwear, furniture and other goods pours from the production lines to be packaged, boxed, warehoused, transported and delivered to customers in every corner of the globe. Other businesses are at work providing services. Electricity generating stations are busy day and night generating power for homes, factories and transport systems. Surgeons are on duty round the clock for emergency cases. Soldiers guard our frontiers because we 'want' peace. Police patrol our streets to bring security.

All this activity can be described in five words: organisation, production, distribution, exchange and consumption. Someone has to set up a basic organisation for each good or service required; these organisations begin to produce the goods or services, then they have to be distributed (if they are goods) or we have to move to them if they are services (like hospital or dental services). At some point we buy the goods, or pay for the services—this is called 'exchange'. Then we enjoy them, which is called 'consumption'. Of course, the word 'consumption' in general use means 'to eat' and we certainly do eat many of the goods we buy, but the consumer also consumes the clothes he wears, the car he drives, the shelter he lives in, etc. A complete picture of the whole process requires only two more words: 'wants' to describe the causes of this immense hive of activity, and 'satisfactions' to describe the results which it achieves. The pattern of the entire working world can therefore be described in brief as:

'WANTS' → ORGANISATION → PRODUCTION → DISTRIBUTION
→ EXCHANGE → CONSUMPTION → SATISFACTION

Of course, as soon as we have consumed one meal we start to think about the next, and the whole process has to start all over again. There

The cycle of production from 'wants' through production and consumption back to 'wants' again.

CONSUMPTION

RESTART HERE

START HERE

'WANTS'

Consumption destroys production and we are back to 4,000 million people throughout the world who want things.

There are 4,000 million people in the world; you could stand them all comfortably on the Greater London Area. All of them 'want' things, food, clothing, shelter, etc.

Mankind in the everyday business of life

EXCHANGE

ORGANISATION

Out step enterprising individuals who set up organisations like sole traders, partnerships, companies, etc.

A marketing system enables us to obtain the goods and services we need.

The goods and services are made available in all areas.

They combine land, labour and capital (the factors of production) to achieve outputs of consumer goods and services.

DISTRIBUTION

PRODUCTION

Fig. 1.1. The cycle of production.

is therefore an endless cycle of production, consumption; production, consumption; production, consumption. This cycle is shown in Fig. 1.1.

1.2 Why are Organisations Formed?

Organisations are formed to provide the goods and services mankind needs. Some of the things we need do not spring to mind straight away. Unlike food, water, clothing and shelter which we need every day of our lives, we only get born once, we only die once, and most people only get married once. The maternity services that help us into the world, the registrar or other appointed person who marries us and the undertakers who lay us finally to rest are not the sort of organisations we need every day.

Although few of us ever go to court, the legal services are there for those who require them; if we travel abroad the passport office will help us make the necessary arrangements; while the Inland Revenue Department collects taxes from the rich to help the poor, like some modern Robin Hood. We don't think how important this is until we strike hard times and turn to our well-organised Department of Health and Social Security for assistance. What a relief it is then to find that they have money available; shelter for the homeless; food for the hungry; wheelchairs for the disabled, etc.

If we list therefore the various reasons why organisations come into existence we find the following main causes:

(*a*) The production of goods for personal consumption (consumer goods).
(*b*) The production of capital assets (often called producer goods), such as factories, tools, machinery, office equipment, heavy motor vehicles, etc., to help the production process.
(*c*) The provision of personal services, such as education, medical and dental care, hairdressing, entertainment, etc.
(*d*) The provision of commercial services, such as banking, insurance, transport and communication.
(*e*) The provision of protective services, including defence, police, fire and rescue services.
(*f*) To legislate: Parliament and local government bodies.
(*g*) The provision of administrative services, such as taxation, Customs and Excise, social security, licensing and control services of all sorts.
(*h*) To administer justice; the Courts system and the prison and related services.

We should note, though, that there is a limit to the wealth that can be created, and therefore each of the types of organisation listed above must operate as efficiently as possible. *In our economic activities the aim is to create the greatest output of useful goods and services from the smallest possible input of resources, for resources are scarce and we try to avoid wasting them.*

1.3 The Private and Public Sectors of the Economy

In all countries some degree of private enterprise is found and some measure of public enterprise is bound to exist too. These two sections of the economy are usually called 'sectors', or parts of a circle. The whole wealth of goods and services of our nation is looked upon as a large round cake, cut into two large portions, one part produced by the **private sector** (business firms) and the other part produced by the **public sector**—local and central government departments.

In a mixed economy like the United Kingdom, then, we have a complex pattern of organisations producing the goods and services we need. The pattern is constantly changing but in general the production of goods and commercial services tends to be performed by *private sector business organisations*, though some goods like coal, gas and electric power are produced by nationalised industries. Services such as education, medical care, broadcasting and television are largely provided by *public sector organisations*, although there is an Independent Broadcasting Authority. Organisations range from one-person businesses (sole traders) to huge organisations with thousands of employees. The largest organisation ever to exist in the United Kingdom was the British Transport Commission, set up under the *1947 Transport Act*, which nationalised the transport industry. It had 900 000 employees. Not surprisingly it was so unwieldy that it had to be broken up into separate organisations for road, rail and waterway transport.

If we list the types of organisation in the United Kingdom we find them to consist of three main types: private-enterprise units, non-profit-making units such as clubs and Co-operative Societies, and public enterprises. The list is as follows:

Private Enterprises
  Sole traders
  General partnerships
  Limited partnerships
  Private limited companies
  Public limited companies
  Holding companies (a more advanced type of public company)

Non-Profit-Making Units
  Clubs of many types
  Co-operative Societies

Public Enterprises
  Autonomous corporations
  Quasi-autonomous national government organisations (QUANGOS)
  Nationalised undertakings
  Local government departments
  Central Government departments

These are the organisations in which we all work. We may set up a business of our own, and become a sole trader. There are more than one million sole traders in the United Kingdom. We may take employment with a large company. There are about 2500 really large companies, some of them so large that they handle every year more wealth than whole nations like the developing countries of Africa or Asia. We may join an autonomous corporation, like the Port of London Authority, or work for a Government department like the Department of the Environment. Whether we choose the private sector or the public sector we shall be providing the goods and services needed, and in return we shall receive a share of the nation's output, so that we are fed, clothed, sheltered, educated, entertained, cured when we are ill and finally buried when we die.

1.4 The Pattern of the Working World in a Mixed Economy

In the mixed economy the pattern of business organisations is therefore as follows:

(*a*) A very large number of small business units, mainly organised as sole trader or partnership enterprises. Frequently they will have employees, but not many, the sole trader or partners playing a leading role and making the crucial business decisions. A great many of these small firms are organised as private limited companies. This has certain advantages which are explained later (see Fig. 1.4) but they do not have to be large firms and many of them are only £100 companies. (This means that the authorised capital subscribed by the owners is only £100, so clearly they are only small organisations.) A recent enquiry into the needs of small firms (the Bolton Report) found that there were 1¼ million of them in the United Kingdom of which about ½ million were private companies. In manufacturing 94 per cent of firms were small (with an average of 25 employees) and in retailing 96 per cent of firms were small, with turnover of less than £1000 per week. These small firms fill the gaps between the very large firms and the huge nationalised organisations. They supply local, or specialised, services in a very wide range of industries.

(*b*) The second major group of business units is the group of large, private enterprises, limited liability companies who form the backbone of the nation's industrial and commercial power. They are not very numerous; there are, for example, only about 2500 **public limited companies**. The name 'public' company is applied to companies whose shares are quoted on the Stock Exchange, and may be sold to the general public. All such public issues have to be made in such a way that they observe the strict rules of the Stock Exchange and comply with the requirements of the *Companies Acts, 1948–81*. Although these companies are not very numerous most of them are very large. Many have over £500 000 000 capital, which contrasts greatly with the £100 companies so common in the unquoted companies mentioned in (*a*) above. In fact, the Bolton Report already referred to showed that in manufacturing the 94 per cent of small firms only did 16 per cent of the work carried out by the industry. In retailing 96 per cent of the firms were small but they had between them only 32 per cent of the turnover. Large firms did 84 per cent of manufacturing, 68 per cent of retail trade, 73 per cent of building and construction, 71 per cent of motor-vehicle production and repair work, 89 per cent of wholesaling and 80 per cent of mining and quarrying.

(*c*) The third group is a relatively small group, the **non-profit-making organisations**. The largest of these is the group of Co-operative Societies, which handle about £1300 million of trade every year. Others, like the Automobile Association, are quite large, but many clubs and societies are very small and serve to meet the needs of members for recreational purposes rather than as major businesses.

(*d*) The fourth major grouping in the mixed economy is the group of **nationalised industries and services**. In the United Kingdom these include industries like gas, electricity and atomic energy, which are completely nationalised; industries like transport, which is partly nationalised and partly free enterprise; and industries like the oil industry. With the latter the British National Oil Corporation has a 12½ per cent stake in North Sea oil, and is only in a very formative state, but as the years go by it will become an oil corporation of the very greatest importance, with huge quantities of oil to refine each year. On the non-industrial side such services as the National Health Service and the social security services are less obviously productive, but their contribution in terms of human happiness and in the relief of distress of every sort is quite incalculable. Because these industries and services are so large and are often monopolies controlling the whole industry or service, they have the capital to set up the most advanced types of organisation. Each nationalised organisation is a study in its own right, employing thousands of workers at all sorts of levels and endeavouring to achieve the very best structure possible for the industry it controls, or the service it provides.

These four groups of organisations make up the **'World of Work'**. What do they need to use when they try to produce goods or services? The answer is three things: *land*, *labour* and *capital*. They are called the **factors of production**. A full explanation of these three factors of production is really the subject matter of Economics and is given in another volume, *Economics Made Simple*. Very quickly we may list them as follows:

(*a*) **Land**. Agricultural land, business sites and premises, the minerals of the earth, the gases of the atmosphere, fossil fuels like oil and coal, forest products, animal products and the bounties of the sea. All these things are usually called **primary products**, because they were provided first by nature. Many of these products are also worked upon and improved into what we call **secondary products**. Crude oil is refined into petroleum, timber is made into furniture, iron ore is made into steel, etc. Clearly the word 'land' covers a great many things provided by nature originally.

(*b*) **Labour**. Before natural products can be turned into useful things work has usually to be performed. Some processes are very simple, like freezing garden peas. Some are more complicated, like using atomic energy to generate electricity. There are many types of skilled and unskilled labour, but all of them are necessary. The man who works a difficult machine to make a motorcar component; the girl who tests and packages it; the driver who drives it to the stores depot near your home and the man who sweeps the roads so that the lorry does not get a puncture are all doing useful work.

(*c*) **Capital**. Capital is often thought of as money, but this is only a special kind of capital, called **liquid capital**. Liquid capital is soon turned into **fixed capital**, which means buildings, machinery, tools and anything else which is used by organisations in the production process.

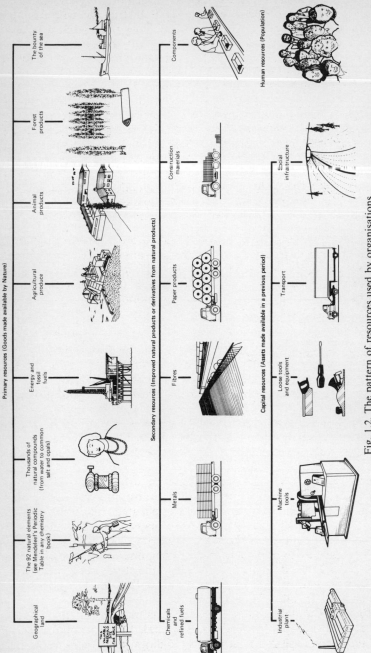

Fig. 1.2. The pattern of resources used by organisations.

These three factors of production—land, labour, and capital—are illustrated in Fig. 1.2. Study this diagram before we go on to consider how the mixed economy really works.

1.5   The World of Work Needs a Money System

One of the results of working our system of production in the way that we do is that we have to invent a 'money' system. Money makes the world go round, but it is only an instrument of human activity, not a governing force. John Stuart Mill, a famous nineteenth-century philosopher who lived in the early days of the capitalist system, was the first man to point this out. We have developed a powerful tool for creating wealth by specialisation. We do not run a simple economy, like Robinson Crusoe on his island, doing a little fishing, and then a little hunting, and then gathering shellfish. We specialise. We take a full-time job in some organisation somewhere and we keep at it. We grow skilled as a result. The tailor makes hundreds of suits a year, whereas Man Friday, and probably Robinson Crusoe too, were naked most of the time. The tailor wears one of his suits, but exchanges the rest for food, shelter, furniture, warmth, light, entertainment, personal transport. He eats out in restaurants, attends pop festivals, flies to the Mediterranean for holidays, has his teeth drilled and his appendix removed, courts his sweetheart, sets up home, educates his children, and it is all done by the money system. To ensure reasonable fair play those with secure jobs and steady incomes pay taxes to help those who have not.

As John Stuart Mill said, having created the wealth it is a matter of human policy only how we share it out. The money system is the method by which our complex society shares out wealth. How this is done is illustrated in Fig. 1.3. Before studying this diagram let us note the stages of activity which are organised by money flows.

(*a*) The factors of production—land, labour and capital—are needed to produce wealth. For the full story of this the reader should read *Economics Made Simple*.

(*b*) The owners of these factors all live in our country. Some have land, some have capital, but most of us, as Karl Marx said, have 'nothing but our labour power'.

(*c*) The owners of the factors supply them to the various organisations and receive in exchange a money reward for the use of the factor. The reward for the use of land is called 'rent'; the reward for the use of capital is called 'interest'; the reward for the use of labour is 'wages'. Any surplus over and above these rewards is called 'profit'. It goes to the owner of the business, which may mean the sole trader or the partners, or it may mean the shareholders of the company. For the public sector, and 54 per cent of British wealth-creating activity is in the public sector, the Government is the owner of the industries and

Departments, and the profit goes to the Exchequer. This is the first flow of money—from the organisations to the owners of the factors of production. Of course, the original flow of this money has to be found from somewhere. It is the capital collected by the organisations from the founders of the firms, and explains why every business needs some money capital.

(*d*) Now we all have money as a reward for using our factors, and as we have created some goods and services, we can begin to consume—but first we must pay our taxes. For most of us the system is called PAYE—Pay As You Earn. This ensures that all those who for some reason are without an income—the sick, the disabled, the unemployed—can be provided for.

(*e*) The rest of our income is now available to be spent on whatever we care to spend it on—consumption.

(*f*) If we have too much income we save it in banks. The banks then lend it:

(i) to organisations who wish to expand their business activities, or

(ii) to Government bodies who are authorised to expand services to the general public. They are also spending tax moneys of course.

(*g*) One other flow that takes place is the flow of foreign trade. Our money flows out to buy imports, and foreigners' money flows in to buy our exports. As these flows must always be made to balance (a Balance of Payments), they do not really affect the money system, but they do enrich the variety of goods we can buy and make our life much fuller and more enjoyable as a result.

(*h*) As the money flows back to the organisations, whether as payment for goods and services or as loans from the banks, they are ready to pay the next week's rewards to factors. The early Socialists used to have a slogan which said: 'We go to work, to get the cash, to buy the food, to get the strength, to go to work, to get ..., etc.' It was a protest against a tyrannical system of work, and in those days the money system was a tyranny. It is really a tyranny no longer. Instead it is an instrument of democratic policy, which alone enables the exchange of goods and services to take place in a modern advanced society. The reader should now study Fig. 1.3 and the notes below it.

1.6 Business Organisations in the Private Sector

A full description of the types of business organisations in the private sector is not appropriate in a book about office practice, and the reader should refer to *Commerce Made Simple* for a full account. It is true though that most offices deal with every type of organisation, and a preliminary comparison of the various types of business units described in Fig. 1.3 above is helpful. This is most easily studied in chart form, and Table 1.1 compares and contrasts sole traders, partnerships, limited partnerships, private limited companies and public limited companies.

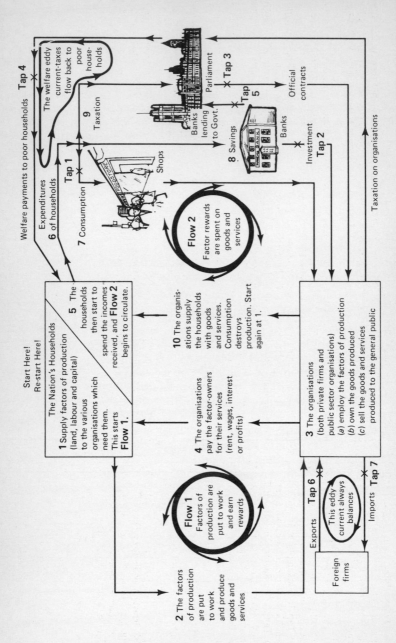

Fig. 1.3. Flows of money round the mixed economy.

Notes

(i) The first flow is of factor services into production and the payment of rewards to the factors, in the form of rent, wages, interest or profits. (Follow Flow 1 round the circle 1, 2, 3, 4: 1, 2, 3, 4, etc.)

(ii) Everything the firms receive in one period is paid out in the next period, either as rent, wages interest or profits—but there is also a very large flow of taxation to the Government which is used to finance the public sector services like defence, education, etc. In the first period these payments must come from the capital provided by those who start the firms up. In later periods the funds come from the sales of goods and services produced in the previous period.

(iii) The second flow is the expenditure of income on goods and services. The owners of the factors spend the incomes they receive. The income flows through a number of taps, which influence the level of activity in the economy. If a tap is closed off for some reason activity in the economy declines (a slump). If taps are opened wide activity in the economy increases (a boom). Let us look at each tap in turn.

(iv) Tap 1: Consumption. If the nation's households are spending a great deal on consumer goods and services business will be booming. If households are pessimistic about the future and only buying essentials, Tap 1 will be partially closed and the economy will slump.

(v) Tap 2: The Savings-Investment Tap. If savings are high consumption will be low (Tap 1 almost closed). This will not matter if the savings are borrowed by businessmen (or by the Government through Tap 5 for the public-sector borrowing requirement—PSBR). An open Tap 2 means strong investment and the economy will keep booming along.

(vi) Tap 3 and Tap 4: These taps are controlled by the government. Tap 4 (welfare payments) allows tax money to flow back to poor families so that they can consume goods and services. This opens up Tap 1 and keeps the economy booming. Tap 3 allows more official contracts for all sorts of things (defence, education, health services, highways, etc.) to be placed. This gives employment to unemployed people and keeps the economy booming. If taxes are not sufficient to pay for these contracts the Government borrows through Tap 5 the money that pessimistic households are saving for 'a rainy day' when they might lose their jobs. The Government contracts ensure that the 'rainy day' never comes.

(vii) Foreign trade always balances (the Balance of Payments) but sometimes it is a bit more difficult than others. The Government does a good deal of manipulating to keep this balance right, and sometimes has to call in the *International Monetary Fund* to overcome a difficult period. Temporarily it is possible for Taps 6 and 7 to affect the working of the economy. A wide-open Tap 6 gives an export-led boom (funds flowing in to UK firms). A wide-open Tap 7 gives an import-led slump (funds flowing out to foreign firms, leaving UK firms starved of orders). However, as explained above, neither of these situations can continue indefinitely. A Balance of Payments has to be achieved. At present we are using floating exchange rates to induce a balance.

(viii) The reader should now return to page 9, section 1.6.

Table 1.1. Comparison of

	Aspect	Sole Trader	Partnership	Limited Partnership
1	Name of firm	Any name provided it is either the proprietor's true name or their names, or a notice giving their names and addresses is displayed at premises and on letterheads, etc.		
2	How formed	By commencing business without formality except (1) above	By agreement, which may be oral or written; limited partnerships must be registered.	
3	Control of the firm	Proprietor has full control	Every partner is entitled to manage	Only the general partner(s) can manage the business
4	Liability for debts	Liability to the limits of personal wealth	Jointly and severally liable for debts to limits of personal wealth	General partners fully liable; limited partners not liable beyond the capital contributed
5	Relationship between owner and business	The business is the owner, or owners, and has no separate legal existence		The business is the same as the general partners; the limited partner is not the business
6	Membership of firm	One	Two or more	Two or more
7	General powers	At will	At will, subject to agreement; if no agreement, *Partnership Act, 1890* applies	
8	Transfer of ownership	By sale of 'goodwill'	Only with unanimous consent	
9	Controlling Acts	None	*Partnership Act, 1890*	*Limited Partnership Act, 1907*
10	Disbanding of firm	At will or by bankruptcy	Firm may go bankrupt or be dissolved by notice, mutual consent or by death of a partner	
11	Advantages	Independence. Personal control of staff and granting of credit. Decisions acted upon at once	Increased capital. Days off and holidays possible. Wider experience of partners. Privacy of affairs	Limited liability for some partners. Larger capital
12	Disadvantages	Long hours. No holidays. Illness affects conduct of business. Unlimited liability. Small capital.	Unlimited liability. Death or retirement ends firm. Profits must be shared	Unlimited liability for the general partners. Also as for partnerships

Profit-making Private-enterprise Units

	Limited Companies	
	Private	*Public*
1	The registered name, registered under the *Companies Act, 1948–80*, with the word 'Limited' for private companies, and the words 'Public Limited Company' for public companies	
2	By registration under the *Companies Acts*, with due legal formality	
3	Directors control the company. Members have no control at all, but may elect a new board at the Annual General Meeting, or at an Extraordinary General Meeting if they wish to do so	
4	Limited liability for all members—only liable to the limit of capital contributed	
5	The business is a separate legal personality from the members	
6	Minimum two, maximum fifty (excluding employees)	Minimum two, no maximum limit (under 1980 Act)
7	As laid down in Memorandum of Association and Articles of Association	
8	Shares may only be transferred with consent of fellow shareholders	Shares are freely transferable
9	*Companies Acts, 1948, 1967, 1976, 1980 and 1981*	
10	Company may go into voluntary or compulsory liquidation	
11	Limited liability. Death of shareholders does not affect the firm. Capital can be found from fifty members. Privacy to some extent on affairs	Limited liability. Death of shareholders does not affect the firm. Very large capital can be collected.
12	Publication now required, but since 1981 turnover need not be revealed unless it exceeds £5 750 000. Only fifty members. Profits need not be revealed if turnover is less than £1 400 000	Full public knowledge of affairs

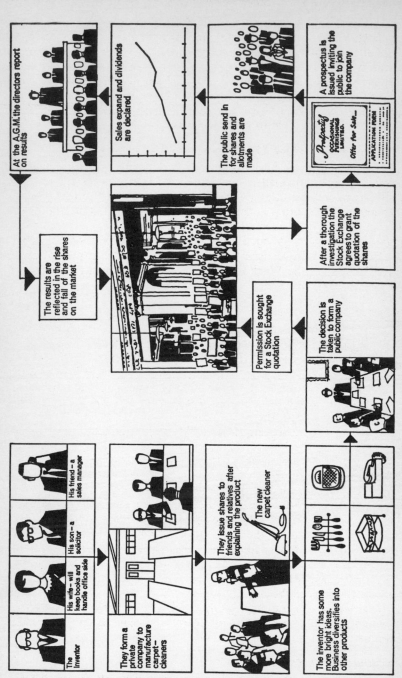

Fig. 1.4. How a company is formed and financed.

The reader should turn to pages 12 and 13 to study this table. For the way in which a company is formed and financed, Fig. 1.4 gives a simple explanation of the general pattern of arrangements. Starting as a small private company the business grows to the point where it is able to meet the strict requirements of the Stock Exchange Council and then 'goes public' by issuing enough shares to make a worthwhile market. This enables extra capital to be collected from the general public and the business is then able to grow more rapidly.

1.7 Non-Profit-Making Units (Clubs and Societies)

A certain number of business units are non-profit-making clubs and societies. They are formed to confer on their members certain benefits in the way of club facilities, discount trading, or value for money. Such clubs and societies often make profits on the year's trading, but these are not profits in the normal commercial meaning of the word. They really represent over-payments by the members for the services they have received, and are usually called 'surpluses'. Examples of such business units are the Working Men's Clubs in the north of England and the Co-operative Societies.

Co-operative Retail Societies

The first successful 'Co-op' store was founded in 1844 in Toad Lane, Rochdale, by 28 weavers nowadays remembered as the 'Rochdale Pioneers'. The idea was to buy foodstuffs at wholesale prices and sell them (to members only) at market price. Profits were divided among members in proportion to the value of their purchases. The share-out (dividend) took place twice a year. By 1845 there were 74 members; the turnover was £710; the profit £22.

The Co-operative Movement spread rapidly. Societies were set up in towns all over the United Kingdom. In 1862 the members voted to set up a wholesale organisation, the Co-operative Wholesale Society. This society not only supplied the retail societies like any ordinary wholesaler but also ran factories, farms, transport services, and even tea gardens to provide everything the retail societies needed. The chief aim in this activity was to ease the serious unemployment of those days. The retail societies joined the wholesale society in exactly the same way as the ordinary members joined the retail society. All the profits of the Co-operative Wholesale Society are shared among the member retail societies, and all the profits of the retail societies are shared among the members. Thus in the end all the profits return to the members of the retail societies, whose purchasing power actually keeps the Co-operative Movement going. These profits in recent years have been distributed by means of a trading stamp scheme.

Agricultural Cooperatives

These are very common in many countries and enable the small-scale farmer to achieve some of the economies of large-scale organisation. They may be marketing cooperatives, which grade, pack and distribute farmers' produce; or purchasing cooperatives, which buy seed, fertiliser and equipment at discount prices, supplying or hiring these items to farmers.

1.8 Public Enterprises

We have seen that the economy is divided into two main parts: the private sector and the public sector. The private sector comprises all those firms described earlier—sole traders, partnerships and limited companies. The public sector comprises all those other institutions set up or taken over by the authority of Parliament for operation in the public interest and not for private profit. There is a wide variety of such institutions, and many of them were set up by Acts of Parliament which approved a unique framework appropriate to the particular industry under consideration. A full discussion of these institutions is a matter for students of the British constitution, and may be studied by those interested in a companion volume, *British Constitution Made Simple*.

Table 1.2 lists some of these major public institutions.

1.9 Local Government Institutions

In every economy an important part of the services required is local in character. Education, health services, drainage and sewerage works are required all over the country and are inappropriate to control by the central Government. A lower order of government, which reaches out to every locality, is required. In the United Kingdom a comprehensive restructuring of local government took place following the Radcliffe-Maude Report. The number of local authorities was reduced from over 1200 to 421. Six of these, not counting London, were designated as metropolitan counties. There are 47 county councils in England and Wales, 35 metropolitan districts or boroughs and 296 non-metropolitan districts or boroughs. Parish councils in England and community councils in Wales operate at the very lowest levels.

Functions of the new authorities. The chief functions of the new authorities include major responsibilities in town and country planning, education, housing, police and fire services, traffic and highways, consumer protection, personal social services and many more. A full description of all these functions is given in *British Constitution Made Simple*.

Municipal undertakings. This type of organisation used to be much more important than it is today, because many water companies, electricity supply companies and gas companies were municipally owned. The nationalisation of such public utility services has reduced the scale of local enterprise, but it is still common to find such institutions as swimming pools, leisure centres, etc., run as municipal enterprises.

Table 1.2. Some Public Sector Institutions

Name of organisation	Reason for operation in public sector	Date of original act of nationalisation
1 Anglian Water Authority	Service of regional importance	1973
2 Atomic Energy Authority	Inappropriate to private sector	1954
3 Bank of England	To unify political and financial power	1946
4 British Aerospace	Government the chief customer	1977
5 British Airports Authority	To ensure adequate facilities	1965
6 British Airways	To foster and develop a costly but vital service	1939 and 1946
7 British Broadcasting Corporation	Inappropriate to allow it to develop in private hands	1926
8 British Road Services	To regulate growth in road transport, as part of integrated service	1947
9 British Gas Corporation	An industry of national importance	1948
10 British National Oil Corporation	To assert a national influence over North Sea resources	1976
11 British Rail	To restore a declining industry	1947
12 British Shipbuilders	To restore a declining industry	1977
13 British Steel	To defeat the influence of powerful firms	1949
14 British Transport Docks Board	Part of a nationalisation of transport in the UK	1947
15 Electricity Council	To secure economies of large-scale operations	1947
16 Independent Television Authority (now Independent Broadcasting Authority)	To license and control programme companies	1954
17 National Bus Co.	Part of integrated transport service	1947
18 National Coal Board	To nationalise a gift of nature in a depressed industry with a history of poor industrial relations	1946
19 National Health Service	To provide a health service to all irrespective of financial status	1946
20 North of Scotland Hydro-Electric Board	Lack of private capital	1943
21 Post Office Corporation	To operate the postal services outside the Civil Service (previously a Government department)	1969
22 County Councils	To provide a wide range of local services, inappropriate to the private sector	1888
23 QUANGOS (e.g. the SITPRO Board)	To fulfil some useful public function (e.g. the Simplification of International Trade Procedures Board represents the UK in international negotiations about documents used in overseas trade)	Various dates. (The SITPRO Board was set up in 1970)

1.10 Central Government Departments

In recent years a certain amount of experimentation (with super-ministries, for example) has caused frequent changes in the running and responsibility of Government departments, so that any list is subject to change at the whim of the Government in charge. In general there are about 20 ministries, with about two-thirds of them sufficiently important for the minister in charge to be of Cabinet rank. The major ministries are the Treasury, the Foreign Office, the Home Office, and those of Defence, Social Services, Employment, Education and Science, the Environment, Wales, Scotland, Agriculture, Trade, Industry and the Department of Energy. All departments have considerable sums of money to spend in pursuing their activities, and are therefore influential in the economy. In 1980 the total expenditure of central Government departments was £86000 million. This is equivalent to a pile of £10 notes 29 times as high as Mount Everest.

1.11 Points to Think About and Discuss

(*a*) 'In manufacturing 94 per cent of the firms only did 16 per cent of the work.' What does this tell us about the importance of large firms in the manufacturing trades? Is it a good thing that so many small firms have so little of the work?

(*b*) When a firm is set up in a district it immediately affects the environment, both natural and human. What are the dangers and what are the advantages which follow from industry moving into a district?

(*c*) 'We already have plenty of goods and services. Let us reduce consumption and preserve the natural world around us.' Do you support or disagree with this idea?

1.12 Rapid Revision

In this book each chapter ends with a test-yourself section, which acts both as a chapter summary and a revision test. Cover the page with a sheet of plain paper and uncover the first question. Try to answer it from your knowledge of the chapter. Lower the paper and read the answer to question 1. Then read question 2 and try to answer it.

Answers	Questions
	1. Why are organisations formed?
1. There are eight main reasons: (i) To produce consumer goods; (ii) To produce producer goods (capital assets); (iii) To provide personal services; (iv) To provide commercial services; (v) To provide protective services (defence, police, fire prevention, etc.);	2. What is the general aim of economic activity?

Answers	Questions
(vi) To legislate (Parliament); (vii) To administer the country (Civil Service, etc.); (viii) To administer justice (the Courts).	
2. To obtain the greatest output of useful goods and services from the smallest input of our scarce resources.	3. Explain the stages in the cycle of production.
3. (a) 'wants', (b) organisation, (c) production, (d) distribution, (e) exchange, (f) consumption, (g) 'wants' again.	4. What are the two sectors of the economy?
4. The private sector and the public sector.	5. Name some private sector organisations.
5. Sole traders, partnerships, limited partnerships, private limited companies, public limited companies, clubs, Co-operative Societies.	6. Name some public sector organisations.
6. Autonomous corporations, QUANGOS, nationalised industries, local and central government departments.	7. How is wealth created?
7. Land, labour and capital are put to work by some type of organisation. The result is a flow of goods or services which can be used to satisfy 'wants'.	8. What part does 'money' play in the 'World of Work'?
8. It enables factors of production to be employed and their reward is paid in money. Then this money is exchanged by the workers, landowners, etc., for the goods and services needed. Each buys a balanced basket of goods for his own family's needs.	9. Go over the page again until you are sure of all the answers.

Exercises Set 1

1. Copy out the lines below and fill in the missing words or phrases. Some answers are given at the end to help you.

(a) From the moment they are born people ...... things.

(b) To satisfy the demands of the public, businessmen engage in ....

(c) Many goods are produced, but we also need many ....

(d) Three industrial concerns would be: (i) a motorcar factory, (ii) a ...... and (iii) a ....

(e) Three commercial activities would be: (i) banking, (ii) ...... and (iii) ....

(f) The two sectors of economic life are the ...... sector and the ...... sector.

(g) A fully developed economy cannot work unless we have a ...... system to arrange the exchange of goods and services.

Answers: services, insurance, public, want, money, production, communications, private, printing works, cotton mill.

2. List the reasons why organisations are set up in society.

3. Distinguish 'personal services' and 'commercial services'. Refer in your answer to the eight services named below, and explain whether you consider them 'personal' or 'commercial'. Are any of them both personal and commercial? The eight services are: (i) dentistry, (ii) a news agency, (iii) surgery, (iv) insurance, (v) a bus service, (vi) road haulage, (vii) education, (viii) satellite communication.

4. Describe the public sector of the economy of your own country, naming major institutions which operate in the public sector, and explaining why they are not privately operated.

5. What is meant by 'the cycle of production'? Why has it continued constantly throughout man's history? Illustrate a typical cycle by reference to the life of one of the following: (*a*) a farmer, (*b*) a coalminer, (*c*) a merchant banker.

6. Make a detailed study of your own workplace, whatever it is, and pinpoint how it is organised. Use the names of official positions (i.e. manager, supervisor, chief clerk, etc.) rather than the names of individuals. Indicate any chains of command which appear to exist. For those in full-time education, study the department in which you are following your main course. Assess the effectiveness of the organisation you have studied and bring out clearly its strengths and its weaknesses. Keep the discussion of such matters impersonal, and consider them objectively (from the point of view of an outsider who is not personally involved).

7. (*a*) Money is the root of all evil!
   (*b*) Money makes the world go round!

Discuss these two views of money and explain which you consider to be the more sensible. In your answer explain how the money system affects a college leaver who is very good at mathematics, but not much else. He is proposing to marry a girl on the same course as himself, in the near future.

8. Why worry about an apprenticeship?—there are plenty of good jobs going in the public sector. Discuss this viewpoint expressed by a careers officer in an area where few apprenticeships were available.

2

THE OFFICE AS THE CENTRE OF BUSINESS ACTIVITY

2.1 The Place of the Office in Organisations

The 'World of Work' is a complex group of organisations of all sorts, sizes and types. We have seen that there are private sector business organisations, public sector corporations, local and central Government departments, Courts of law and many other bodies.

What part does the office play in the business activities of production, distribution and exchange of goods and services? The original meaning of the word 'office' was 'piece of kindness, or service to one's fellow men'. Today it is used more often to describe a room, or building, where clerical processes are carried out to start, develop and control the many activities of a business. There are head offices, branch offices, factory offices, cost offices, transport offices, sales offices and many more. They vary from the magnificent 'board room' of an international company to the single unit of furniture called a 'home office', used by many small businessmen or housewives who carry on agencies in their own homes. Plate 1 shows such an office, which is quite reasonably priced and very convenient for a home agency.

Every single organisation has at its very centre the office which gives life to the whole organisation. Not a wheel turns until the orders go out from Head Office, or Branch Office, or the Departmental Office. It is in the office that projects are conceived, plans made, prototypes devised and practice runs tested out. An office is not therefore a dull and lifeless place. It is more exciting than the busiest transport depot, the most exposed North Sea oil rig, the deepest gold mine and the remotest space station. They can carry out only what the office has planned and authorised.

2.2 The Functions of the Office

The functions of the office include the following:

(a) The starting of any enterprise by the issue of instructions to departments to proceed with projects.
(b) The keeping of all essential documents in good order (filed and indexed) so that they are available when required.
(c) Ensuring that all the requirements of both statutes (Acts of Parliament) and local bye-laws are kept.
(d) Devising report and feedback systems so that the progress of pro-

Plate 1. A compact home office (reproduced by courtesy of MFI Ltd).

jects, sales, etc., can be followed and if necessary stimulated by whatever action seems necessary. **Control activities** are an essential feature of office activities.

(e) The supervision of money flows to ensure that funds are available to meet expenditure at all times.

(f) Routine administration matters; the recruitment and payment of staff, the ordering of equipment and materials and the safeguarding of assets once they have been purchased.

Above all the office, in every aspect of its work, is concerned with **information**, with obtaining and collecting information, sorting, arranging and interpreting it, supplying it to management when required and preserving it for as long as it is useful in promoting the enterprise concerned. The office maintains communications between departments and with outside firms and Government agencies.

The offices of large companies are usually divided into divisions or departments, each of which performs a particular function in the organisation. Fig. 2.1, based on the organisation of an international company, illustrates the structure of a typical firm organised along functional lines.

Public sector organisations, like the Department of Industry shown in Fig. 2.2, naturally have very complex organisations. In this particular case there are seven chief divisions each of which has three or four subdivisions, and these may be repeated in branches all over the country to assist industry in every corner of the land.

2.3 The Major Departments—An Introductory Description

(a) *The General Administration Office.* This department is a nonspecialist department dealing with all those activities which promote the general organisation of the enterprise. The **administrative officer** will be a person of wide experience, to whom all other departmental heads can turn for advice on general office procedures. In smaller enterprises he may be in charge of the appointment of staff, the ordering of equipment and stationery, the general supervision of the premises including security, caretaking and cleaning, canteen or refreshment arrangements and many other matters. Very often this office will have the inward and outward mail arrangements under its general control as well as reception and telephone services, safety and First Aid arrangements and, very often, the typing pool.

(b) *The Personnel Department.* This department supervises all matters to do with staffing. It advertises for and appoints staff of suitable quality for the various activities of the business, runs induction and training courses and prepares updating lectures, demonstrations and seminars. These serve to bring existing staff to higher levels or to introduce new procedures.

The personnel department also preserves records of performance,

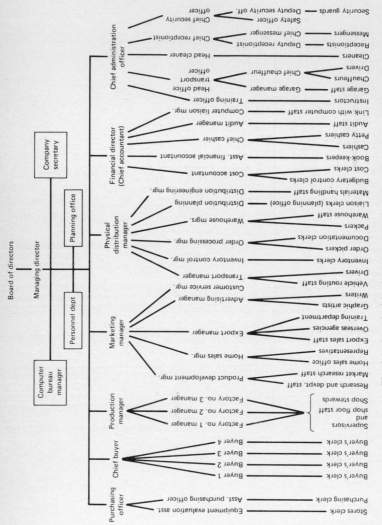

Fig. 2.1. A typical business organisation along functional lines.

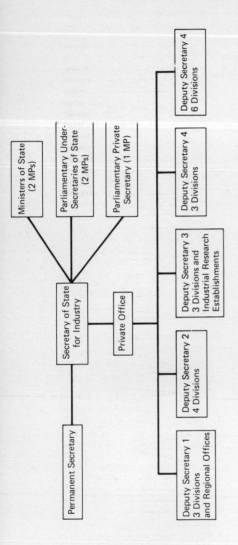

Ministers of State
(2 MPs)

Parliamentary Under-
Secretaries of State
(2 MPs)

Parliamentary Private
Secretary (1 MP)

Permanent Secretary

Secretary of State
for Industry

Private Office

Deputy Secretary 1
3 Divisions
and Regional Offices

Deputy Secretary 2
4 Divisions

Deputy Secretary 3
3 Divisions and
Industrial Research
Establishments

Deputy Secretary 4
3 Divisions

Deputy Secretary 4
6 Divisions

19 Divisions in total excluding Common Service Divisions

The Department is responsible for:

3 Nationalised Industries (Shipbuilding, Steel & Post Office)
6 Industrial Research Establishments
7 Regional Offices
4 Regional Development Grant Offices
11 Small Firms Information Offices
EEC Information Unit

Common Services Divisions
(shared services with Department of Trade)

Establishment Personnel Division
Establishment Management Services & Manpower
Division
Establishment General Services Division
Finance & Economic Appraisal Division
Solicitor's Department
Economics Divisions
Statistics Divisions
Business Statistics Office
Accountancy Services Division
Information Division (part)

Fig. 2.2. Organisational structure of the Department of Industry (November, 1981).

considers candidates for promotion and circularises regular reports for completion by supervisors and departmental heads. It hears complaints from staff and rearranges staffing to avoid conflict, where clashes of opinions or principle appear likely to prove troublesome. Finally, it deals with the dismissal of staff, prepares testimonials for personnel leaving employment and handles welfare problems when necessary.

(*c*) *The Accounts and Costing Departments.* These departments are concerned with the accounting records of the business. The accounts department deals with the book-keeping records of purchases, sales and expense items and with the purchase of capital assets. It carries out **internal audits** to ensure that money is being properly spent. The costing department deals with the estimating of production costs. Some costs, like raw materials, are **direct costs** and may be allocated at once to the product which has been manufactured from them. Others are **overheads**, which cannot be directly attributed to one particular product. They must be spread over all the units of output in some even way. The costing department also attempts to discover rising production costs while they are still changing, so the increases can be controlled or selling prices adjusted.

(*d*) *The Purchasing Department.* This department is responsible for buying the raw materials, machinery, office equipment, stationery and other items needed to produce the firm's products and market them effectively. Purchasing department personnel will evaluate new equipment or new business systems to decide whether they should be adopted, and they will visit exhibitions, demonstrations or suppliers' premises for the purpose of discussing prices and delivery dates.

(*e*) *The Sales Department.* This department is concerned with the marketing of a firm's products at home and overseas. Home sales are usually secured by **commercial travellers** who are allocated a **territory** which they cover at regular intervals visiting established customers and attempting to secure new trade whenever possible. **Export trade** is handled in rather a different way, depending upon the size of the firm concerned. Two other departments are closely associated with the sales department. These are the **advertising department**, which handles day-to-day publicity and special promotions, and the **servicing department**, whose activities preserve **goodwill** by ensuring prompt repairs and the replacement of spare parts.

(*f*) *The Transport Department.* Today the typical method of delivering goods is by 'own account' vehicles. There are great advantages with many products in keeping delivery under personal supervision. Many products are small, technically complex and therefore expensive, and highly desirable as personal possessions. Such products are easily pilfered and difficult to trace once they have been stolen, and a transport department operating vehicles on its own account can supervise drivers much more effectively than can a public transport system. Even where goods are to be rail-freighted, shipped or air-freighted the **transport**

manager, with his professional knowledge of **'freight forwarding'**, will secure the cheapest and most reliable operations for his company's needs. He will also evaluate vehicles, choosing the most useful and economical for his firm.

(g) *The Production Manager's Office.* This office is the centre of a firm's production activities. It is usual to call this the 'factory' rather than the production department. The manager will sometimes be a **production engineer** or **mechanical engineer**, and the office will be devoted to ensuring the most effective means possible of planning and executing production. Costings can be prepared as manufacture proceeds and temporary shortages are overcome by clerks called **progress chasers**, who 'chase' materials required or components being manufactured to ensure that they reach the production line in time.

(h) *The Research and Development Department.* Someone has to take a long-term view in any firm. Today's best seller is tomorrow's 'has-been'. 'Fad today and fade tomorrow' is the rule of modern business. R & D, as it is called, tries to anticipate tomorrow's needs; tomorrow's new look; tomorrow's variation on the well-established product.

There are many small departments which have not been listed above, including the post department, the central filing department, the duplicating department, the addressing and mailing department. As most of these have specialised chapters in this book a discussion of them is left until later.

2.4 The Functions of the Office Manager

These may be listed briefly as follows:

(a) To **think creatively about the purpose of the office**, constantly reassessing its aims and the extent to which these aims are fulfilled efficiently.

(b) To **implement the organisation and methods decided upon in (a) above. Organisation** involves allocating responsibilities and duties to various members of staff, establishing a **chain of command** which enables everyone to act within a particular field of responsibility, and which specifies the person to whom each should refer on matters which are not in his own power to decide.

Methods involves the examination and selection of business systems equipment and machinery to perform the required services efficiently and economically.

(c) To **control** and **direct** both the staff and the environment in which they work so that the office fulfils the aims already agreed upon.

2.5 The Functions of the Office Junior

In every department there are many routine activities which are essential to the proper functioning of the firm as a whole. These activities provide a variety of jobs for young people. All the tasks require a conscientious approach as well as intelligence and common sense; some require manual dexterity of a high order whilst others need special training which may last for a considerable time.

The office junior's main function is to perform the tasks given to him or her as expeditiously as possible, using existing knowledge and skills and adding to these whatever practical training is offered by the employer. Sometimes, day-release courses at the local technical college, or short, intensive courses on the firm's premises will be offered to the junior. Such training helps to develop skills in using calculators, photo-copiers, typewriters and addressing machines, and can lead to the acquisition of valuable, more specialist abilities in accounting and computer techniques. Most young people today are keen to continue their education after leaving school, and whilst many enter the business world with useful qualifications, it is possible to develop their value to an employer very rapidly by building upon the sound basis already laid during their years at school or college.

Common activities performed by office juniors are as follows:

(a) Routine communication activities; copy-typing; audio-typing and junior secretarial work.
(b) Routine calculating and accounting activities; book-keeping; wages calculations; elementary costing activities and petty cashier's work.
(c) Documentation activities; invoicing, the preparation and despatch of statements, the processing of documents and filing of records.
(d) Simple receptionist duties, dealing with visitors of all kinds, relief telephone operating and messenger work.
(e) Postal activities; the collection, stamping and despatch of outward-going mail; the collection of mail inwards and its distribution to departments.

This list is far from complete, yet it illustrates the variety of activities performed by juniors in offices today.

2.6 A Comparison of Large and Small Offices

Offices differ widely, even within the same firm. They may be large, open-plan offices where numbers of employees cooperate together. They may be small, cubicle-type offices where one member of staff, possibly with secretarial help, performs particular aspects of the firm's work, routing each completed section to another department for further processing.

Table 2.1 compares and contrasts these types of offices.

2.7 Studying Clerical Duties and Office Practice

Many students and readers will find the following advice helpful:

(a) Purchase a lever-arch file and keep it as a **subject file**.
(b) Prepare an index, from brown paper or other suitable material,

Table 2.1. Comparison of Large and Small Offices

Large offices	*Small offices*
1. May be open-plan offices, with a high degree of specialisation. Each clerk performs a particular activity on the documents being processed. The work 'flows' round the room, passing successively from clerk to clerk. Plenty of office aids available.	1. The work will be less specialised, each clerk performing several activities.
2. Some clerks find the specialised work boring, because it lacks variety.	2. The employees gain from the variety of their work, and the responsibility they must assume.
3. The office is sociable, but perhaps impersonal—one feels like a mere cog in a big machine.	3. The atmosphere is personal, but lacks the sociable atmosphere of a large office. Close contact with a few people may promote discord instead of harmony.
4. Absence, sickness, etc., are easily catered for.	4. Absence causes difficulty and staff tend to be more closely controlled.
5. The large firm offers social and welfare facilities (canteens, education, etc.) which are attractive to staff.	5. Little social life is possible, and welfare tends to depend upon the employer's personality.
6. Wages and conditions tend to be on scales drawn up after consultation with staff and only remotely connected with personal effort and conscientious work.	6. Wages and conditions depend upon the employer's evaluation of the personal efforts of staff.
7. Career prospects tend to be good since the large organisation can use developed skills and talents better than the small firm.	7. Career prospects may be limited by the small size of the enterprise.

based upon the table of contents of this book, i.e. one section for each chapter.

(c) File away in this index the following items:

(i) Notes prepared while reading the chapter concerned.

(ii) Notes taken of lectures, conferences, etc., attended (if applicable).

(iii) Newspaper cuttings relevant to the subject.

(iv) Brochures and advertisements from firms.

(v) Specimen documents.

(vi) Personal souvenirs of visits made, etc.

The resulting collection is more interesting to revise than an ordinary notebook (see Fig. 2.3).

2.8   Points to Think About and Discuss

(a) Should every office worker learn to type? What would be the advantages and disadvantages of such a rule? What other skills are appropriate to most office workers?

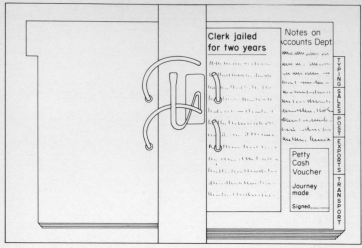

Fig. 2.3. A 'lever-arch' subject file, with index.

(b) What clerical duties would be likely to concern the following:

(i) A retailer in the 'consumer durables' field.
(ii) A salesman in a car showroom.
(iii) A hospital receptionist.
(iv) A costing clerk in a cigarette factory.
(v) A civil servant in the Department of Employment.

2.9 Rapid Revision

Cover the page with a sheet of paper and uncover one question at a time.

Answers	*Questions*
—	1. What are the functions of an office?
1. To start, develop and control the enterprise to achieve its aims.	2. How are these functions performed?
2. (a) Plans are prepared. (b) Orders implement the plans. (c) Reports and feedback systems are instituted to enable management to control operations by a policy of management by exceptions. (d) Routine clerical procedures are instituted to supervise all aspects of the organisation. (e) Information is collected, digested and circulated.	3. What are the functions of an office manager?

Answers	Questions
3. (a) To think creatively about the purpose and aims of the office. (b) To implement the organisation devised to achieve these aims. (c) To direct and control staff.	4. What are the functions of the office junior?
4. (a) To perform a variety of routine activities of a clerical nature. (b) To acquire experience, knowledge and skills necessary to the proper functioning of an office.	5. What are the advantages of large offices?
5. (a) A high degree of specialisation. (b) Plenty of specialised equipment. (c) Few problems with sickness or absence due to holidays, etc. (d) Good welfare facilities. (e) Good career prospects.	6. What are the advantages of small offices?
6. (a) Personal control over the activities of staff easily achieved. (b) Greater responsibility and variety of work for each member of staff. (c) Personal atmosphere—staff are not just a number on a pay-roll.	7. Go over the page again until you feel you are sure of the answers.

Exercises Set 2

1. Copy out the lines below and fill in the missing words or phrases.

(a) At the centre of any organisation we find the ....
(b) In every aspect of its work an office is dealing with some type of ....
(c) An office where each department has its own special job to do is said to be organised along ...... lines.
(d) Large offices with many people working in the same room are called ...... offices.
(e) Small offices where only one or two people work are ...... offices.
(f) The office junior should be prepared to ...... by learning new techniques and handling strange equipment.

Answers: information, cubicle, functional, head office, open-plan, acquire skills.

2. List: (a) three functions of an accounts department; (b) three functions performed by the personnel department.

3. Consider the alternative answers shown below and write on your paper the correct answers in each group.

(a) To evaluate vehicles is: (i) to price them in a series of visits to showrooms; (ii) to consider whether they are appropriate for the needs of your firm; (iii) to empty the carburettor and blow it clear of obstructions; (iv) to estimate the value for insurance purposes?
(b) An internal audit is: (i) a financial investigation carried out by employees of the firm to check whether money has been properly spent; (ii) an operation

on the ear; (iii) routine maintenance on computer wiring and components; (iv) a hearing device for detecting faults inside components?

(*c*) A testimonial is: (i) evidence given by a witness in a magistrate's court; (ii) the will made out by a dying person; (iii) a short-tempered person who is always complaining; (iv) an account of an employee's conduct and ability by the personnel department for the information of another employer?

(*d*) Advertising, if not run as a separate department, would probably be controlled by: (i) the sales department: (ii) the purchasing department; (iii) the personnel department; (iv) the accounts department?

4. What is a general administration office? Explain its functions.

5. List ten different kinds of office. When you have done so write the numbers 1, 2 and 3 against the offices you consider most likely to be found in a small firm manufacturing electrical equipment for use in the home. This firm does *not* engage in the export trade.

6. Suggest a succession of posts leading to high levels of responsibility for the following members of staff:

(*a*) A junior clerk in the accounts department who is studying cost accounting by day-release studies at his local technical college.

(*b*) A copy typist who is studying shorthand at evening classes run by a local youth centre.

7. 'I would like to work in a small office,' said Miss Smith at her interview with the Youth Employment Officer.

'Why does that sort of office appeal to you more?' asked the officer. Suggest six to ten points in favour of small offices.

8. It does not matter whether you are a farmer, an engineer, a printer, a transport driver or a teacher, you will spend much of your time either in office work or in processing documents for office work. Explain the importance of office work in the world today, referring in particular to any two of the professions or trades named.

9. What are the functions of the office?

10. What are the functions of the office junior? Illustrate your answer by reference to one department of a large firm.

11.

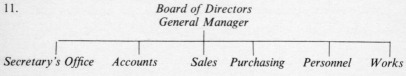

Board of Directors
General Manager

Secretary's Office   Accounts   Sales   Purchasing   Personnel   Works

(*a*) From the organisation chart of a small to medium-sized manufacturing concern given above state the department or official likely to be responsible for:

    (i) Preparing the balance sheet.
    (ii) Training of employees.
    (iii) Making legal decisions.
    (iv) Recommending the rate of dividend payable to shareholders.
    (v) Ordering stock.
    (vi) Maintenance of machinery.

   (vii) Advertising.
 (viii) Despatching goods.
   (ix) Coordinating policy matters.
   (x) Production control.

(*b*) Name the departments (referred to above) in which the following staff are usually employed:

   (i) Cost clerks.   (vi) Invoice typists.
   (ii) Store-keepers.   (vii) Computer programmers.
   (iii) Shipping clerks.   (viii) Welfare officer.
   (iv) Progress clerks.   (ix) Ledger clerks.
   (v) Draughtsmen.   (x) Engineers.

(*c*) Write an account of the work of any *two* of the departments referred to in the chart given above.   (P.S A)

12. (*a*) Draw an organisation chart for a business concern with which you are familiar and state the type of organisation.

(*b*) Explain how the organisation receives its capital.

(*c*) Describe briefly how the following office services are organised throughout the concern: (i) filing; (ii) secretarial (i.e. typewriting, duplicating, etc.); (iii) intercommunication; (iv) mailing.

13. Draw a chart showing the organisational structure you would suggest for a firm engaged in designing and manufacturing office furniture and selling it at home and abroad.

   What additional ancillary services would such an organisation normally employ?

14. Compare the typical organisation of a small firm employing up to ten staff with a large organisation employing five hundred or more staff. Illustrate your answer with organisation charts for both types of undertaking.

15. Draw a typical organisation chart for a limited liability company engaged in manufacturing. Describe briefly the duties performed by the senior staff mentioned in your chart.

3

CLERICAL ACTIVITIES

3.1 The Growth of Clerical Activities

As a nation develops it goes through a series of revolutions. First an agricultural revolution frees the people from the soil and enables them to seek employment in towns. Then an industrial revolution takes place in the production of other goods, so that factory-made clothing, footwear, furniture and equipment replace the craftsmen's products. Finally, a commercial revolution ensures the rapid distribution and exchange of all the goods produced, and the finance and insurance activities necessitated by the growth of business activity. We therefore need more and more clerical activities as we advance in nationhood. **One sign of a mature and advanced nation is the huge number of clerical workers it needs to carry out the complex financial, industrial and social programmes required.**

In Britain the number of office workers exceeds three million people; one in every seven of the working population is directly engaged in clerical activities of some sort, while most of the others depend for their information, orders and instructions on those who work in offices.

3.2 The Five Main Types of Clerical Activity

In the processes of starting, developing and controlling business activities the manager and his office staff take part in many clerical activities. There are five main fields of activity in all offices. They are:

(a) Communications.
(b) Calculations.
(c) Records.
(d) Reports.
(e) Routine procedures.

Whilst many of these activities are described in detail in later chapters a brief look at each of them seems appropriate here.

Communications. Every office is to some extent a communications centre. It receives instructions, information and reports from other offices, and after preparing or processing forms and documents it passes instructions or explanations to those awaiting them. These may be internal memos, or letters to outside bodies.

Information is the chief interest of those who control offices. They need to know as much as possible about the influences at work in the world of business if they are to make the right decisions and run their businesses properly. A lack of information causes costly errors to be made. The chief types of information collected are production reports from factories and mines; sales reports from home and overseas whole-sale and retail outlets; and official statistics from Government or inter-national bodies which show the trends and developments in world population, prices of commodities and growth of national incomes. On the basis of this information, which is arranged and classified into a more digestible form by specialist office employees of various sorts, top management makes **decisions** which are issued out to lower levels of staff as **memos** and **communications** of various sorts.

Nothing is so useful in maintaining good communications as the provision of suitable forms for internal and external use. The **memo form** shown below (Fig. 3.1) will be useful in ensuring that messages state clearly from whom they come and to whom they are sent, that the date is clearly stated and that any difficulties may be clarified by a simple procedure. Sometimes the use of different coloured memo pads for senior staff ensures prompt attention to their urgent requirements.

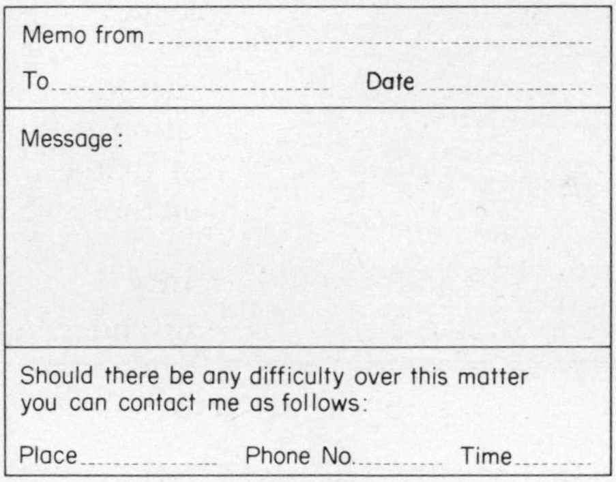

```
Memo from _____
To _____  Date _____
Message :



Should there be any difficulty over this matter
you can contact me as follows :
Place _____  Phone No. _____  Time _____
```

Fig. 3.1. An internal memo form.

A good network of communication trays is desirable and ensures that everyone has a tray in which messages may be left. Trays of the type illustrated in Fig. 3.2 are very economical in the use of space, can be labelled with the names of staff and are often anti-static treated. (Sheets of paper easily become charged with static electricity, and the lowest sheet can often remain in the tray when a pile of papers is removed hurriedly.) Such trays can also be used by a single individual for a variety of work, and labels such as ACTION, FILING, PENDING can be attached to indicate the tray's purpose.

The **telephone system** is an essential link in the chain of communica-

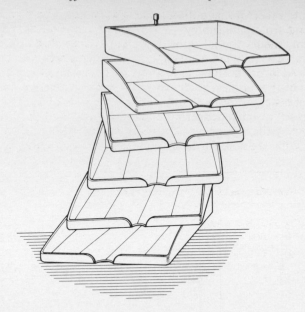

Fig. 3.2. A set of trays for ensuring good communications (reproduced by courtesy of Wilson & Whitworth Ltd).

tions and is fully described in Chapter 6. Direct links over telephone circuits are also possible for the transmission from branches to Head Office of information about sales, daily takings from debtors, cheques banked and so on. This type of information is called 'data' and its despatch or reception and processing by calculators and computers is called **data processing**.

Calculations. Very few of the activities of business can be carried on without calculations or figure work of some sort. Factory output, construction work of all sorts, the consumption of gas, electricity and water, wages payments and countless other items have to be measured, priced and computed. The range of aids to help these activities is now very great, from the simple adding-listing machine and calculator to a computer. They all call for specialist trained labour and a quick, skilful and conscientious approach. A fuller description of calculators and other devices is given in Chapter 13.

Records. Records are important if business is to be conducted efficiently. It is often necessary to prove that contracts were made, or that obligations have been fulfilled. It is vital, too, to be able to answer queries from employees, customers and others efficiently and quickly. Accurate records enable such queries to be dealt with easily, and in many cases they may enable us to compare present performance with past achievements and to detect problems that are arising long before they would otherwise be noticed. Such systematic records have saved many firms from bankruptcy.

Probably the most vital records of all are the book-keeping records which enable us to tell how much we owe our **creditors**, and how much we are owed by our **debtors**. They also enable us to prepare the financial accounts of the business each year so that profits can be ascertained and **dividends** paid to our shareholders.

In Fig. 3.3 a simple ledger account shows a record of our dealings with Henry Wills, a supplier. The position on 1st May reveals that we owe Mr Wills £825.00, for items purchased on 2nd April.

Dr. Henry Wills, 18, High St., Newtown, Essex.								C.L. 107 Cr.
19..			£	19..				£
Apr. 3	To Returns	PRB1	75·50	Apr. 1	By Balance	B/d		50·50
5	„ Bank	C.B.9	48·50	2	„ Purchases	P.D.B.1		900·50
5	„ Discount	C.B.9	2·00					
30	„ Balance	C/d	825·00					
		£	951·00				£	951·00
				19..				
				May 1	By Balance	B/d		825·00

Fig. 3.3. A simple book-keeping record—a creditor's account.

Reports. The basis of control activities is the report. If a member of staff notices something wrong he should report it. The astute office junior who notices that a bill has remained unpaid may save his firm money in future bad debts. Many reports are required as routine procedures from departments to head offices. There the reports are considered and analysed to discover whether the affairs of the firm are being properly conducted. Managers look for exceptions. The vehicle which uses more fuel than the others may have a dishonest driver. The department with the heaviest telephone bill may be poorly controlled. This is known as **management by exceptions**.

Consider the examples shown below of sales figures reported for representatives in six areas of a firm's activities.

Table 3.1. Sales of Product 'X'

Representative	Jan £	Feb £	Mar £	Apr £	May £
Mr A. Area 1	14 000	15 400	17 000	17 000	20 000
Mr B. „ 2	27 000	29 200	33 000	33 900	37 500
Mr C. „ 3	140 000	130 500	141 500	116 000	142 000
Mr D. „ 4	130 000	140 000	147 000	148 500	155 000
Mr E. „ 5	180 000	195 000	199 000	198 500	206 000
Mr F. „ 6	7 250	9 100	10 700	11 000	12 800

Which set is exceptional, and needs to be investigated? An examination of the figures reveals that while most salesmen are selling considerably more, in fact between 14 per cent and 80 per cent more, Mr C is selling a mere 1 per cent more. Clearly he is either experiencing special difficulties or is not doing his job properly. Either way his case should be investigated.

This shows the usefulness of reports.

Routine procedures. Many routine activities must be carried out regularly if the office is to function properly. At the lowest levels these may include the replacement of clock cards ready for a new week or the collection and posting of letters from various departments. At higher levels routine check-ups on the progress of junior staff; following up of overdue credit accounts; checks on vehicle safety and maintenance procedures on plant and machinery are typical routine duties. **The essence of business organisation is the establishment of routine procedures.**

3.3 Subsidiary Clerical Activities

All these types of clerical activity necessitate what may be called **subsidiary activities**—that is, activities which give additional help to the main activities. The subsidiary activities are:

(a) Writing (including typewriting, shorthand and other devices for speeding up the writing process).
(b) Copying (both manually, mechanically and photographically).
(c) Filing (including sorting, numbering and indexing).
(d) Checking.

Staff at all levels perform these activities, but much of the routine work is performed by office juniors. Many of their activities form the subject matter of this book. Here we will briefly refer to some of the more general points about these subsidiary activities.

Writing. This implies the creation of new original records by hand or by typewriting. Decisions that are made have to be recorded; orders must be sent out; enquiries put in hand and explanations given. They must then be communicated to the parties interested by post, or messenger or by being circulated into the in-trays of personnel.

Copying. This is the reproducing of information by carbon copies, spirit or ink duplicators, photographic reproducers or xerography. The communication of instructions to several people, or the entire staff, is most easily carried out in this way. It is of great importance that memos of this sort are read at once by staff who receive a copy. Your employer will be entitled to complain if you fail to act on instructions given in this way. During the Second World War an enthusiastic commanding officer wrote in his daily routine orders that all lower ranks should not only salute their officers, but should shout 'Hi-de-hi' as they did so. To this the officers were to reply 'Ho-de-ho'. Many personnel of both types who had failed to read their memos were charged with an offence against good order and discipline. The commanding officer was, of course, right, but it was several months before derisory cries of 'Hi-de-hi' and 'Ho-de-ho' ceased to ring round the bars and canteens whenever an officer was sighted. It is important to read all memos and routine orders.

Filing (*sorting, numbering and indexing*). Filing is perhaps the most necessary and important clerical activity. No one can run his affairs properly without filing items away in some sensible order where they can be quickly rediscovered. Consider a firm making and installing lifts. As the years go by it becomes responsible for the maintenance and care of lifts in every part of the country. They will vary slightly in many ways. One will invariably be overloaded—another will often break down in a particular way. An accurate file in the maintenance department will warn a fitter—called out in an emergency—which faults are likely; which spares are necessary, etc. He will arrive equipped to correct the fault with the necessary spare parts. The filing systems described later in this book give some idea of the different types of equipment in use, and the different procedures adopted by firms. Do not throw pieces of documentary information away—file them where they can be found when required.

An essential first step in any system of filing is the sorting out of papers into some sensible and convenient order. The 'work-organiser' shown in Fig. 3.4 may be used as a first step in this process. Documents

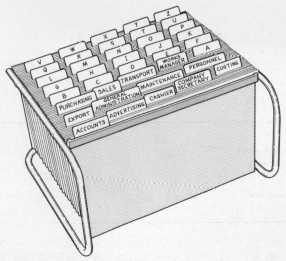

Fig. 3.4. A work-organiser (reproduced by courtesy of Twinlock Ltd).

may be roughly sorted into alphabetical or departmental order first. Then each section is taken to the appropriate filing cabinet and filed. Alternatively the 'work-organiser' may be used to contain folders and papers which could otherwise clutter up the desk. An executive may have tabs prepared for the folders covering the various departmental managers or foremen. Papers referring to departments or activities are sorted into the folders as the mail is opened ready for the day's work. The various managers are then called in; the appropriate folder— containing all the current items for that department—is discussed, and it is then handed over for action by the manager or foreman concerned.

Checking. Checking is necessary at all levels of activity and enormous expense can be saved if careful checks are instituted at all levels. In the United Kingdom today it costs about 14 pence to send the cheapest type of letter. Imagine a firm circulating 5000 customers to announce an exhibition in London. Because of weak checking the date of the exhibition is omitted from the circular. To send out again will cost £700 for postage, besides the cost of envelopes, the second letter and the labour of sending them out. Before this can be done the switchboard will be jammed solid with calls asking for the date of the exhibition. Junior staff should **check their work at every stage, to ensure accuracy**.

3.4 Job Specifications

While most clerical workers expect to do a variety of jobs as the situation requires, some degree of specialisation is desirable and a strong trade union may even insist on a clear designation of duties. This helps in the grading of jobs and also separates the work from the individual doing the work at present. Dr Jekyll may do his present job in a very helpful and cooperative way, doing twice as much as Mr Hyde who succeeds him. Clearly this is not really good for Dr Jekyll or Mr Hyde. The former overworks and is underpaid; the latter slacks and does not really earn his salary. A good 'job specification' will require Mr Hyde to reach a reasonable standard of work, while it may also remind Dr Jekyll that he is overworking and deserves to relax a little.

Good job specifications have the following advantages:

(a) They define the jobs carefully, listing the work to be performed.
(b) They make it easier to decide what class of staff are required, and to appoint properly qualified applicants.
(c) They enable the jobs to be graded for salary purposes.
(d) They enable training schemes to be devised at appropriate levels.

3.5 The Design of Office Procedures

The essence of business organisation is the establishment of routine procedures. No manager can claim to be 'organised' until he has established a routine procedure to deal with the work in hand. Many people who find themselves attending a hospital, or a mortuary, or a police station for the first time are surprised to find that these places have their own routine procedures. What is a memorable event for the member of the public involved in an accident, a burglary or a murder is mere routine to the nurse, the pathologist, the policeman or the judge.

Whenever any new activity is to be started, the manager, or the management team, will consider how the new activity is to be dealt with. They may decide that *A* will be in overall charge of the activity, that mail connected with it will be delivered to *B* who will refer any difficult points for decision to *A*, and who will have *C* and *D* to help with routine activities.

Once this sort of procedure has been devised the whole operation should proceed smoothly, at a minimum cost and under good control right up to top management level. Forms can be designed to assist the activity; for example, a form to list names and record payments or a form to instruct the despatch department daily of the destination of goods to be sent out. The whole activity is systematically performed.

The rules for drawing up an office procedure are as follows:

(*a*) The system must be simple (so that highly skilled labour is not required).

(*b*) It must trigger into action everyone who needs to play some part in it. Thus the passing of a daily 'list of orders' to a typist may trigger her into preparing invoices and labels for the despatch of goods.

(*c*) The procedure should make use, wherever possible, of mechanical aids and labour-saving devices.

(*d*) The principle of 'exceptions' should be followed—that is, only unusual items should be referred to higher authority. The mass of routine matters will be handled by junior staff.

(*e*) Too intricate a system costs money. One famous firm found its system was so involved that paper work was costing millions of pounds. The rules were changed and six million forms were saved every year.

Fig. 3.5 shows a possible plan of procedure for the despatch of a mailing to schools and colleges in connection with a series of books.

3.6 A Manual of Office Procedures

Some firms draw up manuals of procedure to assist new staff in fitting themselves quickly into the organisation. A clear statement of the activities performed in each department is given in the manual, and staff asked to undertake a particular activity are able to read up the procedure for themselves. This is clearly very desirable in some situations—for example, where absolute security of documents is

Spring Mailing Procedure – Educational Textbook Series

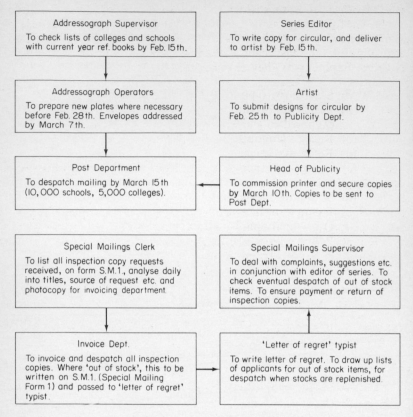

Fig. 3.5. Laying down office procedures.

required, or where dangerous materials are concerned. Documentation in such cases needs to be very carefully checked.

There is the possibility that such handbooks or rules of procedure may become a drawback, rather than an advantage—for example, where they may be used as an excuse to 'work to rule'. Here a group of clerks who perhaps wish to express their resentment of management policies might use the manual of office procedures as a justification for working less hard than normally.

3.7 Points to Think About and Discuss

(*a*) Many young people now stay on at school or proceed to a college or university in order to qualify by examinations and by intensive study for a future career. They then expect to start work at least some part of the way up the promotion ladder. Is this desirable? How can management ensure that the late entrant really does understand the routine office procedures which he or she will one day have to control?

(*b*) The following four jobs are available, for which the six candidates shown below apply. Consider the specification carefully for each post and appoint the 'best' candidate, thus deciding which two must be rejected. Explain why they are unsuitable.

Job (1) (*a*) Some copy-typing
(*b*) Needs to be able to use audio-typing machine—or be prepared to learn
(*c*) Relief telephonist
(*d*) Relief messenger
(*e*) Filing and general duties under supervision (of R. Brown).

Job (2) (*a*) 140 w.p.m. shorthand
(*b*) 50 w.p.m. typewriting
(*c*) Fluent French essential
(*d*) Occasional Spanish and German
(*e*) Public relations responsibility

Job (3) (*a*) 40 w.p.m. typewriting
(*b*) Relief telephonist
(*c*) Occasional use of addressograph equipment
(*d*) Adding-listing machine use required daily
(*e*) Prepared to work to 9 p.m. when required

Job (4) (*a*) Book-keeping to Trial Balance and Final Accounts level
(*b*) Preparation and typing of confidential audit reports
(*c*) Assistance at times to chief accountant in extraction of quarterly figures
(*d*) Presentation of statistical data
(*e*) Occasionally required to visit outlying branches suspected of unreliability over cash payments

Candidate No. 1. Bachelor of Arts Degree. Member of the Institute of Freight Forwarders. No accountancy knowledge. Not interested in salaries below £7000 per annum. Male with a Public School background.

Candidate No. 2. Female. 23 years of age. Reasonable typing. Can operate switchboard and addressograph equipment (but does not like the latter job much).

Candidate No. 3. Typing very good (50 words per minute). Aged 16 years. No shorthand or book-keeping knowledge. Pleasant speaking voice. Likes to meet people. Prefers routine work without too much responsibility.

Candidate No. 4. Fluent shorthand typist. Speaks French excellently and some Spanish. Very sophisticated girl with a charming personality.

Candidate No. 5. At present chief book-keeper in a small firm. Studying accountancy at local technical college. Desires more responsibility. Cannot type but can operate electronic and hand calculators. Male.

Candidate No. 6. Age 16. Types at 40 words per minute. Prepared to learn adding-listing machine and addressograph. Very immature and nervous, but willing.

3.8 Rapid Revision

Cover the page with a sheet of notepaper and uncover one question at a time.

Answers	Questions
—	1. Why are so many people engaged in clerical duties?
1. Because mass production creates a flood of goods which have to be distributed quickly and easily to consumers. This requires documentation, instructions, orders and reports.	2. What are the five main types of clerical activity?
2. (*a*) Communications (*b*) Calculations (*c*) Records (*d*) Reports (*e*) Routine procedures.	3. What are the subsidiary clerical activities?
3. (*a*) Writing, typing, shorthand, etc. (*b*) Copying (manually, mechanically or photographically) (*c*) Filing, sorting, numbering and indexing (*d*) Checking.	4. What is the purpose of a job specification?
4. (*a*) To define the job, so that its difficulty can be assessed (*b*) To grade the job for salary purposes (*c*) To assist the appointment of suitable staff (*d*) To enable staff training schemes to be devised.	5. What is a manual of procedures?
5. It is a book of rules laying down procedures to be followed when an activity is undertaken. It establishes routines for each activity.	6. List five types of document in use in offices.
6. (*a*) Orders (*b*) Invoices (*c*) Statements (*d*) Credit notes (*e*) Petty cash vouchers.	7. List five types of communication used by offices.
7. (*a*) Memos (*b*) Reports (*c*) Internal telephone calls (*d*) External telephone calls (*e*) Letters.	8. Go over the page again until you feel you are sure of the answers.

Exercises Set 3

1. Complete the following sentences by inserting a word or phrase from the group below.

(a) The people who perform clerical duties are called . . . . . .
(b) Clerical duties are performed in a building called an . . . . . .
(c) The branch of mathematical science dealing with numerical facts is called
. . . . . .
(d) Writing letters has been largely mechanised since the invention of the
. . . . . .
(e) The establishment of an internal memo system improves . . . . . . within the organisation.
(f) In order to answer queries from management and customers it is necessary to have a good system of . . . . . .
(g) To . . . . . . things is to store them in such a way that they can be easily rediscovered.
(h) To investigate items that appear to be different from the usual run of things is called . . . .
(i) The reproduction of letters photographically is called . . . . . .
(j) A . . . . lays down all the activities that should be performed by a particular employee.

Word list: office, records, clerks, job specification, communication, file, management by exceptions, statistics, photocopying, typewriter.

2. The following memo is distributed to all staff in their in-trays:
Kindly remember to complete the forms already distributed and return them before 5 p.m.
Prepare a list of criticisms of this memo, explaining why it is an inadequate communication to staff.

3. Select the correct answer or answers to the questions below from the sets of answers supplied.

(i) What is the purpose of regular reports: (a) to record systematically the facts affecting a particular aspect of office work; (b) to welcome visiting personalities; (c) to enable management to assess changing situations, and pursue 'management by exceptions'; (d) to give regular opportunities for supervisors to complain about staff whose activities are below standard?
(ii) Which of the following may be described as clerical duties: (a) the typing of letters from a tape-recorded audio system; (b) the copying of a circular letter to 500 doctors notifying them of changes in Health Service charges; (c) the decision to spend a large sum of money on an extension to the factory; (d) the inspection of burned-out premises for signs of arson?
(iii) What is a manual of office procedures: (a) a list of promotions to be displayed on the office notice board; (b) a handbook made available to new staff describing the system used for certain routine office activities; (c) a hand-operated device used in the training of staff during the induction period; (d) a guidebook reference work as to the status of individuals in a company?
(iv) What is a job specification: (a) a detailed explanation of the materials to be used and the method of construction of a particular object; (b) a remedy

for an illness; (c) a clearly given order; (d) a precise account of the activities to be performed by a particular class of employees?

4. List the chief types of duty described as 'clerical duties' and give an example of each as it might be performed in: (a) the factory office of a large manufacturing firm; (b) the accounts department of a busy Government department.

5. What is a job specification? Make out such a specification for a part-time employee who assists (afternoons only) in the general office. She can type and knows how to keep books, but cannot do shorthand. Invent appropriate activities for her to perform.

6. Explain the functions of a school office in a busy school catering for pupils aged 11–18.

7. List at least five clerical activities. Then choose *one* of the activities you have named and explain its importance to (a) the large office of a public company, (b) the small office of a suburban solicitor.

8. Communication is a major function of offices. How may communication be improved within the office? Refer in your answer to both (a) organisation and (b) mechanical devices.

9. Susan Smith has joined the staff this morning. Suggest how she may be introduced to the various duties she will be required to perform so that she quickly reaches a good level of performance and later may deserve promotion.

10. Suggest suitable clerical assistance for the following senior members of staff: (a) the chief accountant in a busy accounts department; (b) the works manager—a small factory unit only; (c) the head of research and development department; (d) the sales manager; (e) the chief buyer.

You are now told that only nine staff can be employed for clerical duties. What allocation would you make to the senior staff concerned? The sales of the firm are spread over five counties, employing eleven commercial travellers.

11. What is the procedure when complaints are received? Draw up a suitable procedure for dealing with complaints: (a) about the repeated failure of a component you manufacture; (b) about an insufficiently stamped letter which has suffered delay as a result.

12. All business organisations and institutions (e.g. hospitals, colleges, etc.) have offices. Describe the clerical functions that these are likely to have in common.

(RSA Stage II)

4

THE LAYOUT OF THE OFFICE

4.1 The Need for Planning

If an office is merely a haphazard collection of desks, chairs, filing cabinets, telephones, etc., it will be inefficient and inconvenient. The office worker today will not continue in employment where work is badly arranged, facilities are outdated and the work is tiring and laborious. It follows that new offices should be thoroughly planned so that the work is easily performed and conveniently but unobtrusively supervised. Even older offices, which may fall below modern standards in many respects, can be greatly improved if the systems employed and the layout are regularly reappraised. The chief considerations are: (*a*) location of the office, (*b*) conditions, (*c*) the layout and (*d*) the provision of adequate business systems and aids.

We must consider some of the chief points under these headings, although even the best attempts at planning are subject to criticism in the light of actual experience. It follows that the young office worker actually performing the various tasks is often able to offer suggestions which an enlightened management will gratefully accept. Some offices have a **suggestion box** in which staff may place written suggestions. They should in particular report anything they find tiring or irksome, such as uncomfortable seating, poor lighting, unnecessary lifting or walking about. A telephone wrongly placed may cause a junior employee to make endless journeys across a large office. Niggardly behaviour with the paper clips may fray tempers and waste time out of all proportion to the cost of a more generous supply.

4.2 The Location of Offices

Where a completely new office is being built, it is desirable to choose a location which represents the best possible site for the purpose of the business concerned. Important considerations are:

(*a*) The location of other parts of the business, factories, warehouses, depots, etc. It will be of great importance to locate the office as centrally as possible to ensure adequate control.

(*b*) The likely costs, particularly the cost of land, or the rent payable for the use of land. Other costs might include rates for the area, parking costs, etc. The comparison of these costs at various sites may show one site to be more economic than another.

(*c*) Development Authority incentives. Many local authorities, particularly Development Authorities, are keen to attract office development—for example, to areas of inner city decay. They may offer subsidies to assist with building costs, free rental for a period of years, etc.

Other points of interest about the office location are:

(*a*) Its closeness to the bank and the post office. If a local branch of one of the major banks is not available, great inconvenience may be experienced in obtaining money as and when required, or in disposing of cash takings. Similarly, country mail services are less reliable than town deliveries.

(*b*) Its convenience for customers and business contacts. A firm which regularly receives visitors from overseas will wish to set up not far from a major airport. Closeness to a railway station may also be an advantage. Pleasant country surroundings may be very expensive from the point of view of transport for visitors and staff.

(*c*) The availability of suitably qualified staff. If the area surrounding the office cannot offer a sufficient number of suitable employees it will not be a convenient location. Future needs as well as present requirements should be borne in mind.

4.3 General Working Conditions—The *Health and Safety at Work Act, 1974*

In the United Kingdom general working conditions are controlled to some extent by the *Offices, Shops and Railways Premises Act, 1963*, a copy of which must be displayed prominently in all offices for the information of employees. A later Act, the *Health and Safety at Work Act, 1974*, is gradually introducing new regulations and approved codes of practice. The 1963 Act lays down many rules which employers must obey. Premises must be kept clean, adequate floor space must be provided for workers and their equipment, temperature must be kept above a minimum of 16°C, and ventilation must be adequate. Toilet facilities must be available, with running hot and cold water, soap and clean towels. Many employers not only meet these elementary conditions but recognise that good working conditions raise productivity. They therefore pay attention to many points not specifically required by the Act. The main points of interest are listed below.

(*a*) *Decoration*. Walls and ceilings should be tastefully decorated in carefully chosen colours. Furnishing and furniture should wherever possible be chosen to tone or contrast with the decorations.

(*b*) *Lighting*. The Act says that lighting must be adequate for the work required. Modern light fittings are generally inexpensive, and give out light of uniform intensity. Glare is avoided by suitable baffles which screen off the light from anyone who looks directly towards the source of light, yet at the same time the working surface is perfectly lit.

(c) *Safety*. The Act requires that personnel trained in First Aid should be available at all times and that an adequate First Aid box should be provided in every office. The knowledge of First Aid staff should be re-tested every three years. The greatest care should be taken to ensure safety in the office. Electrical and other apparatus should be installed or repaired only by qualified electricians; office equipment should be shielded where necessary—for example, guillotines and other cutting devices—and gangways should be kept clear, even marked out where necessary. Fire exits should be brought to the attention of staff and drills should be held to ensure that procedures are understood. Practical jokes should be severely discouraged—they often cause injuries.

(d) *Noise*. There is little excuse these days for noisy working conditions, since acoustic panels in ceilings and walls, double glazing and cork or rubber flooring can together deal effectively with most internal and external sources of noise. Doors can be fitted with devices which prevent slamming, and many modern machines are quiet in operation. The isolation of noisy equipment in alcoves or rooms where they are least disturbing to the general office is sometimes helpful.

(e) *Ventilation and heating*. Fresh air is essential to efficient clerical activity, but draughts can produce miserable working conditions, cold and rheumatic pains. Temperatures of about 65°–68°F (17°–18°C) are about the best for a busy office.

Generally speaking, the occupier of premises is responsible under the Act for the general working conditions, but where the premises are controlled by an owner who leases off parts of the building to different firms some of the duties and responsibilities are transferred to the owner.

All premises used as offices must be registered with the local authority, who must also be notified of any accident which causes the death, or disablement for more than three days, of any employee.

4.4 Open Plan and Enclosed Offices

Visitors to the House of Commons in London may occasionally be shown 'corridors of power' where all the doors leading off the central passage bear titles such as 'President of the Board of Trade', 'Foreign Secretary', 'Home Secretary' and so on. Small private offices of this type are very convenient for confidential private discussions of important matters, perhaps involving state secrets. On the other hand, enclosed offices of this sort, which are not solely found in Government departments, have disadvantages too. By contrast, many firms have adopted 'open-plan' offices, some of them quite enormous, with three or four hundred people working in the same room. A list of the advantages and disadvantages of open-plan offices would include the following:

Advantages

1. They are cheap to construct since lightweight partitions replace walls.
2. They are often single-storey buildings lit by natural daylight from overhead.
3. They are easy to supervise, since staff are in view at all times.
4. Communication is easy between staff in different departments since it is not necessary to leave the office and perhaps walk long distances to visit colleagues.
5. Changes in the pattern of work and the size of departments are easily taken into account if expanding departments move over into the spaces left by contracting departments.
6. Open-plan offices are easy to decorate. The staff themselves provide part of the decor, making them pleasant places to work in.
7. They are democratic, since all grades of staff are on view. Senior staff must preserve their position by a display of character and efficiency rather than by imposing door-plates and illuminated 'Enter' signs.
8. Layout can be such that the work flows on from desk to desk, each clerk contributing his special knowledge and skill to documents circulated into his in-tray.
9. A planned communications system can reduce movements about the office and put senior staff in instant touch with all departmental managers and clerks.

Disadvantages

1. There is a lack of privacy for confidential discussions.
2. They use land extensively rather than intensively and are therefore less suitable for city offices where rents are high.
3. Idle chatter may disrupt the work of a greater number of people, reducing work output from the more responsible staff.
4. Senior staff may be more easily disturbed than in the cubicle type of office.
5. There are some machines which are inappropriate for open-plan offices, particularly some accounting machines, typewriters, addressing machines, etc. These pieces of equipment must be installed in cubicle type offices on the edge of the open-plan office.

Plate 2 is a photograph of the open-plan office at the computer room of the head office of the Norwich Insurance Co. Ltd.

Plate 2. An open-plan office (reproduced by courtesy of Norwich Union Insurance Ltd).

4.5 Providing a Suitable Layout for an Individual

Layout of the office depends very greatly upon the most careful choice of desks and equipment to ensure the convenience and comfort of the clerk. Clerical duties can be as effectively carried out as the work on production lines in factories if the functions the clerk is to perform are given the same thought beforehand. Since most clerks perform a variety of jobs at different times of the day, the layout should be such that each task is accessible and easily commenced when necessary while at other times it is tidily out of the way.

A firm which specialises in devising equipment appropriate to such a variety of activities is Flexiform Ltd, whose **Master Units**, while mass produced and therefore relatively cheap to purchase, are flexible in nature. The same master unit may accommodate shelving units, pigeon-hole units, filing wallets and boxes, hanging filing pockets, card index drawers, a desk top and many other types of fittings. Such arrangements as those shown in Fig. 4.1 are very convenient, very economical in the use of space and quite inexpensive, especially when their long life is considered.

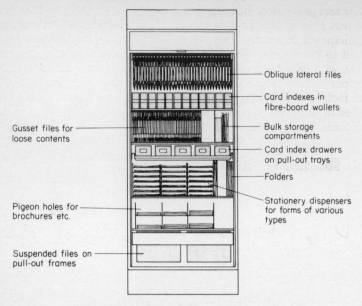

Fig. 4.1. A Flexiform unit (reproduced by courtesy of Flexiform Ltd).

A Case Study on Office Layout

Fig. 4.2 shows the layout of office premises before and after serious thought had been given to the layout by experts from the Flexiform organisation.

Before reorganisation the firm concerned used the main room, and the annexe, to store personnel records, taking 14.5 m² of space. At times personnel records overflowed into the small passageway, shown clear in the diagram. Increased documentation of 20 per cent was anticipated as a result of expansion plans, and additional office area had to be provided. The equipment already in use included:

    36 4-drawer filing cabinets
     1 3-drawer filing cabinet
    10 2-drawer filing cabinets
    33 9-tray visible index cabinets
     2 16-tray visible index cabinets
     1 work table
     3 pull-out working tops with cupboards
     1 20-drawer card index cabinet
     1 4-drawer card index cabinet

After reorganisation the annexe was cleared completely and the main office was able to accommodate not only all the previous records but the anticipated 20 per cent increase as well. The area required had been reduced to 8.8 m², a saving of 5.7 m², despite the increased capacity. Clearly, with office accommodation costing on average £64 per square metre per annum, good office layout can contribute a great deal to the reduction of accommodation costs, and—by reducing distances travelled to secure information stored in the records—can reduce fatigue and increase efficiency.

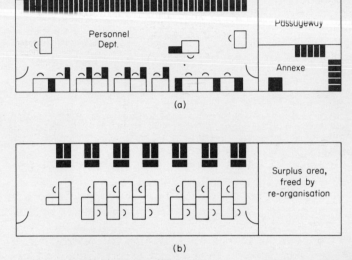

Fig. 4.2. Saving space by improving office layout (reproduced by courtesy of Flexiform Ltd).

4.6　Organisation and Methods (O. and M.)

Work study is a science in its own right today, and during the last twenty years it has begun to take more and more interest in office procedures. There are several reasons why this should be so. First, major economies of large-scale operation in factory production have been achieved in recent years, and many factory systems are now as efficient as they can possibly get. It follows that manufacturers, trying to keep ahead of their rivals in a competitive world, have had to look elsewhere to achieve more economic operations. A great deal of their attention was turned towards the distribution system; transport and warehousing have been revolutionised as more and more attention has been given to the most economic and efficient distribution system. The only other field left where economies can be achieved is in the field of clerical duties and office practice. The O. and M. teams have therefore turned their attention to this new field, and have begun to analyse the work done in offices. A second reason for the new interest in office procedures is the switch to international companies and the international movement of goods. This has required a careful study of documentation to reduce as far as possible the legal disputes which so easily arise when businessmen deal with foreigners who, apart from language differences, have different laws and mercantile customs from ourselves. You cannot hope to secure good arrangements with overseas governments and overseas firms if your own organisation and methods are slipshod and haphazard.

Generally speaking, the O. and M. team are specialists in work study, and do not normally work in the office which is being investigated. They bring an outsider's point of view to bear on the problems, asking employees what they do, what is the purpose of their activities, how long each process takes, etc. The stages of an O. and M. study include the following:

Stages of an O. and M. investigation

(a) Discover and record the present arrangements, including:

(i) What work is performed and by whom?

(ii) What is the purpose of this work in the firm's operations?

(iii) How does the work at present flow through the office? This may best be presented as a flow chart or model.

(iv) What are the links between this office and other departments— what part does this office play in the firm's whole scheme of activities?

(b) Draw up proposals for improving the system, including:

(i) Improvements in documentation; particularly the *alignment* of similar documents (see page 327). (The alignment of similar documents involves putting the same information in the same spot on each document. They can then be typed or run off from a master copy much more easily, using carbon paper or some other reproduction method.)

(ii) Improvements in work-flow; rearranging desks and working positions where necessary to improve the layout.

(iii) Improvements in technology; using labour-saving devices such as accounting machines, calculators, visible-index records, etc. Often convenient visual wall-displays—for example, of telephone numbers, personnel in departmental listing, etc.—improve the speed with which queries are handled.

(iv) Estimates of personnel changes required, including proposals for dealing with redundancy, etc.

(c) Implementation of the policy, including problem-solving where necessary, staff consultation, regular check-ups as the plans take effect and modification of the arrangements in the light of experience.

4.7 Simple Office Aids

There are many minor office aids which promote efficiency, and which every clerical worker should collect for his or her own use. Ideally the management should supply these for all staff. If it does not, and staff are continually having to walk about the office to borrow staplers, rulers and other items then they should point out politely that this shortage of equipment is wasting time and reducing their output of work. The following lists of essential and occasional requirements may help you to judge the adequacy of your own situation.

Essential requirements	Occasional requirements
1. Pencil.	1. Heavy duty stapler.
2. Rubber.	2. Heavy duty punch.
3. Red and blue ballpoint pens.	3. Eyeletting tool.
4. Hand stapling machine.	4. Guillotine (paper trimmer).
5. Staple extractor.	5. Roller damper for envelopes, etc.
6. Light two-hole punch.	6. Electronic calculator, or preferably
7. Scissors.	a printing calculator.
8. Ruler.	
9. Date stamp and pad.	
10. Desk tidy—for pins, paper clips, etc.	
11. Rubber stamps as required.	
12. Rubber stamp rack.	
13. Paste or gum.	
14. Desk diary.	
15. Magnetic pin dispenser.	

Fig. 4.3 illustrates some of these small office aids.

4.8 Points to Think About and Discuss

(a) The professional body for office managers is the Institute of Office Management. What advantages might follow from securing membership of such bodies, which usually require both examination qualifications and proof of experience from applicants?

(b) A delivery man asks you to sign for two tonnes of coke which he has shot into the area at the back of your factory premises. It is lunch-time and no one is on duty in the yard. What is the best course of action? Would you reach a different decision if it was a small, hand-delivered parcel?

(c) Make a plan of any small office that you know, marking in as accurately as you can the following items:

(i) The entrance door.
(ii) The windows.

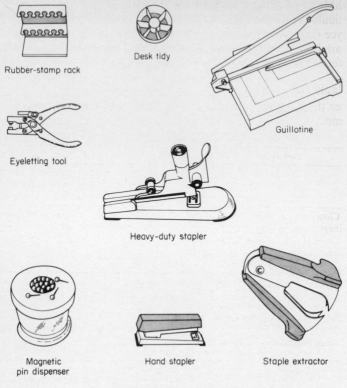

Rubber-stamp rack

Desk tidy

Guillotine

Eyeletting tool

Heavy-duty stapler

Magnetic
pin dispenser

Hand stapler

Staple extractor

Fig. 4.3. Smaller office aids.

(iii) The desk positions and seats.
(iv) Using the letters O.L. mark in the positions of overhead lighting.
(v) Use the letters D.L. for marking in any desk lights.
(vi) Use the letters E.T. and I.T. to mark the position of external and internal telephones. If the same telephone is used for two purposes mark it E. & I.T.
(vii) Mark the position of the filing cabinets, cupboards, work surfaces and other items of furniture.
(viii) Mark the position of any notice boards or display surfaces with the letters N.B.

In a suitable place alongside or below your diagram list any suggestions you have for improving the layout of the office in view of your knowledge of the work done there. Head these suggestions with the title 'Recommendations for improving the office layout'.

(*d*) Consider whether the room you are now sitting in would be acceptable as an office under the *Health and Safety at Work Act, 1974.* In particular consider: (i) cleanliness; (ii) adequate floor space for each employee (how many clerks could it accommodate); (iii) temperature; (iv) availability of toilet accommodation; (v) adequacy of the lighting; (vi) safety aspects, particularly the possibilities of fire.

4.9 Rapid Revision

Cover the page with a sheet of notepaper and uncover one question at a time.

Answers	*Questions*
—	1. List the points to be borne in mind when choosing the location of an office.
1. (*a*) Closeness to other parts of the business, factories, depots, etc. (*b*) General cost considerations, based on costs per square metre per annum. (*c*) Local authority incentives.	2. What other considerations enter into the choice of locality?
2. (*a*) Availability of bank and post office services nearby. (*b*) Convenience of customers and business contacts, particularly overseas contacts. (*c*) Availability of qualified staff.	3. What Act of Parliament controls office conditions?
3. The *Health and Safety at Work Act, 1974.*	4. List the important points in the Act.
4. (*a*) Premises must be clean. (*b*) Adequate floor space for each employee. (*c*) Temperature at about 17°–18°C. (*d*) Toilet facilities and hot and cold water, soap, etc., to be provided. (*e*) Adequate lighting. (*f*) Trained First Aid staff and retesting for these staff every three years.	5. (*a*) With whom are office premises registered? (*b*) What particular events must be notified to them?
5. (*a*) With local authorities. (*b*) Accidents causing death, or incapacity for more than three days.	6. What are the chief types of offices?
6. (*a*) Enclosed offices, or 'cubicle' offices. (*b*) Open-plan offices.	7. What are the advantages of enclosed offices?
7. (*a*) More private for confidential discussions. (*b*) Quiet to work in. (*c*) They isolate noisy equipment. (*d*) They confer status on top-level staff.	8. What are the advantages of open-plan offices?

Answers	Questions
8. (a) They are cheap to build. (b) They are easy to supervise. (c) They are democratic and sociable places to work in. (d) They are adaptable as work patterns change.	9. What is an O. and M. department?
9. A department that appraises organisation and methods and recommends changes in layout and procedure.	10. What aspects might it consider?
10. (a) The present arrangements and system of work. (b) The possible improvements in: (i) general layout, (ii) the documentation procedures, (iii) the 'flow' of work around the office, (iv) the individual work positions, and their layout.	11. Go over the page until you feel you are sure of the answers.

Exercises Set 4

1. Write down on your answer paper the letters (a)–(j), to correspond with the sentences below. Against each letter write the word or phrase, chosen from the word list, which is needed to complete the sentence.

(a) Many .... help firms to find offices in suitable locations.
(b) An idea for improving the working of your office should be contributed to the ....
(c) The Act of Parliament controlling working conditions in offices is the *Health and .... Act, 1974.*
(d) Modern office lighting is fitted with baffle screens to prevent ......
(e) Noise can be reduced by using .... ceiling panels in offices.
(f) Fresh air can be assured by adequate ...... systems.
(g) Greater privacy for senior staff is possible with small ...... offices.
(h) Open-plan offices are easier to ...... than enclosed offices.
(i) Good internal telephone networks reduce the need to ...... colleagues to clarify difficult points.
(j) The department responsible for improving office layout is the ...... and ...... team.

Word List: suggestions box, glare, ventilation, Development Authorities, O. M., enclosed, supervise, Safety at Work, sound absorbent, visit.

2. In each of the following questions select the best answer from the four alternatives given; (a), (b), (c) or (d).
(i) Closeness to a large housing estate may be an advantageous location for an office because: (a) an adequate bus service is sure to be available; (b) there will be a post office nearby; (c) industrial sites are often unpleasant and pollute the atmosphere; (d) a large labour force will be available for employment.
(ii) The *Health and Safety at Work Act, 1974*: (a) lays down clear limitations

on the height of office buildings; (*b*) controls the general working conditions in offices; (*c*) was repealed in 1976; (*d*) nationalised all offices employing more than one hundred staff.
(iii) In all offices there should be, according to the 1974 Act: (*a*) lifts to serve all floors; (*b*) lighting to a standard of 120 lumens per square foot; (*c*) trained First Aid personnel whose knowledge should be retested every three years; (*d*) welfare and recreation club facilities.

3. Which of the following are *not true* of open-plan offices? (*a*) They are often well lit and well ventilated; (*b*) they are easy to supervise; (*c*) they are very suitable for confidential interviews; (*d*) they help the easy flow of documents; (*e*) they reduce the disturbance caused by idle, chattering staff; (*f*) they are generally speaking cheerful places to work in; (*g*) they are democratic, giving all staff the same working conditions.

4. Compare the advantages and disadvantages of the large open office with those of a group of small enclosed offices.

5. What do you understand by 'office methods'? How might they be improved in a firm operating in a traditional way?

6. Tom Smith advertises himself as an 'office consultant'. What services do you think he might offer to businessmen?

7. Write short notes about: (*a*) open-plan offices; (*b*) office fire drill; (*c*) guillotines and similar dangerous equipment; (*d*) document flow.

8. Write a memo for the manager of your office about the provision of minor office equipment items. Advance reasons for increasing the available equipment, and justifying the initial expense. Suggest control procedures to prevent waste of such items.

9. (i) Suggest a layout for a work position, including a diagram if you wish to draw one, for an employee who: (*a*) regularly types for about half her working day; (*b*) spends half of the remainder of her time assembling and stapling speeches of senior executives for distribution as handouts at staff conferences (they are usually at least 12 pages thick); (*c*) is a telephone link-girl for her department answering both internal and external calls.
   (ii) Would you change your layout if she were left-handed?

10. What part can office equipment play in improving the layout of work positions? In your answer refer particularly to: (*a*) filing cabinets; (*b*) wall notice boards; (*c*) desks.

5

THE RECEPTION OFFICE

5.1 The Importance of the Receptionist

Many young people are attracted to clerical positions by the idea of reception work. Receptionists are important because they are often the public's first contact with a firm, and first impressions are often the most enduring. A surly or aggressive reception, or a 'couldn't care less' attitude, can do a firm irreparable damage, by rebuffing clients, customers and potential new staff.

A good receptionist must have many important qualities: a smart appearance; a pleasant speaking voice; a willingness to assist the visitor; and a sound knowledge of the organisation. This enables the receptionist to attend to visitors' enquiries quickly.

The last requirement, a wide knowledge of the organisation, means that it is usually impossible to perform the duties of a receptionist adequately until one knows something about the firm's activities, its layout and its personnel. Perhaps, therefore, twenty years is the minimum age for a receptionist, since by then most young people will have mastered several routine activities and have acquired poise, maturity, knowledge and experience.

5.2 The Work of the Receptionist

Not every firm has such an endless stream of callers that it needs the services of a full-time receptionist although it is important for the reception desk to be manned at all times. It follows that a variety of work may fall upon the receptionist. The type of work performed will vary with the office, but may include the following:

(*a*) Control of the switchboard and telephone system.
(*b*) Supervision of messengers and porters.
(*c*) Book-keeping records—particularly in hotels.
(*d*) Typing, filing and envelope addressing.
(*e*) Petty cashier duties.
(*f*) Small sales—for example of brochures and handbooks published by the organisation.
(*g*) The receipt of packages and messages for onward transmission to departments.

Where the duties of a receptionist are combined with other tasks, posts

Fig. 5.1. The visitor's reception should be friendly and efficient.

are advertised for clerk-receptionist, typist-receptionist, telephone-receptionist or book-keeper-receptionist. Such posts give valuable training to young staff wishing to acquire experience for a later position as a full-time receptionist.

5.3 The Location of the Reception Office

The reception office must be in the entrance hall of the building, or at the entrance to the suite of offices. Often a hall porter will be in charge of the main hall, and will assist visitors to find the suite they require with the help of messenger boys or lift attendants. Where the receptionist is in the main hall he or she will usually have a full working position, including the switchboard, a typewriter, perhaps book-keeping records and other facilities.

Where the receptionist is in a small suite of offices clear instructions to visitors are necessary. Adequate notices reading 'Enquiries' or 'Receptionist' help the visitors to gain immediate access to the suite at the most appropriate point for receiving attention. A bell, or buzzer, should enable them to summon attention at an unmanned reception point. A name-plate, made up of white plastic lettering on a triangular black plastic block, is a great help to visitors who often prefer to know with whom they are dealing. One should be provided for each person who mans the reception position.

5.4 The Reception of Visitors

The following rules are helpful in receiving visitors at a reception point:

(*a*) Do not continue with an obviously trivial task while a visitor waits for attention.

(*b*) If you are engaged on the switchboard you should at least glance up and smile to show that you have noticed the visitor's appearance and will attend to his needs at the earliest possible moment.

(*c*) The best form of greeting is 'Good morning/afternoon. May I help you?'

(*d*) It is useful to make a list of callers, as a routine record of reception activities. This list will often prove helpful, as when the member of staff visited forgot to ask the caller's initial(s) or his telephone number. This register should be prepared quite openly and the caller should be asked for any details he does not volunteer. A typical ruling for such a register is given in Fig. 5.2.

Date	Name of caller	Business or other address	Person or Dept. visited	Time of arrival	Time of departure
19... May 5	J. Goldfarb (Mr.)	San Francisco (staying at Ocean Hotel)	Mr. Lyonnesse	10·30	12·30
5	J. Fellowes (Miss)	20 Golding's Crescent Newtown	Personnel Dept	10·50	11·15
5	R. Bacon (Mr.)	Imperial Typewriter Co.	Miss Hachett	10·55	3·30
5	T. Brownjohn (Mr.)	Elite Display Co.	Advertising Dept.	12·15	12·25
6	R. Lucas (Mr.)	Engineering Consultants Ltd.	Works Manager's Office	3·30	4·45

Fig. 5.2. A reception register.

(*e*) If possible, you should invite the visitor to take a seat while you call the person he wishes to see on the internal telephone system.

(*f*) You should either escort the visitor personally, or call a messenger to escort him. If the interview is to be conducted in a waiting room or vestibule close to the reception room, show him into the room and invite him to be seated until his business contact arrives.

(*g*) It is wise to check up to ensure that the visitor does in fact receive attention; if his contact fails to arrive, remind the contact over the telephone that the visitor is still waiting for attention.

5.5 Problem-solving by Receptionists

In many respects the receptionist is like a buffer between the firm and the world outside. When the private world of the office wishes to make contact with the outside world, or vice versa, the parties concerned will usually make appointments. Visitors who have an appointment present little difficulty to the receptionist, who deals with them in the ways suggested above.

Other visitors may present difficulties; for example, their visit may be unexpected and, therefore, inconvenient. Generally speaking, the uninvited visitor is prepared to wait until someone can see him, or will philosophically accept the fact that his call is so inconvenient that it is quite impossible for him to receive attention. Such a call may result in the receptionist's arranging an appointment, usually in consultation with the personal secretary of the person concerned, for a later date.

A third type of visitor may represent what can only be regarded as an emergency. Such visitors should always be given immediate and courteous attention, according to the urgency of their request. For example, at education offices an irate parent, breathing fire and sulphur against a local head-teacher and demanding to see the District Education Officer, would probably be accorded an interview without a previous appointment. Similarly, a police officer or a journalist from a local or national newspaper would certainly be accorded immediate attention. Quite apart from possible bad publicity resulting from any discourtesy to such people, most firms feel a sense of social responsibility towards the law, the press and local authorities.

Sometimes it is necessary to cover up for a member of staff who for some reason does not wish to see a particular visitor. If there is any likelihood of this it is best to speak impersonally on the internal telephone. Do not say, 'Mr Payne, there is a representative here to see you from Colour Display Co.' Instead, say, 'There is a gentleman here from Colour Display Co. who would like to speak to Mr Payne if he is available, please.' This gives Mr Payne the opportunity to excuse himself. The telling of *white lies* is almost inseparable from reception work. In most cases the motive is to avoid embarrassment to both parties. A direct statement that Mr Payne thinks the Colour Display's Co.'s products are poor value for money and he does not wish to discuss them might upset the representative concerned.

5.6 Confidential Matters

An employee is in a special position with regard to his or her employer. A receptionist is to some extent the employer's agent, acting on the employer's behalf in many matters that arise during the course of the day's work. One of the rules about such agents is that they have a duty of care not to disclose confidential matters regarding the employer's business affairs. An indiscreet receptionist may easily disclose matters which are of use to callers, even by such apparently innocent remarks as disclosing the names of other visitors. Consider the following conversation:

'I have an appointment with Mr Rogerson, I am from Universal Take-overs.'

'I'm so sorry, Mr Rogerson is busy at present. He is having a discussion with the Chairman of Amalgamators Incorporated.'

Clearly the receptionist has 'let the cat out of the bag'. The visitor now knows that the employer is negotiating with two possible purchasers of the business at the same time. This is a breach of the duty not to disclose confidential information.

Similarly, the response to the question 'How's business?' is ideally a non-committal remark like, 'Oh, pretty hectic, you know.' To reply, 'Dull as ditchwater!' will perhaps cause the visitor to revise his ideas of whatever bargain he is making with the firm. He may harden his prices or demand shorter delivery dates than he is normally entitled to expect.

In particular, the receptionist should be careful that visitors do not 'pump' her for information. 'I'm afraid I don't know anything about that', is the discreet answer to *loaded* questions.

5.7 Receiving Parcels

It often happens that parcels, packets and other communications are delivered to the receptionist, and a signature is demanded on a delivery note. Such notes should not be signed without inspection of the goods, since a 'clean' signature—that is, one that makes no comment upon the number and condition of the packages—will usually absolve the carrier from any blame should the consignment be incomplete or damaged.

If the parcel or packet, or number of packets, appears to agree with the description in the consignment note it is best to sign 'Received in apparent good order and condition'. This still leaves the firm free to claim if in fact the contents are damaged and if the damage could not be seen from the outside. If they do not appear to be in good order then it is best to describe on the note the actual condition, i.e. 'Arrived open' or 'Parcel damp and stained—contents may be broken'. This is better than saying 'Signed unexamined', which appears to imply that there was nothing apparently wrong with the parcel.

5.8 A Panel-strip Index

A device called a 'panel-strip index', marketed by Kalamazoo Ltd, is very useful to telephone operators, receptionists and others who need quick references to a range of information. The illustration in Fig. 5.3 shows how it is used. Strips of a specially designed shape are typed or handwritten to give the information required. They may then be inserted in a few seconds in panels which form part of a visual index desk or wall display.

Imagine that a visitor has called and given the receptionist his business card to take to a departmental manager with whom he has an appointment. The receptionist asks permission to return it on his way out.

The register of callers and a visi-index strip are then prepared before he leaves. We now have a convenient visual record of the name, phone number, address and other details and the person he is most likely to wish to speak to. Should someone from his office call him, we will be able to locate him in the building in a few seconds, and similarly we will be able to answer such queries as 'What are his initials?', 'Does he have letters after his name?' etc.

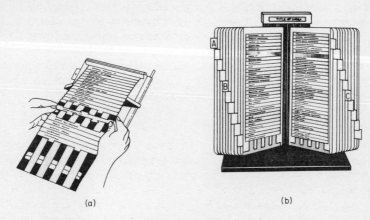

(a)   (b)

Fig. 5.3. A visi-index desk unit holding 3400 strips of information (reproduced by courtesy of Kalamazoo Ltd).

5.9 Points to Think About and Discuss

(*a*) How should a receptionist deal with the following two situations:

(i) A commercial traveller who usually comes on the first Monday of the month for a regular appointment with the chief buyer arrives on the first Wednesday of the month regretting that he has been indisposed.
(ii) An elderly gentleman demands to see the manager in order to lodge a complaint about a product. The manager is on vacation.

(*b*) Three applications are received for a receptionist's post, which involves switchboard operation, keeping a register of visitors, and controlling a staff of three messengers. The ability to give First Aid is also desirable. The three are: (i) a disabled telephonist, male, aged 44, using his own wheelchair, trained Post Office telephonist; (ii) an ex-Post Office telephonist, female, aged 50, a competent typist but untrained in First Aid; (iii) a smart young lady of good appearance, who learned relief telephonist work at her former post, and wishes to 'meet people' in her employment, although she already has a well-paid post as a copy typist.
Discuss the merits of these three applicants.

5.10   Rapid Revision

Cover the page with a sheet of paper and uncover one question at a time

Answers	Questions
—	1. Where should the reception office be located?
1. (a) In the main foyer of the building. (b) In the entrance to the suite of offices.	2. Where a reception point is not manned all the time what arrangements should be made?
2. (a) Clear notices to indicate the reception area. (b) A bell, buzzer or telephone system to attract attention.	3. What attributes should a receptionist have?
3. (a) Good appearance. (b) Pleasant speaking voice. (c) Courteous approach. (d) A good knowledge of the business, its layout and chains of responsibility.	4. What duties are often associated with the receptionist, besides the reception of visitors?
4. (a) Control of the switchboard. (b) Supervision of porters and messengers. (c) Bookings (in hotels) and other book-keeping records such as petty cash. (d) Small sales of brochures, etc.	5. What points must a receptionist watch to prevent the disclosure of confidential matters?
5. (a) Keep conversation with visitors at an impersonal level. (b) Watch out for the visitor who asks leading questions. (c) Talk indirectly over the telephone when notifying the arrival of a visitor.	6. How should parcels, etc., be signed for?
6. So that a 'clean' signature is not readily available—for example, 'in apparent good order' is the best signature to be given. In doubtful circumstances state them, i.e. 'parcel open on arrival'.	7. What is a register of callers?
7. A register recording the names initials and other details about callers, and the purpose of visits made to the premises.	8. Go over the page again until you feel you are sure of the answers.

Exercises Set 5

1. Write the letters (a)–(j) on your answer paper to correspond with the sentences below. Against each letter write the word or phrase from the word list required to complete the sentence.

(a) The receptionist needs a sound knowledge of the firm's ......
(b) The receptionist is the first person in the firm that the visitor meets, and should always try to create a good ......

(*c*) A receptionist should keep her work position tidy and in appearance she should be neat and ....

(*d*) The reception office must be near the ...... to the building or suite of offices.

(*e*) The best greeting is 'Good morning/afternoon. May ....?'

(*f*) Wherever possible callers should have previously arranged an ......

(*g*) It is good practice wherever possible to ask to see a visitor's ....

(*h*) A .... should be kept to assist in recalling later who came, at what time, etc.

(*i*) It is important not to disclose ...... information of use to callers.

(*j*) When using the internal telephone it is best to speak ...... if there is any chance that a visitor may not be welcome.

Word list: impression, impersonally, entrance, organisation, appointment, business card, register of callers, I help you, well groomed, confidential.

2. In the following questions select the best answer out of the four alternatives given:

(i) A receptionist should be knowledgeable about the firm and its affairs because: (*a*) the receptionist can deal with visitors personally instead of bothering other staff; (*b*) the receptionist will feel more confident; (*c*) the receptionist will be able to bring the visitor into contact with the right member of staff with the minimum delay; (*d*) it will save listening-in on the telephone.

(ii) A receptionist should preferably have a name-plate at the reception point because: (*a*) visitors prefer to address the receptionist by name if possible; (*b*) it makes it easier for visitors to 'date' the receptionist; (*c*) complaints about the receptionist's behaviour and attitude may be more easily made; (*d*) it creates an impersonal atmosphere.

(iii) Emergency visitors who arrive without an appointment on very urgent affairs should: (*a*) be given an opportunity to calm down before meeting a member of staff; (*b*) be told that they can receive attention only if they make an appointment in a proper way; (*c*) be invited to wait in a convenient waiting room while the receptionist contacts the most likely person to deal with the matter; (*d*) be taken in at once to the manager, however busy he is.

(iv) The best response to a visitor who expresses his appreciation of your services is: (*a*) 'That's quite all right sir,' (*b*) 'Bring a box of chocolates next time.' (*c*) 'You are very welcome, sir.' (*d*) 'Good morning, sir.'

3. Which of the following are *not* true of a receptionist's work? (*a*) It is easy, routine work; (*b*) it calls for tact in dealing with callers; (*c*) it is of little importance to the firm; (*d*) it makes an instant impression on visitors; (*e*) it needs maturity and a wide knowledge of the firm's personnel and organisation; (*f*) the hours are short and untroubled by emergencies or sudden pressures.

4. What is a register of callers? Draft the likely headings on such a register and enter the name and other details of four visitors.

5. Draw up a message pad which might be of use to a receptionist showing the following points: (*a*) date; (*b*) time; (*c*) to whom addressed; (*d*) message; (*e*) by whom was the message received.

6. You are a relief receptionist in the lunch hour and no one else is available. The canteen is accessible by telephone and has a loudspeaker call system for emergency use. How would you deal with the following situations? (*a*) A traffic

warden informs you that the firm's car is causing an obstruction and must be moved immediately; (*b*) a carrier arrives with two parcels, the smaller of which is clearly damaged and some of the contents may even be missing, and demands an immediate signature; (*c*) a member of a visiting party of foreign buyers arrives to say that he has been separated from his party and is not sure where they are lunching (you know that foreign buyers are always entertained at Rule's Restaurant).

7. One of your duties is the reception of visitors to your chief. List four simple rules to be observed.

8. Suggest five pleasant remarks you might make to a caller while you were waiting for his contact to come down and collect him from the reception area.

9. What do you consider would be (*a*) the pleasant parts of a receptionist's work; (*b*) the most difficult matters to deal with?

10. Your work as a receptionist has grown more and more hectic recently as the firm's activities have expanded. Draft a letter to your employer pointing out the difficulties you are experiencing and suggesting how the work load could be reduced.

11. List the chief qualities you would expect from a receptionist. Select two of these qualities and explain why you consider them to be important.

12. A receptionist is often required to perform routine work during intervals of inactivity. What sort of activities might be carried out in this way? Explain why each is an appropriate activity for a receptionist.

13. A receptionist is faced by the following situations during a busy morning. Explain what action she should take in each case.

(*a*) An important client from overseas is cut off by the receptionist. He was not ringing from his usual office, and the Sales Manager is furious.

(*b*) The office boy is hit by a swing door and his nose bleeds furiously.

(*c*) The local police call in to check security arrangements in connection with their campaign 'Look out—there's a thief about'.

(*d*) The Post department ask her to obtain postage stamps to the value of £10.00.

(*e*) A parcel delivered by special messenger appears damp from internal damage. It also smells strongly, rather like petrol or lighter fuel.

14. Miss Brown, the new receptionist, has been promised that before taking up employment on the first of next month her working accommodation will be improved. What points would you consider when providing her with a satisfactory work-position? The reception office is close to the entrance of your suite of offices in a large multi-occupied building.

15. The receptionist is at lunch from 1 to 2 p.m. There are seven other employees who share the duty of relief receptionist at this time, and also when necessary during the day. They are *A*, *B*, *C*, *D*, *E*, *F* and *G*. *A* is always absent on Monday, and *E* on Thursday. *G* is not to be left in sole charge at lunch-time as she is inexperienced, but it is desired to give her some opportunity of reception work at other times of the day. *C*, by special arrangement, always lunches from 1 to 2 p.m. so that she may care for her invalid mother. Draw up a rota of duties to ensure that the reception desk is always manned.

6

THE TELEPHONE AND SWITCHBOARD

6 1 The Importance of the Telephone Network

When Alexander Graham Bell, a teacher of the deaf, patented the telephone in 1876 he surely could not have dreamed of the revolution he was making in communications, and the effect it would have on the business world in particular. The whole quality of our lives has been transformed by this facility to speak personally and instantaneously to almost anyone else in the world. It is now possible to dial business associates almost everywhere in the world directly, without any assistance from the operator. Half the world's population watches pictures of a royal wedding, a presidential assassination, or an Olympic Games. There seems to be no limit to the technical skill of the telecommunications engineer. Already proposals are being made that the telephone system should read our gas and electricity meters for us without any human assistance. Television-linked telephone circuits, which enable us to see our caller, are already in use, and may be said to have perfected Alexander Graham Bell's invention, for they enable the deaf person to lip-read what his caller is saying to him.

The telephone is the most vital communications link in business. It is direct, personal and immediate. The most modern switchboards are miracles of ingenuity, linking department to department, branch to head office, international company with foreign subsidiary, ship to shore, aircraft to base; with every refinement to ensure speed, economy and, if necessary, secrecy. The telephone operator holds one of the key positions in any organisation. Consequently, the young office worker should always be prepared to learn how to operate the switchboard. It brings immediate recognition of his or her ability, and a knowledge of the affairs of the firm which cannot be acquired so quickly in any other way.

6.2 The Principle of the Telephone

Fig. 6.1 illustrates the principle of the telephone. Note carefully:

1. The human voice makes sound waves which strike the diaphragm of the microphone in the telephone hand-set.
2. The pressure waves cause the diaphragm alternately to compress and release the carbon granules behind it. This alternately increases

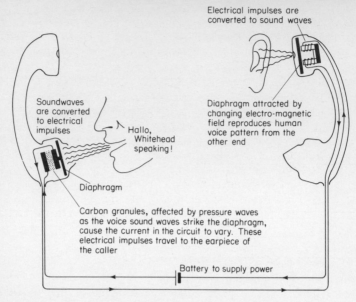

Fig. 6.1. The principle of the telephone.

and decreases the flow of current in the circuit passing through the telephone network to the earpiece of the caller's hand-set.

3. In the earpiece the current is led around an electro-magnet which becomes more or less magnetised as the current varies. The strong current attracts the earpiece diaphragm strongly—the weaker current releases the diaphragm.

4. This movement of the diaphragm imitates the movement of the human voice box miles away which is causing the current to vary, and we hear the same sounds the speaker is making.

6.3 Advantages and Disadvantages of the Telephone System

These may be listed as follows:

Advantages

(*a*) It is a very fast communications system, taking only fractions of a second to bridge gaps of hundreds of miles.

(*b*) It is a direct link person to person, giving an extremely individual and personal character to the contacts made in this way.

(*c*) It is relatively cheap, especially if good control can be exercised.

(*d*) Calls can be received on automatically operated telephone answering services, at any time of the day or night. This enables agents and commercial travellers to phone in cheap calls at off-peak periods for attention the next day.

Disadvantages

(*a*) There are no written records of the calls—though they may be tape-recorded at some expense. Contracts made by telephone therefore are difficult to prove in court. Generally speaking they are most useful to those bodies which, by a custom of the trade, are binding in honour—for example, Stock Exchange contracts, Lloyd's insurance contracts and other contracts made by those who live by the motto 'My word is my bond'.

(*b*) Although relatively cheap, telephone services may be abused—for example, for private purposes of staff. Good control is necessary; or devices like 'trunk barring' may reduce the abuse.

(*c*) Since the caller cannot be seen, the personal contact established depends upon the voice; one cannot see facial expressions or gestures which may convey much in a completely personal confrontation.

6.4   Making a Telephone Call from an Office

Simple Installations

Whether an office is small or large the owner will apply to British Telecom for telephone services to be connected to the premises. A hire charge is made for the use of facilities installed, and also for the calls made, which are metered automatically. Quarterly accounts are then rendered to the subscriber. It follows that telephone calls from an office do not involve the insertion of money in coin boxes. Special booklets are distributed to subscribers called *Telephone Dialling Codes* for the area in which the subscriber lives.

The simplest installation merely consists of a hand-set which is connected directly to the telephone system. Other systems have a simple hand-set with a switch and connection to another hand-set. The switch has four positions. By repositioning at points (*a*), (*b*), (*c*) or (*d*) it is possible to connect: (*a*) to the exchange to make or receive outside calls; (*b*) to the other extension (in this case the outside caller cannot hear what is being said); (*c*) the outside caller to the extension; (*d*) the two hand-sets as an intercom unit.

In either of these cases, immediately the hand-set is lifted a dialling tone is heard, and the subscriber may then dial any number he requires in the enormous range of numbers given him in the booklet. There are about 3000 exchanges within call, with thousands of subscribers on each exchange, so that virtually anyone in the country is within reach. For these simple installations the best course of procedure is as follows:

(*a*) Find out the telephone number of the person or firm you wish to ring.

(*b*) Then find the dialling code for that exchange from the dialling instructions booklet. This will also tell you the rate of charge.

Charges vary between the three classes, and with the time of day. There is a peak rate, a standard rate and a cheap rate.

(c) Lift the receiver and listen for the dialling tone (a continuous purring sound).

(d) Dial the exchange code first, and then the personal number of the business associate. When dialling, it is best to dial carefully but quickly—do not leave too long an interval between each digit. The dial should be allowed to return freely to its starting point between each digit.

(e) Wait for an interval of anything up to 15 seconds.

(f) Listen for either:

  (i) a ringing tone (burr-burr) which tells you the number is being called;

  (ii) an 'engaged tone', a repeated single note, which tells you to try again later;

  (iii) a number unobtainable note (a steady note). You should replace the receiver, check your information about codings, etc., and then re-dial.

(g) At the end of the call replace the receiver carefully. It is this action which disconnects the charging equipment. A badly replaced receiver may cost a great deal of money if the charging meter is not disconnected.

Private Branch Exchanges

Most large firms have some sort of PBX or PABX installation.

The letters PBX stand for **private branch exchange** and imply that a

Plate 3. The SL-1 attendant's console (reproduced by courtesy of Reliance Systems Ltd).

firm with this type of switchboard has a small exchange of its own, similar in many ways to the telephone exchanges set up in every area to serve the general public. From PBX a staff operator will find numbers for the staff, make calls for them and so on. However, the pace of technology has rendered such an exchange less and less useful in the last few years. The growth of STD circuits (subscriber trunk dialling), using equipment called GRACE (group routing and charging equipment), has rendered the operator less necessary than formerly as far as external calls are concerned. Connections to GRACE are made by dialling 0 and the code required. Thus all London numbers are 01 numbers. All Birmingham numbers are 021, etc.

PABX stands for **private automatic branch exchange**. While many firms still use the PBX equipment, the new automatic branch exchanges, one of which is illustrated in Plate 3, will gradually replace them. The attendant, instead of a complex switchboard with electric wiring, has a compact electronic console which simply sits on the desk-top. They are electronic miracles, offering a variety of services to a large number of extensions.

The Features Offered on a Modern (Computerised) PABX

A modern PABX offers a huge range of services to the subscriber, which may be selected or rejected when the original installation is made and adapted easily from time to time as business patterns change. The SL-1 system illustrated in Plate 3 and Fig. 6.2, for example, is very flexible. The flexibility of the SL-1 system stems from the fact that the central control is a computer. The system's features and services are defined by a software program rather than circuit wiring. Features can be added, deleted or modified by changing the soft-ware program rather than the hardware.

In the description of the features and services of the SL-1 system below the author is grateful for permission to use material supplied by Reliance Systems Ltd.

Access to paging. Extension users and attendants have access to loudspeakers or radio-paging equipment.

Access to dictation. Extension users have access to and control of dictation equipment, so that they may dictate letters to a typing pool.

Digital transmission multifrequency calling (DTMF) allows the use of telephones equipped with pushbutton dials to transmit digits via audible tones to the switching equipment.

Access to services and trunks. Extension users can either dial or press a key to gain trunk lines or services from the telephone exchange.

Call forward—First number busy. This service automatically routes incoming calls to a pre-selected extension when the called directory number is busy. A busy executive can thus pass calls to a secretary or assistant.

Call forward—First number does not answer. Automatically routes incoming

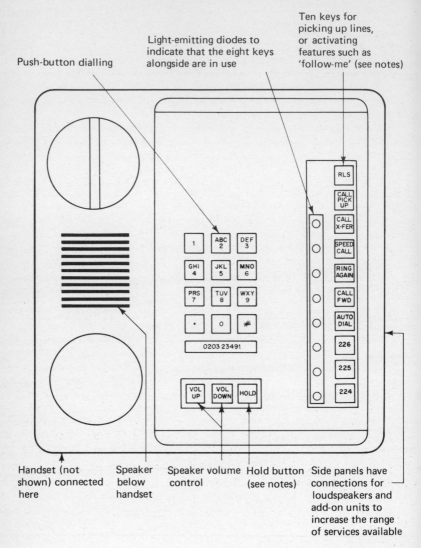

Fig. 6.2. The basic SL-1 telephone (reproduced by courtesy of Reliance Systems Ltd).

calls to a pre-selected extension when the called directory number does not answer within a prescribed time.

Call forward—Follow-me. Automatically routes incoming calls to an extension defined by the absent extension. An executive who has to see a colleague elsewhere in the building can route all his calls to the extension concerned.

DTMF to dial pulse conversion. Automatically converts DTMF signals from a key telephone for transmission over rotary-dial-only trunk lines.

Direct inward dialling (DID). Allows an incoming call from the exchange network to reach a specific extension without assistance from the attendant.

Direct outward dialling (DOD). Allows an extension user to gain access to the exchange network, without assistance from the attendant, by dialling an access code.

Class-of-Service restrictions. This enables managements to control calls originating from extensions—for example, to prevent junior staff using outside lines at peak periods in the day.

Code restrictions. Denies or allows selected extensions access to international, national and local public exchange codes. The degree of restriction provided can be automatically varied at pre-selected times of day and on switching to night service.

Hunting. This service routes a call to an idle extension number in a pre-arranged group, when the called extension number is busy.

Extension-to-extension calling. An extension user can dial other extensions within the same system directly without the assistance of the attendant.

Night service. Allows incoming calls to be directed to selected extensions or directory numbers after normal business hours or at times when the console (switchboard) is unattended.

Call pickup. Allows an extension user to answer an incoming call to another extension belonging to the same call pick-up group.

Handsfree operation. Permits the extension user to speak without using the handset.

Hold. Allows an extension user, without assistance from the attendant, to hold any active call and use the telephone to call another number for consultation purposes. The user may then return to the held call and continue the interrupted conversation.

Call transfer. Allows an extension user, on any established two-party call, to hold the existing call, and originate another call to a third party for a private consultation. The user may either release from the consultation and return to the original call or transfer the original call to the third party.

Call waiting. Informs an extension user by tone buzzing and lamp flash signals, that another call is waiting to be connected during an established call.

On-hook dialling. Allows a user to dial without lifting the handset.

Override. Enables an extension user, after reaching a busy number, to override the busy condition and enter the existing conversation on a bridged basis, preceded by a warning tone.

Conference (three-party). Allows an extension user, while on any two-party connection, to hold the existing call, and originate another call to a third party for a private consultation. The user may then add the held party to the call for a three-party conference.

Conference (six-party). A similar feature to Conference (three-party) except that six conferees are allowed.

Pushbutton dialling. A dial pad consisting of 12 non-locking pushbuttons (4 × 3) is provided on all SL-1 telephones and consoles.

Release key. A dedicated key can be provided on the SL-1 telephone which allows an extension user to release from an active call without having to go on-hook.

Telephone expansion. The complement of key/lamp facilities on the SL-1 telephone may be expanded by simply installing add-on key/lamp modules on the right-hand side of the basic telephone.

Tone buzzing. Provides an audible tone through the speaker to alert the extension when on-hook.

Voice calling. Allows the originating extension user to page over the speaker in the called party's SL-1 telephone.

Volume control. Provides independent volume control of tone buzzing, tone ringing and voice calling.

Ring again. Alerts a calling extension when a busy number becomes idle.

Speed calling. Permits an extension user to dial frequently-called numbers using only one or two digits.

6.5 Answering the Telephone

Just as the receptionist is the caller's first link with the firm, and it is important to receive callers courteously and attend to their needs promptly, the telephonist is the telephone caller's first introduction to the firm. Always answer calls promptly, deal with callers courteously, and ensure that you convey, by your interest in the callers and their requirements, the impression that your firm is efficient and businesslike. Under the STD system all calls are metered and charged. Formerly many local calls were not metered and were very cheap. A businessman who is kept waiting for an extension today may elect to ring again later since he will be charged for the call while he is waiting. Time can be saved to callers if the following procedure is adopted, not only by telephonists but by all who answer extension telephones:

(*a*) Announce your identity, and state the name of the firm, or the department. 'Whitehead speaking. Accounts department. May I help you?'

(*b*) Listen to the caller and assess the quality of the enquiry. The following alternatives may occur:

(i) It is a routine enquiry which can be answered directly. Do so courteously and fully, without being repetitive. The caller will be satisfied and ring off.

(ii) It is a specialised enquiry but one which the telephonist is competent to deal with. In this case it is useful to make a note of the call and a pad of scrap paper should be handy to record any necessary details. It is sometimes difficult to remember exactly what was said without a note of this sort. A phrase like 'Told him we'd deliver by the 30th' may prove invaluable next day when trying to recall the conversation.

(iii) The person the caller wishes to speak to may not be available. The telephonist has a choice between taking a message for the absentee, or asking the caller to wait while he locates him. It is often cheaper for the caller to leave a message and the responsibility then rests upon the telephonist to ensure that it reaches the absent colleague.

The best way to take a message is upon a printed message pad which conveniently reminds the operator of most of the essential details. Fig. 6.3 shows such a pad, with spaces for the date, time, name and address of the caller, his telephone number and the detailed message. It is best to read the message back to the caller.

```
┌─────────────────────────────────────┐
│        Telephone Message Form         │
│                    Date_____   │
│                    Time_____   │
│                                       │
│  Caller's name_____  │
│  Address_____  │
│  Telephone No._____ Ext. No._____  │
│                                       │
│  Message for_____  │
│  Message:_____  │
│  _____  │
│  _____  │
│  _____  │
│  _____  │
│  _____  │
│  _____  │
│                                       │
│        Message taken by_____    │
└─────────────────────────────────────┘
```

Fig. 6.3. A telephone message form.

The pay-pips. Sometimes when answering the telephone a high-pitched series of rapid pips is heard. These are the 'pay-pips' which sound to tell a caller in a public call box that it is time to insert the money into the slot machine. As the caller can hear nothing until this is done the person answering the call should wait for the pips to end before announcing the firm's name. The call may later be interrupted by a further series of pips. This requires the caller to pay again. The person answering should hold on in case the caller inserts a further coin.

6.6   Special Telephone Services

A wide range of services is available to the general public and all subscribers through the telephone system. The most important of these are as follows:

(*a*) *The emergency services.* Dialling 999 gives everyone a priority answer from an operator, who will ask which service is required. The services available are Fire, Police, Ambulance, Coastguard and Lifeboat services. The operator connects the caller to the service, who will then ask for the address where help is needed. In public call boxes a press-button connection, instead of a 999 call, enables direct contact with the operator to be made without the payment of money in the slot machine.

(*b*) *A. D. and C. calls.* Sometimes subscribers wish to know the charge for a particular call—possibly to charge a member of staff for it. The phrase 'Advise duration and charge' is used to book such a call through an operator. When booking the call the subscriber says 'and may I have A.D.C. please'. The operator meters the call and a few minutes after the end of the call she will ring back to say, 'Your call to New York was timed at 3 minutes 48 seconds and cost £6.40.'

(*c*) *Alarm calls.* Subscribers who have urgent early morning business appointments can ask for an early call. 'Alarm' calls can also be booked for any time of the day or night. The charge is 24 pence. Precautions are usually taken by the Post Office to avoid overlooking the call; they usually ask two operators to ring the number.

(*d*) *Information services.* These can be very valuable, particularly the weather reports and the motoring reports. The 'speaking clock' service is one of the most widely used services in the country. A teletourist service supplies information on shows, sporting events, etc., in five languages, for tourists visiting London. Test Match scores, cookery recipes, share prices and other information are also available.

(*e*) *Transferred charges, telephone credit cards and Freefone services.* These services help the subscriber who wishes to pay for incoming calls. It is, for example, convenient when travellers wish to call head office, or businessmen who are away from home wish to call their families to transfer the charge and have it added to the ordinary tele-phone bill. The only additional cost is a small charge to pay for the recording of the transfer. A **credit card** system operates differently. Selected staff, usually commercial travellers, are given a credit card which they use from any ordinary telephone box in the country. By dialling the operator and giving details of the credit card account the caller will be connected free, and the charge will be passed on to the credit account. The Freefone service enables a businessman to instruct all callers that he will pay the charges. This may be an attraction to customers. The caller simply asks the operator to connect him. The charge is recorded against the subscriber, with no charge to the caller.

(*f*) *Person to person calls.* These are available, at a small extra charge, to enable long-distance callers to save time on their calls. By paying the 'personal' charge, whether or not the person required is available, they ensure that they are not charged for the time spent locating their business contact. Only one personal charge is made in any 24-hour period even if two or three attempts are necessary before the call is finally connected.

(*g*) *Data transmission services*. Businessmen very often wish to receive data from branches, factories, etc., with the utmost possible speed. A series of **Datel services**, i.e. 'data by telephone' services, is available either over public or private circuits and at speeds of up to 48 000 bits per second. These fantastically fast services enable the head offices of firms to keep abreast of world trends in business.

(*h*) *Fixed time calls*. For a small extra charge a call can be booked to a subscriber at or about a given time, to ensure that contact can be made with the subscriber even if lines are busy.

6.7 Intercommunication Links

Intercom units are widely used as an adjunct to the telephone service. A typical intercom unit has 20 buttons, each bearing the name of an executive. The time of top executives is expensive, and any device which saves them time pays for itself in a very short while. Such a unit, giving direct contact with departmental managers at the press of a button, and with loudspeaker and microphone circuits built in, enables them to carry on with their written or other work while discussing points with the departments concerned. If confidential discussion is required they have only to lift the hand-set to cut out the loudspeaker and discuss matters privately. When departmental managers call in, the buttons light up to indicate which department is calling. The end two buttons in the bottom row may be connected up to lights outside the executive's door reading 'Wait' or 'Enter'.

6.8 Paging Devices

A paging device is one which will find executives wherever they are and either bring them to a telephone or enable them to hear a message, and perhaps also reply to it, immediately. It is most useful in such situations as the hospital service, where night duty doctors may be called from wherever they are working at present, to be acquainted with an emergency situation somewhere in the building. Similarly, in dock or workshop areas contact with key supervisory staff can be readily achieved.

A recent development is radio-paging, which extends the paging service to almost all areas of the country. Executives designate which area they wish to be paged in, and are given a radio-paging number. When this is dialled on any telephone a computer will transmit a bleep in the designated area which will activate a bleeper in the executive's possession. The executive then phones in for the message.

Non-slip telephone pad

Dialling ball-pen

The telerest

Rubber suction
'Neverstray' parking device

Fig. 6.4. Small aids for the telephonist (reproduced by courtesy of Wilson & Whitworth Ltd).

6.9 Small Telephone Aids

Like other office employees, the telephonist has special problems which have received very careful attention by office equipment manufacturers. There are several devices which make life easier for the busy telephonist, or for those who frequently need to answer extension telephones. Some of these are shown in Fig. 6.4. They include:

(a) Telephone mats, to prevent the extension telephone from moving when dialling is taking place.
(b) Dialling ball-pens, which give much more efficient dialling, and can

be popped into rubber suction holders on the telephone when not in use.

(*c*) Telerests, which hold the telephone against the ear so that both hands are free to refer to correspondence, etc.

Although small equipment of this type will usually be provided by the employer some clerks prefer to provide their own. They can then ensure that they have everything that is needed in order to work with maximum efficiency. If they do change employment they arrive at the new post complete with many gadgets, each quite inexpensive in its way, and each of which heightens their effectiveness in the new office.

6.10 Points to Think About and Discuss

(*a*) British Telecom is much concerned about the needs of handicapped people. In the 'green pages' at the front of the latest telephone directories they list various aids for handicapped people. Find out what these are. Then consider: (i) Why it is desirable that the telephone system should pay particular attention to the needs of handicapped people? (ii) How the telephone can be made more readily available to: (*a*) the bedridden at home; (*b*) the chronically sick in hospitals; (*c*) the disabled?

(*b*) The 'yellow pages' are added to ordinary directories as a supplement, giving a classified list of business addresses. What are the advantages of this arrangement to (i) the subscribers and (ii) the businesses. Are there any disadvantages to either party?

6.11 Rapid Revision

Cover the page with a sheet of notepaper and uncover one question at a time.

Answers	*Questions*
—	1. Who invented the telephone?
1. Alexander Graham Bell.	2. How does it work?
2. Voice sound waves are converted by the microphone mouthpiece into electrical waves which travel to the earpiece of the person called. Here they are reconverted to sound waves.	3. What do the letters PBX and PABX mean?
3. PBX = private branch exchange PABX = private automatic branch exchange	4. What are the meanings of STD and GRACE?
4. STD = subscriber trunk dialling. GRACE = group routing and charging equipment.	5. What do these systems do?
5. They enable the subscriber to dial directly to all parts of the country without any need to call the operator at the exchange.	6. How should the telephone be answered?

Answers	Questions
6. (*a*) Announce your identity, and the name of the firm or department. (*b*) Answer directly if it is a routine matter which you are competent to deal with. (*c*) Answer a specialist matter which you are competent to deal with and record any vital details on a telephone memo pad. (*d*) Other callers should be connected to someone competent, or a detailed message should be taken.	7. Explain the following: (*a*) How to use the emergency services. (*b*) What is an A.D.C. call? (*c*) What are transferred charges, credit card services and Freefone services? (*d*) What are person-to-person calls? (*e*) What are data transmission services?
7. The answers are too involved to describe here. The reader should refer to the text.	8. What is a paging device?
8. It is a device to call members of staff who are busy about the building.	9. What organisation runs the telephone system in the United Kingdom?
9. British Telecom.	10. Go over the page again until you feel you are sure of the answers.

Exercises Set 6

1. Write down the letters (*a*)–(*j*) and against them write the phrases from the word list necessary to complete the following sentences:

(*a*) The telephone was invented by ....
(*b*) The sound waves of the caller are turned into .... in the telephone circuit and are then reconverted to sound waves at the receiver's telephone earpiece.
(*c*) PBX stands for ....
(*d*) PABX stands for ....
(*e*) The more modern switchboards, where many of the connections are made automatically, are called ......
(*f*) GRACE stands for ....
(*g*) STD stands for ....
(*h*) Yellow-page directories are ...... directories, listing firms under the type of trade or service performed.
(*i*) The letters A.D.C. stand for ....
(*j*) Devices which locate busy staff wherever they are working in a building are called ...... devices.

Word list: Alexander Graham Bell, private automatic branch exchange, classified, group routing and charging equipment, advise duration and charge, electrical waves, private branch exchange, subscriber trunk dialling, paging, consoles.

2. On a half sheet of A4 paper type or write out a Telephone Message Form as shown in Fig. 6.3. Then record on it the following message. 17th May 19...
Mr A. A. Kenningham of Moulded Plastics Ltd wishes to speak urgently with Mr R. Roberts of Sales Dept. He particularly wishes to know the prices of 'ordinary' and 'extra quality' shelving units, and to know whether both qualities

of shelving can be mounted on the same brackets. If not, what are the gauges and prices of the 'extra quality' brackets. Will Mr Roberts phone him at Burdon 13475, Ext. 12, before 5.15 p.m. If Mr Kenningham proves to be not available will he leave a detailed message with Miss Chalmers. Message taken by R. Ford, telephonist.

3. In the following questions choose the best answer to the question from the answers given, (*a*), (*b*), (*c*) or (*d*).

(i) The principle of the operation of the telephone is: (*a*) that the voice travels along a wire to the receiver's earpiece; (*b*) that the pressure waves of the voice striking the diaphragm of the mouthpiece cause a pressure wave to flow along the copper conductor; (*c*) that the sound waves of the voice patterns are converted into electrical waves along a conductor to the earpiece of the receiver, where an electro-magnet reconverts them to sound waves which can be heard by the person called; (*d*) the movement of molecules of copper along a conducting wire.

(ii) The good telephonist will always answer calls: (*a*) by saying 'Hallo'; (*b*) by announcing his/her identity, or the firm's identity; (*c*) in strict rotation as they arrive at the switchboard; (*d*) by saying 'Hold on. I'm busy.'

(iii) Trunk call barring is a system used on PABX consoles: (*a*) to stop junior staff making long-distance calls; (*b*) to stop unauthorised staff making long-distance calls; (*c*) to prevent anyone having private calls; (*d*) to stop long-distance calls coming in without going through the operator.

(iv) A telephone credit card: (*a*) enables a credit-worthy businessman to buy telephone equipment on credit; (*b*) enables senior staff to draw money from any branch of the 'Big Four' banks; (*c*) enables a caller to credit his charges to his own home telephone account; (*d*) enables the bearer, by quoting the number of the credit account, to telephone any number and have the call charged to the head office of his organisation.

4. Which of the following could be said to be true of the work of the telephone operator: (*a*) it requires tact and diplomacy at all times; (*b*) it is not essential to most offices; (*c*) it has been made easier by the use of automatic devices; (*d*) it sometimes requires the telephonist to deal with emergency situations coolly; (*e*) it never has spells of intense activity; (*f*) it sometimes requires the telephonist to act in other capacities, for example as a receptionist; (*g*) it is best carried out by someone who knows the organisation of the firm very well; (*h*) it does not require special training.

5. Suggest four ways in which a manager, wishing to cut the cost of telephone services, could economise in its use without reducing the effectiveness of the service.

6. The telephone gives direct communication between businessmen and their clients or customers. What are the advantages of such links? Are there any disadvantages?

7. A new junior has been appointed in your office, one of her main duties being to answer the telephone. List four *practical* hints to help. (RSA)

8. Name three of the special telephone services provided by British Telecom which give, by dialling particular codes, immediate information on certain matters or events. (RSA)

9. What do you understand by the following terms: (a) STD; (b) fixed-time calls; (c) data transmission services; (d) the speaking clock?

10. Write about eight lines about each of the following: (a) personal calls; (b) early morning alarm calls; (c) transferred charge calls; (d) cheap rate calls.

11. What is subscriber trunk dialling? How has it changed the work of the telephonist as far as outgoing calls are concerned? What difference has it made to local calls?

12. What do you understand by the terms PBX and PABX? Explain the use of these systems to a business house conducting a major part of its business by telephone.

13. 'Under this system housewives wishing to order goods from your mail-order house will be able to phone them through cheaply after your offices are closed and their orders will be able to receive attention first thing the following morning.' What system was the speaker referring to? Describe the likely sequence of events between the housewife lifting the receiver to send her order for a vacuum cleaner and its arrival in a railway delivery van.

14. (a) How is the charge for STD calls calculated? (b) What are the advantages and disadvantages of STD? (RSA)

15. You are employed in the office of Super Stationery Limited and at 10.30 a.m. on 3rd June you receive the following telephone call:
'John Brewster here, Bennington Limited; is Mr James there?'
You are the only person in the office, so you ask if you can take a message; Mr Brewster replies:
'Yes, please. We're shipping agents and Mr James has an African consignment. Will you tell him that there's some cargo space available on ss *Orono* to Mombasa. It's loading at Tilbury Dock, London. They're starting on the 7th June and won't take anything after the 11th. I'd like confirmation before 4.30 this afternoon, so ask Mr James to ring back, please, before then. Would you like to take the number? It's Maxwell 37184. If I'm out ask for Mr Smith—he'll be able to deal with the job. Thank you, goodbye.'
Draw up a suitable telephone message form for general use, and record the essential points of the conversation ready for Mr James' return. (RSA)

16. (a) What should a junior do to ensure that an incoming call is dealt with intelligently? (b) Some firms forbid personal calls for their employees. Why do you think this is done? (c) Why do people sometimes make 'Personal calls?' What is the procedure? (RSA)

17. (a) You are looking after the telephone switchboard and also the paging system. A visitor, Mr Blake, has called to see Mr Martin, the Chief Engineer, by appointment. The visitor is on time but Mr Martin is at the other end of the factory. Write out the exact message you would speak into the microphone of the paging system. (b) What is the main advantage to a business of an internal telephone system? (c) What particular advantage is it for a business to install a PABX switchboard? (d) A company has branches in the six largest cities in the United Kingdom. The Managing Director has some urgent news to pass on to the Branch Managers. Ideally he would like to tell them all at once and at the same time have some opportunity for a brief discussion in which they could all participate. Discuss how this could be done. (RSA)

18. (*a*) In what circumstances might you wish to make use of: (i) a telephone answering machine; (ii) the transferred charge call service; (iii) a telephone credit card; (iv) the personal call service? (*b*) Explain fully *one* of the above telephone services. (RSA)

19. (*a*) Draw up a list of instructions for the guidance of junior office staff on the use of the telephone; (*b*) draft a suitable press advertisement for a telephone switchboard operator in your firm. (RSA)

20. Your employer is concerned because a number of incoming messages received by telephone have not been dealt with efficiently. (*a*) Draft a telephone message form which could be used on all occasions when the person required is not available. (*b*) What would you do if a telephone caller would not leave a message?

21. Automatic subscriber dialling has recently been introduced into your district for both local and trunk telephone calls. Draw up a set of rules for the use of the telephone to guide the office staff, taking into account the special requirements of STD.

22. Your employer has received complaints that telephone messages are either not conveyed to the persons concerned or are incorrectly recorded. Clients have also expressed disappointment that the office telephone is not manned during the luncheon period and on Saturday mornings. Examine the situation and write a memorandum to your employer suggesting an improvement in the arrangements for telephone messages. (RSA)

7

MAIL INWARDS

7.1 Introduction

Mail inwards and mail outwards are clearly both connected with the postal services, but they are not handled in the same way. While mail outwards involves the weighing, stamping and actual despatch of letters and parcels, and is usually the main function of the post department, mail inwards does not involve quite the same sort of routine activity.

In many firms much of the correspondence is addressed to the firm as a whole, not to particular persons or departments. Some firms even print on their letter headings 'All correspondence to be addressed to the General Manager' or some other official. It follows that a preliminary sort-out is necessary to ensure that letters reach the proper department. This preliminary sort-out is best carried out by experienced staff, often the personal secretaries of the various departments or even the office manager himself. Sometimes members of lower management staff open the mail together, sorting it into departmental trays. In other offices a supervisor controls the incoming mail, with more junior staff doing the routine activities of opening letters and rough sorting.

7.2 Collecting the Mail

Mail is usually delivered to the addressee by the postman, and it arrives at times convenient to the Post Office organisation. Firms wishing to collect at times convenient to them may do so through the 'private box' or 'private bag' service. The former enables the firm to hire a box in the Post Office sorting department into which their mail will be placed, and from which it can be collected. The 'private bag' service enables a firm to send a driver to collect the firm's mail which will be handed over in a suitable locked bag provided by the firm. The bag must conform to the Corporation's specifications. The charge—at the time of writing—is £20 per box or per bag per annum. A separate box or bag is required for parcels, and if one or the other is used for both, a double fee is payable.

The services enable firms to ensure that mail is collected, opened and distributed to departments early in the day, so that correspondence can be read and action taken at the earliest possible moment. It is usual for mail inwards staff to start work earlier than other employees and this is sometimes operated on a rota basis.

7.3 Rules for Opening Incoming Mail

Mail should be opened systematically, with particular attention to the security of incoming cheques or money. It is also important to ensure that all the contents of envelopes are removed and secured together before the envelope is thrown away. Some departments prefer to keep envelopes with the contents: for example, Personnel Departments can often learn a lot about an applicant from the way an envelope is written. The following rules might apply, but every office will have its own special procedures, which the reader should discover on taking up employment.

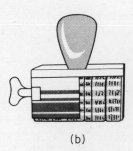

(b)

This date stamp can be altered to read Answered, Supplied by, Ordered, Cancelled, Invoiced, Checked, Delivered, Received, Entered, Telephone, Acknowl'd, and Paid

(a)

A self-inking date stamp

Fig. 7.1. Devices for date-stamping letters (reproduced by courtesy of Wilson & Whitworth Ltd).

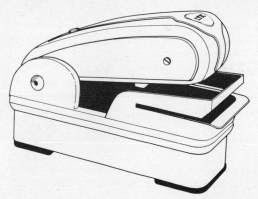

Fig. 7.2. A device for time-stamping mail inwards (reproduced by courtesy of International Time Recording Co. Ltd).

Rules for dealing with mail inwards

(*a*) *Carry out a preliminary sorting.* Separate the **first-class** from the **second-class letters**. Arrange both types in tidy packs with the addresses all facing the same way.

(*b*) *Extract the personal letters.* Extract any envelopes marked 'Private', 'Confidential', 'Personal' or 'To be opened by addressee only'. Stamp these letters on the envelope with a **date stamp** to show the date of arrival, and perhaps the time of arrival, using a stamp such as those in Figs 7.1 and 7.2. Then place them unopened in the trays of the individuals to whom they are addressed.

(*c*) *Open the non-confidential sealed letters.* Sealed letters should be opened, either with a **paper knife** or with a **letter opening machine**. This is a machine that shaves off a very tiny sliver of paper from the edge of an envelope, so that the contents may be removed. The small slice is only about two thousandths of an inch thick, so that it is impossible to damage the contents of the envelope. Fig. 7.3 shows such a mail opener.

(*d*) *Remove and sort the contents.* After removing the contents the clerk should ensure that the envelope is empty by holding it up to a desk light. Then the correspondence removed should be opened out, and date stamped with the date, or time and date, of its reception.

If it has any 'enclosures' mentioned at the foot of the letter ensure

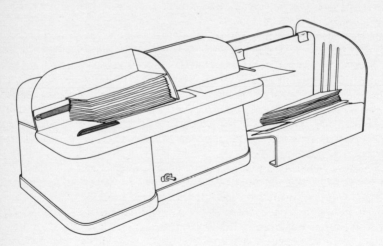

Fig. 7.3. A mail opening machine (reproduced by courtesy of Messrs Pitney-Bowes Ltd).

Notes

(i) Mail of varying sizes and thicknesses is placed in a stack on the feed plate.

(ii) An electric drive feeds the letters into the machine, where two rotary knives cut off a thin strip, without damaging the contents.

(iii) The opened letters are stacked in a hopper ready for the removal of their contents. The 'chips' cut from the letters are ejected into a separate hopper.

that they were in fact enclosed. If any are missing make a note of the fact against the 'enclosure' and sign it—for example, 'Not enclosed— R. Smith'. The supervisor should be informed so that action may be taken. Finally, sort the correspondence into the most appropriate tray.

(*e*) *Record important documents in the mail inwards register*. It sometimes happens that important documents arrive in the ordinary post; at other times they arrive in special post such as registered or recorded delivery post. Many offices require the supervisor to record all such mail in an **Inwards Mail Register**. Solicitors, for example, might record the receipt of deeds, conveyances and depositions. Publishers might record manuscripts of books, or artwork, and most offices would record registered and recorded delivery letters. The arrival of money, cheques, bills of exchange and so on should be recorded in a **Remittances Inwards Book**. Payments, whether by cash or cheque, should be compared with the **remittance advice note** which accompanies them. Registered letters should preferably be opened only by the supervisor. Any disparity between either cheques or money and the advice note should be reported at once. When all the mail has been opened, the cashier should be requested to sign the Remittances Inwards Book for those items involving payments, to confirm that he has received them. Where **loose postage stamps** are received—for example, in requests for samples, patterns and recipes or to cover return postage—the cashier will eventually pass them on to the post department for use, charging them out as part of the **petty cash imprest**. Alternatively, the Post Office will repurchase them subject to a 10 per cent discount.

Special note on recorded delivery. A lot of important mail is sent **recorded delivery**, which is a way of proving that the posted item reaches its destination, and a less expensive method than registering it. For example, colleges often use recorded delivery to send certificates to students who have passed examinations. Such deliveries must be signed for on an individual basis, otherwise no responsibility is accepted by the Post Office. Thus where five recorded delivery letters arrive at the same time, each one should be signed for; it is incorrect to bracket them together and sign once only.

(*f*) *Prepare circulation slips if necessary*. In many offices it is the practice for certain types of mail to be circulated to several departments, so that all are informed of the latest developments. The duplication or photocopying of such documents gives each department a file copy, and a full record of events. Less expensive, however, is the affixation to the correspondence of a **circulation slip** which shows the order in which the correspondence should circulate. Thus, in Fig. 7.4, the circulation slip is routed to all the directors of the company, and the company secretary and the accountant. Sometimes a rubber stamp is used bearing the names of the persons or departments to be circulated, but a circulation slip overcomes the difficulty met when there is insufficient space on the item for a rubber stamp.

Circulation Slip	
Please read the attached correspondence, and pass at once to the next person on the list	
Name	Please initial when read
Director No. 1	
„ No. 2	
„ No. 3	
„ No. 4	
„ No. 5	
Company Secretary	
Chief Accountant	
Received by Mail Inwards department and circulated on :-	
Date Stamp here	

Fig. 7.4. A mail inwards circulation slip.

(*g*) *Open the unsealed letters.* These should be opened and the contents—often circulars—put into the trays of those most likely to be interested.

(*h*) *Distribute the trays of mail.* Finally, trays should be distributed carefully to the individuals concerned, so that none of the contents is lost. Empty envelopes should be kept for three days at least in case they are needed for reference and before finally being disposed of they should be checked again to make sure they are empty.

7.4   Sorting the Mail—A Desk Sorter

If mail is sorted into departments, without being opened, a *desk sorter* is a convenient piece of equipment. It consists of a flat base-plate, to which is connected a series of hinged metal flaps. Each flap projects a short distance beyond the previous one, and bears a visible index panel which can show the various names of the departments. Letters and documents placed between the flaps are held in position by the weight of the flap. Other sorters consist of filing pockets conveniently arranged in concertina style, pigeon-holes and work-organisers such as the one illustrated earlier (see page 39). Fig. 7.5 shows an Ambidex desk sorter of the type mentioned above.

7.5   Points to Think About and Discuss

(*a*) As an office manager it is your duty to draw up a roster of staff to come in half an hour early each week and open the incoming mail. Miss Smith, a personal secretary, objects to taking her turn on this duty. (i) What arguments could be used to justify the requirement to

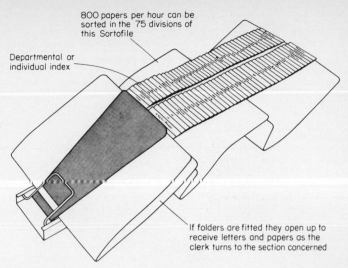

800 papers per hour can be sorted in the 75 divisions of this Sortofile

Departmental or individual index

If folders are fitted they open up to receive letters and papers as the clerk turns to the section concerned

Fig. 7.5. An Ambidex desk sorter (reproduced by courtesy of Ambidex Equipment Sortofiles).

come in early? (ii) Miss Smith refuses point blank to come in. How should the problem be dealt with?

(*b*) A registered letter addressed to 'The Administration Office' was opened by a junior member of staff who reported that money was short. Upon telephone enquiry the chief cashier of the firm concerned reports that on making up the registered envelope for post he called two witnesses to see the notes inserted in the envelope and sealed it in their presence. What should be done about the £2 that is missing?

(*c*) In a small office there are five people. They are: (i) Mr Jones, the manager, who never arrives until 10.15 a.m.; (ii) Mrs Pike, his secretary, a very experienced and trustworthy member of staff; (iii) Mr White, chief clerk and cashier; (iv) Miss Trimble, a junior secretary who joined the firm last week; (v) Miss Brown, the postal clerk. What arrangements should be made in such an office with regard to the opening of mail, much of which is remittances inwards for mail order goods advertised in the national press?

(*d*) A burglary during the night has meant that the cash in the petty cash till and the postage stamps have been stolen. It is proposed to claim from the insurance company for these losses, and also for the cost of repairs by a carpenter, a locksmith and a glazier. How would you set about discovering the correct sum to be claimed?

7.6 Rapid Revision

Cover the page with a sheet of paper and uncover one question at a time.

Answers	Questions
—	1. How is mail collected for a large office?
1. Usually through the private box or private bag system.	2. List suitable rules for opening incoming mail.
2. (*a*) Carry out a preliminary sorting. (*b*) Extract the personal letters, marked 'confidential' or 'private'. (*c*) Open the non-confidential sealed letters, and sort them. (*d*) Record remittances inwards. (*e*) Prepare circulation slips if necessary. (*f*) Sort the unsealed letters into appropriate trays. (*g*) Distribute the trays of mail.	3. Which type of staff should open and sort the mail?
3. (*a*) Responsible staff of middle management level or personal secretary level. (*b*) A specialist mail inward supervisor.	4. Why do some firms ask correspondents to address all mail to 'The General Manager', or some similar addressee?
4. It gives better control of correspondence and reduces undesirable, or corrupt, practices.	5. What is a mail opening device?
5. It is a device which cuts a thin sliver off sealed envelopes without damaging either the contents or the envelope.	6. What action should be taken when money reputed to be enclosed in a letter is reported short?
6. Rigorously investigate the affair to determine the cause of the shortage.	7. What should be done with envelopes after opening mail?
7. Keep them for 2–3 days until it is quite certain they will not be required. Check them against a desk light before final disposal.	8. Go over the page again until you feel you are sure of the answers.

Exercises Set 7

1. Choose the best word or phrase from the word list below to complete these sentences.

(*a*) Mail should be distributed .... after it is received from the Post Office.

(*b*) Mail marked ...... or ...... should not be opened.

(*c*) Important letters such as registered letters or recorded delivery letters should be recorded in a ....

(*d*) A paper knife is a device for ...... letters.

(*e*) A .... will remove a tiny sliver of paper from the edge of an envelope.

(*f*) Always test envelopes to see if they are ...... before discarding them in the waste paper basket.

(*g*) All mail should be .... on arrival to indicate when it was received in the mail inwards office.

(*h*) If a letter has ...... sent with it the fact will usually be noted at the foot of the letter.

(*i*) It is best if the ...... opens letters likely to contain money or cheques.

(*j*) A .... may be made out if a letter has to be read by several members of staff.

Word list: personal, confidential, opening, as soon as possible, letter opening machine, date stamped, circulation slip, mail inwards register, supervisor, enclosures, empty.

2. Suggest why mail inwards should be opened only by experienced staff.

3. In what ways may mail inwards reach the office? How should it be dealt with on arrival?

4. Describe the procedure that would be adopted by a large organisation for the speedy opening, sorting and distribution of the morning post. What special security precautions might be introduced?

5. A firm frequently receives: (*a*) registered letters; (*b*) cheques; (*c*) loose postage stamps in payment for items requested by customers. How should these be dealt with on arrival, and what will eventually happen to each?

6. What action would you take about: (*a*) an envelope that arrived empty; (*b*) a registered envelope, signed for by the telephonist, which proves to have been carefully cut at the bottom? The valuable contents are missing.

7. You are in charge of the mail inwards room. Write out a list of instructions to guide your relief in dealing with the incoming mail each day, whilst you are on holiday.

8. Today's incoming mail includes the items listed below. You have instructions to sort mail into four departments:
(*a*) Accounts; (*b*) company secretary and administration office; (*c*) purchasing department; (*d*) sales department. List the items suitable for each department.

(i) the telephone account.
(ii) a brochure on electronic calculators.
(iii) four orders from customers.
(iv) a credit note from a supplier.
(v) a bank statement.
(vi) an insurance policy for a commercial traveller's car.
(vii) 12 invoices from suppliers.
(viii) the deeds to a new factory.
(xi) the monthly correction list for the *Post Office Guide*.
(x) a testimonial regarding an applicant for employment.
(xi) a brochure about office equipment.
(xii) a Home Office enquiry about a work permit for an overseas trainee from a foreign branch.

9. An important document, received in the post at 8.30 a.m. and recorded in the Mail Inwards Register, did not reach the company secretary in his tray. Suggest a procedure for tracing the missing document.

10. Write against the items of mail listed below the most likely department to be interested in them: (*a*) new booklet of tax instructions; (*b*) price list of office equipment; (*c*) notification about trainee schemes for transport staff; (*d*) the Lloyd's shipping list; (*e*) an invoice for goods ordered from a supplier; (*f*) a cheque from a debtor; (*g*) a request for information from the Chamber of Trade; (*h*) a Department of Health leaflet about earnings-related contributions; (*i*) a copy of a Government White Paper on the auditing of company accounts; (*j*) an employee's P45 from a previous employer.

11. In what circumstances should incoming mail be:
(*a*) photocopied; (*b*) recorded in an Inwards Mail Register; (*c*) handled by the supervisor only; (*d*) left unopened?

12. There have been complaints from the other departments in your organisation that the postal and telephones department, in which you work, is often left unattended at lunch-times. The lunch hour may be taken from 12 to 1 or from 1 to 2. There are six girls in the department:

A a switchboard operator
B a receptionist who can also deal with the switchboard
C a postal clerk responsible for all outgoing mail
D a postal clerk who can also operate the photocopiers
E a girl in charge of photocopying of incoming and outgoing mail
F a junior responsible for preparing parcels, franking envelopes and preparing letters for the post.

Make out a lunch rota which will ensure that there is always someone in the office who can deal with post and telephones. D and F are on day-release courses on Tuesday and Wednesday respectively. (RSA)

13. Explain fully a procedure for the handling of incoming office mail so that it is dealt with systematically and efficiently. (RSA)

14. The senior executives of your firm have complained that the morning's mail is late in being delivered from the mail room to their offices with a consequent delay in starting the day's business. The office manager has asked you to investigate the present method of handling the incoming mail and to devise a more satisfactory system which will not only ensure that the correspondence is available for distribution before the senior executives arrive in the morning, but will also take into account the need for security in the handling of remittances. Write a memorandum to the office manager setting out the procedure you would recommend. (RSA)

15. You work for a manufacturing company and you are responsible for the incoming mail. In this morning's post you found: (i) a letter from a skilled operator asking for a job in the factory; (ii) a credit note for returnable containers; (iii) a letter making a special offer of an exceptionally large discount on some raw materials used in your company's manufacturing processes; (iv) a cheque, accompanied by a remittance advice, in partial settlement of one of your customer's accounts.

(*a*) To which departments of your office will you direct these documents?
(*b*) What action will then be taken within those departments? (RSA)

16. Give *four* practical hints for a junior clerk to help him in his duties of opening and sorting incoming mail in a large organisation. You should bear in mind the importance of getting everything to the proper recipients as quickly as possible. (RSA)

8

THE POST DEPARTMENT—MAIL OUTWARDS

8.1 Introduction

The post room is one of the most important departments in any firm, and one where many office juniors start their employment. It is an excellent point to begin work, for by spending some time in the post department the young clerical worker quickly learns the layout of the firm, its organisation and staff, and the chains of responsibility in various departments.

In former times the postal services have been the chief means of communication between firms, and an enormous staff was at one time employed in the General Post Office to provide an efficient service. In Queen Victoria's time seven deliveries a day was not uncommon. Today the postal services are supplemented by the telephone and telex systems, so that less emphasis is placed upon speed in the postal services. Two deliveries a day are usual; only one in some areas. Firms with urgent business to transact do it by telephone; the written documents which eventually travel by post merely confirm the oral agreements made on the telephone. Some years ago the Post Office in the United Kingdom ceased to be a Government department, and began to operate as an independent corporation, **The Post Office**. The telephone service has now been separated off as another corporation, **British Telecom**.

8.2 Organisation of the Post Department

The size of a firm dictates the organisation of this department. In many firms a single individual called the **postal clerk** will handle all outwards postal transactions. Often it is convenient in such firms to make this person a **petty cashier** as well (see below).

In larger firms a more complex organisation may be required, and some firms like **mail order houses** even have complete post offices controlled and operated by The Post Office built into their premises to handle the enormous volume of mail outwards.

The following rules should apply to most 'Mail Outwards' departments:

(*a*) Good links should be established with all departmental managers to ensure that they lay down firm procedures about outgoing mail. The late despatch of 'emergency' correspondence will thus be reduced to a minimum.

(*b*) Collection points and collection times should be clearly designated, and adhered to rigorously.

(*c*) Staff should be trained to mark in pencil in the top right-hand corner all special mail, i.e. airmail, foreign mail, recorded delivery and registered mail.

(*d*) First-class mail should be rubber-stamped 'First-class' in the **top left-hand corner**.

(*e*) Practices should be established for the recording of important letters as they are despatched, and for the checking of 'enclosures' by the clerk responsible for folding and sealing mail after signature.

(*f*) Franking machines should be used wherever possible, and procedures established for recording the use of adhesive stamps.

(*g*) Rules should be laid down to prevent the despatch of private correspondence at the expense of the firm.

(*h*) Establish procedures for recording and preserving receipts from the Post Office for registered letters, recorded delivery letters, COD packets and other parcels.

8.3 The *Post Office Guide*

This is a reference book of great importance which is issued annually. When a copy is purchased the buyer is also given a card which he may complete and send to his local postmaster, requesting up-to-date supplements as they appear. Since postal charges vary, not only with government budget decisions but because of international agreements with foreign postal authorities, the *Guide* cannot avoid being out of date when it reaches the post offices for sale. By applying for the supplements a postage clerk is able to update the *Guide*, sticking the latest changes over the pages where alterations are required.

It is quite impossible to describe all the services offered by the Post Office (the *Guide* has over 600 closely printed pages), but some of the major ones are listed below:

(*a*) The inland and foreign postal services.

(*b*) The telegraph, telephone and telex services to home and overseas destinations, and to ships and aircraft.

(*c*) Remittance services for sending money payments to home and overseas creditors.

(*d*) Savings services for small investors, such as the National Savings Bank, the Savings Certificate scheme, Premium Bonds, and so on.

(*e*) Licensing services for television, motor-vehicle taxation, driving and many others.

8.4 Collecting Mail Outwards

Every firm must have an adequate system for posting outgoing mail and for avoiding sudden rushes of post which would overwhelm the staff. Points to be considered include the following:

(*a*) *Collection points.* A tray for outgoing mail should be placed in every department where mail can be conveniently collected by a messenger and brought down to the post department for despatch. Regular times should be arranged for the collection—say at every even hour, 10 a.m., 12 noon, 2 p.m., 4 p.m., etc. This will not only spread the work of the post department over the working day but will ensure more rapid handling by the postal authorities. Letters posted early in the day are cleared easily and quickly by the Post Office, but the great mass of post despatched in the early evening is inevitably subject to some delay. In particular, a final collection time should be laid down by which mail must be ready if it is to be handled by the post department that night.

(*b*) *Unusual mailings.* Many firms circularise their customers at regular intervals. Such mailings put the post department under pressure, but this can be avoided if the mailing can be arranged to fall at a time when routine postal activities are likely to be slight. Also much of the work can be avoided by using the **bulk mailing service** of the Corporation. Letters may be delivered in bulk to the Post Office, together with a cash payment for the total postage. At their convenience the Corporation will then frank the postage paid onto each envelope and despatch the letters.

(*c*) *Letters for signature.* When letters have been typed and are ready for signature they should be checked, signed and put into the departmental post tray at once. If a manager delays doing this until late in the day he will cause a pressure of work in the post department which is unnecessary. The postal clerk is entitled to protest if a particular department offends regularly in this way.

8.5 The Petty Cash (Imprest) System

In many small offices the postage clerk acts as a petty cashier. The word 'petty' means 'small' or 'minor'. A petty cashier is responsible for all sorts of cash payments—for example, the refund of bus fares to messengers. Since postal clerks must have sums of money available for stamps and other items, and must account for these expenditures, it is a simple matter for them to account as well for other small items. It saves the time of the chief cashier who prefers not to be interrupted for trifling payments of this kind. A special type of system, the **imprest system**, is used to control the sums of money spent. Under this system the postal clerk is given a sum of money called the **imprest** or **float** for use in purchasing stamps, etc. Suppose an imprest of £20 was agreed as being sufficient for a week's activities. As money is spent, the petty cashier records it in a Petty Cash Book. At the end of the week the book is totalled and presented for checking. After this the cashier **'restores the imprest'**—the money spent is replaced. The postage clerk thus starts the new week with a £20 imprest.

Fig. 8.1 illustrates the imprest system. The notes explaining the

Dr.											Cr.
	Date	Details	PCV	Total	Postage	Fares	Cleaning	Sundry Expenses	Stationery	Folio	Ledger A/cs
20.00	19.. Mar. 25	To Imprest	CB9								
	25	By Stamps	1	1.50	1.50						
	26	,, Postage	2	0.65	0.65						
	26	,, Cleaning	3	0.45			0.45				
	27	,, Sundries	4	0.32				0.32			
	27	,, Fares	5	1.45		1.45					
0.30	28	To Telephone Call	L3								
	28	By R. Jones	7	1.34						L19	1.34
	29	,, Cleaning	8	0.65			0.65				
	29	,, Sundries	9	0.40				0.40			
	29	,, Travelling	10	1.65		1.65					
	30	,, Envelopes	11	0.45					0.45		
	30	,, Office Equipment	12	1.65						L15	1.65
	30	,, Sundries	13	0.15				0.15			
	31	,, Totals	—	10.66	2.15	3.10	1.10	0.87	0.45		2.99
	31	,, Balance	c/d	9.64							
20.30				20.30							
					L5	L11	L27	L36	L49		
9.64	Apr. 1	To Balance	B/d								
10.36	1	,, Restored Imprest	CB11								

Fig. 8.1. The Petty Cash Book.

Notes

The following points will explain the operation of the Petty Cash imprest system, shown in Fig. 8.1 above

(*a*) The page is divided into two parts, debit and credit, but the 'centre' of the book is offset towards the extreme left of the page. This gives only a very small amount of debit side, while the credit side is expanded to make room for a series of analysis columns.

(*b*) The details are written on the credit side, since there is no 'Details' column on the debit side.

(*c*) The chief source of cash received is the cashier, who provides the original imprest, but other small sums may be received from staff, for telephone calls, etc. All receipts are debited.

(*d*) On the credit side, money spent is first entered into the total column, but is then extended out into one of the analysis columns. This enables the total postage, fares, etc., to be collected together. A special column at the end is used to extend out any items which cannot be mixed with other items—for example, the payment to R. Jones' account.

(*e*) At the end of the week, or when the imprest is nearly all used, the petty cashier rules off the page in such a way as to total the 'Total' column, and the analysis columns. These are then cross-totalled to ensure accuracy. The balance is found; the book is closed off and the balance is brought down.

(*f*) The cashier then checks the petty cashier's work and restores the imprest by providing enough cash to raise the balance to the original imprest figure.

(*g*) The book is now posted to the ledger accounts, using the totals of the analysis columns and the individual special items in the end column. Folio numbers are entered as shown.

(*h*) The petty cash vouchers, which authorise the payments made, are arranged in order, numbered and the PCV numbers are entered in the column provided. The petty cashier is now ready for a further week's business.

kccping of the Petty Cash Book (see page 99) have been set across the page for easier reading.

8.6 The Franking Machine or Postage Meter

Postage stamps are easily stolen, difficult to identify, unhygienic to lick and difficult to handle in large quantities. Much better control and more efficient methods are made possible by the use of a **postage meter** or **franking machine.**

The rules for using these machines are as follows:

(a) The machine must be presented at a specified office for meter setting with the amount required, say £100, which is paid in advance.

(b) The mail franked by the machine must be posted with all the letters facing the same way and securely tied in bundles, at a named post office.

(c) At the end of every week, whether the machine has been used or not, a docket must be tendered showing the meter readings at the end of each weekday.

(d) The licensee must have the machine tested at least twice every six months by the manufacturer to ensure clear impressions on envelopes and packet labels, and accurate records of the postage paid.

Fig. 8.2 shows an electric postage meter mailing machine. The caption notes bring out the advantages of the machine. Plate 4 shows an electronic version, the mail processor, capable of handling 12 000 items of postage per hour. Letters of all sizes and thicknesses can be moistened, sealed, imprinted with postage and postmarks, counted, recorded, printed with a personalised advertisement chosen by the user and stacked ready for despatch.

The Post Office maintains a check on postage machines to prevent fraudulent manipulation of the meters. It consists of a **weekly control card**, which must be handed in to the Post Office on Fridays or Saturdays, showing the numbers of units used during the week and the total units deposited. This figure of units paid for in advance must clearly agree with the Corporation's records of moneys paid by the licensee. A typical control card is shown in Fig. 8.3.

8.7 The Postage Book

In earlier days it was usual for a note to be made of every letter despatched, so that some proof was available that letters had actually been sent and accurate checks on postage could be maintained. Today this is not the usual practice: clerical labour is too expensive and the volume of post is too great. There are, however, certain offices where it is essential to keep a record of at least some of the mail despatched— solicitors, for example, might keep a record of conveyances or other important documents despatched by post, and Government offices

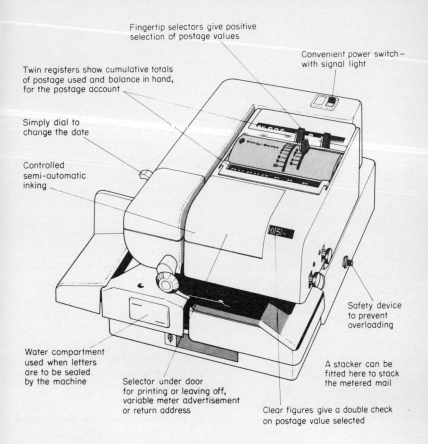

Fingertip selectors give positive
selection of postage values

Convenient power switch—
with signal light

Twin registers show cumulative totals
of postage used and balance in hand,
for the postage account

Simply dial to
change the date

Controlled
semi-automatic
inking

Safety device
to prevent
overloading

Water compartment
used when letters
are to be sealed
by the machine

A stacker can be
fitted here to stack
the metered mail

Selector under door
for printing or leaving off,
variable meter advertisement
or return address

Clear figures give a double check
on postage value selected

Fig. 8.2. An electric postage meter franking machine (reproduced by courtesy of Pitney-Bowes Ltd).

Notes

(i) The machine operates automatically as soon as an envelope is inserted; the motor is switched off until that moment.

(ii) The postage set on the meter is automatically deducted from the balance in hand to show the amount of postage still stored in the machine.

(iii) The letters franked by the machine do not have to be 'cancelled' like stamped letters, but go straight into the sorting office for despatch.

(iv) The machine prints gummed labels with the correct postage for use on parcels, packets and envelopes too large to be fitted into the machine.

(v) Advertisements and sender's address (for return if undelivered) can be printed on every franking.

dealing with passports would keep a record of such mail outwards. Very often this type of mail would be sent by **registered post** or **recorded delivery** and receipts would be obtained anyway. Fig. 8.4 shows a typical ruling for a Postage Book.

Franking Machine Control Card

Licensee........ _WHITELAW DESIGN CO. LTD._

Meter Office
(as shown on Record Card)....... _NEWTOWN G.P.O_

Machine (or Meter) No........ _L 18475_

Setting or Recording Unit........ ½p

    I certify that the following particulars in respect of the above described machine for

week-ended........ _24-11-19.._ ....are correct:—

	All machines	Locking machines	All machines
	Reading of Ascending Register (Totalisator)	Reading of Descending Register (Credit Meter)	Last entry in col. "Total Deposits" or "Total Settings" on Record Card
Mon.	18, 579		20, 000
Tue.	18, 919		20, 000
Wed.	21, 240		25, 000
Thur.	21, 350		25, 000
Fri.	23, 420		25, 000
Sat.			

Note 1. Whether or not the machine has been used this card must be posted on Saturday, or on Friday if no postings are made on Saturday.

Note 2. The daily entry must be made on completion of each day's postings.

Signed...... _M. Thomas_

.... _24ᵗʰ Nov_ ....19....

Fig. 8.3. Controlling the use of postage meters.

	Postage Book			Page 1
Date	Addressee	Address	Type of Enclosure	Postage value
19.. April 4	T. Hill	7, Coombe Lane, Exeter	Conveyance for signature	0.22
4	R. Jones	15, Hill Rise, Newtown	" " "	0.22
5	M. Peters	21, Lodge Lane, Grays	" " "	0.22
6	L. Long	17, Hill Rd, Buxton	Deposition	0.24
6	R. Smart	34a, Lorings, Newtown	Conveyance for signature	0.22
7	M. Smith	15, High St, Leamford	Will (duplicate copy)	0.24

Fig. 8.4. A postage book for important mail outwards.

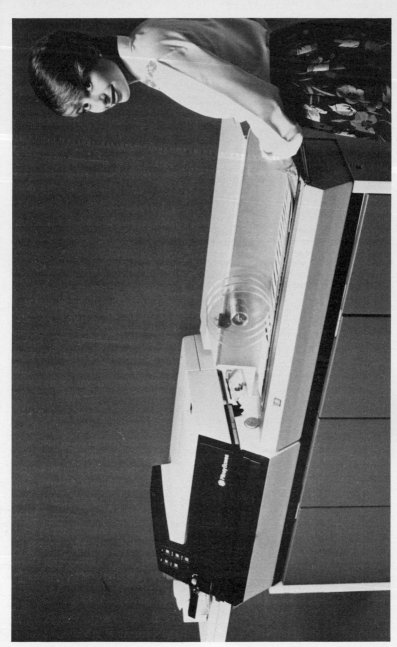

Plate 4. An electronic mail processor (reproduced by courtesy of Pitney-Bowes Ltd).

8.8 Some Post Office Services

The following special services, among others, are offered to the general public by The Post Office:

(*a*) *Registered Post.* This is a first-class letter service which offers the transmission of valuable items in return for a registration charge. It covers compensation up to various levels, reaching a maximum of £800 at the time of writing. Registered letters must be handed to an official of the Post Office, who will issue a certificate of posting which also acknowledges payment of the registration charge. Packages may also be registered, if posted at 'first-class' letter rate. Parcels are no longer accepted as registered mail, but on payment of an extra 'Compensation Fee' the Corporation will pay compensation up to a maximum limit of £225.

The undermentioned postal packet has been registered and posted here this day

Certificate of Posting   **Post Office**

| Regn. No. | Regn. fee paid | Minimum Fee Paid |
| | | p |

Date Stamp

Accepting Official's Initials   For Regulations see over

Fig. 8.5. A 'registered letter' receipt (reproduced by permission of The Post Office).

(*b*) *Recorded Delivery.* This is a service designed to ensure safe delivery. Compensation is available only to a nominal amount (£18 at the time of writing). The Post Office issues a certificate of posting to the sender, and obtains a written acknowledgement of delivery from the addressee. This is useful in many circumstances—for example, when

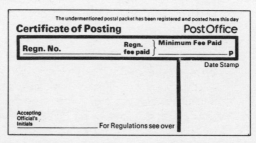

P 2297 B   FINAL DECIMAL   **CERTIFICATE OF POSTING**
P 707821   **FOR RECORDED DELIVERY**

Note. MONEY must not be sent by RECORDED DELIVERY. See over for Conditions of Acceptance and Instructions.

Date Stamp

Enter below in ink the name and address as written on the letter or packet.

Name.................

Address ....

....

Accepting Officer's Initials.................

GP. 1867 C.P. LTD. 1/71

P 707821 Recorded Delivery

Fig. 8.6. A 'recorded delivery' receipt (reproduced by permission of The Post Office).

legal documents, certificates of educational qualifications and other important papers are sent through the post.

(c) *Express Services.* The range of express services provided by The Post Office is much reduced these days, since the telephone and Telex systems have reduced the numbers of people requiring an express service. There is a **special delivery** service which may be requested (at a fee of 80 pence) from the delivery office, i.e. on the last stage of the letter's journey, but such a special delivery will only be made if it is likely to be an improvement on the ordinary postal service. Thus a letter reaching a delivery office at noon when all deliveries for the day had ceased would be specially delivered, but one arriving at 6 a.m. would simply be delivered with the morning post.

An **express post** service is available in London and certain other towns as a fast messenger collection and delivery service. Details are available from local postal representatives. A service called **Swiftair** is available for airmail letters to and from foreign countries. Swiftair packages receive accelerated attention during transit and accelerated delivery in the country of destination. Post Office services to exporters are described in Chapter 23.

(d) *Railway and Airway Letters.* By arrangement with the Post Office railway and airline authorities accept packets and letters up to a weight of 1lb for rapid transit over the passenger train or airline services. On arrival at the destination the letters may be called for, or if requested the authorities will put them into the local postal system for delivery by the postal authorities. Railway letters and airway letters are addressed in the following ways:

> T. Brown Esq.,
> Parcel office,
> York Station.
> (To be called for)

or

> T. Brown Esq.,
> Green Gables,
> Rufforth,
> Nr York.
> (York Station—to be posted on arrival)

(e) *Poste Restante.* The phrase 'poste restante' means 'remaining at the post office'. It is a useful service for travellers, and is limited in time. It may not be used for more than three months in any one town. Letters are addressed as follows:

> J. Green Esq.,
> Poste Restante,
> Post Office,
> Richmond,
> Surrey.

Instead of 'Poste Restante' the words 'To be called for' may be substituted.

(*f*) *Business Reply Service.* Under this service a businessman who wishes to obtain an answer from clients without putting the client to the expense of postage, may obtain a licence from the local head postmaster to enclose reply paid cards or leaflets in his correspondence with customers. A deposit is required of an estimated month's postage likely to be incurred under the scheme. The design of the card or leaflet proposed must be included with the application, and must conform to the specifications laid down in the *Post Office Guide*. The licensee pays the postage, and a further charge of ½p per card, as well as a licence fee of £15. This service is very popular with business houses seeking custom through postal and magazine advertisements.

8.9 A Large Mailing—Mechanisation of Mailing Activities

When a large mailing of advertising circulars is being prepared it will usually be the work of particular sections of the firm to undertake special functions connected with the mailing. The post department may play some part in these activities, or even undertake the whole mailing in slack times. In such circumstances there are a number of machines available which will remove most of the drudgery from the mailing and are worth purchasing if mailings are a regular feature of the firm's activities. If mailings are a rare event it is cheaper to type the envelopes individually.

The machines which are most helpful are:

(*a*) *The addresser-printer machine.* This machine makes use of address plates. There are several types, but the one illustrated in Fig. 8.7 can be embossed with nine lines of data with 46 characters per line. Up to 35 plates can be stored in hoppers which feed the plates into the addressing machine. After printing the plates are collected automatically in a further hopper, ready for storage until required again.

These plates, once prepared and checked, enable successive mailings to be made without the need to check envelopes for incorrect addresses.

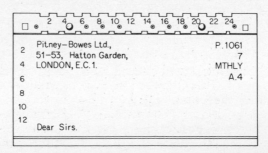

Fig. 8.7. An address plate (reproduced by courtesy of Pitney-Bowes Ltd).

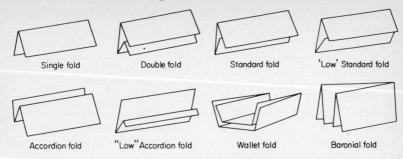

Fig. 8.8. Folds made by a folding machine (reproduced by courtesy of Pitney-Bowes Ltd).

They should be proofread to ensure correct initials, house numbers, postal codes, etc. There will then be no possibility of transcribing mistakes, mis-spelled names to offend customers or transposed street addresses to misdirect cheques, invoices, etc. Once the plate is perfectly prepared every mailing from it will be perfect.

(*b*) *The folding machine.* The impact made on the customer by a leaflet or other document may depend upon the folding of the document. Fig. 8.8 shows eight possible folds which can be made by a typical folding machine. The folding of leaflets, etc., is a time-consuming activity, disliked by staff who are sometimes loaned to the post department from their ordinary duties to help with a mailing. The folding machine, with a single operator, can fold between 5000 and 12000 sheets per hour, giving clean, accurate folds, never taking more than one sheet or skipping a sheet, and eliminating the need for overtime payments in busy periods.

(*c*) *The collating–inserting–sealing–mailing machine.* This machine, with a single operator, can do the work of many people. It will collate (arrange several sheets in order, neatly, for insertion into the envelopes), insert, seal, stamp, count and stack ready for posting as many as 7500 envelopes per hour.

(*d*) *The mail tying machine.* These machines will tie packages of any size or shape in a few seconds. They are particularly useful for mail order houses and for individuals such as nurserymen who send trees and plants by post at certain times of the year.

8.10 Posting Lists

When a firm sends registered or recorded delivery letters it is tedious having to wait for the Post Office counter clerk to write out the receipts. The Post Office prefers firms to keep a book for each of these types of letter, and present it at the Post Office as a '*posting list*'. The registered lists are prepared in duplicate, giving the names and addresses of all the letters to be sent. The counter clerk only needs to fill in the registered numbers and to stamp the book—tearing out one copy for Post Office use. With recorded delivery letters he simply stamps the list of recorded delivery letters to acknowledge that the Post Office has taken charge of them. This system of posting lists saves much time in busy post offices and should be adopted by all firms who send registered and recorded delivery letters regularly.

8.11 Points to Think About and Discuss

(a) Office juniors working in the mail inwards and outwards section are complaining that they have to arrive earlier than other staff and invariably leave later. They also complain that the last hour of their working day is so exhausting that they are quite unable to enjoy the evening even when they do finally get away. What improvements could be made to meet these objections?

(b) A firm with an address-list of 15 000 customers is introducing two new models of its most important machines. At the same time it is diversifying into a related field, producing a range of equipment likely to appeal to about two-thirds of the firms only. Leaflets cost $\frac{1}{2}$p each to produce and postage will be 14p per letter. Would you recommend:

(i) sending all three leaflets to all the firms?
(ii) sending separate mailings, the leaflets about the new models going to all firms and the leaflets about the new range of equipment going under separate cover to the ten thousand firms likely to be interested?
(iii) some other scheme?

Give your reasons.

8.12 Rapid Revision

Cover the page with a sheet of paper and uncover one question at a time.

Answers	Questions
—	1. What organisation conducts the postal services in the United Kingdom?
1. The Post Office.	2. Which reference book describes the services offered.
2. The *Post Office Guide*.	3. Outline a suitable system for dealing with mail outwards in a large organisation.
3. (a) Arrange suitable collection points in the departments; (b) fix the last time for collection from these post trays; (c) lay down rules to arrange an even despatch of mail throughout the day; (d) lay down rules for marking letters with the service required (first-class; recorded delivery, etc.); (e) collect and despatch mail at regular intervals.	4. What is a postage meter?

Answers	Questions
4. A meter which automatically franks letters with the required postage, so that stamps are unnecessary.	5. How does The Post Office control the use of postage meters?
5. It requires the daily completion of a form, which is submitted on the last day of the week to the Post Office where the machine is registered for use.	6. What system is used for Petty Cash?
6. The imprest system.	7. What is an imprest?
7. A sum of money set aside for a particular purpose.	8. What are the advantages of the imprest system?
8. (a) It saves bothering the main cashier; (b) little risk, and little temptation; (c) it trains young staff; (d) it saves time on posting to the Ledger because of the analysis columns; (e) it is easily checked.	9. Where is the 'middle' of a page in a Petty Cash Book?
9. Set towards the left-hand side of the page.	10. Why is this done?
10. Because the petty cashier does not often receive money.	11. When is money received?
11. (a) When the imprest is drawn from the cashier; (b) when members of staff pay for telephone calls, etc.	12. Why does the credit side need more room than in an ordinary Cash Book?
12. Because there are extra analysis columns.	13. What is the point of these analysis columns?
13. To collect together similar minor expenses and to make it possible to post the total each week to the Ledger with only one posting per column.	14. Go over the page again until you feel you are sure of the answers.

Exercises Set 8

1. Copy out the sentences given below, and complete them by using an appropriate word or phrase from the word list.

(a) The postal services are provided by an organisation called ....

(b) Postal deliveries are less frequent today than in earlier times because other means of ...... are available.

(c) The postal clerk in many firms also acts as the .... disbursing small sums of money as required.

(d) The most important reference book for a postal clerk is the ....

(e) A .... is a machine which prints the postage paid onto letters, so that they need not be stamped.

(f) To prevent excessive work in the post department late in the day, departmental managers should read and ...... letters for despatch as they are typed throughout the day.

(g) A .... is used to record important outgoing letters.

(h) Letters which are sent by the .... service travel through the mail system in the usual way but are delivered by special messenger if they arrive at the destination office after the usual mail delivery has taken place.

(i) The business reply service is one where the ...... is prepared to pay whatever postage is due when he receives the letter.

(j) A ...... is a machine which arranges papers or leaflets in order for despatch by post, or in readiness for a meeting.

Word list: communication, sign, postage book, *Post Office Guide*, special delivery, addressee, The Post Office, petty cashier, collator, franking machine.

2. In each of the following select the best answer (*a*), (*b*), (*c*), or (*d*) to the question.

(i) A poste restante letter: (*a*) is one addressed to the local head postmaster; (*b*) is one addressed to a post office for collection by a genuine traveller; (*c*) is one delivered to a letter box mounted on a post at the end of a long drive; (*d*) is a type of express delivery?

(ii) A service by which a letter is sent out to the addressee by Post Office messenger if it has missed the daily delivery is called: (*a*) 'express all the way'; (*b*) express at the request of the addressee; (*c*) special delivery; (*d*) Swiftair.

(iii) An addresser-printer is: (*a*) a Post Office employee who rewrites badly written envelopes to save unnecessary delay; (*b*) a printer who specialises in mailing systems for other firms; (*c*) a machine for printing envelopes from special embossed address plates; (*d*) a machine for filing, stamping and despatching bulk mailing?

(iv) A posting list is: (*a*) a list of registered envelopes to be sent off at the same time, presented to the Post Office counter clerk for signature; (*b*) a list of staff transfers to other departments; (*c*) a selection of the *Post Office Guide* listing postal charges to foreign countries; (*d*) a disability suffered by postmen as a result of carrying heavy sacks of mail?

3. What are the advantages gained by the use of 'postal franking' over the use of postage stamps?

4. Outline procedures for the efficient handling of outgoing mail in a large organisation. What equipment would be useful and what records should be kept?

5. Write about five to eight lines on any *three* of the following. Refer to the *Post Office Guide* if necessary.
(*a*) Postal franking; (*b*) the *Post Office Guide*; (*c*) how to address an envelope; (*d*) postage books; (*e*) recorded delivery; (*f*) registered parcels.

6. Draw up a list of instructions for a junior member of staff with respect to: (*a*) collection of mail outwards from departments; (*b*) duties as a messenger with respect to registered letters, recorded delivery letters and parcel post.
Use such imaginary names of individuals and departments as will make the instructions sensible.

7. What points would you pay particular attention to in preparing address plates for a mailing system?

8. Use the *Post Office Guide* to discover: (*a*) the cheapest way to send a book

by airmail to Dar-es-Salaam in Tanzania (weight 250 grams); (b) the correct method of address for a letter to the purser of a merchant ship in home waters.

9. Explain the steps that are necessary to post: (a) a registered packet; (b) a recorded delivery letter; (c) an airmail letter for Hong Kong; (d) an airmail letter to West Africa. Refer to the *Post Office Guide* where necessary.

10. What is an international reply coupon? What is a phonopost package? Refer to the *Post Office Guide* if necessary.

11. What mechanical aids are available to make the stamping and despatch of mail outwards more efficient?

12. In what circumstances would you despatch a letter by 'recorded delivery' rather than ordinary post? Describe the 'recorded delivery' service.

13. Your firm proposes to mail 24 000 customers with a special leaflet about a new product. Describe stage by stage the procedure you would use in such a mailing, referring to any machines that would be helpful. You may assume that such mailings are made regularly by your firm.

14. Describe briefly the Post Office services you would use in each of the following instances: (a) to enable customers in this country to reply to you without having to pay postage; (b) to enable customers abroad to reply to you without having to pay postage; (c) to collect money from customers in mail order transactions; (d) to send a legal document in which proof of delivery may be required in a court of law; (e) to ensure that an airmail letter to Nigeria received the most expeditious delivery possible; (f) to obtain correspondence in advance of the normal time of delivery; (h) to send £15 required the same day in another part of the country. Refer to the *Post Office Guide* if necessary. Give reasons for your answers.

15. (a) What are 'window' or 'aperture' envelopes and when are they used? Mention their advantages and disadvantages.

(b) What happens if: (i) a letter bears insufficient stamps; (ii) a letter bears no stamp; (iii) there is no reply when a postman brings a registered letter?
(RSA I)

16. What are the differences between: (a) a money order and a postal order; (b) registration and recorded delivery; (c) airmail and surface mail; (d) a posting list and a postage book?

17. Write fully about the following postal services (refer to the *Post Office Guide* if necessary): (a) business reply service; (b) redirection of letters; (c) cash on delivery.
(RSA I)

18. You are responsible for the franking machine in the postal department of Graham Stubbs & Co. Ltd.

(a) Draw up a franking machine control card as in Fig. 8.3 (page 102), with the following details for the week ended 5th July.
The meter office as shown on the record card is Huddersfield GPO and the Machine Number is D4361. The machine is operated on the basis of ½p units. At the commencement of business on Monday, 1st July, the number of units used (taken from the previous week's card for reading of ascending register) was 87 412 and the number of units purchased, i.e. total deposits, was 90 000.

Monday:	used 2007 units
Tuesday:	paid £50 to the Post Office
	used 1560 units
Wednesday:	used 2408 units
Thursday:	used 1976 units
Friday:	used 1841 units

(b) What was the balance of credit at the end of the week?   (RSA I)

19. If you were sending the following articles by post, which service would you use? Give reasons briefly: (a) legal documents which are valuable (not in terms of money) and for which you wish to have proof of delivery; (b) a gold and diamond ring, value £80; (c) an envelope (16 × 23 cm) containing a letter with enclosures (not valuable) and weighing about 150 grams.   (RSA I)

20. If you had to send banknotes by post, what method would you use to ensure their safety? Explain fully, referring to the *Post Office Guide* if necessary: (a) the steps you would take in packaging; (b) the Post Office service you would use; (c) the procedure you would follow at the Post Office; (d) the precautions the Post Office would take in order to ensure safe delivery of the package.

21. Compare the following two Post Office services in relation to cost, security, and compensation: (a) recorded delivery; (b) registered mail. When would you use each of these services?   (RSA I)

22. You are employed in the mailing department of a large organisation, which is shortly to be reorganised and equipped with modern equipment. The office manager has asked you to give him your views on the procedure and equipment necessary for dealing with the outgoing mail. Write your recommendations in report form.   (RSA II)

23. Outline the necessary action which has to be taken in the post department when dealing with the following: (a) Post Office docket for your franking machine; (b) twelve registered letters to be despatched at once; (c) printed papers and samples to be posted in bulk; (d) parcels for despatch abroad.

24. You are employed in the mailing department of a large organisation. Name three machines which would simplify and speed up the handling of incoming and outgoing mail. Describe these machines and their functions.

25. Rule up a Petty Cash Book with analysis columns, and enter the following items:

19..

		£
March 2	Balance in hand	2.56
	Received from cashier	17.44
	Bought stamps	3.00
3	Postage on parcel	1.25
	Bus fares	0.36
	String and gum	0.45
4	Bought pencils	0.36
	Surcharge on letters	0.18
	Tea and milk for office teas	1.55

Balance the book on 5th March.

26. From the information in the following Petty Cash Book (which is kept on the Imprest System) answer the questions given below.

Cash Received £	Date 19..	Details	Totals £	Postages and Telegrams £	Carriage £	Stationery £
						Cr.
4.61	Jan. 1	Balance				
15.39	2	Cash				
	3	Postage	1.10	1.10		
	5	Stationery	3.41			3.41
		Carriage	2.45		2.45	
	6	Postage	1.25	1.25		
	7	Telegrams	0.45	0.45		
		Carriage	1.55		1.55	
	8	Stationery	5.18			5.18

Dr is at the top left and Cr. at the top right of the table.

(*a*) What is the amount of the petty cash float? (*b*) What was the balance of petty cash on the first day of the year? (*c*) How much was spent in postage and telegrams during the period? (*d*) How much was spent in stationery during the period? (*e*) What was the total amount spent during the period? (*f*) How much must the Petty Cashier receive at the end of the period to make up the float?

27. (*a*) Whose signature(s) will appear on a petty cash voucher? (*b*) What will be pinned to the voucher whenever possible? (*c*) What is a 'float'? (*d*) What is the imprest system of petty cash?

28. You are responsible for writing up the Petty Cash Book in your office. The three analysis columns are headed 'Office Expenses', 'Postage and Stationery', and 'Cleaning'.

(*a*) State under which heading you would enter the following payments: refills for ballpoint pens; laundering of towels; erasers; tea, milk and sugar; stamps; tip for a van driver; a roll of Sellotape; magazines for waiting room; dishcloths; airmail letter forms. (*b*) What do you understand by analysis columns? (*c*) Explain fully the uses of the Petty Cash Book.

9

THE GENERAL ADMINISTRATION OFFICE

9.1 Offices which Serve the Whole Organisation

However large an organisation may be, there are some departments which influence the work in every other department. We have already looked at the work of the reception office, the telephone system, the 'mail inwards' department and the 'mail outwards' department. Each of these departments may be said to serve the whole organisation and forms part of the interdepartmental team which promotes the firm's general activities. Standing at the very centre of this general activity is the **general administration office**, under the **administration officer**.

9.2 Functions of the General Administration Office

This office performs a wide range of activities providing office services for the more specialised departments such as production, buying, sales, advertising, despatch and transport. In particular, it often provides centralised services such as typing and audio-typing pools or duplicating and photocopying services. It may act as a **resource centre** providing handouts, publicity material, display facilities, etc., and it usually acts as a general reserve force to assist activities in other departments which come under pressure at times of peak activity.

The administration officer must be a person of wide experience and sound ability to whom colleagues at all levels can turn for help and advice in handling problems that arise. He will usually have some control of the disbursement of funds between departments, and a general responsibility for the choice and supply of office equipment and business systems, both the hardware (machinery and equipment) and the forms and documentation. This will usually involve some decision-making about the provision of centralised office services.

9.3 Centralised Office Services

We live in a world where there are great economies to be achieved by the use of large-scale organisation. A large firm can usually manufacture, distribute and sell more cheaply than a small firm, and a large office can similarly produce letters, circulars, invoices and other documents more economically than a small office. Top-class machines, highly skilled staff and subdivision of labour into specialised jobs and processes reduce the costs of each unit of office activity just as they do in a factory.

What is Centralisation?

Centralisation is a system where control is exercised from the centre on the activities of all departments and branches. Detailed instructions on methods and procedure to be followed are issued from Head Office, and a system of 'reporting back' is instituted to keep Head Office informed of developments. In addition, those cost centres that can be more efficiently operated as large units—for example, accounting centres, typing pools and resource centres—are removed from the specialised departments and operated as central services. Very advanced equipment can therefore be employed at these service departments, including computerised accounting and data processing installations and multi-user audio-typing systems.

The advantages and disadvantages of centralised services may be arranged appropriately in tabular form as follows:

Centralisation of Services

Advantages	*Disadvantages*
1. More economical operation. The specialist staff can perform the work more quickly and easily with proper facilities which are utilised more fully.	1. Impersonal nature of the employment. Some of the gains in economy of operation are lost in frustration of individuals resentful of the impersonal nature of the work.
2. Better administrative control. The supply and use of hardware, software, ancillary equipment and staff time are more easily controlled in specialist centralised offices.	2. Greater bureaucracy. Form filling and similar time-wasting activities may mean an increase in 'red tape' and bureaucracy. Where departments are dependent on coopera-
3. Better use of staff. Skilled staff can be more fully utilised, since interruptions by telephone calls or visiting staff can be circumvented.	tion from other departments a growth of interdepartmental committees and other time-wasting bodies is inevitable.
4. Cheaper labour costs. Routine work can be performed by less skilled staff. Centralisation gives a variety of graded employments at all levels of difficulty.	3. Impersonal activity is subject to delay. Delays may occur in more important activities—for example, senior staff must dictate letters in full instead of giving a secretary brief instructions like 'Write and
5. Better layout and use of mechanical aids. Machines can be more fully utilised, and they can be isolated if they are noisy, away from the general office.	say—no, we're sorry'. Boredom reduces work output if tasks become too repetitive and bright staff go elsewhere.
6. Greater flexibility in the use of resources. Central pools enable flexible use to be made of available staff and equipment. A statistical department makes fuller use of statistically programmed mini-computers, and the capital tied up	4. Impractical orders and procedures. The remoteness of managers from the actual scene of events leads to some procedures being unworkable or inappropriate.
	5. Segregation of staff. Many of the

Advantages	Disadvantages
in this equipment is more intensively used. 7. Greater variety of service. A centralised service will usually be able to afford a variety of equipment which will increase the choice available to staff. For example, in reprographic activities, documents and brochures may be produced in black ink, colour, spirit, with or without illustrations and with a variety of typestyles. The resulting output will be appropriate to its final use—from board-room reports of high quality to cheap handouts and documents for more routine activities.	routine office practices which are most easily centralised employ less experienced staff. This separates staff into categories and reduces 'esprit de corps', the essential unity of the organisation. 6. Job motivation is reduced. The routine work of centralised departments retards the training and development of personnel. The opportunities to experience all facets of business life are reduced, and work becomes a daily round of office chores. This must be overcome by planned progression from department to department to assist young staff to gain general experience.

9.4   Services Commonly Controlled by the General Administration Office

In the largest offices the general administration office would usually control:

(*a*) Mail inwards and outwards.
(*b*) The telephone and telex systems.
(*c*) Caretaking, cleaning and routine maintenance services.
(*d*) Reception and messenger services.
(*e*) Canteen, refreshment breaks and machine vending services.
(*f*) Stationery and office supplies.
(*g*) Holiday, sick relief and other staff rotas.
(*h*) First Aid, fire and safety services.

It would be influential in appointing staff and supervising the following central services:

(*a*) Duplicating and reprographic services.
(*b*) Typing and audio-typing pools.
(*c*) Filing and records services.

The centralised services are dealt with more fully in the chapters which follow.

9.5   Overcoming the Disadvantages of Centralised Services

The boredom that results from specialised activities can be partly overcome by a rota system in which a group of clerks or operators perform activities in turn. Thus the processing of a particular document may be substituted after a while by a mechanical operation with an adding-listing machine, which may be followed by a short period of calculating or accounting. Wherever possible the employee should be encouraged to plan the day's work personally, while achieving a full coverage of necessary activities and reaching a satisfactory level of **productivity**. Almost every type of office work is measurable, and a supervisor can tell whether the volume of work done is a fair output for an employee of that grade.

A second solution to the tedium of these centralised services is to raise the salary payable. This compensates the workers for the monotony of the employment by enabling them to obtain better leisure enjoyment, good vacations, etc.

A solution to the impersonal relationships between staff requiring services and those giving them from centralised services may lie in some degree of specialisation. For example two or three typists in a typing pool might always attend to the correspondence, invoices and other documents required by the sales department, and thus build up a strong link with that department as well as an expertise in its requirements.

9.6   Public Relations

Every organisation has to maintain relations with the general public, not only in order to maintain sales of goods or services but also to meet the many obligations which arise in the course of everyday life. The public today are very conscious of the need to preserve the environment, indeed there is a huge **Department of the Environment** to control the impact of industry on our national heritage. One nationalised industry which runs cross-channel ferries made a decision to change from paper cups to plastic cups. It was in the habit of dumping rubbish overboard in mid-channel. The new plastic cups, unlike the paper ones, did not become waterlogged and sink, but floated ashore where they proved to be a source of almost permanent litter. Quite apart from this nuisance the matter brought to light the fact that to save emptying a few dustbins at each end of the journey the seas were being polluted with all sorts of waste products. Naturally the industry concerned had to revise its policy to meet the public indignation that arose.

The general administration officer often assumes responsibility for public relations in small firms. Larger organisations will appoint **public relations officers**, who are often members of the **Institute of Public Relations**.

9.7   Points to Think About and Discuss

(*a*) A hospital has been storing its x-ray records departmentally; the various departments such as the orthopaedic department, ear, nose and throat clinic, casualty department, etc., keep their own records. The registrar is proposing to centralise all hospital records, and suggests a centralised x-ray records department. Discuss the advantages and disadvantages of such a system.

(*b*) The office has been supplied twice daily with tea, served to staff at their desks from a mobile trolley with urns. A vending machine system is suggested instead, located at convenient points on each floor and available at all times. Discuss the advantages and disadvantages of such a change.

(*c*) Argue a case for, or against, a change from a system where personal secretaries with shorthand and typing skills serve executives' correspondence needs, to a system where executives are connected by a hand microphone to a centralised dictation machine and letters are typed by a pool of audio-typists.

9.8   Rapid Revision

Cover the page with a sheet of paper and uncover one question at a time.

Answers	Questions
—	1. What are the functions of the General Administration Office?
1. To control a wide range of activities within the firm, particularly the care and cleaning of buildings, the security arrangements and the provision of centralised services used by other departments.	2. Which services are often centralised?
2. (*a*) The telephone service; (*b*) typing pools; (*c*) calculation and accounting services; (*d*) stationery and office resources.	3. What are the advantages of centralisation of these services?
3. (*a*) More economical operation; (*b*) bulk purchase of supplies; (*c*) the best and most sophisticated equipment becomes economical; (*d*) better use of staff time; (*e*) cheaper labour can be employed because every activity becomes routine.	4. Are there any disadvantages?
4. (*a*) The work becomes impersonal; (*b*) a bureaucratic attitude may develop; (*c*) delay may occur because of the indirect nature of orders to staff; (*d*) segregation of staff causes resentment; (*e*) job motivation is reduced.	5. What type of person is required for the post of chief administrative officer?
5. A person of wide interests and abilities, who is equally at ease with all classes of visitors and staff.	6. Where is the General Administration Office usually situated?

Answers	Questions
6. Near the entrance to the building, on the ground floor, where it is at the centre of activities.	7. Go over the page again until you feel you are sure of the answers.

Exercises Set 9

1. What do you understand by the designation of 'Chief Administration Officer'? What responsibilities would such a post carry in the large office block of an international company?

2. 'Every one of these dictation machines will save you the wages of six short-hand-typists.—Salesman to general administration officer.

You are one of the shorthand-typists. Write a report objecting to the adoption of dictation machines, and justifying your opinion.

3. Your office has six members of staff who can do relief telephone operating. The telephonist has lunch from noon to 1 p.m. and coffee breaks from 10.30 to 10.45 a.m. and 3 p.m. to 3.15 p.m. Draw up a rota for relief telephone duties so that the work is fairly allocated between *A*, *B*, *C*, *D*, *E* and *F*. *C* cannot be available any morning and *F* cannot do any lunch-time work. *A* has Thursday off and *D* has Friday afternoon off.

4. What is meant by 'centralisation'? What is meant by 'centralised services'? In your answer consider the application of these two principles in (*a*) the retail supermarket trade *or* (*b*) an oil company controlling a chain of garages *or* (*c*) a university with fifteen colleges.

5. You are asked to produce a holiday rota for the ten members of your staff covering the months of June, July and August (a period of thirteen weeks). The staff consists of yourself and your assistant, one telephonist and a relief telephonist-typist, two general clerks, two shorthand-typists, one copy typist and a junior trainee clerk. Each member of the staff is allowed to take two weeks' holiday. Draw up the necessary rota, ensuring that the department's work is adequately covered.

6. In office practice there is an increasing tendency towards specialisation and centralisation of functions. State your views as to why this is happening and explain the advantages which can be obtained. Illustrate your answer by reference to one specific office procedure.

7. As administrative officer it is your duty to cover the absence of any clerk or specialist employee. Johnson, an export documentation clerk, is jealous of his specialist knowledge and secretive about the various functions he performs. Suggest arguments which you would use to change his attitude. If he stubbornly refuses to train a replacement how would you suggest this should be overcome?

8. Considerable trouble has developed among the caretaking staff in the Massive Office Company. The administration officer discovers the following chief complaints: (*a*) Bill Bloggs, the assistant chief caretaker, is universally disliked for his bad temper and foul language; (*b*) female cleaners consider that they receive an unfair allocation of the heavy work; (*c*) persistent grumbling by supervisors about the late arrival of cleaning staff is caused by the fact that

the first bus does not reach the area until ten minutes after the official starting time. This grumbling is resented by the cleaners; (d) there is a shortage of cleaning materials of every sort although prices have not risen and the allocation of money has not changed; (e) increased bus fares have not been reflected in any increase in wages for the lowest paid staff. Higher ranks have had a 10 per cent increase in pay; (f) department 'D' is notoriously slovenly in its behaviour. Staff cleaning this department are thoroughly disgusted with the condition of desks and floors, which seems to be related to the installation of a coffee machine.

Suggest remedial action the administration officer should take on each of these points.

9. 'Central services are more efficient than departmental services.'

'The impersonal relationships between staff and the central services who are supposed to be supplying them with correspondence, etc., lead to a reduction in efficiency.'

Discuss these two opposing views of central services. Which view is the more correct in your opinion?

10. Segregation of the sexes frequently results from a change to centralised services. Why is this? What solutions can be found to this problem?

10

CENTRALISED SERVICES—THE TYPING POOL

10.1 Typewriting

In the nineteenth century most letters were handwritten, and the chief requirement of a clerk was—in W. S. Gilbert's words the ability 'to copy all the letters in a big, round hand'. Today the typewriter, in the hands of a competent typist, produces letters of good appearance; neat, legible and well displayed. It is not the work of a moment to achieve competence as a typist, and to learn to display material well and at speed requires patience, perseverance and intelligence on the part of the typist.

The following grades of typist may be identified:

(*a*) Trainee junior typists
(*b*) Copy-typists
(*c*) Audio-typists
(*d*) Shorthand-typists
(*e*) Personal secretaries

Whilst all typists require reasonable intelligence and manual dexterity, the higher classes of typists require a sound background of general education and business experience. Many personal secretaries have university degrees and experience in public relations and other fields. Such labour is expensive, and much of the routine correspondence of the office must be typed more economically by some system of copy typing or audio-typing. This type of correspondence is best prepared by typing pools, which have certain advantages over the system where departmental typists prepare work for their own particular section of the business.

10.2 The Typing Pool

Under the typing pool system most of the typists in a firm are collected together in a central office where they type the vast majority of the correspondence required. Probably only the senior executives, with their personal secretaries, will not have their correspondence prepared by the pool. Everybody else, either by manuscript (hand-written copy) or audio-tapes or by dictating to one of the pool typists who can do shorthand in one or other of its forms (Pitman, Gregg, Speedwriting, Teeline, etc.) will make their requirements clear to the typing pool supervisor,

122 *Office Practice Made Simple*

who will allocate the work to the typists and audio-typists in the pool. The advantages of this system may be listed as follows:

Advantages of the Typing Pool

(a) It makes economical use of typist labour, since the idle time inevitable in departmental organisation—for example, while managers are at meetings—is filled by other·work.

(b) Sickness and holiday difficulties are easily overcome since the absence of a typist can be met by allocating work to others.

(c) A broader experience of the work of the office is given to the typists in the pool. This particularly improves the training of young staff, who can be employed on less essential activities like routine envelope addressing, etc., as they learn the keyboard. They can then be raised to better levels of work as they acquire competence.

(d) Interruptions to the work are avoided—telephone queries can be intercepted and dealt with by the supervisor, and a body of trainee staff is available for taking messages, conducting searches, etc.

(e) More correct work results, not only because the supervisors check work before returning it to departments but also because greater skill results from specialisation in a particular class of work.

(f) Less time is wasted—in departmental offices there is a tendency to lose typing time due to a variety of interruptions.

(g) Noise is confined to the typing pool, and goes unnoticed, whereas departmental typists disturb their departments.

Against these advantages may be set the disadvantages of most centralised systems, which include a lack of personal contact between typists and executives, an increased need for messenger and collection services and the dissatisfaction of staff segregated from the general and wider activities of the enterprise to perform a limited, if useful, specialist activity.

10.3 Types of Typewriter

Rapid developments in typewriter design, particularly the application of electronics to give **'word-processing'** facilities, have revolutionised the secretarial side of office work. Usually an experienced buyer will evaluate the machines to select those which are most suitable for the particular requirements of the typing pool, departmental or personal secretaries concerned. The range of typewriters now includes:

(a) Standard manual typewriters
(b) Portable typewriters
(c) Electric typewriters
(d) Golf-ball typewriters
(e) Electronic typewriters
(f) Word processors
(g) Dual-feed machines
(h) Continuous stationery machines
(i) Carbon-ribbon machines
(j) Hectograph carbon-ribbon machines

A few words about each type of machine seems appropriate at this point.

Manual Typewriters

As their name implies, manual typewriters are operated by hand, the typists striking the keys so that the typeface strikes the ribbon and prints the required character on the paper. It is essential to develop an even touch so that the text is printed uniformly on the paper. It is not the purpose of this book to teach typewriting, which is a specialist study in its own right. Many readers will be introduced to the typewriter as part of their office studies, and it is indeed desirable that everyone should learn to type. Manual typewriters are so cheap today that almost everyone can afford to own a typewriter for personal use, and readers are strongly recommended to take time to learn this useful skill.

```
                    Pica Typestyles

        This paragraph has been typed on a
'Pica' machine.  Pica typestyles are
designed with 10 characters to the inch
(10 pitch).  They give a clear, legible
typescript and are used for the vast
majority of business correspondence.


             Elite Typestyles

        This paragraph has been typed on an 'Elite'
machine.    It has 12 characters to the inch
(12 pitch).    Elite typestyles give a smaller, more
personal  appearance to the typescript.


        Although manufacturers have now designed
many interesting typefaces, all typefaces are
based on 'pica' or 'elite', with 10 or 12
characters to the inch.
```

Fig. 10.1. 'Pica' and 'elite' typestyles.

The two main typefaces are 'pica' and 'elite'. Pica is the traditional typeface for office work. It gives a standard ten characters to the inch, and is bold in appearance. Elite gives twelve standard characters to the inch but for special purposes both these styles can be obtained with more or less characters to the inch.

Standard machines have six lines to the inch and may usually be set either to single, double or triple line spacing. Half line spacing is also possible on some machines. Fig. 10.1 shows pica and elite typefaces.

Portable Typewriters

These are lightweight models which are very convenient for typists who travel about a great deal. Thus journalists, authors and others who travel in pursuit of news stories or background information essential to their craft find a portable machine of great convenience. They usually have carriages 9" or 12" long, which is adequate for most ordinary purposes. Since the framework is less robust than standard machines they are more suitable to experienced typists than to learners, and many parents who buy their teenage children a portable typewriter would do better to supply them with a standard model. The extra expense is offset by reduced servicing charges eventually.

Electric Typewriters

These have many advantages over manual machines, of which the following may be noted:

(i)   The typist does not tire so easily, since the merest contact on the keys is enough. The powered machine then drives the key forward to strike the ribbon, and as it drives all the keys uniformly the typescript is even and easy to read.

(ii) Automatic carriage return saves the typist time and effort, automatically operating the line spacer at the same time.

(iii) 'Repeat characters' are provided, if not on all characters at least on certain ones. Thus, the underscoring of words is carried out automatically, and the space bar can be operated automatically. These features save the typist much physical effort.

(iv) A carbon copy control enables the machine to be adjusted when several carbon copies are required. The physical effort required to take, say, 10 carbon copies on a manual machine is very great, but by increasing the power behind the keys of an electric machine as many as 20 copies may be prepared.

Golf-ball Typewriters

Some years ago a revolutionary type of electric typewriter which has been extensively copied, appeared on the market. This is the **IBM Selectric machine**. Here the characters are moulded onto a spherical 'golf-ball' head. When a key is depressed the machine selects the shortest path for the head to rotate and tilt so that the correct character strikes the ribbon. The machine is capable of typing up to 15 characters per second, which is about twice as fast as most typists can type.

Because of the single typing element the carriage does not move, the golf-ball typeface travelling across the stationary paper sliding on a guide shaft. The machine is therefore quieter, uses less desk space and operator-effort is minimal. The golf-ball may be changed to give different typefaces—see Plate 5—which enables variety of presentation to

ماشین تحریر کارت مغناطیسی فارسی شکل تازه ای به کار شما خواهدبخشید .

پس از این لزومی ندارد نگران اشتباهات خود بشوید . اکنون تمام کارهای تحریری خود را میتوانید بصورت پیش نویس ، یعنی آسان ترین نوع ماشین نویسی تهیه کنید . اگر اشتباهی کردید کافیست به عقب برگشته و دوباره روی آن ماشین کرده و بکار خود ادامه دهید . در پایان یک نسخه بدون

... صحیح بودن متن تحریر شده ، کیفیت غیر قابل قیاس ... های شما خواهد داد .

Plate 5. A golf-ball electric typewriter—with Arabic typeface (reproduced by courtesy of IBM (UK) Ltd).

be incorporated into the typescript. Plate 5 shows one of the interchangeable 'golf-ball' typing elements, for which different typestyles are available.

Electronic Typewriters

Electronic typewriters have recently replaced the golf-ball typewriter as the latest thing in typewriting. The more complex machines become part of a full word-processing system, which is described later. The chief features of an electronic typewriter are as follows:

(a) The functions traditionally performed manually by the typist, such as margin setting, numerical alignment, tabulation, underlining, title centring, etc., are performed by a central logic unit in the typewriter.

(b) A one-line memory holds each line typed long enough for corrections to be made using a correction key. After the correction another key automatically returns the printing element to the position where the last character was typed.

(c) At the end of the line the print unit automatically returns to the start of the next line and adjusts the paper vertically.

(d) There is an automatic space bar, and every character can be repeated.

(e) By means of the 'Centre' key every heading can be perfectly centred automatically, and also all dates, salutations, signatures, etc., can be automatically justified to the right-hand margin.

(*f*) Automatic vertical lines can be typed in to give separation of the paper into columns for tabulation.

(*g*) The print unit consists of interchangeable daisy wheel printing elements, capable of typing 17 characters per second.

When linked with a visual display unit (VDU) such typewriters enable a whole document to be reproduced on the visual display before typing. The whole document is then typed out at 7 characters per second (about 200 words per minute), and in perfect layout as previously displayed on the visual display unit. Such a system is illustrated in Plate 6.

Word Processors

Word processors are sophisticated electronic typewriters linked to a memory stored on a magnetic medium. Usually the storage medium is a 'floppy disc', but in some cases it is a magnetic card or tape cassette. There is an electronic keyboard, and a display unit which shows everything that is typed. The actual line being typed is held in a buffer memory which enables the typist to correct any errors before the line is actually printed. Sometimes a whole page is displayed and corrected before printing. The machine can then print the line, or the page, and in some cases it can start from either end according to where the printing element is at the time. A line may therefore be printed backwards if this will be quicker. Before the line is printed, automatic spacing spreads the wording to fill the line exactly, giving right-hand margin justification— just like a printed book. The type is stored on interchangeable daisy-wheels, so that a selection of typefaces is available. Plate 7 shows such a printing unit.

There are numerous applications of word processors; for example, we may list:

(*a*) *Standard form letters.* A letter frequently sent to many customers can be stored in the memory and recalled whenever it is required. The word processor will stop at the date, reference section, internal address, etc., and enable the console typist to type in these variable details. The machine will then print the letter at speeds up to 400 words per minute.

(*b*) *Repetitive typing.* Standard paragraphs from contracts, leases and similar legal documents can be called forward and printed to save the typist typing them out.

(*c*) *Revision typing.* Reports and similar documents can be recalled from the memory to the visual display unit and corrected, updated or changed. The extra material will be accepted and the following material reshuffled to take account of the insertion.

Dual-feed Machines

These machines are used for accounting. The word 'feed' refers to the way paper is inserted into the machine. Where a summary sheet

Plate 6. An electronic typing system: the Olivetti ETS 1010 (reproduced by courtesy of British Olivetti Ltd).

Plate 7. A 'daisy-wheel' printhead (reproduced by courtesy of British Olivetti Ltd).

is required showing all the work done—for example, when making ledger entries for sales invoices—the summary sheet is fed into the machine in the usual way by the rear feed. The ledger card and the statement are fed into the front feed, or into a second feed at the back, and positioned so that they are correctly aligned with the next clean line on the summary sheet. The details of the goods supplied are then typed on the statement, and repeated on the ledger card and the summary sheet below. The operator then removes the ledger card and statement from its feed, but the summary sheet merely moves up one line ready for the next customer's account to be inserted. A full description of this system is given in *Book-keeping Made Simple*. Fig. 10.2 shows a more advanced accounting machine, which has both alphabetical and numerical keyboards. The ledger cards are fed into the front feed guides and position above the next clean line of the rear-fed summary sheet.

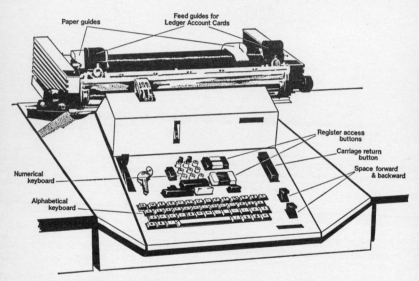

Fig. 10.2. A dual-feed machine for accounting (courtesy of British Olivetti Ltd).

Continuous Stationery Machines

One of the irksome tasks of the copy-typist is the need to insert paper and carbons into the machine at regular intervals. This problem can sometimes be overcome by using a continuous pack of stationery which will be automatically fed with carbon paper each time a new sheet is used. This is most useful when invoices and credit notes are being dealt with by the same typist for much of the working day. The weight of the stationery as it is fed in must be taken by a friction mechanism, which also enables the carbon paper to be automatically inserted between the copies. Fig. 10.3 illustrates a typical machine of this type.

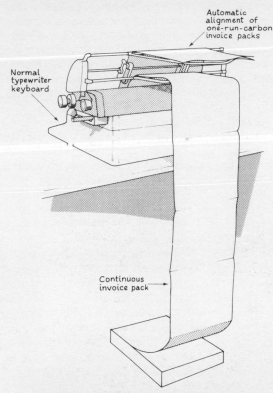

Fig. 10.3. A continuous stationery machine.

Carbon-ribbon Machines

These machines produce a clear, black impression from the type, giving correspondence a distinguished appearance favoured by many executives. It is also ideal for photocopying and for offset-litho masters. The ribbon is used once only, and then has to be replaced, so that there is no chance of quality declining as ribbons wear out.

Hectograph Carbon-ribbon Machines

Hectograph spirit masters can be prepared on these machines, which use a ribbon of hecto-carbon to print the masters. Once again these are consumable, the ribbon being used once only, but the resulting spirit master is of high quality.

10.4 Audio-typing

Audio-typing has developed rapidly in the last twenty years since the tape-recorder has been perfected. Its name implies that the typist types what she hears. Since most people speak faster than a typist can type (the late President Kennedy was reputed to speak at 400 words per minute) she needs a machine which can be interrupted with a foot switch. The typist listens, memorises a phrase, stops the machine and types the phrase. A variety of dictating machines is marketed, and the choice is therefore very wide.

Advantages of Audio-typing Systems

Audio-typing systems separate the executive from the typist, so that he can dictate when it suits him and the typist is then free to type the letters at a convenient moment for her. Portable dictating machines enable the executive to dictate correspondence when travelling or when absent from the office. Multiple installations enable an executive to connect himself to one of a central bank of dictation machines and dictate letters immediately he opens his mail or immediately after a telephone conversation or interview with a client or customer. There is a considerable saving in labour costs, since audio-typists are usually paid less than shorthand-typists and may do more work because of the specialist nature of the activity. The shorthand-typist must be absent from her desk to take dictation for much of the time. The audio-typist can work only at her own installation and therefore tends to produce a greater volume of finished work. Work is more fairly shared between typists, who do not work for a particular executive but for a group of executives. It is also easier to take over a spool of magnetic tape when a typist is absent than to take over her dictation book, which is full of personal 'short forms' she has invented to speed up her note-taking.

Disadvantages of Dictation Machines

Typists tend to resent dictation machines which render their short-hand unnecessary and reduce freedom to move about the office taking dictation from executives. The typist loses that sense of personal service which is so valuable in a firm, and becomes instead a clock-watcher who is anxious only to escape from the tyranny of the machine.

Whereas shorthand-typists never break down or suffer from power failures this is not uncommon with electronic machines and considerable inconvenience and delay may result—for example, at times of industrial unrest in the power industry.

Qualities of the Good Audio-typist

The audio-typist must have the following qualities:

(*a*) The ability to type at a good basic speed.

(*b*) The ability to spell and punctuate properly. Since typing is carried out directly from what is heard on the stethophones, it is very important that the typist can turn this directly into a properly spelled and punctuated letter.

(*c*) The ability to display material properly.

It follows that an audi-typist should already be a trained typist, and should convert to audio-typing by a short conversion course. Resentment will be reduced if the typist is not a shorthand-typist but has previously been engaged as a copy-typist only.

Using the Dictation Machine

An executive dictating letters for the first time has to grow used to the impersonal nature of the system. It is essential to speak distinctly and give clear instructions about requirements, the number of copies needed, the type of paper to be used perhaps and the distribution of any copies within the firm.

In dictating to a shorthand-typist, the executive who ponders what to say next gives the secretary a chance to read through and improve the notes. The executive who dictates to a dictation machine stops the machine when not actually speaking, since this saves tape. As a result the typist receives a continuous spool of dictation material.

The latest machines overcome many of the defects of earlier machines. For example, if the executive pauses for more than four seconds the machine will automatically cut out to save tape time. When tape is being replayed the machine senses the material being replayed and cuts out immediately at the end of the replay. If the user releases the machine when it has been replaying it automatically tracks forward to the end of the dictation and stops ready for any further dictation by the user. An automatic privacy lock on multi-user equipment prevents anyone back-tracking onto another user's dictation. The latest portable machines have quick-release cassettes which can be posted into the typing pool by travellers and executives working at home.

Corrections can also be indicated on modern machines. A coordinated correction sheet, divided into sections, enables the user to mark in the point where corrections have been made, and where the new wording is to be found on the tape. With magnetic machines it is possible to re-record the correct wording over the top of the old wording.

Types of Recording Media

Dictation machines record in a variety of ways. The chief types are:

(*a*) Magnetic recordings made on wire, plastic tape, plastic belting or magnetic sheeting. Magnetic recordings can be erased or printed over with a new set of dictation so that they can be used again and again. The magnetic sheeting is particularly convenient since it can be clipped to documents, correspondence, etc., filed away in filing systems and posted in an ordinary envelope. Fig. 10.4 illustrates the convenience of this type of magnetic recording.

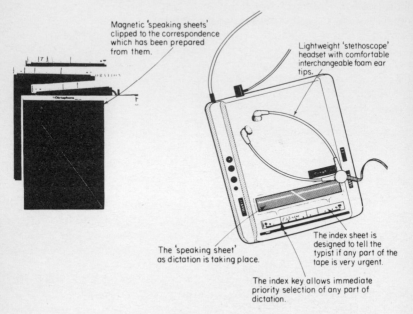

Magnetic 'speaking sheets' clipped to the correspondence which has been prepared from them.

Lightweight 'stethoscope' headset with comfortable interchangeable foam ear tips.

The 'speaking sheet' as dictation is taking place.

The index sheet is designed to tell the typist if any part of the tape is very urgent.

The index key allows immediate priority selection of any part of dictation.

Fig. 10.4. A 'speaking sheet' dictation machine (reproduced by courtesy of Dictaphone Ltd).

(*b*) Inscribed recordings. Here a diamond stylus cuts a permanent record into a plastic tape. This visible record is filed away after transcription as a permanent record of the correspondence.

Types of Installation: Centralised Systems

(*a*) *Multi-bank system.* Here there are a number of recording machines in a central bank, to which executives are connected by wire through the ordinary PABX telephone circuits or the private internal telephone network. The number of recording machines is commonly one to six executives. Executives are automatically connected to a free recorder. A supervisor distributes dictated recordings to the members of the typing pool. Each typist has a transcription machine for playing back the recordings, varying the speed by a foot pedal control. The system is very impersonal but relatively cheap because the ratio of recorders to transcribers is 6:1 or even 8:1, which is economical.

(*b*) *Tandem system.* Here the executive calls a control panel on the ordinary telephone and is automatically routed to the next available secretary, who has a 'tandem' system. This consists of two dictation machines, each of which is available for recording or playing back. The executive dictates the letter to the machine that is recording, while at the same time the typist is transcribing a previously recorded piece of work. When this is completed a switch is thrown, the roles of the machines are reversed and the typist transcribes the letter just recorded while the tandem machine is available for recording purposes.

A refinement on this system permits the executive to rewind and playback letters. Once again a confidential lock prevents one executive listening to a recording made by another executive. A phone link enables the typist to check details with the supervisor, or with the executive. Plate 8 illustrates the 'tandem' system.

Plate 8. A typist operating a tandem dictation system (reproduced by courtesy of Peter Williams Group Ltd).

Disadvantages of Centralised Dictation Facilities

These may be listed as follows:

(*a*) The capacity is limited, and may result in queuing for free recorders at certain busy times of the day. In such circumstances calls are routed to the supervisor who may have difficulty assessing priorities.

(*b*) In some circumstances an executive who is interrupted tends to hold the connection for it is impossible to reconnect. This intensifies the problems when capacity is fully utilised.

(*c*) Power failures and breakdowns hold up the whole system.

(*d*) The initial capital cost is high.

(*e*) Some systems do not enable the secretary to know how long the letter is that is to follow, nor that corrections have been made later on in the tape. This may mean that the work has to be done again.

10.5 Points to Think About and Discuss

(*a*) What are the likely costs, and benefits, of installing an audio-typing pool instead of the existing departmental secretary system? Consider under these two headings the financial, social and psychological aspects of the change.

(*b*) To what exent should the following matters influence management in its business decisions:

(i) Profit.

(ii) Good employer–employee relationships.

(iii) Status in the locality?

(*c*) A firm is considering rearranging its work to meet changing requirements. The changes will have the following effects:

(i) The dismissal of 100 personal secretaries and their replacement by 60 audio-typists. All staff are recruited locally.

(ii) A reduction of 5 per cent in prices to the customers.

(iii) An increase in profits of £200 000 per year is expected, estimated to represent a 1 per cent increase in dividend to shareholders.

The firm is the largest employer in the area in a highly competitive international field. What are the implications of these changes?

10.6 Rapid Revision

Cover the page with a sheet of paper and uncover one question at a time.

Answers	*Questions*
—	1. List the advantages of a typing pool.
1. (*a*) Higher typist output. (*b*) Cheaper labour used than the personal secretary type of employee. (*c*) Greater variety of work received and hence wider experience for the typists. (*d*) Improved training and supervision possible. (*e*) Less noise in other offices.	2. List the disadvantages of a typing pool.

Answers	Questions
2. (*a*) Loss of personal convenience to departmental executives. (*b*) Reduced use of their skills by some trained shorthand typists. (*c*) Increased messenger and collection services required. (*d*) High cost of audio systems.	3. List five types of typewriter besides the standard manual typewriter and the electric machines.
3. (*a*) Electronic machines (*b*) Word processors. (*c*) Dual-feed machines. (*d*) 'Golf-ball' machines. (*e*) Carbon-ribbon machines.	4. What is a word processor?
4 A machine which produces an electronic record of typed material which can be amended at will and reproduced faultlessly. The machine can accept revisions and alterations, adjusting the stored text to fit in afterwards, with justified right-hand margins.	5. What is a continuous stationery machine?
5. One which feeds a continuous pack of stationery into a machine to save typist time when invoicing, etc.	6. What is a golf-ball machine?
6. A machine with interchangeable typing units, mounted on a moving typing element which traverses across the paper. There is no moving carriage to this type of machine.	7. What are the advantages of audio-typing systems?
7. (*a*) They free the executive from the secretary, so that dictation may take place at any time. (*b*) They raise productivity since the audio-typist can work only at the machine, and is under constant supervision. (*c*) Peaks of work in particular departments are smoothed over the whole organisation. (*d*) Cheaper labour is used.	8. What are the requirements from a good audio-typist?
8. (*a*) The typist must be able to type at a good speed. (*b*) It is essential to spell, punctuate and display work properly.	9. What are the chief types of recording media?
9. (*a*) Re-usable magnetic tape. (*b*) Permanent record plastic tape. (*c*) Magnetic sheeting.	10. What are the chief types of centralised dictation service?
10. (*a*) Multi-bank dictation systems to which executives are connected by their desk telephones. (*c*) 'Tandem' systems.	11. What is a 'tandem' system?

Answers	Questions
11. A system where each audio-typist has two machines one of which is recording while the typist is transcribing from the other.	12. Go over the page again until you feel you are sure of the answers.

Exercises Set 10

1. Complete the sentences below by selecting the correct word or phrase from the word list.

(*a*) A non-electric typewriter possessing the usual characteristics (10 or 12 characters to the inch and 6 lines to the inch) is often spoken of as a .... machine.

(*b*) A typist who types directly from a tape-recorder is called an ....

(*c*) A carbon-ribbon typewriter gives a clear black typescript very suitable for ....

(*d*) A room in which many typists work from shorthand notes, manuscript copy or from dictation machines is known as a ....

(*e*) Portable typewriters are less ...... than standard machines and are therefore easily strained by inexperienced typists.

(*f*) Electric typewriters save typist effort by features such as .... return.

(*g*) Electronic typewriters which permit the recall of text for additions or alterations, which can be accepted at any point, the disturbed material being automatically moved to accommodate it, are called ....

(*h*) Multiple copies of invoices which need interleaved carbon are most easily fed into the machine by using ....

(*i*) When an audio-typist has two machines, one of which records while the other is transcribing, she is said to have a ....

(*j*) It is vital for an audio-typist to be able to ....

Word list: audio-typist, robust, standard manual, typing pool, continuous stationery, spell and punctuate, automatic carriage, word processors, offset litho masters, tandem system.

2. List the advantages and disadvantages of having the vast majority of the correspondence of a firm typed in a central typing pool.

3. What advantages does an electric typewriter offer to a businessman? What arguments would you use to counter his comment that 'the advantages don't outweigh the extra cost'?

4. It is proposed to establish a typing pool using a central bank of dictating machines to which executives are connected through their ordinary desk telephones. Jenny, a shorthand-typist, opposes the idea. Anne, a copy-typist, is in favour. Suggest reasons for their opposing views and discuss the possible advantages and disadvantages of the scheme.

5. In what ways do any four of the following special-purpose typewriters differ from standard typewriters: (*a*) carbon-ribbon typewriters; (*b*) typewriters with a dual-feed device; (*c*) a word processor; (*d*) a continuous stationery typewriter; (*e*) a 'golf-ball' typewriter; (*f*) an electronic typewriter.

6. During the day you have typed the following: (*a*) 24 invoices for goods sold to customers on credit; (*b*) an agenda for the monthly industrial relations meeting between shop stewards and management (20 copies); (*c*) a memo to the head caretaker about a heating appliance which is not working (2 copies).

Explain what processes will follow in each case before the efforts you have made are brought to final fruition.

7. Describe briefly the use of: (*a*) a tandem dictation machine system; (*b*) a word processor; (*c*) a portable typewriter.

8. The question of replacing shorthand-typists by audio-typists and purchasing dictating machines is under consideration by your firm. Write a memorandum to the head of your department giving your views on this matter and setting out the advantages and disadvantages of recorded dictation

9. What is a typing pool? What are its advantages and disadvantages?

10. (*a*) Your office manager has invited you to choose a dictating machine for your office. Write a memorandum to the office manager stating the type of machine you would prefer, giving reasons for your choice. (*b*) What would you do to correct a mistake made when dictating on the machine you have selected in (*a*)?

11

CENTRALISED SERVICES—COPYING AND DUPLICATING

11.1 The Development of Copying Services

As offices have expanded, there has developed a greater and greater need for copies of documents, information bulletins and memos. No longer can the proprietor of a business keep the whole organisation under his eagle eye. Management must instead design a system of information services which brings significant details of the business's affairs to its attention, and enables it to direct the activities by a stream of communications to depots, branches and industrial plants scattered throughout the country, or around the world.

Historical Developments

The earliest copies were made by clerks, who simply copied out important documents, promulgations and court records in a 'big round hand'. The first attempts to replace these human copyists with some sort of mechanical copy centred around the use of a stencil. These were already in use in the textile trade for stencilling patterns onto cloth. The stencil was a metal sheet, with the pattern cut into it in the form of holes, through which the colour could be pressed to decorate the material. What was needed was a material that was not metal, but could be easily pierced with the shapes of letters. Early attempts were made in America by Thomas Alva Edison and others, using needles to pierce the letter shapes in a paper stencil, but it was laborious work. The final breakthrough was made by a man whose name became synonymous with the duplicating process—David Gestetner.

What Gestetner (1854–1939) invented was a wheeled pen with sharp teeth. The earlier inventors had tried using a blunt metal pen—called a stylus—to rub holes in paper laid on a rough surface. The stylus, pressing the paper down on a rough metal surface, caused the rough metal under the paper to pierce it so that a pattern of letters appeared in the paper. These stencil marks were very imperfect. Gestetner's stylus had a little toothed wheel fixed to the end, which revolved as the writer's hand moved, cutting a succession of tiny holes through the paper.

He gave the name 'cyclostyle' (wheeled stylus) to this device, and later improved the design so that the hand holding the stylus could move exactly as if it was holding a pencil. The new device was called a neo-cyclostyle, and by the 1890s the armies of copy-clerks in the offices

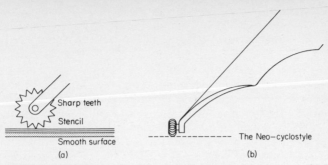

Fig. 11.1. David Gestetner's stencil cutter (reproduced by courtesy of Gestetner Ltd).

were being replaced by this simple duplicating apparatus. Fig. 11.1 illustrates the wheeled pen and the way in which the teeth cut into the paper stencil.

The actual duplicating process depended upon ink being rubbed through the stencil from above. The stencil was held in a hinged frame while it was being written upon, but when the letter or document had been accurately copied the frame could be lifted. A piece of paper was inserted below the stencil, the frame was lowered and an inked roller run across the stencil. The ink penetrated through the tiny holes, so fine that they were only as wide as a pen would write, and a whole page of 'copy' was produced in a few seconds. Although today the majority of duplicated letters are typed on a stencil in a typewriter, the rolling-ball stylus which is a development of the neo-cyclostyle is still used for signatures, or for drawings and maps which are added to stencils by hand after the typewritten passages have been cut into the stencil. David Gestetner's neo-cyclostyle has been developed to give a variety of sizes—from fine writing to broad print—and with the improved stencils made possible by the use of plastic coatings still provides one of the cheapest and simplest copying services.

Modern Developments

In recent years the variety of processes available for making accurate copies has increased, and now includes the following:

(*a*) Carbon copying.
(*b*) Photocopying, dyeline copying and thermocopying.
(*c*) Spirit duplicating.
(*d*) Ink-stencil duplicating.
(*e*) Offset lithography.
(*f*) Xerography or electrostatic copying.

Each of these is dealt with separately in the pages that follow. Before examining them closely we must first consider the general problem of **reprography**, a term which implies any sort of process which enables a copy, or a succession of copies, to be reproduced from a master copy. This master copy may be the original document or may be a specially prepared 'master', written or typed or electronically prepared.

11.2 Choosing a Copying System

It is easy to decide that we need a copy, or a number of copies, of a document, letter, newspaper article, photograph or diagram. It is more difficult to know which is the best device to purchase to produce the copies needed, and a machine which would be suitable for one particular purpose might be totally unsuitable for another. Contrast the managing director, who wants to send a single copy of a very secret document to the chairman of the board, with the Scotland Yard detective requiring 5000 copies of a 'Wanted for Murder' poster. It is unlikely that the process used to produce the single copy would be equally appropriate for a run-off of 5000 copies.

All copying is really a system that can be used over and over again. Before purchasing such a system it is necessary to evaluate the copying requirements that arise over a period of several months, and to decide the most likely needs of the department or firm. It is a matter of **cost-benefit analysis**, setting the costs of any particular system against the benefits to be obtained, and thus deciding on the best buy. The following considerations would need to be taken into account:

(*a*) Does the office need one-off copies or long production runs? Some machines are suitable for long production runs and are robust enough to stand up to hour after hour of work. Others are intended only for occasional copies, and cannot work for long periods without over-heating or breaking down.

(*b*) Is speed necessary? Some machines produce a copy in seconds. Others take time to produce the first copy but then run off many copies more quickly. Clearly such machines are unsuitable for a firm needing one-off copies very quickly.

(*c*) Do we need to copy one side only or do we need to copy double-sided originals?

(*d*) Many machines cannot be purchased, but only hired from the manufacturers, who usually charge on a 'usage meter'. Usually the first copy is very expensive, the next few copies fairly expensive, and subsequent copies very cheap. It follows that before hiring such a machine we should estimate how many short-run, medium-run and long-run copies we are likely to want per week, month or year. This will enable us to evaluate the machine, and whether it is wise to hire it.

(*e*) What is the nature of the material to be copied? Some copiers work only if there is carbon in the ink. A ballpoint pen or a blue ink will not 'copy' on such machines. This difficulty has been overcome in the so-called dual-spectrum machines.

(*f*) What are the likely running costs of any particular system? For example, how much are the masters; how much is the paper; how many copies per year or month will be required? A few simple calculations will then help the businessman to choose a system he can afford.

A Resource Centre. Perhaps the best idea of all when choosing a copying system is to set up a centralised resource centre. This will enable a variety of the most suitable machines to be purchased for the general use of the whole office or institution. Staffed by trained technicians who quickly master the peculiarities of different machines, and know the most appropriate process for a particular requirement, such resource centres can give an economical and efficient service. The capital equipment purchased is more fully utilised, so that better value is obtained for the money expended.

The controller of such a resource centre also acquires the knowledge and expertise to carry out the evaluation of equipment suggested under (*a*) to (*f*) above. By visiting the business equipment firms and exhibitions like the International Business Show, the supervisor will represent the firm as an informed and knowledgeable buyer, not buying on impulse, or after listening to a salesman's glib tongue, but buying that selection of proven equipment which meets the firm's requirements.

Sometimes the objection is raised to a resource centre that it often delays a department's work because it closes for lunch or for a tea-break; often these are times when an individual requiring copies of a document, etc., can come to the centre and use its facilities. While it cannot be too strongly emphasised that departments should think ahead about their requirements it is also true of all centralised services, but particularly reprography, that rota systems should ensure that the centre is manned at all times.

11.3 Carbon (and NCR) Copying

Carbon paper is paper which is coated with a layer of carbon, either on one side or on both sides. It used to be a very messy method of copying, but modern carbon paper, which is usually single-sided, is treated so that it does not come off until actually written upon or typed upon. It produces simultaneous copies, and where several copies are produced this is called 'manifolding'. Usually, four good copies can be obtained, but with special thin carbon paper and an electric typewriter up to twenty copies can be obtained.

However, the labour involved in interleaving paper and carbons is tiresome. Many stationers prepare business documents in pre-packed sets, which can be inserted into a typewriter conveniently without the need to interleave carbon paper. The documents have a carbon surface wherever necessary on the back of each sheet, so that the necessary information will be copied onto the copy below it. This carbon will never be used more than once, so it is a cheap 'one-off' type of carbon coating. Furthermore, a document lower down in the pack may not need to have all the information stated, and the manufacturers arrange for these details to be omitted—by leaving out the carbon above that copy. For example, a delivery note does not need to have the prices on it—it is often better if the carman does not know how valuable the packages are that he is carrying. By leaving out the carbon at that point the information does not appear on the carman's copy.

The advantages of carbon copies are listed in Table 11.2 (page 162).

NCR Paper

A system which eliminates the need for carbon paper is that known as NCR paper (No Carbon Required). Here the paper is coated with chemicals which are themselves colourless, but when combined they form a coloured liquid. The surface is coated with millions of microscopic globules of chemical. The pen—preferably a ballpoint pen—or the typewriter keys fracture the crystals on the paper, producing a visible copy on the pages below. There is one difficulty with such paper. If the user is not aware of the nature of NCR paper he may waste a whole pad of forms by writing on the top one. They must be torn off the pad in sets before using them. It is even sadder when someone uses the pad as a resting place for a piece of scrap paper. The message 'Please phone Mr Smith before 2.30—very urgent', will appear on all the forms below it, and will make that telephone message a very expensive one. NCR forms are very useful for any document where two or three copies only are required, and save time in busy offices since carbon paper does not have to be interleaved.

The advantages and disadvantages of NCR paper are listed in Table 11.2.

11.4 Photocopiers, Thermal Copiers and Dual-spectrum Machines

Photocopiers depend upon the action of light upon chemically treated paper. The special light-sensitive paper is exposed in the photocopier and then developed by passing through the chemicals. Such photocopiers are declining in use becasue the liquids in the process are inconvenient, giving 'wet' copies, while the photographic paper has a short shelf-life. The development of 'dry copiers', which may be either dyeline copiers, thermal copiers, dual spectrum copiers or electrostatic copiers, is eliminating wet copiers and the use of liquid developers. The term 'plain paper' copiers is applied to most types of electrostatic copiers which do not require chemically-treated paper but only use good quality plain white paper.

Dyeline Copiers

The dyeline process depends upon the action of ultraviolet light on sheets of paper coated with diazo salts. When a sheet of such paper is exposed to ultraviolet light it is bleached white, and the developer used upon the paper in the second process produces no colour at all. Where a master letter or document which is to be reproduced is placed on top of the diazo coated paper, and both are exposed to the light, the light passes through the white paper of the master, but cannot pass through the printed or typewritten parts. The diazo paper is therefore not bleached in those places where the light was unable to penetrate, and when passed through the developer a perfect copy of the original is produced on the diazo paper. By a careful choice of coatings and developer, blue, black or red copies may be produced. The more translucent the original the better the copies, and the less powerful the source of light required.

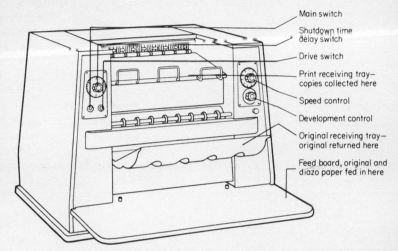

Fig. 11.2. A dyeline copier (reproduced by courtesy of Ozalid (UK) Ltd).

Advantages of Dyeline Copiers. Dyeline copiers are very cheap—$\frac{1}{2}$p per copy, which is very economical if only a few copies are required. While other methods are more suitable for long production runs the dyeline is very competitive where small numbers of copies are required. It is very versatile, especially for firms which send out bills monthly or quarterly, of exactly the same amounts—for example, water boards, office laundry services, plant hiring firms and so on—the copies produced each month from the master, taking only a few seconds each, being less expensive than addressograph or similar services. Unfortunately inflation has affected the usefulness of dyeline machines for this sort of routine billing, since the quarterly charges tend to rise regularly. One disadvantage is that some dyeline machines need to be vented to atmosphere, because of dangerous fumes. Fig. 11.2 illustrates a dyeline machine.

Thermal Copiers

These machines depend upon the action of the infra-red end of the spectrum of light waves. They are not strictly speaking photocopiers, since the infra-red rays are not visible but can only be felt as heat. The original and the copy paper are fed into the machine only once, taking about four seconds to make a copy. Whatever is printed on the original, provided there is a carbon base to the ink that has been used in its preparation, absorbs the infra-red heat rays and warms up. This warmth acts upon the heat-sensitive paper, producing a copy of the original.

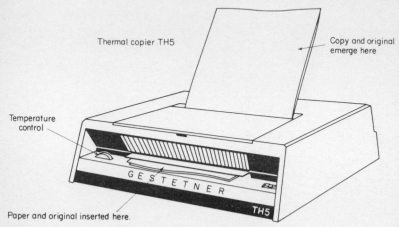

Thermal copier TH5

Copy and original emerge here

Temperature control

GESTETNER

TH5

Paper and original inserted here.

Fig. 11.3. A desk-type thermal copier (reproduced by courtesy of Gestetner Ltd).

Fig. 11.3 shows a typical thermal copier. These machines are small, compact and simple and inexpensive to operate. Few working parts ever go wrong, but they are at best suitable for medium outputs.

They can make duplicating and spirit stencil masters and can also produce transparencies for overhead projectors. Despite their many uses they cannot 'see' originals unless they have carbon in the ink and are likely to be replaced by dual-spectrum machines.

Dual-spectrum Copiers

Dual-spectrum copiers overcome the difficulty of thermal copiers by using both invisible sets of rays at either end of the light spectrum. The ultraviolet light rays are used to take a negative picture of the document to be copied. This is then fed through the machine a second time to produce a thermal copy of the original, which is positive. Since the ultraviolet light can 'see' anything, whether it has a carbon base or not, and the heat-sensitive copy is sensitive to the intermediate negative, the dual-spectrum machine will photocopy practically anything.

11.5   Spirit Duplicating

Spirit duplicating is a very simple method of producing copies from a master copy which has been made with a special type of material, called hectograph carbon. This carbon master yields up a tiny portion of its hectograph carbon every time it comes into contact with a sheet of run-off paper which has been damped with spirit, and as many as 300 good copies can be produced from a single master. The process is as follows:

(*a*) A sheet of master paper, very smooth and white, is placed into contact with:

(*b*) A sheet of hectograph transfer paper. This hectograph carbon is thick and used to be messy to handle, especially as the best colour to use is purple. Fortunately, it can now be coated with a surface that prevents it marking anything until the coating is pierced by a typewriter key or a ballpoint pen in the actual preparation of the master. The reader should note that the white master and the carbon are in direct contact; in other words, the carbon is facing upwards—the reverse of the usual way carbon paper is used.

(*c*) The typist types onto the white sheet and the back of the white master then receives a mirror image in the form of dislodged carbon from the coated transfer sheet. Similarly, any drawing that is drawn in by an artist with a ballpoint pen will be in mirror image form.

(*d*) Colours can be changed by changing the coated hecto-paper. Most firms produce seven colours. This is a unique feature of the spirit duplicating process, which is the only system where multiple colours can be reproduced onto copies with a single pass through the printing machine.

(*e*) The result is a master sheet which can be fitted onto the revolving drum of a spirit duplicator. As the smooth copy paper is fed into the duplicator it is damped by a spirit damping roller. It then comes immediately into contact with the master as it revolves on the drum. A tiny deposit of the hectograph carbon is dissolved by the spirit on the smooth run-off paper, giving a clear copy of the information on the master.

A name that is synonymous with spirit duplicators is BANDA—the trade name of Block and Anderson Ltd, now part of the Ozalid Group. Plate 9 shows a modern spirit duplicator of the type suitable for small office use. It has many applications in advertising, producing circulars, educational material and documentation.

Aspects of Spirit Duplication

The following points are of interest:

(*a*) It is a very cheap system, the price of copies falling quickly to approach the price of the run-off paper itself.

(*b*) Masters may be filed away for future use, but as they produce only about 300 copies they do need to be renewed. A new process, using the thermal copier as a source of heat, enables a new spirit master to

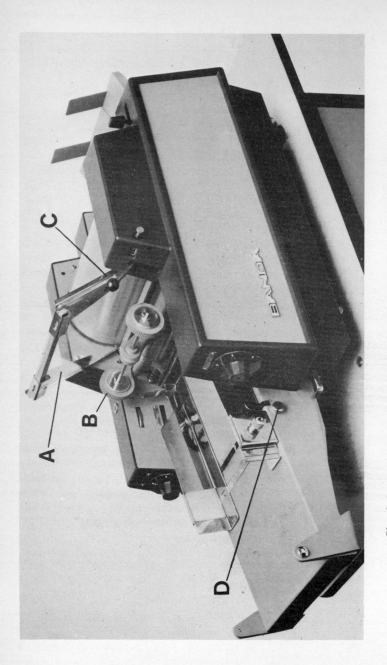

Plate 9. A general-purpose spirit duplicator (reproduced by courtesy of Ozalid (UK) Ltd).

A Master insertion plate.
B Auto feed rollers.
C Master clip opening lever.
D Fine setting control.

be prepared in a few seconds, so that the short life is not now any real disadvantage.

(c) One of the most valuable uses of spirit duplication is in the preparation of **aligned documents**. These are described more fully in another volume (*Commerce Made Simple*). The point here is that many documents require several copies, and an aligned series of documents—say an invoice, a bill of lading, an insurance policy, a shipping note, a dock dues note, etc., all relating to the same consignment—may need between them twenty or thirty copies. The spirit duplicator gives a cheap master, easily corrected, which can then run off up to 300 copies—a very useful master indeed which will print all the documents required.

(d) A spirit master is easily corrected with a special correcting fluid which obliterates the incorrect text. It can then be retyped to give a correct master.

Advantages and disadvantages of spirit duplication are listed in Table 11.2.

More Advanced Applications of Spirit Duplication

The ingenuity of manufacturers in this field seems endless, and the latest electronic machines are miracles of ingenuity. **Line-selection machines** have the ability to produce from a single master sheet a succession of job cards which will initiate activity at all levels to get a particular succession of jobs under way. For example, they have been used on the Concorde project. A master is first prepared listing the processes necessary to be carried out in succession for the manufacture of a particular component on the project. When the list has been checked to ensure that every task has been listed and in the correct sequence the master is inserted into the line-selection machine. The programme of selections needed is then punched into the instruction panel in a few seconds. The machine will then produce, in correct sequence, a set of job cards each of which has the heading of the master, to tell everyone what part he is making and where it fits into the total project. The machine, having printed the heading, then skips to the single line of instructions appropriate to the particular job, and prints that line only out of the mass of instructions on the master. It is difficult to think of a more labour-saving device. Formerly such cards were hand-typed or handwritten, with all the chances of errors this involves. Plate 10 illustrates such a line-selection machine.

11.6 Stencil Duplicating

(Permission to draw upon an article 'Stencil Duplicators' by W. B. Proudfoot, late of Gestetner Ltd, is gratefully acknowledged as source material for this section.)

Aspects of Ink-stencil Duplication

While many of the copying processes already referred to are satis-

Plate 10. A line-selection spirit duplicator (reproduced by courtesy of Ozalid (UK) Ltd).

factory when only 1–5 copies are required, they suffer from the disadvantage that the cost of copies does not reduce as the number required rises. Stencil duplicating has the advantage that as many as several thousand copies can be prepared from a single master. Even if only 20 copies are required it will be cheaper to cut a stencil, and if several hundred are required the cost falls as low as the cost of the paper itself.

The copy. The copy has the following advantages:

(*a*) It can be of print-like quality, or a mere typewritten sheet.
(*b*) The class of paper can be varied to suit the use of the copy—cheap paper for internal use, educational handouts, etc.; quality paper for advertising purposes or 'prestige' material.
(*c*) Coloured inks can be used, on a range of coloured papers.
(*d*) Both sides of the paper may be used, which reduces costs.
(*e*) Copies need not be checked—since the master has been checked and corrected before copies are run off.

Table 11.1. Everyday Uses of the Ink Duplicator

Communications	Reports	Lists	Data
Notices	Conference	Price	Catalogues
Bulletins	Departmental	Reading	Time-tables
Information	Branch	Book	Inventories
Memoranda	Financial	Stock	Statistics
Itineraries	Statistical	inventories	Servicing and
Directives to	Research	Library	procedure
branches	Technical		manuals
Invitations			
House			
magazines			

Advertising	Education		Business systems
Circulars	Lesson notes	Invoices	Petty cash
Booklets	Class handouts	Price lists	vouchers
Leaflets	Diagrams	Internal	Quotations
Folders	Graphs	documentation	
Press releases	Questionnaires	Office stationery	
Illustrations	Tests		
	Examination	Export	
	papers	documentation	
	Transparencies		
	for overhead	(In the items named above the permanent	
	projectors	matter—firm name and address, etc.—can	
		be pre-cut on the stencil. The typist adds	
		the variable data, and the whole stencil is	
		then run off.)	

The capital cost. Stencil duplicators are essentially robust machines capable of long-run outputs over considerable periods of time. They are not expensive, yet they are durable and have relatively few working parts to go wrong. The initial capital cost is therefore spread over several years, and is out of all proportion to the benefits derived from the stream of memos, bulletins, documents and data which follow from the original outlay.

The Advantages of the System

(*a*) It is a versatile, clean, economic method of producing from 20 to several thousand copies.

(*b*) The stencils are cheap, familiar to every class of typist (each of whom learns to cut stencils as part of any basic typing course), and may be prepared by a variety of methods extremely quickly. Illustrations, artwork, diagrams and charts can be cut in, or electronically stencilled in a matter of minutes. A new method of producing a stencil in a few seconds from an existing original by means of a thermal copying process already referred to above (see page 143) has further reduced the time required to prepare a stencil.

Applications of the System

The stencil duplicator lends itself to many routine applications in every type of office. Some of the most common are listed in Table 11.1 on page 149.

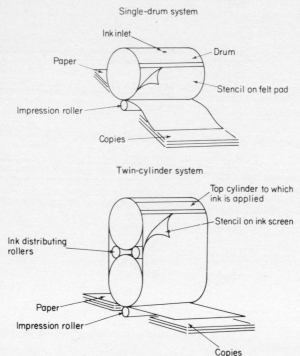

Fig. 11.4. The two kinds of rotary stencil duplicator (reproduced by courtesy of Gestetner Ltd).

Stencil Duplicators Described

The original duplicators designed by David Gestetner were flat-bed duplicators, now largely replaced by rotary duplicators. The stencil is wrapped around a drum, or cylinders, operated by turning a handle or by an electric motor. Fig. 11.4 illustrates the two systems.

In the more advanced twin-cylinder system, the ink is applied to the top cylinder and transferred to the lower by the ink-distributing rollers operating in a gap between the two cylinders. The ink screen—made of silk or Terylene—passes round both cylinders and allows the ink through to the stencil which is supported upon the screen. The ink passes through the holes cut in the stencil by the typewriter or rolling-ball stylus and makes the copy as the paper is forced between the impression roller and the stencil.

All modern rotary duplicators have a mechanical paper-feed mechanism which feeds the paper a sheet at a time from the paper feed-board through the duplicator to a delivery point where copies are collected and stacked. Automatic inking devices and automatic counters are features of the most recent machines, which can also be varied to speeds between 30 and 175 copies per minute. The precision feed mechanism is adjustable to take all types of paper from airmail to thin board, the feed-board rising automatically to maintain the paper at a correct height for entry to the machine. It can also be adjusted to

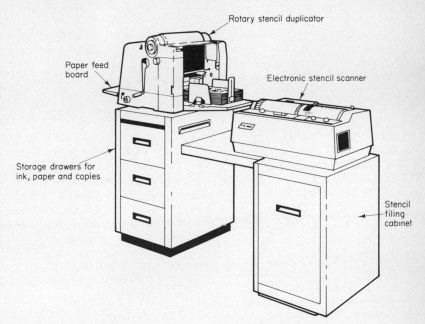

Fig. 11.5. A combination unit giving a duplicating department in a deck-sized space (reproduced by courtesy of Gestetner Ltd).

centralise the copy on the paper to allow for poor positioning of the typescript on the master.

Fig. 11.5 shows a combination unit which gives all the requirements of a small office duplicating department in a desk-size space. Everything needed for a wide variety of duplicating work is provided, conveniently grouped to save operating time and unnecessary motion.

Making a good master. A copy is only as good as the master from which it is prepared. The aim of the stencil maker should be to produce a perfect stencil containing all the required information, neatly and attractively displayed without errors of any sort. The following check-list covers most of the points to which attention should be paid.

(*a*) Is the stencil appropriate for the purpose required? There are many different kinds of stencils, which vary in size, quality and in the pre-cut style of heading and format.

(*b*) Is the type clean, and has the typewriter ribbon been disengaged so that the type strikes the stencil clearly? When cutting a number of stencils the type should be cleaned periodically.

(*c*) Is the stencil correctly aligned in the typewriter and has the pressure setting on an electric machine been correctly adjusted?

(*d*) Is the copy that is about to be typed correctly positioned on the stencil? While it is possible to adjust the duplicator to make allowances for minor mispositioning, any major errors in positioning will result in a poor appearance of the eventual copies produced.

(*e*) Are insets, or artwork, going to be inserted into the stencil after typing? If so the space of the inset must be marked faintly with a soft pencil mark around the paper guide card indicating the shape to be left clear. After the typescript has been completed this shape is cut out, and the inset is inserted, and cemented into position with stencil cement. Alternatively an electronic stencil can be cut from a paste-up of the typescript and the artwork required.

(*f*) On completion, the stencil should be checked for literals (errors in spelling or punctuation). Any ruled lines which are required may now be inserted—preferably with a tracing scope such as the one illustrated in Fig. 11.7. If a signature is to be added it should be written with a rolling-ball stylus onto the stencil, preferably backed by a signature sheet. Finally, a check should be made that all the vital material is included in the text. It frequently happens that important items like the date, time and place of meetings are omitted from memos and circulars. Such errors lead to expensive follow-up memos, extra postage costs, etc.

Correcting a stencil. Fig. 11.6 illustrates the proper procedure for correcting stencils. The process takes only a few minutes. It is a false economy to cut a stencil and then proceed hurriedly to duplicate copies without first checking the master. Corrections may then have to be made

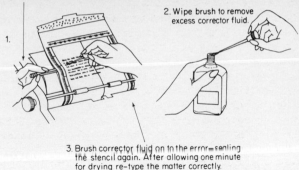

1. Raise stencil clear from typewriter platen and insert pencil between stencil and backing sheet.

2. Wipe brush to remove excess corrector fluid.

3. Brush corrector fluid on to the error—sealing the stencil again. After allowing one minute for drying re-type the matter correctly.

Fig. 11.6. Correcting a stencil with corrector fluid.

on hundreds of copies. A master is simply corrected with the use of corrector fluid, as shown in Fig. 11.6.

A stencil scope. Where a large volume of work is being prepared on stencils there will inevitably be much checking to be done, and frequently artwork, letters and ruling up will be required. The best device for such work is a scope such as the Gestetner-scope illustrated in Fig. 11.7. Here is a drawing and tracing frame specially developed to make the preparation and checking of stencils a simple matter. The scope is illuminated from underneath by a glare-free diffused lighting, and enables a stencil to be held firmly while it is ruled and drawn upon. A T-square can be snapped on, used in any position on the stencil to ensure perfect alignment for lettering guides.

Electronic stencil cutting. Fig. 11.5 shows a combination unit which includes an electronic stencil scanner. This is a very versatile machine which will prepare stencils from practically any sort of printed or illustrated master. The master may be a sheet of typescript, a photograph, a coloured illustration or a newspaper article.

An electronic stencil scanner consists essentially of two rotating cylinders on a common axis, so that the original to be copied and a specially coated electronically conductive stencil can be rotated side by side. As the original is rotated it is scanned by a beam of light reflected to a photoelectric cell. The electric impulses picked up are used to control a spark gap which is scanning the stencil. At every point where the photo-cell senses a dark spot the spark cuts a hole in the stencil. The scanner can be varied between 200 lines to the inch and about 750 lines to the inch. The more lines to the inch the clearer the picture, but the longer it takes to cut. The machine is fully automatic once it has started scanning and the operator does other work until the scan is complete.

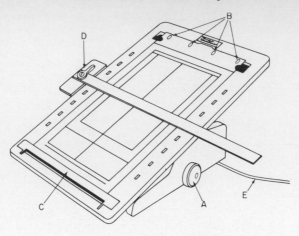

A— Scope clamp–to vary the angle of the scope for convenient ruling and drawing.

B— Studs to locate the stencil heading.

C— Stencil clamp, keeping stencil steady when written upon.

D— Snap–on Tsquare which moves to required position and may be clamped firmly.

E— Electric cable to diffused lighting.

Fig. 11.7. A Stencil-scope (reproduced by courtesy of Gestetner Ltd).

In a few minutes a perfect stencil will have been reproduced from a paste-up master.

Thermal stencil cutting. The type of thermal copier already illustrated in Fig. 11.3 can now be used to reproduce a master stencil in a few seconds. The heat rays of the thermal copier are absorbed by the image area of any master inserted into the special stencil folder. The image area heats up, and melts the special surface of the stencil, which is in contact with it, thus reproducing the master perfectly on the stencil. The result is a facsimile (exact copy) of the letter or illustration in the stencil. The master is undamaged and is removed. As with most thermal copiers the ink from which the master is prepared must be carbon based.

Storing stencils. Many institutions need to use stencils repeatedly and they may be stored quite easily. Thus schools and colleges may store lecture notes and class handouts for re-use at a later date. The best method of storage is in a hanging file cabinet (part of the combination unit shown in Fig. 11.5), the stencil being enclosed in an absorbent file folder which can be suspended by a simple plastic hanger—as illustrated in Fig. 11.8.

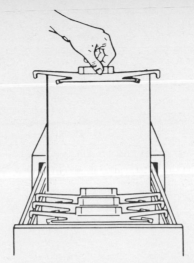

Fig. 11.8. Storing ink stencils for future use.

11.7. Offset Litho Duplicating

The offset litho process is a duplication system which offers very high-quality reproduction on hard papers. It is capable of excellent colour work, great accuracy and high speeds. It enables even the small office to produce most of its own handouts, advertising circulars, statistical and factual reports and documents for office use.

Principles of Offset

(*a*) *Oil and water don't mix.* The process depends upon the well-known principle that oil and water—or, more truthfully in this case, grease and water—don't mix. A greasy image of the printing, artwork, etc., which is to appear on the copies is produced on the offset litho plate. This may be done with a special lithographic ribbon, or with special offset pens, pencils, brush ink, stamp pads and ruling and writing ink, using a paper plate. Alternatively, a photographic plate may be prepared. The whole plate is then damped and the water covers the plate, except where it is repelled by the greasy image. Then the ink is rolled across the plate. This ink is also greasy and is repelled by the damp parts of the plate but accepted by the greasy image. We now have a greasy, inked picture of the original matter.

(*b*) *The offset process.* This inked picture is now transferred from the plate to a rubber-covered cylinder called the blanket cylinder, which picks up a reverse picture of the original material. In any printing process the print comes out back to front. Ordinary printers spend their apprenticeship learning to set type back to front, so that when

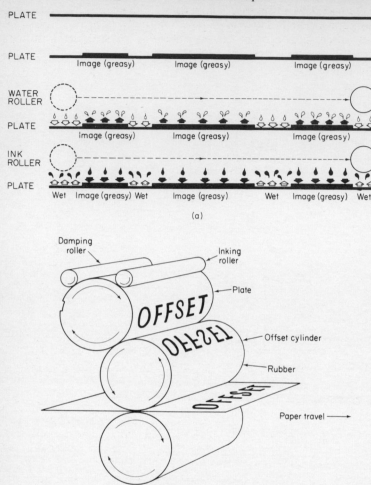

Fig. 11.9. The principles of offset lithography: (*a*) grease and water don't mix; (*b*) a reverse print of a reverse print is legible (reproduced by courtesy of Gestetner Ltd).

it is pressed down upon the paper by the printing press the printed matter will be the right way round. The ordinary reader can then read it. The offset process overcomes this setting difficulty by off-setting the print on to a blanket of rubber. The typist who prepared the plate prepared it with an ordinary typewriter. This will be reversed onto the offset blanket, and reversed again onto the copy paper as the offset blanket comes into contact with it. This double reversal gives a readable copy. Fig. 11.9 illustrates these offset-litho principles.

(*c*) Why 'litho'? The word 'litho' means stone. The earliest uses of this method of printing used engravings on limestone. The word is not really appropriate today, and its use is gradually dying out. The process is now often spoken of as 'offset duplicating'. The illustration in Fig. 11.10 is a machine described by the makers as a Series 211 offset duplicator.

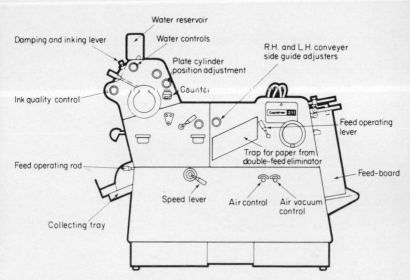

Fig. 11.10. An advanced offset duplicator (reproduced by courtesy of Gestetner Ltd).

Making Plates

The master plates for offset duplicating may be prepared on paper plates which have a life span of up to 2000 copies. The manufacturers can prepare metal plates with a very long life for customers who require long reprographic runs. Photographic plates may also be made by customers on their own premises using their own electrostatic equipment.

11.8 Xerography or Electrostatic Copying

The word 'xerography' really means 'dry-pictures', and distinguished this process from photocopying, which was a process using wet developer. Today there are other dry copiers besides the Rank Xerox, for this type of copier is manufactured by other firms. However, the name 'Rank Xerox' is synonymous with the electrostatic copying process, and the author is indebted to this firm for the source material for this section.

Most readers will be familiar with static electricity, which charges up many articles in everyday life, such as a fountain pen rubbed upon a coat sleeve or a glass rod rubbed with silk. Such static charges may be used to hold minute powdery particles of developer on paper. This may then be heated so that the developer melts and fuses into the paper, reproducing whatever shapes and patterns the static charge had taken. The Xerox copier arranges the static charge as an image of any document that is to be copied. Fig. 11.11 shows how the system works.

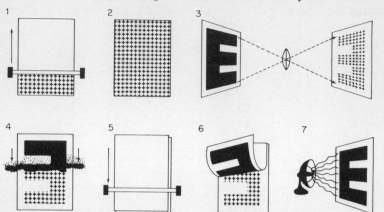

Fig. 11.11. How xerography works (reproduced by courtesy of Rank Xerox Ltd).

Notes
1. The surface of a coated plate (or drum) is sensitised by an electrically charged grid which moves across it.
2. The coating of the plate is now fully charged with positive electricity.
3. The original document (E) is projected onto the coated plate. Positive charges disappear in areas exposed to light. A pattern of charges is left on the coated plate of exactly the same shape as the dark part of the original document.
4. A negatively charged powder is dusted over the plate and adheres to the positively charged image.
5. A sheet of paper is now placed over the plate and receives a positive charge.
6. The positively charged paper attracts powder from the plate, forming a direct positive image.
7. The print is fixed by heat for a few seconds to form the permanent image.

This entire process takes only a few seconds, and can be arranged to take place repeatedly so that copies are delivered at the rate of one every second. The Xerox 3600 model illustrated in Plate 11 takes its name from its ability to deliver 3600 copies every hour. The sorting device attached at the end will arrange up to 50 copies of a succession of pages so that they are in correct order ready to be stapled into booklet form. A report can thus be prepared—for example, for every member of the Board of the company—in a very short time indeed once an initial copy is typed for use as a master.

Other Plain-paper Copiers

Other plain paper copiers have been developed from the xerographic process using the electrostatic principle, but they do not give perfectly

Plate 11. The Xerox 9500 with sorter (reproduced by courtesy of Rank Xerox Ltd).

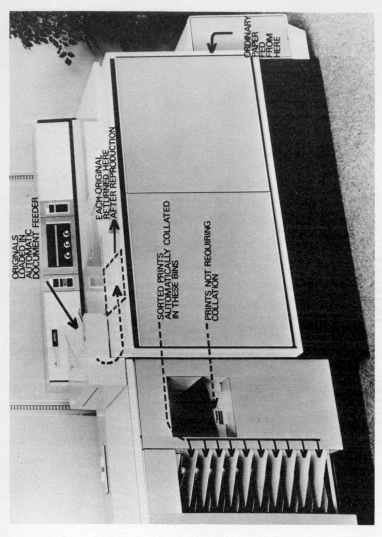

Plate 12. A liquid-toner plain paper copier: the Nashua 1215 (reproduced by courtesy of Nashua Copycat Ltd).

dry copies. Instead of the electrostatic charge attracting dry particles of powder, the copying material (the toner) is carried in a petrol-based liquid. In the Nashua Copycat machines, for example, the liquid toner contacts the drum directly and passes the image directly onto the paper. This is very economic in the use of toner, does away with the dusty particles which give problems in the dry machines, and also eliminates the need for heat to fuse the toner to the paper. There is no warm-up time while the heaters reach the necessary temperature, and a machine need not be switched on all day. In fact, Nashua machines switch off automatically and only take a second or two to warm up.

Plate 12 shows a Nashua 1215 plain-paper copier. Its compact size reflects the elimination of bulky heaters needed in dry copiers to fuse the image to the paper.

Electrostatic Platemaking for the Offset Duplicator

Returning for a moment to the offset litho process, we see that the electrostatic copier enables any office to prepare photographic plates of high quality for the offset litho machine.

The plate is prepared in the electrostatic platemaker, but it is removed before any fusing takes place so that the image can be examined for blemishes. The blemishes, remember, will be of a developing powder held to the paper only by an electrostatic charge. These can be removed by a magnet—surely the easiest way of rubbing-out ever invented. The girl in Fig. 11.12 can be seen cleaning up the image, before inserting it into the fuser, which in this example is a separate heating unit shown alongside the copier. Not only can the blemishes be removed, but also a whole paragraph of unwanted text can be removed by the magnet.

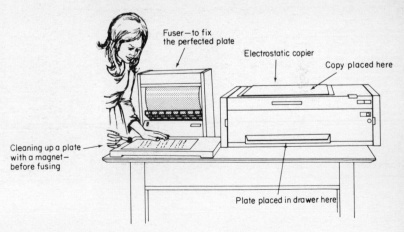

Fig. 11.12. An electrostatic platemaker for an offset litho duplicator (reproduced by courtesy of Gestetner Ltd).

Table 11.2. A comparison chart for reprographic methods. (The most representative methods at present have been chosen.)

Aspects considered	Carbon Copies	No Carbon Required (NCR)	Dyeline Copying	Ink Stencil Duplication	Spirit Duplication	Dual-transfer Photocopying	Offset-litho duplicating	Electrostatic and plain-paper copiers
1 Materials required by the process.	Carbon paper. Flimsy copy paper.	Prepared sets of specially coated documents.	Paper coated with diazo salts and sensitive to ultraviolet light. Translucent originals.	Stencils with wax or plastic surface. Absorbent run-off paper. Black or coloured inks.	Spirit master paper. Hecto carbon paper. Run-off paper. Spirit.	Intermediate paper. Copy paper.	Greasy ink. Water. Paper, metal or photographic plates.	Run-off paper. Ink powder or toner.
2 Quantity produced.	Up to 4 copies. Up to 20 with electric typewriter.	Up to 4 copies.	Any number—but cheapest from 1–15 copies.	Thousands if necessary. It is economical over 20 copies.	Up to 300 copies. Less for some colours.	Single copies or runs of up to 25 on automatic models.	Paper plates up to 2000 copies. Very long runs on metal and photographic plates.	Very long runs possible.
3 How operated.	Typewritten or handwritten.	Typewritten or handwritten.	Electrically operated.	Hand or electrical models available.	Hand or electrical models available.	Electrically operated.	Electrically operated.	Electrically operated.
4 Suitable for reproducing (a) Black typewritten. (b) Coloured typewritten. (c) Handwritten. (d) Drawing. (e) From photographs. (f) On both sides of paper.	(a) Yes (b) — (c) Yes (d) Yes (e) — (f) —	(a) Yes (b) — (c) Yes (d) — (e) — (f) —	(a) Yes (b) Yes (c) Yes (d) Yes (e) — (f) —	(a) Yes (b) Yes (c) Yes—but less satisfactory. (d) Yes (e) Yes (f) Yes	(a) Yes (b) Yes (c) Yes (d) Yes (e) — (f) If thicker run-off paper used.	(a) Yes (b) — (c) Yes (d) Yes (e) Yes (f) —	(a) Yes (b) Yes (c) — (d) Yes (e) Yes (f) Yes	(a) Yes (b) — (c) Yes (d) Yes (e) Yes (f) Yes but not all machines on the market.
5 Applications: (a) Small circulations. (b) Medium circulations. (c) Large circulations. (d) Documentation. (e) Reports. (f) Advertising. (g) Educational.	(a) Yes (b) Yes (c) — (d) Yes (e) Yes (f) — (g) —	(a) Yes (b) — (c) — (d) Yes (e) Yes (f) — (g) School reports.	(a) Yes (b) Yes (c) — (d) Yes (e) Yes (f) — (g) —	(a) — (b) Yes (c) Yes (d) — (e) Yes (f) Yes (g) Yes	(a) — (b) — (c) Up to 300. (d) Yes (e) Yes (f) Yes (g) Yes	(a) Yes (b) Yes (c) — (d) — (e) Yes (f) — (g) Makes transparencies.	(a) — (b) Yes (c) Yes (d) Yes (e) Yes (f) Yes (g) Yes	(a) Yes (b) Yes (c) Yes (d) Yes (e) Yes (f) Yes (g) Yes

6 Costs: (a) Capital outlay. (b) Costs per copy.	(a) Typewriter needed. (b) Low.	(a) None. (b) Fairly low.	(a) Fairly large. (b) Cheap ½p.	(a) Not very great. (b) Falls to cost of run-off paper only, therefore cheap.	(a) Not very great. (b) Falls to cost of run-off paper only, therefore cheap.	(a) Not very great. (b) Every copy costs the same, i.e. expensive for long runs.	(a) Fairly expensive. (b) Costs per copy fall almost to cost of run-off paper, therefore cheap.	(a) Machines expensive to hire. (b) Usage meter—cheaper for long runs.
7 Maintenance requirements.	None.	None.	Regular servicing advisable. Some machines need venting.	Regular servicing advisable (reasonable charges).	Regular servicing advisable (reasonable charges).	Occasional servicing advisable.	Regular servicing advisable.	Sophisticated machinery must be maintained regularly—but service free to hirers.
8 Advantages.	I. Simultaneous copies. II. Cheap. III. No special skill needed.	I. Simultaneous copies. II. No carbon required. III. No skill required—public can use them easily.	I. Instant copies. II. Cheap for low runs. III. Good copy quality. IV. Adaptable for certain work. V. Only 1 original prepared. Easy to correct. VI. Economical of labour in business systems work (i.e. monthly statements).	I. Cheap. II. Simple. All typists can cut skins. III. Writing and drawing can be added to typed stencils. IV. Electronic stencil cutting very effective. V. Very long runs possible. VI. Colour possible. VII. Simple storage. VIII. Heat master very quick.	I. Cheap. II. Simple. III. Colour very effective. IV. Drawing simple. V. Storage simple for masters. VI. Ideal for aligned documentation.	I. Copies at colours. II. No skill required. III. Dry copies. IV. Makes overhead projec- or transparences. V. No errors.	I. Very long runs. II. Cheap copies. III. Wide variety of uses. IV. Very high-quality work possible.	I. Very quick II. Very simple to operate. III. Facsimile copies. IV. Overlays available for aligned documentation.
9 Disadvantages.	I. Not easy to correct. II. Only a few copies possible. III. Carbons do dry out in long-term storage. IV. Quality of copies falls away.	I. More expensive than ordinary forms. II. Cannot be altered. III. Can be spoiled easily and wasted.	I. Fairly expensive machine. II. Every copy costs the same. III. Ammonia machines need a vent to atmosphere.	I. A little bit messy with cheaper model machines. II. Uneconomic below 10 copies.	I. No good for very long runs. II. Masters can be spoiled by inexperienced operator. III. Fluid inflammable, needs careful storage.	I. Too expensive for individual hand feeding on cheaper machines.	I. Not convenient or cheap for small runs.	I. Expensive. II. Skilled servicing required.

A master need not therefore be cut about if a certain passage is not wanted for this particular copy. A quick wipe with the magnet before the plate is fused removes all unwanted material.

11.9 Choosing Reprographic Equipment

Table 11.2 is an attempt to assist the reader to evaluate the different reprographic methods outlined in this chapter. It lists various aspects of the equipment and compares these aspects across the range of equipment that is available.

11.10 Points to Think About and Discuss

(*a*) Jones, the manager of the sales department, is anxious to establish a resource centre which would be able to afford the most expensive reprographic equipment, and would supply the advertising material he considers essential. Bloggs, in charge of production, maintains that the sales department's inability to produce the copies it needs from its own resources is solely due to inefficiency, and failure in the past to buy wisely with the budget of money allocated to Jones. His own department is well supplied with reprographic equipment. Consider these two points of view.

(*b*) In what ways would a reprographic service be of use to the following people or institutions?

(i)   An infants' schoolteacher
(ii) The secretary of a residents' association
(iii) An estate agent
(iv) The Ministry of Housing
(v)   A bank manager
(vi) An inwards mail clerk
(vii) A 'multiple shop' organisation
(viii) A building society

11.11 Rapid Revision

Cover the page with a sheet of paper and uncover one question at a time.

Answers	*Questions*
—	1. Why is the copying and duplicating of documents so important today?
1. Because businesses are large, and everyone must be kept informed if all are to function efficiently as a team.	2. Who first perfected a copying process?
2. David Gestetner, 1854–1939.	3. List ten methods of copying.
3. (*a*) Carbon paper; (*b*) NCR paper; (*c*) stencil duplicating; (*d*) spirit transfer; (*e*) thermal copying; (*f*) photocopying; (*g*) dyeline copying; (*h*) xerography; (*i*) plain-paper copying; (*j*) Offset duplicating.	4. What do we call an office that prepares copies for other departments?

Answers	Questions
4. A resource centre.	5. What problems must be overcome in setting up a resource centre?
5. (a) The work of the firm must be analysed to decide the types of document, brochures, etc., required. (b) The most suitable and economic ways to meet these requirements must be decided upon. (c) The necessary equipment must be purchased or hired. (d) Staff procedures must be laid down to ensure efficient operations.	6. What aspects enter into the choice of any particular piece of reprographic equipment?
6. (a) How simple is it? (b) How clean is it? (c) How expensive is the master? (d) How expensive are the copies? (e) How expensive is the capital equipment required? (f) How many copies will it make? (g) Is it continuous in operation or does it need to be 'fed' by an operator?	7. Using the chart shown on pages 162 and 163, compare the methods of copying under each of the headings shown. Make up a rapid revision page for each copying process if you find this method of study helpful.

Exercises Set 11

1. Copy paragraphs (a)–(t) onto a sheet of paper and write against them the correct word or phrase from the word list to complete the following sentences.

(a) The earliest form of reprography was a flat-bed duplicator with a stretched wax paper on which the text was written with a ...... pen.

(b) Early photocopiers suffered from the disadvantage that they required liquid ......

(c) A special department devoted to the production of handouts, display material and advertising circulars is a ....

(d) Before purchasing reprographic equipment it is best to consider carefully the ...... of your firm or institution.

(e) NCR paper is paper which produces copies but .... is ......

(f) A copier which works by infra-red heat rays is called a ...... copier.

(g) Dual-spectrum copiers use both heat rays and .... rays.

(h) A hectograph ribbon could be used in the preparation of a ....

(i) Documents which are similar in layout (...... ......) are simply prepared from a spirit master, which can be used to run off as many copies as are needed.

(j) The name ...... is synonymous with ink-stencil duplicating.

(k) Most modern duplicators print from a master secured to a revolving drum, and hence are known as ...... duplicators.

(l) Since any errors on a master will be reproduced on every copy that it produces it is essential that masters are ....

(m) A device which cuts stencils by burning holes in the stencil at the same point as an electric eye 'sees' a dark spot on the master copy, is called an ...... stencil cutter.

(n) Lithography refers to a printing process originally carried out with ......

(*o*) The offset process is one which reproduces an image from a greasy ......

(*p*) The image in offset lithography is offset onto a .... and from there to the copy paper.

(*q*) ...... gives dry copies.

(*r*) If a copy is produced from an electrically charged plate it is called an ...... process.

(*s*) An electrostatic plate may be cleaned with a ......

(*t*) To ...... a reprographic machine is to attempt to judge its suitability for your office.

Word list: developer, requirements, cyclostyle, ultraviolet, spirit master, rotary, stone, plate, electrostatic, magnet, thermal, electronic, no carbon required, resource centre, rubber blanket, aligned documents, Gestetner, carefully checked, xerography, evaluate.

2. List some of the chief reasons for a copying service in: (*a*) an architect's office; (*b*) a technical college. How would a resource centre help each of these establishments? What are the advantages and disadvantages of a resource centre?

3. Consider the alternative answers shown below and write on your paper the letter which in your opinion gives the best answer.

(i) Reprography means: (*a*) the production of copies by photographic methods; (*b*) the reproduction of pictures by some mass production process; (*c*) the copying of mathematical diagrams; (*d*) the production of copies of any material, whether typewritten, handwritten or artwork by a variety of technical processes.

(ii) Spirit duplication is: (*a*) the production of copies made in hectograph carbon on spirit-damped copy paper; (*b*) part of the art of séance-holding spiritualists; (*c*) the production of copies in coloured ink on white or cream paper; (*d*) the doubling of copies by mirror image methods so that the copy appears on both sides of the paper.

(iii) The cyclostyle is: (*a*) a bicycle with solid tyres for cross-country journeys; (*b*) a toothed scraper for artwork which facilitates shading in large circular areas; (*c*) a toothed-wheel pen which makes impressions on paper when run across it in the action of drawing or writing; (*d*) an instrument for counting the number of copies printed.

(iv) Electrostatics is: (*a*) the science of thunderstorms; (*b*) the phenomena observed when electrical charges are applied to objects; (*c*) a stationary electric motor which drives machinery by belt systems; (*d*) the stationary part of an electrical power supply into which office machinery is plugged.

4. Your employer visited the International Business Show and was very impressed by the offset duplicators on show. You are asked to compare offset duplicating with the stencil and spirit duplicators at present in use in your office. Prepare a tabulated statement making comparisons of the three machines under the following headings:

(*a*) Duplicating process (state the materials you would use).

(*b*) Applications, i.e. its suitability for the production of: (i) black typewritten work; (ii) coloured typewritten work; (iii) handwriting/drawing; (iv) photographs.

(*c*) Quantities produced.

(*d*) Type of paper employed for copies.
(*e*) Other remarks. (RSA II)

5. You have been asked by the office manager to give your views on whether your office should have a spirit duplicator or an ink duplicator, and whether it should be electrically or hand operated. Write a memorandum explaining your views, indicating fully the types of work which can be performed by each. (RSA I)

6. (*a*) Explain *in detail* how you would obtain one copy of a printed document from an office copier; (*b*) name the type of machine you would use and say why you would choose it; (*c*) what are the advantages and disadvantages of photocopying? (RSA I)

7 Photocopying and dual transfer copying are processes used in modern business. Define these terms and say in what circumstances the processes are useful. (RSA I)

8. (*a*) Describe three different processes of photocopying; (*b*) summarise the circumstances in which each would be used. (RSA I)

9. Describe two of the following methods of reprography, outlining the advantages and disadvantages and commenting on the type of copy commonly produced by each method: (i) dyeline equipment; (ii) spirit duplicating; (iii) offset duplicating. (RSA)

10. (*a*) Give three ways of making copies of office documents; (*b*) for what kinds of work would you choose each method; (*c*) list the advantages of each method and any disadvantages. (BEC General)

11. Describe briefly: (*a*) the spirit method; (*b*) the stencil method of duplicating and the relative advantages and disadvantages of both. (RSA)

12. Write notes on the preparation of a master for a spirit duplicator and the subsequent rolling off of 200 copies. Mention the advantages and disadvantages of this method of duplicating. (RSA)

13. State, with reasons, whether you would or would not suggest using a photocopying machine for the following items. If you would not recommend using a photocopying machine, what other machine would you use, assuming its availability? (*a*) A single copy of a pocket street map; (*b*) 5000 copies of a circular to school parents; (*c*) 12 copies of an itinerary; (*d*) 200 copies of a handout for pupils visiting your factory.

14. A new spirit duplicator is to be installed in your office. What supplies will be necessary for its use? Briefly explain the purpose of these, and their use. (RSA)

15. Your employer has asked you to suggest the most efficient means of producing the following, bearing in mind the cost in money and time: (*a*) 60 copies of a circular letter (one foolscap sheet), now in rough handwriting, to be distributed internally; (*b*) five additional copies of a single-spaced typewritten letter, consisting of two quarto pages; (*c*) similar to (*a*) but 600 copies required. Give your reasons for choosing the various methods. (BEC General)

16. (*a*) State which method of reproduction you would choose to produce copies of the following:

(i) 100 copies of an internal telephone directory; (ii) 4 copies of a small diagram; (iii) 2000 copies of time sheets for use by employees in the factory; (iv) 20 000 copies of price lists, printed in two colours, for circulation to customers and prospective customers.

(b) What are the main advantages of offset reprography?   (BEC General)

17. Give six practical points to be observed when using the rotary ink duplicator. (Do not include the cutting of the stencil.) State THREE advantages of this type of duplicating.   (BEC General)

18. (a) When would you use an ink duplicator in preference to other methods of reproduction? (give your reasons); (b) explain how you would prepare a stencil for this type of machine; (c) what precautions should you take:

(i) to ensure that the resulting copies are good.
(ii) to ensure that the duplicator is kept in satisfactory working order?
    (BEC General)

19. What method of reproduction would you consider most suitable to produce copies of the following? Give reasons for your choice: (a) 6 copies of a newspaper article containing a detailed illustration; (b) 12 copies of a notice to staff containing a rough plan, using three colours; (c) 300 copies of an examination paper for internal use in a college; (d) a confidential report to three departmental heads.   (BEC General)

20. The stencil duplicator in your office is to be replaced and the office manager is uncertain whether to purchase the same type again or to change to another process. He asks you to give him your views on the matter and to explain the principal features of two other methods of duplicating. Write your reply to the office manager in report form.   (RSA I)

21. Describe the methods of using the plain paper copier and the stencil duplicator, mentioning the kinds of work for which you would use each of them.

22. A firm wishes to make copies of documents for the following purposes: (a) issue to six departmental heads; (b) issue to a staff of 1500. Describe methods which could be used in these circumstances.   (BEC General)

23. It is proposed to issue a six-page monthly report to 500 customers. Write a memorandum to your employer explaining the steps you would take and the equipment you would use in preparing and despatching the report.
    (BEC General)

24. Describe briefly (a) the spirit method and (b) the stencil method of duplicating and the relative advantages and disadvantages of each method. (RSA)

25. What masters are required for the following: (a) an ink duplicator; (b) a plain paper copier; (c) an offset duplicator; (d) dyeline?

26. What are: (a) The advantages of (i) a flat-bed type of photocopier; (ii) a Xerox machine; (b) The disadvantages of dry-heat photocopying?   (RSA)

27. (a) Give two materials of which offset plates can be made. (b) Give two ways in which offset plates may be prepared for offset printing. (c) Give two advantages of using an offset machine instead of a stencil duplicator. (RSA)

28. Describe in non-technical terms a system of stencil duplication and a method of photocopying with which you are familiar.

29. (*a*) Describe the process known as offset reprography; (*b*) what advantages and disadvantages can be claimed for this method of printing? (BEC General)

30. What particular method would you use to produce 1000 copies of a circular letter? Explain the various stages in the production of this letter. (BEC General)

31. Discuss the advantages and disadvantages of a resource centre, in a large institution such as a university or teachers' training college.

12

CENTRALISED SERVICES—FILING, INDEXING AND RECORD KEEPING

12.1 Introduction

Every firm receives and despatches a great deal of correspondence daily. These letters, circulars, information bulletins and reports must be put away where they can be found when required for reference purposes. This work is called **filing**. Filing may be defined as the storing of letters and documents in a systematic way so that they may be retrieved at a later date for reference purposes. The work of filing is the responsibility of filing clerks and the supervisors of centralised filing systems. The organisation may vary from a simple filing cabinet to a huge, but compact, electronically controlled storage system such as Conserve-a-trieve, a system controlled by a single operator. A piece of correspondence may be retrieved when required by calling electronically for its storage container. Plate 13 illustrates the system.

12.2 Essentials of a Good Filing System

A good filing system should have the following characteristics:

(*a*) *Simplicity*. The system should be easy to follow and simple to operate, even by a non-specialist member of staff.

(*b*) *Security*. The system should be as secure as is required by the matter concerned. Personnel records, wages records, company policy records, etc., should be very secure. Catalogues and similar items should be more generally available and accessible to all staff.

(*c*) *Compactness with comprehensiveness*. Clearly it is not easy to reconcile these two opposite requirements. Generally speaking, we need files to be comprehensive about the matter they are concerned with but we need a compact system to enable files to be stored conveniently and with easy access. A clear policy of **document retention** will enable compactness to be more easily secured. If documents have to be retained for ever, then adequate reserve storage should be provided, and a clear policy about transfer into the reserve stores should be laid down. If documents may be destroyed after a given time then this should be clearly laid down and **document shredders** might well be provided. (A document shredder reduces a document in seconds to a mass of paper waste, which may be used as packing materials in the despatch department.)

Plate 13. Automated electronic filing.

(*d*) *A clear cross-reference system* to enable staff who look for documents in a wrong section to find the correct section where the file required has been stored (see page 177).

(*e*) *A systematic 'tracer' and 'follow-up' system*. Senior staff may call for a file at any time to deal with an emergency situation. If the file required is out they may be in difficulty unless it can be traced. An 'out' card tracer system (see page 178) will overcome this difficulty. Similarly, a 'follow-up' system (see page 179) will chase up files kept for longer than necessary and reduce the numbers of files missing from the filing system. Should they be required these files will then be available for special action.

(*f*) *An appropriate classification system*. There are a number of alternative methods of storing records. The most satisfactory system should be selected, bearing in mind the requirements of the business. This sometimes leads to conflicting systems in some businesses, one department preferring records to be arranged geographically, for example, while another prefers a subject classification. Conflict is most likely where the adoption of a centralised system is forcing departments which have formerly pleased themselves to align their arrangements.

12.3   Centralised Filing Systems

Whether or not it is advisable to centralise filing systems depends upon the size of an organisation and the extent to which different departments need to consult the same records. Centralised filing is never desirable for confidential records, such as personnel records, or wages and salary records. Briefly the relative advantages and disadvantages may be set down as follows:

Advantages of a Centralised Filing System

(*a*) Clear responsibility will be laid down for filing. Adequate equipment will be provided and qualified staff will be appointed or trained.
(*b*) Related matter from all departments will be filed together, so that staff consulting a file will be fully informed.
(*c*) Records will be better maintained, better supervised and properly controlled by management. Staff who are inefficient in their attitude to record-keeping will be pinpointed, and may be educated and trained to improve their attitude.

Disadvantages of a Centralised Filing System

(*a*) It is time-consuming to have to order files and wait for them to appear.
(*b*) Filing staff cannot have the departmental knowledge which is so helpful when filing departmentally. They must therefore rely upon the filing indications given by the departmental staff submitting material for filing.

(c) Filing in departments is often used as a routine time filler which enables staff to employ themselves busily at times when other work is not available. If these activities are performed centrally by specialists, then total staff employed must rise.

12.4 Filing Systems

In ordinary filing, correspondence is placed in a **file folder**, and is given a title before being filed under one or other of the major filing systems. It is worth starting a file folder for correspondence only if there is some probability that a lengthy course of correspondence will develop with that firm. Other letters are filed in a **miscellaneous file**, in alphabetical order with the letter A on the top, B below it and so on. When several letters for the same firm have accumulated it is worth opening a file for that particular correspondence.

The major filing systems may be listed as follows:

(a) The alphabetical system.
(b) The numerical system.
(c) The alpha-numerical system, which combines the above systems.
(d) The subject system.
(e) The geographical system.

The Alphabetical System

The alphabetical system of filing is the commonest in business. It is most easily understood, and is direct. This means that the filing clerk goes directly to the filing tray with the correct initial letter and searches it to find the file, which will be in alphabetical order in the tray. To assist her to find the file quickly the following guides are available:

(a) The trays have a name-plate in the front to indicate the contents, e.g. A–E.
(b) Primary guide cards are inserted with the visible portion sticking up on the left-hand side of the tray.
(c) Secondary guide cards are inserted with the visible portion sticking up in the centre of the tray.
(d) The labels on the individual files are placed at the right-hand end of the file.

A good filing clerk will therefore cast her eye first to the left to locate the primary section she requires, then to the centre, to locate the subsection required, and then to the right to pinpoint the actual file. Fig. 12.1 overleaf illustrates these points.

To assist the reader with the many rules of alphabetical filing a special section at the end of this chapter (see page 190) explains them fully.

The Numerical System

The numerical system of filing has an advantage in that there is a

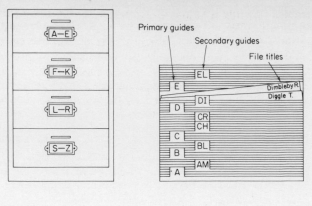

Primary guides

Secondary guides

File titles

Dimbleby R.
Diggle T.

EN	English, H.
	Empson & Co. Ltd.
	Ellis, J.
	Ekland, B.
E	Edwards, B.
	Dorkins, S.
	Dope, T.
DO	Donegal, R.
	Distrophy Society
	Displays Ltd.
	Dimbleby, R.
DH	Diggle, T.
	Demitracapolous, J.
	Delta, W. Ltd.
	De Froberville, J.
	Dear, H.
D	Dean, R

D—E

Fig. 12.1. Alphabetical filing.

vast range of numbers that can be used, whereas there are only 26 letters in the alphabet. It is not direct, like the alphabetical system, for it is impossible to go directly to the file in the cabinets. Instead the filing clerk must refer to a reference index, to find the number allocated to that file. This reference index is itself in alphabetical order, and is known as the alphabetical index file. The index gives the numbers of the files which may then be found in the filing cabinets. Fig. 12.2 shows the two different arrangements. The numerical system shown is the simpler of the two possible numerical systems. It is called the **consecutive digit**

system, since a new file is simply given the next consecutive number.

A variation upon the numerical system, which has the advantage of spreading the new files over the range of filing cabinets, is called the **terminal digit filing system**. The idea is to put new files into successive filing cabinets rather than into the same filing cabinet, as with the consecutive digit system. Since new files tend to be more active than old-established files, a large number of new files in the same drawer may

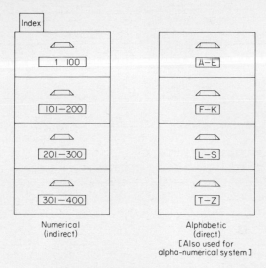

Fig. 12.2. Filing systems.

cause delays. Several staff may wish to consult a file in the same drawer. If the files are filed in the cabinet displaying the terminal digit, only every tenth new file will be in any given drawer. More advanced terminal digit systems can be used where each indexed item will be given three numbers: a document number, a file number and a cabinet number. These might read 32:14:03. The letter concerned will be the 32nd item in the 14th file in the 3rd cabinet.

The Alpha-numerical System

This system is a combination of the other two systems. Files are entered in the major sections of the system in alphabetical order, but each letter section is then filed in numerical order, with a **guide card** at the start of each section listing the numbers of the files in that section of the filing system. A typical guide card would be as shown in Fig. 12.3. The index letter would indicate clearly the start of files beginning with L. The guide card would then pinpoint the particular file required. Periodically the filing clerk would update the guide card, putting the files listed into alphabetical order. As the reader will notice, the early

L

	No.		No.
Lanham, E.	7	Lucey, R.	1
Lawrence, T.H.	2	Luckford, H.	6
Lee, J.	5	Larkin, T.	10
Lott, R.	4	Lee, V.	11
Love, P.	9	Leary, P.S.	12
Lovegrove, S.	3		
Lovett, T.D.	8		

Fig. 12.3. An alpha-numerical guide card.

files are listed alphabetically, but filed numerically. Recent additions are listed numerically, but at a later date will be incorporated into the alphabetical list.

Classifying Files by Subject

Some firms find it convenient to file under subjects, at least for part of their work. Thus, the general administration office may file items under the main subject headings of its activities, premises, staffing, insurance, equipment, contracts, telephones, sublettings, etc. As the firm grows, some subdivision within these major headings may become necessary. Premises may require files on leases, repairs, cleaning, lighting and heating, plant layout, drainage, electricity and telephone systems, etc. Once again primary and secondary guides will lead the filing clerk through the intricacies of the system, and an alert clerk will be ready to recommend to a superior any subdivisions that become necessary. For example, the clerk might receive repeated requests for a file for the Alpha Omega Repair Co. Ltd. The clerk knows that this material is filed under 'General Repairs', but it might be more convenient to allocate this correspondence to a separate file since the company's services are being used repetitively for a wide variety of repair jobs.

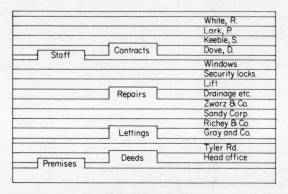

Fig. 12.4. Filing by subjects.

Card indexes for 'subject' filing systems. Whenever we have a subject filing system we must have a card index showing the names of all correspondents and the files where their information is filed. For example, a request from a departmental head to 'Bring me the file for Porlock and Sons' might be difficult to fulfil if the filing clerk was not sure which subject was involved. A reference to a card index would quickly reveal that Porlock and Sons were lift repairers, and their correspondence was filed under lift repairs.

Fig. 12.4 shows a typical subject classification, with primary, secondary and tertiary guides.

Classifying Files by Geographical Area

It is sometimes convenient to file information geographically. Thus a large sales force may be divided into counties, with the representatives or agents in each county filed alphabetically. An export house may file under the countries to which exports are sent. Within these main filing divisions the material may be filed under firms, or under subjects. Once again a card index would be necessary if a 'subject' classification is adopted.

12.5. Cross-referencing

It often happens that a name consists of several words, and staff will request files in different ways. Thus British Air Ferries Ltd might be wrongly requested as Air Ferries Ltd, or even as 'the air ferry firm'. To save trouble in future the filing clerk should make out a cross-reference card (for a card index system) or a cross-reference sheet for an alphabetical system. The next time she receives a request for Air Ferries Ltd the index card, or reference sheet, will tell her 'Air Ferries Ltd—see British Air Ferries Ltd'.

A cross-reference card, or cross-reference sheet, should be made out whenever a file may be requested under a title other than its true title.

Cross-references may also be recorded on the **file title** itself, on a special guide card, or on the cover of a file folder. The latter method is most useful where one firm is a subsidiary of another, so that two files of correspondence might well be in existence. Thus if Supergrowers Ltd have a subsidiary Chemical Fertilisers Co., the file for Supergrowers Ltd might bear the cross-reference (see also Chemical Fertiliser Co.) while the file for Chemical Fertiliser Co. would bear the cross-reference (see also Supergrowers Ltd).

Many foreign names are confusing to filing clerks. The Chinese always begin with the surname, while Mohammedans have all their names as surnames, taking the father's name, the grandfather's name and the great-grandfather's name. Often they will use these names in any order.

As an alternative to cross-references it is sometimes better to make a photocopy of an important letter. This is then filed in the less important file; the original letter is filed in the more frequently requested file cover.

Some typical cross-reference guides, or guide cards, are illustrated in Fig. 12.5.

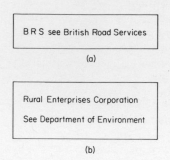

(a)

(b)

Fig. 12.5. Typical cross-reference cards.

12.6 'Out' Markers

When a file is removed, or when a letter is removed from a file, it should be replaced with an 'out' marker. These may be of several types. One of them is shown in the Expandex Filing System illustrated in Fig. 12.9 on page 186. It shows the 'out' tab sticking up to indicate which file has been removed. On the card itself spaces are ruled so that information can be written in as to the destination of the file and the likely date of return. This information will enable the file to be traced and retrieved after it is no longer required. A system of follow-up procedures can be instituted to ensure that files are returned.

Sometimes, instead of recording this information, the 'out' card has a simple pocket into which the original **request slip** for the file can be inserted. This saves time, since the person requesting the file has already written all the information on the request slip.

A further method of recording files which are out is to keep a book record of the files sent to staff. This is like a 'day book' in accounting, recording every file going out and its destination.

We thus have three methods of recording 'out' files. These are:

(*a*) 'Out' cards, the same size as a file, with a projecting tab saying 'out', and room to record where the file has gone. On return the file is replaced, the 'out' card is removed, and the line recording who had this particular file is closed by inserting the date of return in the space provided. The 'out' card may then be re-used elsewhere.

(*b*) 'Out' cards with a pocket for 'request slips'. On return the file is replaced, the 'out' card removed and the request slip destroyed.

(*c*) A 'files requested' day book which lists all files sent out, and records their return.

Each of these methods may then be used in some sort of follow-up system.

12.7 Follow-up Systems

One of the chief problems with any filing system is the tendency of executives and other staff to hold on to files and documents longer than necessary. This makes serious difficulties for the filing clerk, since correspondence is arriving all the time and the file will be out of date, and letters awaiting its return must be stored in a temporary file. The filing department therefore operates a follow-up system.

The follow-up systems most commonly in use are as follows:

(a) The Daily Scanning System

Here a small filing system is scanned every morning by the chief filing clerk, who lists any overdue files. The member of staff who has borrowed the file is then requested to return it, or to book it out for a further period. This daily scanning system is very easy if the 'files requested' day book is in use since it is only necessary to look through the book to see which files are still out, and overdue.

(b) The 'Tickler' System

This is a more useful system in many ways, since it provides a method of securing not only the return of files, but also other regular check-up procedures. For example, the production manager might wish to review the progress made on a particular project at regular intervals, and might therefore request that the file on this project be sent to him as a matter

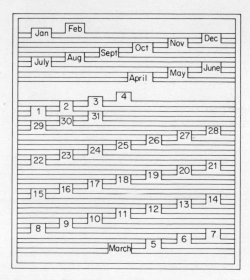

Fig. 12.6. A 'tickler' system.

of routine on the fifteenth day of every month. This request would be recorded in the 'tickler' system and would 'tickle' the filing clerk's memory on the correct day. Similarly, a bad payer's file might be requested by the accountant, who would stop further supplies to the customer if the account had not been settled by a certain date each month.

The 'tickler' system consists of two sets of cards, a set headed with the names of the months, and a second set headed with days, 1–31. The system enables records to be placed in the system at a point where action is to be taken, and a daily and monthly review can thus be made. The system is illustrated in Fig. 12.6.

Its use may be described as follows:

Daily system. When files are sent out, the file requisition slip is placed in the section of the daily list at the point where the file should be retrieved. Thus, a file requested on the 10th for three days should be returned on the 13th. The request slip would be inserted into the 'tickler' system on the 14th, by which time it will definitely be overdue. If it is returned before that date, the request slip will be extracted and destroyed. If it is not returned, the member of staff will be contacted and the file retrieved.

Monthly system. Some routine procedures are carried out at regular intervals—for example, the removal of 'dead' files to storage. The monthly card system enables such routine work to be spread around the year adequately. For example, it might be best to review these matters in months which were known to be 'slack' months, when little other work was available. This would be recorded on the monthly card system and the necessary action taken. Similarly, certain actions, such as the renewal of fire insurance premiums, occur only in a particular month of the year. A record on the monthly card system that Mr Jones was to receive the fire insurance file on the Lea Bridge Road premises on the 15th day of October every year would remind Mr Jones that he must review the policy and contact the insurers if any updating of the 'cover' is necessary.

Every day, and every month, the card for that day or month is moved to the back of the file and the next day, or month, with its duties, is commenced.

12.8 How to File a Letter

To file a letter the following procedure should be followed:

(*a*) Discover whether there is a file folder for that particular letter. This may mean looking straight into the files if the system is alphabetical, or there may be a card index to help the search.

(*b*) If there is a file folder, find it and place the new letter on top, since letters are filed in date order with the most recent letter highest in the pile. This order of filing is called *chronological order* (from the Greek word *khronos* = time). Letters filed in chronological order assist staff who know roughly when a letter was written, or a contract made, and can turn, in the correspondence, to that date and search through until they discover the letter concerned.

(*c*) If there is no file folder, file the letter in the miscellaneous file. Here the letters are filed in alphabetical order, i.e. Allen before Allsop, and Barker before Brown, and in each firm's correspondence the new letter is placed on top of the batch. If half a dozen letters have accumulated, consider whether a file folder for that set of correspondence should be opened.

(*d*) Consider whether any cross referencing is necessary. If the letter relates to more than one aspect of the business and should be filed in two or three places we can either copy it and file the copies in each place, or put the letter in the chief place and a cross-reference to it in the other places.

12.9   How to Find a Letter

To find a letter the following procedure should be followed:

(*a*) Discover whether there is a file folder for that particular letter. This may mean looking straight into the files in an alphabetical system, or there may be a card index to help the search.

(*b*) If there is a file folder, find it and remove the file.

(*c*) If the whole file is to be sent to a particular person, record its destination by the use of an 'out' marker.

(*d*) If the file is the 'miscellaneous' file, remove only the desired correspondence from it, marking its position with an 'out' marker placed in the pile of correspondence at the appropriate point. Send the correspondence required in a temporary file folder to the person who wants it.

(*e*) If the request slip calls for only a particular letter from a file, remove that letter, mark its position with an 'out' marker and send it in a temporary file folder to the person requiring it.

(*f*) If the office uses a 'tickler' system, record in the system that the file is out and its destination so that it does not get lost and its return can be requested at a later date if the applicant fails to return it.

12.10   Microfilm Filing

Photographic processes enable the size of stored records to be reduced very considerably. An ordinary letter of A4 or quarto size can be reduced to thumb-nail size, and over 8000 sheets can be reproduced on a small spool of film. This method is most appropriate for storing records which must be kept for many years; it is particularly valuable for historical and museum records, for official government records and Court records, etc. The cost of the initial equipment is high, and only worth while if extensive records are to be kept in this way. The process requires the following:

(*a*) *A camera*, usually using 35 mm film, which may have an automatic feeding device. Documents in batches are inserted into the feeding device, which passes them forward to be filmed in correct sequence. The camera may be able to photograph both sides of a document at the same time. Exposed film is sent to the manufacturers for processing.

Indexing the documents is a time-consuming but important process. Each batch may be given a batch number, followed by an individual number for each document. Alternatively, captions can be added to a document to indicate its contents.

(*b*) *A scanner unit*. This projects the filmed documents onto a screen where they may be read by the clerk or official consulting the records. A print of any required document can be supplied by some machines enlarged sufficiently to be read by the naked eye.

Recent developments in microfilm filing have made it much more versatile for ordinary business use. 'Jackets' have been developed which can hold photographs of 60 documents in a packet of 150 mm × 100 mm. One rarely has more than 60 live documents in any particular batch of correspondence. When anyone requires a file the 'jacket' is placed in a 'jacket duplicator' and photocopied. The whole duplicate jacket is sent to the person who requested it, and the original is re-filed. No need for 'out' markers here. A file is never 'out'. The person requesting the file reads it in 'file reader' and when he has finished with it the copy is placed in the waste paper basket, or destroyed if it is a security file.

Two photographs of a camera and viewer respectively, for microfilm filing may be seen in Plate 14.

12.11 Filing Equipment

There is an enormous range of equipment available from hundreds of different business equipment manufacturers, many of whom have become household names. It is impossible to illustrate the full range in a book of this size but some of the more specialised items are illustrated in the sections which follow. In describing the various methods of filing below, reference is made to these illustrations. The reader is urged to visit exhibitions like the International Business Show, held at regular intervals in Birmingham, and similar displays of office equipment and business systems.

Files

There are many varieties of files including:

Box files. These have a solid box-like construction and a spring-loaded compression pad inside holds down the filed material firmly.

Plate 14. A microfilm camera (*top*) and viewer-printer (*below*) (reproduced by courtesy of Kodak Ltd).

Letters, leaflets, catalogues, etc., are simply inserted into the file and the spring-loaded arm is released to hold them in.

Lever-arch files. These have already been illustrated in Fig. 2.3 and retain correspondence rather more safely than box files. Individual letters can be extracted without disturbing the file.

Concertina files. These are made up of a succession of pockets into which similar documents can be collected ready for processing. They are particularly suitable for items like **petty cash vouchers**.

Visible index files. These are particularly useful for ledger records, personnel records, membership records, sales records, attendance and marks registers in schools, etc. (see Fig. 12.7).

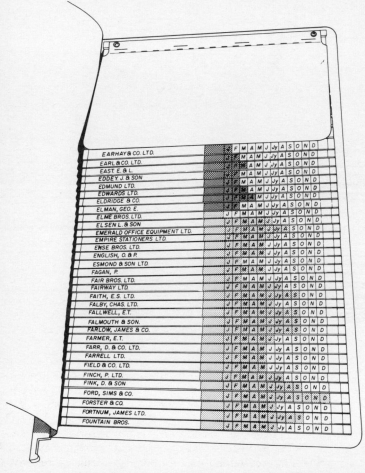

Fig. 12.7. A visible record system (reproduced by courtesy of Expandex Ltd).

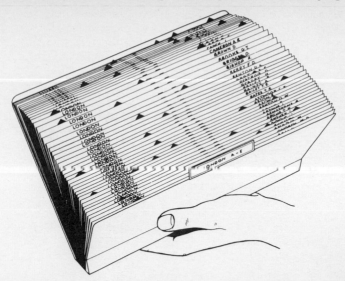

Fig. 12.8. The Vistafan visible card system for commercial travellers (reproduced by courtesy of George Anson and Co. Ltd).

A variation is the Vistafan system (Fig. 12.8), which is extremely compact and can be easily inserted into a commercial traveller's jacket pocket, yet it opens to reveal the names and records of fifty customers in a particular area. As many as 2000 records may be stored in a small tray on the seat of the traveller's car, and he can update records after each call before driving off.

Suspended horizontal files. With this type of filing a metal framework is fitted into the top of each drawer of the filing cabinet, to give a raised rail from which pockets are suspended on metal rods. These rods may have nylon runners fitted to reduce noise as they move up and down the rails. Some are in concertina style so that it is impossible to have documents or file folders inserted between the pockets. Documents and correspondence are filed in file folders, suspended vertically in the pockets, each of which will hold several file folders. Index strips give a visible index (see Fig. 12.9).

Lateral files. With this type of filing the conventional three- or four-drawer filing cabinet is replaced by a taller, cupboard-like cabinet with neither front doors nor a back. The files are suspended, rather like clothes in a wardrobe, from rails fitted across the cabinet. As many as six ranks are possible at normal working heights, and since the files suspended in the pockets are accessible from both sides it is possible for the filing clerks to work at the same cabinet from opposite sides. There is a considerable saving in floor space and the physical effort of opening and closing drawers is avoided.

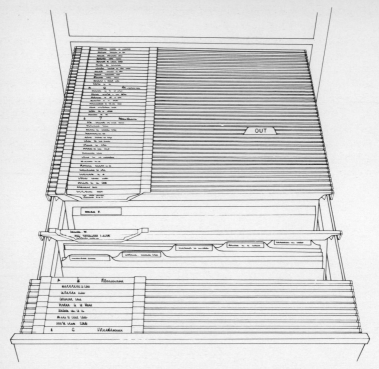

Fig. 12.9. Horizontal suspension filing (reproduced by courtesy of Expandex Ltd).

Vertical files. This name is confusing, since today practically all filing systems are 'vertical' in the sense that documents are rarely stored flat with one document on top of another. Here it is used to describe a type of file which is supported by a plastic spine, in a vertical rack. The papers inside must be secured, either by a plastic thong or in pockets. The Anson vistafile is an excellent example, the spine being sufficiently wide to be used as an index and flash-board, where coloured flashes indicate certain types of information. When used, for example, in garages, it may indicate the type of car owned by the customer and the date he is due for his next service. A reminder can then be sent out with a booking for the service.

Automated electronic filing. This type of filing system (illustrated in Plate 13, see page 171) consists of two facing banks of storage containers. The touch of a button directs an electronically controlled conveyor situated between these banks to any position within the system in order to locate the selected container, which is then drawn onto the conveyor, and in seconds is delivered to the work station. After completing the filing activity the operator presses a RESTORE button, and the container is automatically returned to its original position.

Ring, thong and post binders. Many documents are most conveniently stored in binders. **Ring binders** have spring-loaded split rings which may be opened to release the documents. Some have ingenious mechanisms for moving documents up and down, so that a visible index can be opened to admit a further visible index card at the correct place for its insertion in alphabetical order (see Fig. 12.10). **Thong binders** have a plastic thong to thread through documents, and **post binders** have metal posts which may be separated off to insert further sheets. These are most widely used in accounts departments where **Day Books** are not kept—since they require much effort and provide only a permanent record of the documents. A set of documents carefully preserved in a post binder can itself act as the 'Day Book'.

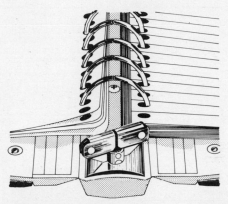

Fig. 12.10. An ingenious ring binder with visi-index records (reproduced by courtesy of Twinlock Ltd).

Circular rotary filing. There are many types of rotary files, which enable a great many records to be filed in wallets or pockets around a central vertical pillar. They are economical of space, very accessible and can be used by several filing clerks at the same time (see Plate 15).

Safety first and filing cabinets. Since filing cabinets are accessible only when drawers are open, there is always a danger that they will fall forward if more than one drawer is opened at once. This is particularly likely to happen if the lowest drawer is filled with light objects, such as handbags, boxes of paper handkerchiefs, etc. Such objects should always be stored in the top drawer rather than the bottom drawer.

12.12 Indexes

An index is a device for finding the position of records in a system quickly and easily. Several references to indexes have already been made, but a full list includes the following:

(*a*) *Page indexes*, such as are found in the back of a book. It is often

Plate 15. Circular rotary filing (reproduced by courtesy of Flexiform Ltd).

helpful to include items more than once. For example, in this book the index not only shows Filing—with many subheadings under that entry—but also each of the individual entries in its own place in the index—for example, concertina files appears under C. Page indexes may be used in ledgers, sales departments, etc.

(*b*) *Card indexes.* These have already been referred to (see page 177).

(*c*) *Visible card indexes.* These have again been referred to (see above and page 184).

(*d*) *Wheel indexes.* These are a form of rotary card index which enable a very large number of records to be found very speedily by rotating the wheel until the card required is found (see Fig. 12.11).

Fig. 12.11. A wheel index (reproduced by courtesy of Rotadex Datafind Ltd).

(*e*) *Strip indexes.* These have already been referred to (see Fig. 5.3, page 65).

(*f*) *Vowel indexes.* These indexes are used to split up a group of names into six columns, to make each name easier to find in the lists. Thus, a list of names beginning with 'P' would be divided up into columns according to the first vowel in the name. 'Palmer' would come under

A	E	I	O	U	Y
Palmer, P[11] Patterson, T[16]	Penrose, R[73] Pemberton, Q[1] Peterson, S[94]	Pilsner, S[147]	Potterton, H[72] Posy, R[89]	Phurrey, R[71] Plume, T[15]	Pyrford, H[5]

Fig. 12.12. A vowel index.

the 'a's and 'Potterton' under the 'o's as shown in Fig. 12.12. Y is regarded as the sixth vowel.

12.13   Selecting a Suitable System

Filing will be most efficiently carried out if a suitable system, which will achieve the aims of the firm, is adopted from the very beginning. All systems become out-dated, and need reviewing, preferably with the help of a specialist adviser from the supplier whose systems are being considered. Once a system has been installed it is expensive and wasteful to change it, but updating of procedures is always helpful. Some of the commonest types of filing problems are mentioned in the table following.

Matter to be filed	*Suggested methods*
(*a*) Correspondence	Horizontal suspension filing, vertical suspension filing, lateral suspension filing, conventional filing cabinets.
(*b*) Invoices, credit notes and other documents	Post binders, lever-arch files, box files— for small businesses concertina files.
(*c*) Ledger cards—sales and purchases	Visi-index files, posting trays supplied by systems manufacturers.
(*d*) Confidential staff records	Vertical vistafiles with thonging and pockets for documents. For security reasons the cabinet must be lockable.
(*e*) Used stencils	Special stencil-storing cabinets.
(*f*) Dictating machine belts	Special storage racks from dictation machine manufacturers.
(*g*) Data processing paper tapes and magnetic tapes	Special storage racks from specialist suppliers.
(*h*) Large drawings and charts	Special chart-storing devices from specialist manufacturers.

12.14.   Rules for Filing Alphabetically

To assist the reader with the many rules of alphabetical filing the next few pages have been divided into a series of **alphabetical filing rules**. Each group has been given a number, and short practice exercises are included to help the reader to master the rules. The answers are given at the end of this section (see page 195).

Alphabetical Filing Rules I—Indexing Units

The ordinary alphabetical index is used in alphabetical filing to decide in which order the files shall be stored. The sequence is decided by considering the name of the person, or firm, and regarding every element in it as an **indexing unit**. Thus, Margaret Potter has two indexing units, while J. V. H. Knott and Overseas Groupage Forwarders Ltd each have four indexing units.

These indexing units are then inspected to decide which is the first indexing unit. With personal names the surname is usually chosen as the first indexing unit, and the 'given' names or initials then follow, as second, third, etc., indexing units. With impersonal names, such as the Borough Council of Newtown and the Diocese of Oxford, the first indexing unit is the first word that distinguishes that body from all other bodies. Thus:

> Borough (there are many boroughs)
> Council (there are many councils)
> Newtown (this is—if not unique—at least very distinctive)

We would therefore index the title as: Newtown, Borough Council of.

Two important rules are 'nothing comes before something' and 'short before long'. Thus Potter comes before Potter, H., which comes before Potter, Harry.

Practical exercise 1. Select the correct first indexing unit in the following names (for the answers see page 195)

(*a*) Alfred J. Marshall
(*b*) Peter R. Cummings
(*c*) Daniel Daniels
(*d*) M. V. T. Potterton and Co. Ltd
(*e*) Liverpool Wheat Exchange
(*f*) R. S. V. Paterson & Co. Ltd
(*g*) Zoological Gardens of Chester
(*h*) Chartered Institute of Transport
(*i*) Terry Mendoza (Photographics) Ltd
(*j*) Seamen's Society

Alphabetical Filing Rules II—Indexing Personal Names

As already explained, the most important indexing unit, the surname, is placed first. Margaret Potter becomes Potter, Margaret, and J. V. H. Knott becomes Knott, J. V. H.

Since K comes before P they would be arranged in sequence as follows:

> Knott, J. V. H.
> Potter, Margaret

Practical exercise 2. Arrange the following names in alphabetical order, correctly indexed (for the answers see page 195).

(*a*) Peter Jones, Daniel Wheddon, Harry Hawke
(*b*) Silas T. Lark, Samuel P. Larkin, Ruby M. Lazarus
(*c*) A. J. Cronin, Charles Dickens, Rudyard Kipling, H. Melville

When the surnames have the same first letter, the second letter of the surname is used to decide the sequence, or if necessary the third letter of the surname.

Thus, Tom Driver, Roy Drover and Peter Dimbleby would be indexed in the order shown below:

Dimbleby, Peter
Driver, Tom
Drover, Roy

Where the entire names are identical the sequence is decided by the address. Thus David Jones, Cardiff; David Jones, Bramhall; David Jones, Stepney, would appear as:

Jones, David, Bramhall
Jones, David, Cardiff
Jones, David, Stepney

Practical exercise 2a. Arrange the following names in correct sequence (for the answers see page 195).

(*a*) R. Chambers, R. Chalmers, Eric Chalmers, Edith Chumleigh
(*b*) R. Fortescue & Sons Ltd, R. Fortescue, R. Forte, Peter Forth
(*c*) Howard Proctor Ltd, Peter Howard, P. T. Howard
(*d*) Gurr & Co. Ltd, Ben Gunn, B. Gunn Ltd, B. Gnu, B. Gnutsen
(*e*) R. Marshall & Co. Ltd, R. Marshall, Rosemary Marshall
(*f*) P. Lane, Penny Lane, Penelope Lane, Penelope P. Langdon
(*g*) Glover & Sons Ltd, Grover & Go., Glouceston Ltd, P. Grimes Ltd
(*h*) Murray, John Murray, John Martin, Joan Martindale
(*i*) Lyons of Dumbarton, Lyons of Doncaster, Lyons of Lyonnesse
(*j*) Armstrong (Dover) Ltd, Armstrong (Middlesex) Ltd, Armstrong (Manchester) Ltd

Alphabetical Filing Rules III—Titles, degrees and decorations

Titles, degrees and decorations are *not* looked upon as indexing units. They are placed after the name, but are ignored. Thus the following would be listed in the manner shown:

Mrs Rose Godley, Sir George Godley, Rt Revd Thomas Godley

Godley, Sir George
Godley, Mrs Rose
Godley, Rt Revd Thomas

Practice exercise 3. List the following groups of names in correct alphabetical order (for the answers see page 195).

(*a*) Mrs M. L. Gilbert, M. Gilbert, OBE, Professor Martin Gilbert
(*b*) Dr Howard Jones, MD, R. Jones, DFC, Mrs Rita Jones
(*c*) Mrs D. W. Heather, Lady Doreen Heather, Sir Dennis Heather, CH.

Alphabetical Filing Rules IV—Names with a Prefix

Many names have prefixes, such as O', Mc, Mac, Da, Du, Van and

Von. With all such names the whole name is the first indexing unit, so that Peter van Tromp appears as

> Van Tromp, Peter

and Leonardo da Vinci as

> Da Vinci, Leonardo

Two different methods are used for Mac and Mc. Sometimes a special section in the files is given to these names. If so Mac and Mc are treated as if they were the same, and all names with these prefixes are filed in the special section under the letters that come after the prefix. Thus Macadam, Macnamara and McCardy would be filed as:

> Macadam
> McCardy
> Macnamara

If there is not a special section then the names are filed as they are written, and the three names listed above would be rearranged as:

> Macadam
> Macnamara
> McCardy

Another group that is often given a separate section is the group of names beginning with Saint or St. If there is a separate section, usually in the 'sa' part of the index, the names are treated as if spelled out in full, i.e. Saint, and this is treated as the first indexing unit. Some indexers put all the Saints together, followed by the St's. Others mix them in together, treating them all as Saints and using the second indexing unit to determine the correct order.

Practice exercise 4. List the following groups of names in correct alphabetical order (for the answers see page 196).

(*a*) Thomas O'Leary, Michael O'Loughlin, Peter Osgood, Mary O'Callaghan
(*b*) Peter Du Bois, Oscar Van Tromp, Pieter de Raat, Roger McCardy
(*c*) Thomas McEvoy, Peter MacIlven, Roger McInnes, the Right Honourable Hugh McGrath. (Assume that a special place is reserved for Mac and Mc.)
(*d*) Saint, A., St Andrew's School, St Aloysius College, St Trinian's, Saint James' Academy
(*e*) Roberto da Costa, Rita de St Angelo, Irene d Eye, Peter de Gout

Alphabetical Filing Rules V—Hyphenated Names

Where a name is hyphenated it is usual to treat the two words which are joined as separate indexing units. There are exceptions to this rule, as shown below, but it holds good for the vast majority of names. Thus Peter Anson-Large, John Wilkes-Browne, John Lampeter-Smythe and Thomas Walker-Upjohn would be filed in order as:

> Anson-Large, Peter
> Lampeter-Smythe, John
> Walker-Upjohn, Thomas
> Wilkes-Browne, John

The exceptions to the rule are names which although hyphenated really make a single word, each part being incomplete without the other. Thus Ultra-sonics Ltd or Super-heaters Ltd, would be treated as having only two indexing units.

Practice exercise 5. Arrange these groups in correct order (for the answers see page 196).

(*a*) Ian Forbes-Adam, Roberta Forbes-Robertson, Mildred Forbes-Poynter
(*b*) Peter Knapp, Roger Knapp-Fisher, Alan Knapp-Anderson
(*c*) Klockner-Knoeller Ltd, Arthur Klockner, Jane Klockner-Stubel
(*d*) Alan Ross, Peter Ross-Whyte, Clifford Ross-Whittingham, David Ross-White
(*e*) Ultra-electric Co. Ltd, Ultra-violet Ray Co. Ltd, Ultra-sonics Ltd

Alphabetical Filing Rules VI—Separate Words

Names where separate words occur are treated as if each word was a separate indexing unit, though here again there are exceptions. The rule may be illustrated by:

> Make Your Own Board Co. Ltd
> Making Merry Wine Co. Ltd
> Mending While-U-Wait Co. Ltd

The exceptions are geographical names such as Isle of Man Gas Board. Here Isle of Man is treated as one indexing unit.

Practice exercise 6. Arrange these groups in correct order (for the answers see page 196).

(*a*) J. R. South and Co. Ltd, South Western Gas Board, Southern Railway
(*b*) Harry South, South Hampstead Cricket Club, H. L. Smith
(*c*) W. C. Stewart, Stew and Simmer, Stewart Ward Coins Ltd
(*d*) Whiter Wash Co., White Sea Canal Co., R. J. White
(*e*) Sweeney Todd, Todd, S. J., Today's Wear, Toddler's Wear
(*f*) Canvey Island Motors Ltd, J. R. Canvey, John Canvey, Peter Canvey.

Answer Section. The answers to the practice exercises are given below:

Practice exercise 1. The first indexing units are:
(*a*) Marshall (*b*) Cummings (*c*) Daniels (*d*) Potterton (*e*) Liverpool (*f*) Paterson (*g*) Chester (*h*) Transport (*i*) Mendoza (*j*) Seamen's

Practice exercise 2
(*a*) Hawke, Harry
Jones, Peter
Wheddon, Daniel
(*c*) Cronin, A. J.
Dickens, Charles
Kipling, Rudyard
Melville, H.

(*b*) Lark, Silas T.
Larkin, Samuel P.
Lazarus, Ruby M.

Practice exercise 2a
(*a*) Chalmers, Eric
Chalmers, R.
Chambers, R.
Chumleigh, Edith
(*c*) Howard, P. T.
Howard, Peter
Howard, Proctor Ltd

(*e*) Marshall, R.
Marshall, R. & Co. Ltd
Marshall, Rosemary

(*g*) Glouceston Ltd
Glover & Sons Ltd
Grimes, P. Ltd
Grover & Co.
(*i*) Lyons, Doncaster, of
Lyons, Dumbarton, of
Lyons, Lyonnesse, of

(*b*) Forte, R.
Fortescue, R.
Fortescue, R. & Sons Ltd
Forth, Peter
(*d*) Gnu, B.
Gnutsen, B.
Gunn, B. Ltd
Gunn, Ben
Gurr & Co. Ltd
(*f*) Lane, P.
Lane, Penelope
Lane, Penny
Langdon, Penelope P.
(*h*) Martin, John
Martindale, Joan
Murray
Murray, John
(*j*) Armstrong (Dover) Ltd
Armstrong (Manchester Ltd
Armstrong (Middlesex) Ltd

Practice exercise 3
(*a*) Gilbert, M., OBE
Gilbert, Mrs M. L.
Gilbert, Professor Martin
(*c*) Heather, Mrs D. W.
Heather, Sir Dennis, CH
Heather, Lady Doreen

(*b*) Jones, Dr Howard, MD
Jones, R., DFC
Jones, Mrs Rita

Practice exercise 4

(a) O'Callaghan, Mary
O'Leary, Thomas
O'Loughlin, Michael
Osgood, Peter

(c) McEvoy, Thomas
McGrath, the Rt Hon. Hugh
MacIlven, Peter
MacInnes, Roger

(e) Da Costa, Roberto
De Gout, Peter
De St Angelo, Rita
D'Eye, Irene

(b) De Raat, Pieter
Du Bois, Peter
McCardy, Roger
Van Tromp, Oscar

(d) Saint A.
St Aloysius College
St Andrew's School
St James' Academy
St Trinian's

Practice exercise 5

(a) Forbes-Adam, Ian
Forbes-Poynter, Mildred
Forbes-Robertson, Roberta

(c) Klockner, Arthur
Klockner-Knoeller, Ltd
Klockner-Stubel, Jane

(e) Ultra-electric Co. Ltd
Ultra-sonics Ltd
Ultra-violet Ray Co. Ltd

(b) Knapp, Peter
Knapp-Anderson, Alan
Knapp-Fisher, Roger

(d) Ross, Alan
Ross-White, David
Ross-Whittingham, Clifford
Ross-Whyte, Peter

Practice exercise 6

(a) South, J. R. and Co. Ltd
Southern Railway
South Western Gas Board

(c) Stew and Simmer
Stewart, W. C.
Stewart Ward Coins Ltd

(e) Today's Wear
Todd, S. J.
Todd, Sweeney
Toddlers' Wear

(b) South, H. L.
South, Harry
South Hampstead Cricket
Club

(d) White, R. J.
White Wash Co.
White Sea Canal Co.

(f) Canvey, J. R.
Canvey, John
Canvey, Peter
Canvey Island Motors Ltd

12.15 Points to Think About and Discuss

(a) Firm *A* has its filing carried out in the departments, each of which has a single filing clerk. Firm *B* has its filing handled centrally. The staff consists of a filing supervisor, a chief filing clerk and eight filing clerks. Discuss the likely difficulties to be met with in Firm *A* that will not be met in Firm *B*, and vice versa.

(*b*) Miss A says: 'Filing is tedious work, I am bored to death half the time.' Miss B says: 'I find it fascinating to control this enormous collection of documents, each of which is important in some way.' Discuss these two attitudes to filing. Prepare a two-minute speech by each young lady justifying her point of view.

12.16   Rapid Revision

Cover the page with a sheet of notepaper and uncover one question at a time.

Answers	Questions
—	1. What is filing?
1. Filing is the storing of correspondence in a retrieval system, whence it may be obtained for reference.	2. What happens to the correspondence?
2. It is placed in a file folder which is given a title and is then stored in one of the five systems.	3. What are the five systems?
3. (*a*) Alphabetical. (*b*) Numerical. (*c*) Alpha-numerical. (*d*) Subjects. (*e*) Geographical.	4. Suppose there is only one letter from a particular correspondent?
4. Place it in the miscellaneous file.	5. How are letters in a miscellaneous file filed?
5. Alphabetically, with the A's on top.	6. In a busy file how are the letters filed?
6. With the most recent letters on top.	7. What do we call this order?
7. Chronological order.	8. What are the essentials of a good filing system?
8. (*a*) Simplicity. (*b*) Security. (*c*) Compactness. (*d*) An appropriate classification. (*e*) Clear cross-references. (*f*) Adequate tracing of out-files. (*g*) Adequate follow-up of out-files. (*h*) A properly laid down document retention policy.	9. List the chief types of filing system.
9. (*a*) Box files; (*b*) lever-arch files; (*c*) concertina files; (*d*) visible index files; (*e*) card files; (*f*) horizontal suspension filing; (*g*) vertical suspension filing; (*h*) electronic filing.	10. Go over the page again until you feel you are sure of the answers.

Exercises Set 12

1. Prepare a report to your office manager on the advisability of transferring all the departmental filing systems to a central filing department. Set out clearly in your report the advantages and disadvantages of the two systems.

2. Describe: (*a*) vertical filing; (*b*) horizontal (flat) filing.

3. (*a*) What is: (i) a strip index; (ii) a vowel index; (iii) a visible card index? (*b*) Design a visible card suitable for indexing the customers of a firm. Make use of a signalling device to show the kinds of product sold.   (BEC General)

4. (*a*) Describe the uses in filing of three of the following items of equipment: (i) collator; (ii) posting tray; (iii) suspension file; (iv) transfer case. (*b*) What is meant by three of the following: (i) a cross-reference sheet; (ii) an outguide; (iii) document retention; (iv) a follow-up system.   (BEC General)

5. (*a*) List the following names in the order in which they would appear in an alphabetical filing system: (i) Department of Education and Science: (ii) John Smith & Sons Ltd; (iii) Dr A. P. Sherbert; (iv) United Nations Organisation; (v) The Playboy Club; (vi) De la Rue Ltd; (vii) ABC Co. Ltd; (viii) David Aaronson; (ix) J. McDougall & Co.; (x) J. MacFarlane & Co.
   (*b*) Explain the essential features of a numerical system of filing and mention which organisations would be likely to use the system.   (BEC General)

6. (*a*) What are the essential requirements of a good filing system? (*b*) List the following names in alphabetical order for indexing purposes: (i) K. White & Co. Ltd; (ii) R. Atkins Ltd; (iii) Dolman Ltd; (iv) Dr W. O'Brien; (v) R. McBride; (vi) Hotel Metropolitan; (vii) Department of the Environment; (viii) British Rail.

7. Explain the uses and advantages of visible card indexes.

8. The following terms are used in filing: explain fully what they mean. Give examples of diagrams where appropriate and explain their uses: (*a*) out or absent card; (*b*) guide card; (*c*) cross-reference; (*d*) chronological order.

9. (*a*) Describe a suitable system of filing and classification for use by an international company with branches in large cities in many parts of the world. The company manufactures disinfectants, fertilisers and detergents; (*b*) draw and complete a primary guide card and a secondary guide card to be used with this system.

10. 'A good filing system is essential in an efficient office.' Comment on this statement and outline the factors which must be taken into account when devising a filing system.

11. (*a*) Arrange the following names in order for alphabetical filing: (i) Morgan Groceries Ltd; (ii) The British Council; (iii) 5-Star Supermarket Ltd; (iv) The CBC Gas Appliance Co.; (v) Dr T. B. Ruston; (vi) G. O'Connor; (vii) The Halifax Building Society; (viii) The YWCA; (ix) National Council of Women; (x) Hotel Supreme; (xi) Elder Dempster Ltd; (xii) The Prime Meat Co.; (xiii) BBC; (xiv) British Oxygen Co. Ltd; (xv) Dawson and Cook Ltd.
   (*b*) You have two files with identical surnames. Show by two different

examples how you will decide which comes first in the alphabetical method. (*c*) What rule governs the alphabetical placing of the name McAndrews?
(RSA)

12. There are six departments in your firm and each keeps its own files in its own way. There is talk of a central filing system but several departments object. Draw up in two columns a list of arguments for and against a central filing system.

13. (*a*) What system of filing requires the use of a card index? (*b*) What information would you include on a card? (*c*) Which of this information must be easily visible? (*d*) Explain how and why these cards are used.

14. Describe in detail two filing systems. Mention their advantages and their suitability for certain businesses or departments.

15. Describe the construction and employment of: (*a*) lever-arch files; (*b*) box files; (*c*) concertina files.

16. Why do we file documents? What are the requirements of a filing system?

17. What system would you use or install so that files could be removed from the filing system and their return could be ensured after a reasonable time?

18. State what you regard as the essential requirements of a good filing system.

19. Explain briefly the following filing systems: (*a*) alphabetical: (*b*) geographical; (*c*) numerical; (*d*) subject.

20. (*a*) Why is the filing of documents indispensable in a large firm? (*b*) List the following names in alphabetical order for filing or indexing purposes; (i) Urban District of Wakefield; (ii) Albert Johnson; (iii) Sir Samuel Miles; (iv) The Ritz Hotel; (v) BIC Ltd; (vi) John Smith; (vii) London Co-operative Society; (viii) Professor Hugh Redman; (ix) Royal Northern Hospital; (x) School of African Studies.

21. (*a*) What is the purpose of filing? Answer as fully as possible. (*b*) When is it best to do the filing? Give your reasons. (*c*) What is the purpose of a miscellaneous folder?
(BEC General)

22. Alphabetical and numerical filing systems are used widely. Write fully about them, suggesting for which kind of business organisation or department each may be best suited. Give your reasons.

23. Explain fully the meaning of the following expressions: (*a*) lateral filing; (*b*) an 'out' or 'absent' card; (*c*) a miscellaneous folder; (*d*) a secondary guide card. Give examples or diagrams where suitable.

24. Draft some 'Hints on Filing' for an inexperienced filing clerk. Answer fully.

25. What do you understand by: (*a*) suspension filing; (*b*) alphabetical order; (*c*) guide cards; (*d*) 'nothing' comes before 'something'? Answer fully, giving examples or diagrams where suitable.

26. (*a*) Arrange the following names in order for alphabetical filing: (i) Hoyland Urban District Council; (ii) Ministry of Transport; (iii) D. R. Donnison; (iv) Corona Soft Drinks; (v) Grants of St James's (Northern) Ltd; (vi) Frank Coker

(Contractors) Ltd; (vii) Dr T. J. O'Connor; (viii) Royston Parkin & Co.; (ix) Royal Insurance Co. Ltd; (x) Old Denaby Motors.

(b) Why are index cards necessary in numerical filing? Give an example of the layout of the card you would use. (RSA)

27. (a) Say what you understand by a cross-reference and give an example; (b) make an observation about the bottom drawer in a filing cabinet; (c) what are 'dead' files and how should they be treated? (d) what is an 'out' or 'absent' card and how is it used?

28. List the methods of filing (including the type of equipment and system) you would use for: (a) petty cash vouchers; (b) stock record cards; (c) dictating machine belts; (d) correspondence with suppliers; (e) used stencils wanted for further use; (f) large-size drawings and photographs in the publicity department. Give reasons for your answers. (RSA)

29. (a) Why is it necessary to follow a set of rules when filing? (b) What does date order mean? (c) When is it useful to pre-sort correspondence for filing? (RSA)

30. Which method of filing would you use for the sales department of the following: (a) a small cutlery business; (b) a large concern with a thousand credit customers; (c) an exporting firm, with agents in many overseas countries? Give your reasons for your choice. (RSA)

31. Why is a card index necessary with numerical filing? Draw up two sample cards and fill in the details. When would you use this system of filing? (RSA)

32. Write a description of a filing system with which you are familiar. You should make reference to the following: (a) the type of cabinets used (e.g. vertical); (b) the system of classification (e.g. alphabetical); (c) the nature of the documents handled; (d) the method of controlling files taken away from the cabinet; (e) the method of transferring documents no longer required; (f) any additional information about the system that you consider important.

33. The filing clerk complains that he is short of space for storing current correspondence and that the files are becoming very bulky and difficult to handle. He also experiences difficulty in locating papers in the files (indexed under subject headings) after other members of the staff have been engaged on filing. Examine the filing clerk's complaints and prepare a report to the office manager setting out your findings and making recommendations to improve the efficiency of the filing system.

34. The head of your department has asked you to examine some new systems of filing and recording information with the object of saving office space and at the same time having the records available for quick and easy reference. In a memo to your head of department explain the features of: (a) microfilming; (b) lateral filing; (c) one other method which you consider should be introduced.

35. (a) It is claimed by some people that a good filing system for correspondence does not need a separate index. Give your views on the truth or otherwise of this claim and illustrate your answers by reference to the various methods of filing.

(b) What method and equipment would you use for filing: (i) sales ledger cards; (ii) stock record cards?

36. In order to record details of several thousands of customers, your office has a card index system which consists of rather small cards stored upright in wooden drawers. Explain the disadvantages of this arrangement and give your suggestions for converting it to a modern visible system.

37. What effect is mechanisation having on filing procedures? Select any one procedure to illustrate your answer.

38. (*a*) You are short of space in your office which is used to house the firm's filing cabinets and you no longer have room to accommodate all the old records. Reference to the information on some of these old records will, however, need to be made periodically in the future. Suggest how you would deal with this problem, (*b*) How would you record and control the files which are temporarily removed for reference from the central filing room?

39. Describe the methods of filing, type of equipment, and indexing (if any) which you would use for keeping any *four* of the following: (*a*) invoices received from suppliers; (*b*) confidential staff records; (*c*) catalogues received from wholesalers; (*d*) minutes of meetings; (*e*) petty cash vouchers; (*f*) used stencils required for subsequent use.

40. (*a*) Place the following names in the correct form and order for indexing: (i) Walter Jones & Co. Ltd; (ii) The Beverley Mills Ltd; (iii) J. Robert Skinner; (iv) Smith and Robinson; (v) De La Rue and Co. Ltd; (vi) Thomas Slater; (vii) The Borough Council of Bigtown; (viii) P. R. McGrath; (ix) Department of Employment; (x) Dr John Peters; (xi) F. B. O'Sullivan; (xii) 20th Century Supplies Ltd.

(*b*) Describe in detail two 'follow-up' systems which could be used to ensure that replies are received to letters sent from your office.

13

CENTRALISED SERVICES—
CALCULATIONS AND DATA PROCESSING

13.1 Introduction

Many activities in the office require calculations. There are the simple pay-roll calculations necessary to provide employees with a correct wage packet each week and complex financial calculations necessary to achieve correctly judged budgets for departments, or correctly costed goods and services.

The equipment available to assist in these calculations varies enormously. At one end of the range is the hand-operated adding-listing machine. At the other end is the computer, producing complete pay-rolls, debtors' and creditors' ledgers or scientifically simulating the activities of chemical plants still on the drawing board, from information fed into its memory.

All the information used in the office is known as data. These data have to be processed to achieve the desired result. This may be the calculation of an invoice price, or a monthly stock re-order point, or a budget telling a buyer how much he may spend in the month ahead. This range of activities is known collectively as **data processing**. Today we think of data processing chiefly as an activity performed by computers, which carry out more and more of the routine work of businesses.

13.2 Centralised and Departmental Services

Calculating services may be provided both departmentally and centrally. Clearly many simple calculations will be performed on a pad of paper by the individual requiring them. In many cases, as with simple additions, an adding-listing machine or calculator will be provided in each department. For major calculations a centralised system will be advantageous because the volume of work available will justify the purchase of more sophisticated machines, the training of specialist operators, or the purchase of a computer.

13.3 Adding-listing machines

Much of the routine numerical work in an office consists of additions and subtractions. Many of these will originally be done mentally, and will subsequently be checked by the use of an adding-listing machine. Such machines provide a printed list of the numbers pressed into the keyboard by the operator, and any subtotals requested. Earlier machines simply showed the final totals in registers on the machines. The add-lister is very convenient, because the checklist can be used to sort out any discrepancy between the total arrived at mentally and the one arrived at with the machine. It is also extremely useful in the accounting field, since bunches of invoices, credit notes and other **posting media** may be totalled before being passed to the accounting machine operator. The operator, after entering the documents, ensures that the total added to the ledger concerned does in fact agree with the total shown on the add-list clipped to the batch of documents. Any mistake in the postings is thus discovered immediately.

13.4 Ready Reckoners

For many calculations the ready reckoner is still the simplest way to arrive at the required answer. Office juniors and invoice typists engaged in regular preparation of documents involving simple price calculations often find it convenient to draw up their own ready reckoners. An odd half-hour when there is little other work to do spent in this useful way may ease pressure at busier times. A quick reference to the chart pinned over the desk will indicate the sum required to be inserted on a particular invoice. Ready reckoners available in bookshops contain an enormous number of calculations, and the reader is strongly recommended to purchase one.

13.5 Electronic Calculators

We live in an age of electronic chips, where a complex electric circuit can be built upon a 'chip' of silicon no bigger than a fingernail. The result is a whole range of electronic calculators, which can add, subtract, multiply, divide, give percentages and do other calculations in a fraction of a second. A multiplication sum involving ten digits in both the multiplier and the multipland, for example:

$$2\,786\,495\,236 \times 1\,598\,721\,686$$

would be performed in one-fifth of a second. The answers are shown in a display panel of lighted figures.

Other models of electronic calculators are available with print-out facilities instead of display panels so that a permanent record of the answers to the calculations performed is available from a roll of paper, like the tally roll of an add-listing machine. Typical business calculators for desk use are shown in Plates 16 and 17.

13.6 Punched Card Systems

Punched card systems are rapidly being replaced by computerised systems, but it is convenient to refer to them here since the punched card is one of the chief methods used to 'input' information into a computer. Basically a punched card system is one where a body of information, recorded by punched holes in manilla cards, is manipulated

Plate 16. An electronic calculator (reproduced by courtesy of Addo Ltd).

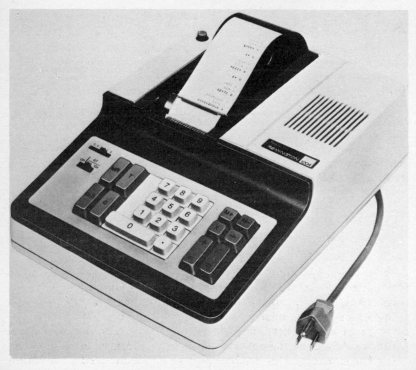

Plate 17. An electronic printing calculator (reproduced by courtesy of Sperry Rand Ltd).

and analysed by mechanical means to provide control information for management.

A punched card. A punched card consists of 80 columns of information, each column of which has twelve positions which may be punched. The surface of the card is divided into 'fields' (each consisting of one or more columns); each of these fields is a heading under which information may be analysed. Thus the day, month and year might constitute three separate fields for analysis, while customer number might be a fourth. It is a relatively simple matter to read off the information punched onto the card once the 'heading' of the field is known. Fig. 13.1 illustrates a punched card, whilst the illustration on page 218 illustrates typical fields into which the card may be divided. One corner has been cut off to prevent cards being put into a file the wrong way round.

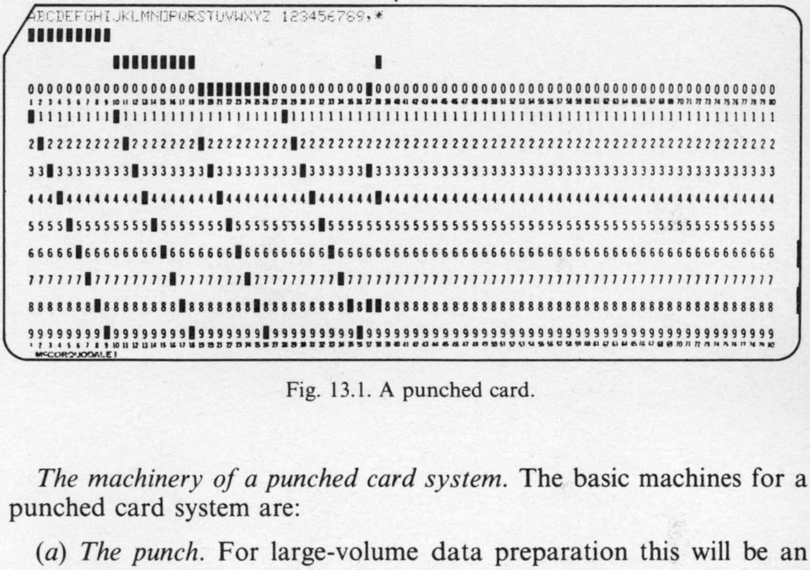

Fig. 13.1. A punched card.

The machinery of a punched card system. The basic machines for a punched card system are:

(*a*) *The punch.* For large-volume data preparation this will be an automatic machine punching holes in cards in response to keyboard depressions.

(*b*) *The verifier.* This machine checks the correctness of the punching, and today is usually automatic. It punches a notch at the end of a column which has an error in it, and a verified card with no errors is notched at the end in one of four selectable positions.

(*c*) *The sorter.* This sorts a single column at a time, the position of the holes being sensed. Similar cards are trapped automatically at an appropriate point in a 'pocket' where they collect in correct order. Successive sortings will analyse the cards to furnish the information required.

(*d*) *The tabulator.* This machine prints out the analysed information which it senses on the cards fed into it, adding up the various totals required.

13.7 Edge-punched Cards

For the small firm a variation on punched cards known as edge-punched cards provides a cheap and convenient method of analysing certain information. The thin manilla cards have ranges of information printed upon them, which can then be punched with a very accurate hand punch, through the edge of the card. For example, an estate agent may type onto the card the name and address of each applicant for housing accommodation. Around the edge of the card are printed ranges of information—for example, Bungalow, Flat, Terraced House, Semi-detached House and Detached House. The customer may be interested in a bungalow, and this section out of the range given will be clipped out. Lower down, in the price range section of the card, there may be sections: less than £15 000; £15 000–20 000, etc. If the customer is prepared to pay up to £27 000 the section which includes this price will be clipped out. By inserting wires through the cards at appropriate points all the customers interested in a type of property which has become available may be quickly discovered. Plate 18 illustrates the method of selection used by one edged-card system—the Kalamazoo system.

Edge-punched cards follow several different systems for indicating numbers. Some follow a system based on 1, 2, 4 and 8. All the numbers from 1 to 15 can be punched by combining these numbers. For example, 5 may be indicated by punching 4 and 1. Others have a grid pattern which can indicate larger numbers by punching at two points on the grid. Where the two punch marks meet on the grid is the number indicated.

13.8 Computers

In the last quarter of a century the development of computers has revolutionised office practices. A **program** of instructions is fed into the computer which enables it to process any data supplied. Thus a payroll program would enable the computer to calculate the salaries due to staff, no matter how complex the calculations required. This **data processing** can save an enormous amount of clerical effort. Whilst a detailed knowledge of computer hardware is not necessary, it is useful to be familiar with their operation and application.

The computer scheme in Fig. 13.2 shows the main components of a general computer configuration. Computers are designed for a specific set of applications, and therefore configurations may differ depending on scientific or commercial usage. To deal with differing company requirements a variety of hardware is needed. Fig. 13.2 shows a configuration appropriate to commercial applications. However, the diagram includes all the equipment for 'inputs' to the computer and

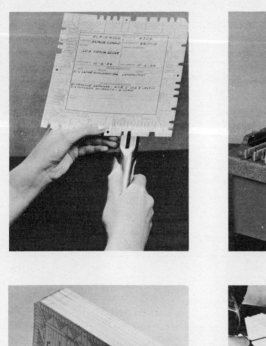

Plate 18. Edge-punched cards: punching the card (*top left*); sorting the cards (*top right*); particular cards offset by the sorting mechanism (*bottom left*); restoring cards to correct sequence (*bottom right*) (reproduced by courtesey of Kalamazoo Ltd).

'outputs' from it, and firms would purchase only those input devices and output devices which were necessary for their particular class of work. The main components are as follows:

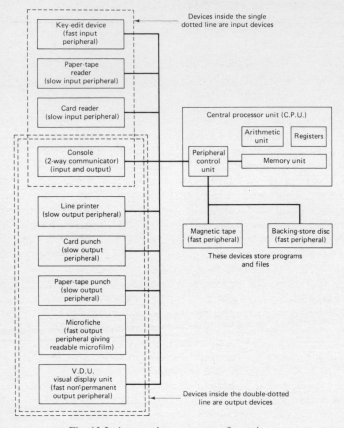

Fig. 13.2. A general computer configuration.

(*a*) *The Central Processor Unit* (*CPU*), comprising: (i) the memory unit; (ii) the arithmetic unit; (iii) the registers; (iv) the peripheral control unit (or units).

(*b*) *Slow input devices*: (i) the card reader; (ii) the paper-tape reader.

(*c*) *Fast input devices*: (i) the key edit device; (ii) magnetic tape; (iii) backing-store discs.

(*d*) Slow output devices: (i) the card punch; (ii) the paper-tape punch; (iii) the line printer.

(*e*) *Fast output devices*: (i) magnetic tape; (ii) discs; (iii) microfilm; (iv) VDUs (visual display units).

(*f*) *A communicating device*—the console. This is both a slow input device and a slow output device.

Information is fed into the computer using the input devices, but once the central processor unit has processed it that part of the information which is to be retained in the computer for temporary or permanent storage is created by the computer on magnetic tape or discs. These are fast input and output devices, usually known as **backing store** devices.

A Description of Computer Hardware

Briefly the functions of the components named above may be described as follows:

(*a*) *The Central Processor Unit.* The CPU is the main section of the computer and contained within it are the **memory unit**, the **peripheral control unit or units**, the **arithmetic unit** and the **registers**.

The memory unit of the CPU determines the power of the computer, since it is here that the actual computer programs, used for the processing of data, are stored. The central processor works so fast that it outpaces the data being fed in and the results being printed out. The trend in modern computers is to produce multi-programming machines which can handle several programs at once. While one program is inputting or outputting data, the central processor switches to another program. Thus, the core is used more efficiently.

The arithmetic unit is located in the CPU, and here the calculations such as multiplication and division are performed. The computer works on a simple current-on, current-off basis whereby 1 and 0 can be represented. **Binary arithmetic**, as the reader who knows his 'New Mathematics' will remember, is a system of arithmetic which uses only 1 and 0. All numbers can be represented by combinations of 1 and 0. Similarly, all letters can by represented by 1 and 0.

The answers, and partial answers, to the calculations are stored in the **registers** temporarily, from where they may be transferred to the memory unit for subsequent output to tape or disc storage.

Peripheral control units are designed to deal with all the ancillary equipment used for input and output of information. **Data transfer** is the name given to the movement of information over the link between the CPU and all outside components. Outside components are known as **peripherals**. The word 'periphery' means 'outside boundary' and the peripherals may be regarded as surrounding the CPU. Note that in some instances the peripheral control units are themselves peripheral to the CPU.

(*b*) *Input Peripheral Devices: Card readers and paper-tape readers.* These are slow peripherals. The transfer of data into the computer may be achieved by these two devices. Original master programs and data to be processed are punched onto cards. These are read, and converted into machine language by the card reader. A modern card reader can process up to 2000 cards per minute, each card consisting of a maximum of 80 characters—that is 160 000 characters per minute. A similar system using a paper-tape reader replaces the punched card by a punched paper tape. Once a program has been proven it is stored on a fast peripheral medium, such as magnetic tape or disc.

Key-edit device. This is a fast input device, which feeds information in by magnetic tape. The term 'edit' refers to the ability of the device to detect when an operator miskeys and feeds an error into the system.

Magnetic tape or disc. These are fast peripheral devices of several types. Their speed is commonly in the region of 80 000 characters per second for tape and 200 000 for disc. These fast media can only be used once the original data has been supplied by the slow peripheral or by the key-edit device. The fast medium then retains the more permanent data, such as files and programs, which will be required on subsequent runs. For example, on a pay-roll run the programs, personal detail files, tax tables, etc., can be held on fast peripheral media, because of the unchanging nature of the data. Details of current hours worked by employees, which vary from week to week, would have to be input weekly on slow peripherals.

(*c*) *The Console.* During running time communication can be achieved by means of the **console**, which can be used like a normal typewriter to feed instructions directly into the computer. Messages from the computer can also be received. This device is for the computer operator's use. For example, a certain program may be required and the operator will tell the computer to find it and load it into the core. The computer will notify the operator with a message such as 'Program loaded O.K.'

(*d*) *The Programs.* These consist of instructions which manipulate the data supplied. The data might be the hours worked, the rate of pay, the tax code number, and various deductions to be made from the employee's salary. The employee is represented by his clock number. The program will itself perform the calculations, to produce the net pay to which the employee is entitled.

Fig. 13.3 shows a small portion of such a pay-roll program, written in **Cobol**. Cobol is a high-level computer language. It is the most commonly used language for commercial programs. Cobol stands for Common Business Oriented Language.

```
        CALC.
                MULTIPLY RATE BY HOURS GIVING GROSS-PAY.
                IF S-F-INDICATOR=1 SUBTRACT SUPERANNUATION FROM GROSS- PAY.
                ADD TAX, NAT-INS, HSA TO TOTAL-DEDUCTS.
                SUBTRACT TOTAL-DEDUCTS FROM GROSS-PAY GIVING NET-PAY.
        PAY SLIP.
                MOVE PAY-DETAILS TO PRINT AREA.
                WRITE PAY-RECORD AFTER ADVANCING 2.
                GO TO FILE-UPDATE.
```

Fig. 13.3. A portion of a pay-roll program.

(*e*) *Output Peripheral Devices. The line printer.* The chief method of output in the final stage is the **line printer**. This prints out the result of the processed data. It is the computer's chief means of communication since it can be read by the human user. Speeds vary with the type of device but an output of 1300 lines per minute, each line having a maximum of 132 characters, is representative. Several of these components are illustrated in Plate 19. A recently developed process in multi-program computed systems is 'off-line' printing. Since the printer is much slower than the central processor unit, it is inconvenient to print directly from the processor. Instead, the processor records all its final results on a fast peripheral such as magnetic tape or disc, and these fast peripherals then pass the results to the printer when they are **'off line'** and the central processor is busy with other programs.

VDU and microfilm output. A fast method of output is the visual display unit (VDU), which shows an instantaneous picture on a television screen. This can be used directly for hotel bookings, hospital appointments, etc. If firms wish to avoid masses of bulky line-printer print-out they can have the information photographed from the VDU to give a microfilm, which can be viewed in a microfilm reader (see microfilm filing).

Minicomputers and Microcomputers

The development of silicon chip technology has made computers available much more cheaply in recent years, and the units have become so small that they can sit on a desk in an ordinary office instead of requiring special air-conditioned dust-free premises. These mini- and micro-computers (the difference is largely in the size of the memory available) are very cheap, yet will perform all the requirements of many small businesses. Input is usually achieved by a fast-input device—the floppy disquette—and instructions are given from the minicomputer console. Plate 20 shows a typical configuration in a small business office.

The Role of the Computer in Data Processing

Data have to be processed at two levels. First, there is a lower management level where many routine activities in the accounting, cost control and production control field must be carried out. Above this level, top management is faced with daunting problems affecting the conduct of the enterprise, and even the industry. The computer is a specialist machine which can perform both these types of activity well if it is properly programmed.

First, it will perform the traditional office functions—pay-roll, sales accounting, purchasing, stock control and production control—very quickly and accurately. In the past these have been treated as isolated activities and computerised individually. The more modern and sophisticated approach is to discover the links and connections between these

Plate 19. Components of a medium-sized business computer (reproduced by courtesy of International Computers Ltd).

Plate 20. A PET computer in a small office, with floppy disquette, tractor printer and VDU accessories (reproduced by courtesy of Commodore Business Machines (UK) Ltd).

individual activities. Integrated systems are now being designed which avoid the repetition of slow inputs necessary when the activities are treated separately. The computer itself determines which data are required for the separate lower-level activities, and, while performing these elementary functions, collates the information, analyses it statistically and prepares for top management an integrated report on the firm's activities. The role of the computer in data processing, at its highest level, is to alert management to the dynamic trends developing in the firm, so that corrective measures may be taken to ensure maximum efficiency.

The routine uses of a computer include:

(*a*) *The pay-roll.* The computer calculates gross pay, tax liabilities and other compulsory or voluntary payments to be deducted, and hence net pay due can be determined. It prints out statements of pay, and credit transfer slips or cash analyses.

(*b*) *Stock control.* The computer updates its records of stock as sales are made. Stock is coded with bar codings, vertical black lines arranged in patterns which can be used to give the computer and the electronic till associated with it information about the item sold, its price and stock reference number. As the customer passes the check-out point the bar code is read with an optical reader which not only rings the price up on the till but also records the sale in the stock records. The computer has already determined the optimum reorder points of all stock items, and as the stock level falls to the minimum it will print out a requisition for the Buying Department. It will also print out a stock list when requested, which can be compared at stocktaking time with the actual physical stock, to determine losses due to pilfering, staff theft, breakages and other wastage. Plate 21 shows a typical bar code.

Plate 21. A bar code for stocktaking purposes (reproduced by courtesy of Spicer-Cowan Ltd).

(*c*) *Sales accounts records.* The many necessary features of any sales accounting system can be programmed into a computer. Thus debtors' ledgers will be maintained, overdue debtors pinpointed, and credit controls may be established to ensure that debtors do not order more than can be safely permitted.

(*d*) *Costing and budgetary controls.* The chief features of these systems, designed to control costs and to reveal where planned expenditures are being exceeded, can be programmed into a computer. The computer will then alert management when actual performance varies from planned performance, so that corrective action may be taken.

(*e*) *Production planning.* It often happens in production that a delay in the arrival of a particular component, or a breakdown in a particular section of the work, interrupts the planned programme. Re-scheduling of the work becomes necessary and a new **critical path** has to be decided upon. A critical path is the shortest path to be followed in production to ensure completion of the project, whatever it may be. A computer programmed to make decisions about such matters will enable management to decide the best procedure when any hitch or breakdown requires plans to be reassessed.

Advantages and Disadvantages of a Computer

The advantages of computerisation may be listed as follows:

(*a*) Very fast operation at electronic speeds.

(*b*) Accuracy of the figures derived.

(*c*) Reduction of routine activities saves labour at lower levels.

(*d*) Improved management control because management is more fully informed.

The disadvantages are:

(*a*) A period of upheaval is inevitable and as much as two years may be necessary before the full advantages are revealed. During this time unskilled and semi-skilled staff may be displaced and computer-orientated staff may have to be employed or trained.

(*b*) Capital outlay is considerable, and there is a risk of obsolescence if forward planning is disregarded.

13.9 Points to Think About and Discuss

(*a*) Computers are popularly believed to cause unemployment by taking over work formerly performed by clerical staff. Discuss the implications for (i) the employees, (ii) the firm and, (iii) the nation of a general adoption of computers.

(*b*) In the last few years the adding-listing machine has largely replaced the adding machine. It is confidently predicted that the electronic printing calculator will replace the electronic calculator. What are the advantages of having a printed record of the calculations you have performed?

13.10 Rapid Revision

Cover page with a sheet of paper and uncover one question at a time.

Answers	Questions
—	1. What is the main part of a computer?
1. The Central Processor Unit (CPU).	2. What does it contain?
2. (a) The memory unit; (b) the arithmetic unit; (c) the registers; (d) the peripheral control unit or units.	3. What name is given to a body of instructions fed into the computer?
3. A program.	4. How is the program fed into the computer?
4. An input device, either a card reader or a paper-tape reader or a key-edit device, reads the program and turns it into machine language.	5. What is the basis on which a computer works?
5. A simple current-on, current-off system which represents 1 and 0.	6. What arithmetical system is used?
6. The binary system.	7. What is a peripheral unit?
7. It is a unit outside the CPU, standing, as it were, on the periphery or boundary of the system.	8. What are the two fast peripheral devices?
8. Magnetic tape and disc.	9. How fast do these peripherals work?
9. Between 80 000 and 200 000 characters per second.	10. What is the function of the fast peripherals?
10. To store the more permanent data which will be needed in later runs, and load them into core as and when required.	11. What is the console?
11. A device for communicating with the computer and receiving messages from it.	12. What is the final output of a computer most likely to be?
12. A print-out by the line printer of the processed data.	13. How fast does it print out?
13. Commonly at about 1300 lines per minute.	14. Go over the page again until you feel you are sure of the answers.

Exercises Set 13

1. What office procedures require calculations? How may these calculations be performed?

2. Write fully about three machines for making calculations.

3. The following table shows the sales of coal and coke in January:

	Coal (tonnes)	Coke (tonnes)
Week 1	1850	3836
Week 2	1720	3725
Week 3	1964	4426
Week 4	1874	3526

(*a*) What were the total sales of each commodity? (*b*) What were the average weekly sales of each commodity? (*c*) If coal sells at £28 per tonne and coke at £31 per tonne, what was the value of the sales of each commodity in the first week?

4. Name four simple books or pieces of equipment which help with the adding, subtracting, or multiplication of sums of money.

5. Your employer is considering purchasing a calculator. Supply the answers to the following questions in memorandum form: (*a*) In what specific ways will a calculator be of use in the office? (*b*) What is the difference between an adding-listing machine and a calculator?

6. Should calculation services be provided departmentally or centrally? Outline circumstances where each of these two alternative systems might be advantageous.

7. What is a punched card? How is it used in business systems?

8. 'Edge-punched cards combine a card record system with a rapid process of sorting.' (*a*) Explain the meaning of this statement; (*b*) state the uses of edge-punched cards; (*c*) describe briefly any other methods which are available for sorting information in offices.

9. What is a microcomputer? For which types of business is it suitable and what functions can it perform?

10. You are employed by a large manufacturing company which intends to computerise a number of office routines. This change will have a considerable effect upon some of the procedures used in the sales, purchasing, accounting, and production departments.
   What action should be taken, and by whom, in order to ensure: (*a*) that all the staff concerned are made fully aware of the implications of the change before it takes place; (*b*) that the details of the new procedures are kept in the minds of staff after the change?

11. What are the advantages of using computers in office work?

12. Explain briefly the operations performed by an electronic computer.

13. Electronic computers are being used increasingly in offices. Give a list of office functions for which a computer can be used and outline the advantages of using a computer as compared with other methods.

14. What factors would you take into consideration when selecting the most appropriate means for performing calculations in your office?

15. (*a*) From the edge-punched card shown on p. 218 state the numbers represented by the slots for: (i) product; (ii) size; (iii) pack; (iv) customer classification; (v) area; (vi) factory; (vii) transport.
   (*b*) Discuss the uses and advantages of edge-punched cards.

16. (*a*) In connection with computers: (i) what are input media; (ii) what does 'off-line' mean; (iii) what is magnetic tape used for?
   (*b*) Read the punched card shown below and write down the information given in the 'fields' for: (i) Account No.; (ii) Area; (iii) Date; (iv) Order No.; (v) Product No.; (vi) Quantity sold; (vii) Invoice No.; (viii) Rate per item.

(*c*) Calculate the amounts for gross value, trade discount, and net value. The trade discount is 25 per cent. Apart from trade discount there are no other deductions to be taken into account in arriving at the net value.

(*d*) Why are the top right-hand corners of punched cards cut off, as shown in the illustration below?

14

THE ACCOUNTS DEPARTMENT

14.1 The Functions of the Accounts Department

The accounts department is one of the most important departments in any firm, and the accountant is always a senior member of staff, often with a seat on the board of the company. In earlier times accounting was chiefly concerned with keeping a record of the transactions between the firm and other firms. Debtors' and creditors' accounts were kept, using a system of **double-entry book-keeping**. Although these records are still very important, the work of the accountant has extended to cover every aspect of the enterprise. The accounts department will account to the following:

(a) The individual employee for wages, expenses, commission, etc.

(b) The supplier for goods and services supplied.

(c) The management for the profitability or otherwise of the enterprise.

(d) The Government for its share of the profits (corporation tax or income tax) and for value added tax (see Chapter 15), national health payments, etc.

(e) Outside institutions where it collects funds on their behalf—for example, contributions to charitable bodies like Dr Barnardo's Homes are often deducted by firms from employees' salaries.

Within the firm the **cost accountant** will prepare costing figures which not only show what units of production are costing but also show future **cost estimates**. As production proceeds a check on actual costs against estimated costs can be made. If actual costs are greater than estimated costs an enquiry can be made into the reasons for the difference, and corrective measures can be taken.

Similarly, the financial accountant will prepare **budgets** for each department's expenditure and will watch to see whether a department is overspending. An urgent memo to the head of the department will lead to a reduction in expenditure in line with the budget of money available.

14.2 Double-entry Book-keeping

The accounts department keeps its records by a system known as double-entry book-keeping. This system was developed in the Middle Ages by the merchants of Lombardy in northern Italy, who later gave

(1) Every transaction has an original Document

Invoices from other firms, all different shapes and sizes, our Purchases

Second Copies of our own invoices, our Sales to other firms

Credit Notes from other firms, our purchases returned

Second Copies of our Credit Notes, sales returned to us

Invoices for Assets Bought

Letters about Errors

Bankruptcy Notices

Our Statements — Recd. with thanks

And cheques from the Debtors

Other Firms' Statements

And our cheques

Petty Cash vouchers

(2) These documents are entered in the Books of Original Entry

Purchases Day Book

Sales Day Book

Purchases Returns Book

Sales Returns Book

Journal Proper

Cash Book

Petty Cash Book

Credit the Cash Book

(3) These books are then posted to the Ledger—

Debit the Purchases A/c with Total

Credit the Personal A/cs of Creditors

Debit the Personal A/cs of Debtors

Credit the Sales A/c with Total

Debit the Returns in the Creditors' A/cs

Credit the Purchases Returns A/c with Total

Debit the Sales Returns A/c with Total

Credit the Returns in the Debtors' A/cs

Debit the A/c Required

Credit the A/c Required

Debit the Personal & Nominal A/cs

Credit the Personal & Nominal A/cs

Debit the Nominal & Personal A/cs

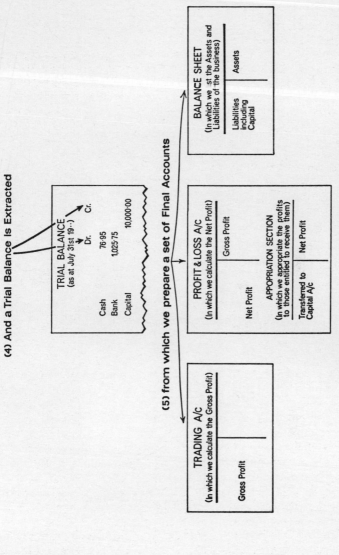

(4) And a Trial Balance Is Extracted

TRIAL BALANCE
(as at July 31st 19-·)

	Dr.	Cr.
Cash	76·95	
Bank	1,025·75	
Capital		10,000·00

(5) from which we prepare a set of Final Accounts

TRADING A/c
(In which we calculate the Gross Profit)

Gross Profit

PROFIT & LOSS A/c
(In which we calculate the Net Profit)

Gross Profit

Net Profit

APPROPRIATION SECTION
(In which we appropriate the profits to those entitled to receive them)

Transferred to Capital A/c

Net Profit

BALANCE SHEET
(In which we st the Assets and Liabilities of the business)

Liabilities including Capital

Assets

Fig. 14.1. Double-entry book-keeping.

their name to Lombard Street, the banking centre of the City of London. Fig. 14.1 illustrates the system, and although it is an involved diagram, the reader will find it repays close study, using the following notes as a guide:

(*a*) *Every transaction has an original document*. These documents, many of which are described in this book (for a full description, see *Book-keeping Made Simple*), may be:

(i) Invoices	(v) Statements
(ii) Debit notes	(vi) Receipts
(iii) Credit notes	(vii) Petty cash vouchers
(iv) Cheques	(viii) One of many other documents.

Whenever any business transaction takes place which requires an accounting record a document will be prepared and a copy passed to the accounts department.

(*b*) *These documents are then entered in the books of original entry*. Books of original entry are often called **Day Books**, because we enter items in them day by day in chronological order. The French word for a day book is 'Journal', so some firms call them Journals. The most common in use are:

(i) A Purchases Day Book
(ii) A Sales Day Book
(iii) A Purchases Returns Day Book
(iv) A Sales Returns Day Book
(v) A Journal Proper (this is used for all the rarer entries, like dishonoured cheques, bad debts, purchases of assets, etc.)
(vi) Cash Books
(vii) Petty Cash Books.

(*c*) *The day books are then posted to the Ledger*. The Ledger is the most important book of account. It consists of a collection of pages, each one of which is an 'account' of the firm's transactions with some person, or firm, or good. A simple creditor's account is illustrated on page 37. The detailed work of posting Ledgers can be tedious, and mechanised or computerised systems reduce the labour involved. It is possible to learn to operate book-keeping machines and microcomputers in as little as two days.

(*d*) *A trial balance of the Ledger is then extracted*. This checks the accuracy of the book-keeping and marshals the accounts ready for the preparation of the final accounts of the business.

(*e*) *The final accounts are prepared*. The final accounts are the trading account, which is used to discover the trading profit, and the profit and loss account, which is used to decide the final **net profit**. The net profit is the clear profit made after all expenses have been deducted.

When the final accounts have been prepared and the profit has been added to the owner's capital account (or the loss has been deducted from the owner's capital account) the accountant has established what degree of success the business has achieved. All he needs to do now is to summarise the final position of the business by drawing up a balance sheet which shows the assets and liabilities of the firm. This is the general pattern of double-entry book-keeping.

14.3 Simple Accounting Records—Simultaneous Entries

One of the most time-saving and ingenious ways of keeping records is the 'simultaneous record' system. Many firms now produce this type of system, which is particularly useful for the smaller business. The most famous name is probably Kalamazoo. The system described and illustrated in Fig. 14.2 by kind permission of Kalamazoo Ltd is called the 'Compact System'.

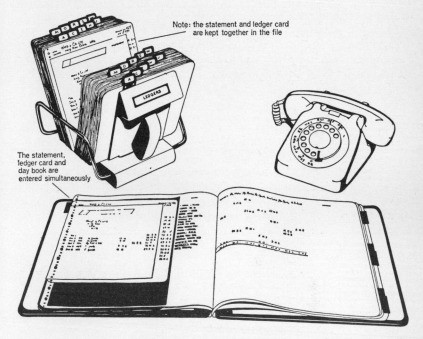

Fig. 14.2. Records made simultaneously (reproduced by courtesy of Kalamazoo Ltd).

The basic idea of the system is the simultaneous entry of invoices in the Day Book, the Ledger, and also on the statement. A statement is a document sent out at the end of the month to all debtors, requesting them to settle their accounts. The Day Book takes the form of loose-leaf sheets housed in a binder. The same binder can hold both the Purchases and Sales Journals, and the Returns Journals.

The interesting feature of the system is the line of holes punched down the edge of the Day Book pages, which enable a flat board called a **collator** to be secured under the Day Book page by the studs which stick up through the holes down the edge. The page is raised a little, the collator slipped underneath so that its studs stick up through the holes, and a sheet of carbon paper is placed on top.

The Ledger card and the statement, which are always kept together in a 'Mini-Tray', are now positioned over the Day Book page so that what is written will occupy the next clean line on all three records. The invoice details are then written, and simultaneously bring the statement, the Ledger card, and the Day Book up to date. The Ledger card and statement are replaced in the tray, the next account due to be entered is selected and positioned, and a further entry is made from the next invoice. Checks are built into the system to ensure that the total value of invoices received or despatched that day equals the total value entered in the Day Books. The Day Book then provides the figures for posting to the nominal accounts, and also any analysis figures required about particular departments.

The Ledger cards, or accounts, have already been posted, and no errors in posting can have occurred, while the statements are kept up to date and are ready for despatch on the last day of the month.

It is difficult to imagine a more simple or efficient system.

A further example of these methods is given on pages 264–5.

14.4 Mechanised Accounting

In order to speed up the work of the accounts department an enormous range of book-keeping machines, accounting machines, data processing equipment and computers is available. The ingenuity of these machines seems endless and some firms with the most advanced techniques literally know by the end of each working day how much profit the enterprise has made during the day. The work of punched card systems and computers has already been described (see pages 206–15).

Although mechanical systems of book-keeping are still in use, the advantages of computers and minicomputers is such that new installations are invariably electronic.

14.5 Statements of Account

Although it has many functions, an accounts department is particularly engaged in collecting accounts receivable and paying accounts due. The document rendered when an account is payable is called a 'Statement of Account'. Most firms render accounts on the first day of the month so that each account rendered includes all items up to the last day of the preceding month. Others carry out what is known as **'cyclical billing'**. This involves spreading the work out over the whole month, so that each day about 3 per cent of the customers' accounts are rendered. This also tends to spread the receipt of cash payments more evenly over the month.

Discounts

The chief types of discount met with in business are **cash discounts**, **settlement discounts**, **quantity discounts** and **trade discounts**.

Cash discounts and settlement discounts are very similar. Cash discount is given to customers who pay 'prompt cash'. Settlement discount is given to debtors who pay promptly for their goods when the time for payment arrives. It is a great inconvenience to a businessman to have debtors who are slow in settling their accounts, because it

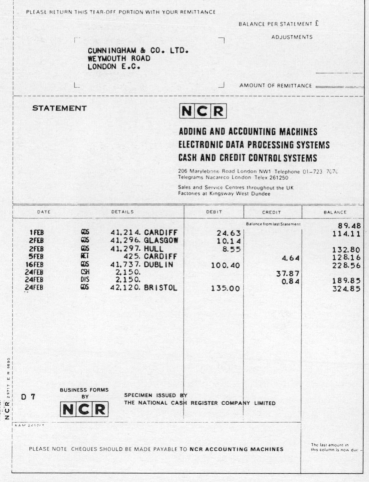

Fig. 14.3. A computerised statement of account (reproduced by courtesy of NCR Ltd).

means that his capital is being used by somebody else. To encourage prompt payment a cash discount is offered. Naturally this means a smaller total profit than he would otherwise earn, but it may be cheaper to give this discount than to allow debts to accumulate and perhaps suffer bad debts.

The other types of discount are not connected with the payment of accounts, but are concerned with purchasing and sales policies. They are dealt with more appropriately elsewhere (see pages 292 and 295).

Fig. 14.3 illustrates a computerised statement of account. The reader who is not very familiar with accounting should note that the debit column indicates that the customer has received goods, and the balance owing increases by the amount debited to his account. The credit column indicates that the customer has given value, perhaps returns, or cash paid, and the outstanding balance has therefore decreased at this point.

The customer wishing to claim discount will write on the account—less discount £x—and will deduct it. He will then pay the net amount by cheque, or credit transfer, or in some other way.

14.6 Credit Control

Many small businessmen display signs saying 'Please do not ask for credit, as a refusal may offend'. For many firms, especially those in very competitive trades, the granting of credit is inevitable in modern conditions. Cash payments are very inconvenient; credit enables a host of transactions to be settled with a single payment. Some credit enthusiasts are beginning to talk of 'the cashless society', where people do not need to carry cash about with them at all, merely signing their names for fares, goods, meals, theatre and cinema tickets, etc. Whether we shall ever reach this idyllic situation seems rather doubtful. At least it is essential for all accounts departments to exercise strict **credit control** policies.

The following points may be listed as important features of a credit control system:

(*a*) Always take up references on new customers before granting credit. A banker's reference, or a reference from a trade association or professional body, is easily obtained by credit-worthy customers.

(*b*) Exercise strict control of credit levels until a customer is well known and well regarded. A customer who wishes to exceed his credit level for some reason is free to ask that the level be raised, but goods ordered in disregard of the agreed level will not be supplied, except on COD (cash on delivery) terms.

(*c*) An overdue account should be placed on a 'stop' list. Coloured flashes are sometimes used, particularly on visi-index systems, to indicate a 'stop' on an account.

(*d*) Similar 'flashes' may be used to indicate habitually slow payers.

Here supplies will be stopped whenever shortages arise, preference being given to customers who pay promptly.

(e) Persistent follow-up of overdue accounts is essential. The first statement should be followed by a copy statement, and then by a personal letter or telephone call. When all else has been tried legal action to secure payment may be taken. This may result in the debtor being bankrupted—a legal process which sets the debtor free from debt, but only after his effects have been sold to pay as much as possible of the sums owed. He is also prevented from obtaining any further goods on credit. Some firms, known as **debt factors**, buy up the bad debts of other firms, usually for about half their value. By making appropriate arrangements to collect the money owed, often by instalments, they eventually make a profit on their purchase. A businessman who is too busy to collect such debts himself, and who feels that legal action will injure his goodwill in the locality, may think this assignment of debts to a debt factor the best way to 'cut his losses'.

(f) In the case of limited companies particular care is necessary in granting credit. The only really safe way to deal with a limited company is to make a preliminary examination of its affairs by consulting the records at Companies' House, in London and Cardiff. These will indicate the size, profitability and rate of growth of the company. If the records are not kept up to date, this fact alone is enough to create suspicion in the mind of a shrewd accountant, and credit should not be granted.

Hire purchase is a rather special type of credit which is dealt with elsewhere in this book (see page 320).

14.7 Internal and External Audits

Auditing is the systematic checking of accounting activities. Internal audits are those conducted within the firm by employees of the accounts department called auditors. External audits are those carried out by an independent firm, appointed as required by Section 159 of the *Companies Acts*. This requires all companies to appoint auditors, and pay them an adequate remuneration for checking that all aspects of the firm's accounts have been properly kept, and that they comply with the accounting requirements of the *Companies Acts*, 1948–81.

A basic principle of auditing is that a thorough check of all aspects of the firm's accounting should be made from time to time, without prior warning being given. This makes it impossible for staff to cover up improper practices before the auditors arrive. Often, where a firm is large, investigations are made on a 'random sample' basis. This means that some sampling method—for example, drawing names out of a hat—will decide which departments are subject to rigorous checks, and which to less thorough investigations.

14.8 Points to Think About and Discuss

(*a*) Two young men, who know nothing about accounting, are proposing to set up in business, making a technical product which they are competent to produce. They ask you to advise them about a system of accounts. They believe the turnover will not exceed £30 000 in the first two years, and they have limited capital available. What alternative solutions are available to their accounting problems?

(*b*) The accountant has many responsibilities; to the management, to the creditors, to the employees. Consider these three responsibilities in detail, listing the headings under which these different parties will hold him accountable. Do their interests conflict?

14.9 Rapid Revision

Cover the page with a sheet of paper and uncover one question at a time.

Answers	Questions
—	1. What system of book-keeping is used in an accounts department?
1. Double-entry book-keeping.	2. Who first devised this system?
2. The merchants of Lombardy, in northern Italy, who gave their name to Lombard Street in London.	3. Which is the most important book of account?
3. The Ledger.	4. What is a trial balance?
4. It is a means of checking the accuracy of the book-keeping.	5. What is meant by a 'simultaneous records' system of book-keeping?
5. It is any system where the original document, the day book and the Ledger card are prepared at the same time.	6. Which firm is particularly famous for these 'simultaneous record' systems?
6. Kalamazoo Ltd.	7. Why does book-keeping lend itself particularly to mechanisation and computerisation?
7. Because: (*a*) the book-keeping processes are logical and simple; (*b*) the work is repetitive and easy programs can be devised; (*c*) the controls which can be built into the system are an enormous advantage to the accountant.	8. How can an accountant establish a good system of credit control?
8. By insisting upon: (*a*) references being taken up on all new customers; (*b*) credit levels being set on all customers until they are well-known and respected clients; (*c*) overdue accounts being placed on a 'stop' list; (*d*) persistent follow-ups on overdue accounts; (*e*) careful control of new accounts with limited companies.	9. Go over the page again until you feel you are sure of the answers.

Exercises Set 14

1. Select the correct word or phrase from the word list to complete the sentences given below.

(*a*) All accounts departments keep records based upon a system of .... book-keeping.

(*b*) Every transaction commences with the preparation of a business ....

(*c*) A document made out when goods are returned is a ....

(*d*) When documents arrive they are usually recorded in books of ....

(*e*) The French word for 'day book' is ......

(*f*) A trial balance checks up on the accuracy of the entries made in the ......

(*g*) When two or three records are made up at the same time—for example, the statement, ledger card and sales day book—these are called .... systems of accounting.

(*h*) Kalamazoo is the name of the firm which produces many .... for the small firm.

(*i*) A microcomputer uses circuits printed on small ....

(*j*) A discount taken by a customer who pays his account in the normal way directly it is due, is called a ...... discount.

Word list: document, journal, Ledger, settlement, simplified business systems, original entry, double entry, silicon chips, credit note, simultaneous entry.

2. Select the correct answer from the groups (i)-(iv) in each section below.

(*a*) A monthly statement is: (i) a regular report made to the police about security measures; (ii) a balance of all the accounts in the Ledger; (iii) a request for settlement of an account that has now fallen due; (iv) a notification to an employee of the salary paid into his account by credit transfer.

(*b*) A debt factor is: (i) a person who makes a debtor bankrupt when he fails to pay; (ii) a man who buys up debts and collects them in the best way he can; (iii) a fraction, payable on a debt by an insolvent debtor; (iv) a part of a factory handling hire purchase orders only.

(*c*) Cyclical billing is: (i) a system of rendering accounts in rotation a few each day so that a backlog of work does not build up in the accounts department; (ii) the name used in the hire purchase trade for agreements dealing with the purchase of bicycles; (iii) a rotary index which enables sales Ledger accounts to be found quickly; (iv) a type of bill-hook, or sickle, sold by ironmongers for use in country activities.

(*d*) An audit is: (i) a hearing aid; (ii) a device which listens to electronic impulses in computerised accounting and picks out overdue or fraudulent accounts; (iii) a man who checks book-keeping records; (iv) a systematic check on accounting records to detect defalcations.

3. (*a*) What is a statement of account? (*b*) Who sends it to whom and why? (*c*) From what book-keeping records are the figures taken to complete this document? (*d*) Where will the document eventually be filed?

4. The management of a medium-sized firm, using traditional book-keeping methods, is thinking of purchasing a computer. Describe briefly the type of work this machine will perform and the advantages likely to be derived from its purchase.

5. Your firm, quite a small one, has been doing its accounts by hand. A salesman has tried to sell your employers a microcomputer. Another salesman has recommended a 3-in-1 system on billing boards.

Your employer asks you whether you know anything about either of these and asks you to write out some notes stating how both types of equipment could be used. Set out your notes in the form of a simple report.

6. What is meant by 'internal audit'? How can the expense of auditing accounts be justified?

7. You are asked to take charge of petty cash controlled by the *imprest system*, and to record receipts and payments in a Petty Cash Book, *using analysis columns*. Explain clearly and fully what is meant by the words in italics.

8. (*a*) Office accounting procedures have become increasingly computerised in recent years. Explain the advantages which are obtained from computerisation and illustrate your answer by reference to one particular office routine; (*b*) what factors should be considered before deciding whether any given office procedure ought to be computerised?

9. Write short notes about the following: (*a*) the central processor; (*b*) off-line printing; (*c*) electronic printing calculators; (*d*) auditors.

10. What are 'bar codes' in the retail trade? How do they assist traders as far as (*i*) till records and (*ii*) stocktaking are concerned?

11. Why is it important to keep overdue accounts to a minimum? What steps should be taken when accounts are outstanding for a long period?

12. Outline the stages of credit control likely to be exercised by an accountant over transactions with a new customer, Bigorder Ltd.

VALUE ADDED TAX

15.1 What is Value Added Tax?

On 1st April, 1973, a new taxation system was introduced in the United Kingdom, replacing two other forms of taxation, purchase tax and selective employment tax, which were abolished on that date. The new tax was designed partly to bring the United Kingdom taxation system into closer alignment with Common Market systems, but it has also spread taxation over a wider range of consumer products, making taxation fairer than in the past. The disadvantage of the new tax system is that it requires about 1 500 000 businesses, many of them quite small, to keep VAT records. This has meant that VAT routines have become part of office practice for every firm in the country.

The principle of VAT is that tax is levied on the value added to goods at every stage as they pass from the natural raw material stage to the finished product, and then onwards to the final consumer. Every middleman along the way buys goods and uses services which have already had some tax levied upon them. When he in turn sells goods or provides services, he levies tax on the price he charges his customers. The amount he is liable to pay over to Customs is the difference between his 'output tax' levied on customers and the 'input tax' levied upon him by his suppliers. It is proportional to the value added.

Table 15.1. Calculations—Value Added Tax

Business	Cost price free of tax	Sale price free of tax	Value added	Final charge to customer (incl. 10% tax)	Input tax	Output tax	Tax payable
	£	£	£	£	£	£	£
1. Farmer	0	200 (tree trunk)	200	220	0	20	20
2. Sawmill Co.	200	500 (sawn planks)	300	550	20	50	30
3. Furniture Manufacturer	500	3000 (coffee tables)	2500	3300	50	300	250
4. Retailer	3000	5000	2000	5500	300	500	200

Imagine an oak tree cut down in a farmer's field, taken to a sawmill and cut into planks, sold to a manufacturer and turned into 500 coffee tables eventually retailed at £11 each including tax. The list in Table 15.1 of values added, etc., might be calculated. Tax has been levied at 10 per cent.

The effect of the tax is that the final consumers pay a total price of £5500, of which £5000 is the true value of the coffee tables they bought and £500 is tax. This £500 will be accounted for as shown in the tax payable column of Table 15.1.

15.2 Office Activities made Necessary by Value Added Tax

A businessman must perform the following activities to comply with the regulations for the new tax:

(*a*) Complete and send off to the Customs and Excise authorities a registration form VAT 1, which registers the business as a 'Taxable Person'.

(*b*) Record his outputs. These are the charges for goods and services which he makes to his customers, and to which he adds the tax payable to the customer. This enables him to calculate his *output tax* for any tax period.

(*c*) Record his inputs. These are the charges made to him by his suppliers of goods and services. The tax charged to him by these suppliers is called **input tax**.

(*d*) Complete his VAT return (Form VAT 100) at intervals, and account for the tax due.

(*e*) Keep records and accounts that are adequate for these purposes.

An explanation of these items in greater detail is given below.

Registration Form VAT 1

Everyone carrying on a business after 1st October, 1972, whose taxable outputs (i.e. charges for goods and services supplied to customers) are likely to exceed £15 000 per annum must complete a form VAT 1. This makes the individual, firm or company a 'taxable person' under the regulations. He is then required to act virtually as the collecting agent of the Customs and Excise, charging his customers tax on goods and services supplied, and remitting it (less any tax he is entitled to recoup on inputs) to the department. A person whose business is so small that the turnover is not more than £15 000 need not be registered, and all his output will be exempt. He does not charge his customers tax but is not entitled to deduct the tax he pays on goods and services received. He is therefore very much like a consumer, paying tax on all goods and services he receives.

Output Records and the Rate of Tax

Every 'taxable person' must keep records of the goods and services he supplies to his customers, and must add to the charges made the

SALES INVOICE No. 74   14 August 1979
To A Retailer Ltd.
48 North Road, London N12 5NA.
From: Foundation Trading (UK) Ltd.
Bowman Street, Chester.   VAT Regd. No. 987 6543 21
Sale

Quantity	Description and Price	Amount exclusive of VAT	VAT Rate	VAT Net
		£	%	£
6	Radios, SW14 at £21.30	127.80		
12	Record Players P38 at £9.80	117.60		
6	Amplifiers J27 at £11.80	70.80		
		316.20	15	45.06*
	Delivery (strictly net)	6.00	15	0.90
Terms: Cash Discount of 5% if paid within 14 days		322.20		45.96
	VAT	£45.96		
Tax Point: 14/8/1979	TOTAL	£368.16		

*Calculated on the discounted price.

Fig. 15.1. Illustration of a tax invoice.

correct rate of tax. Tax was originally chargeable at 10 per cent, but is now charged at 15 per cent (the standard rate) on all goods. The multi-rate system in use earlier was found to be very inconvenient.

Certain goods and services are taxable, but at the zero rate. These include food, water, books and newspapers, items for the blind, fuel and power, building work, export services, transport and drugs supplied on prescriptions. It might seem pointless to say an item is taxable and then tax it at the zero rate, but in fact this enables a businessman who is not charging his customers tax on his outputs to reclaim the tax on his inputs, which he had paid to suppliers. There is a class of **exempt goods and services**, which are not taxed at all. These include the leasing of land and buildings, insurance, banking, finance, postal services and lotteries. The suppliers of these services do not need to register or keep records, but they are unable to claim back any tax paid on inputs.

The final effect of keeping 'output records' is that the businessman is able to calculate the total tax which he has added to his customers' statements, and which he must account for to the Customs and Excise authorities.

Input Records

A taxable person who is collecting tax from his customers as in (*b*) above, does not have to pay the full amount over to the Customs and Excise. He is entitled to deduct from the sums collected as 'output tax', the total sums paid to his own suppliers. These are revealed by keeping 'input records' which show the value of goods and services supplied to him by other firms, and the tax that these firms have charged him— his 'input tax'.

The Tax Return (Form VAT 100)

The taxable person must render a return of the tax outputs and inputs of his business and pay tax every three months. The three-monthly intervals arc known as 'tax periods' and the return and any tax due must be sent in within one month of the end of the tax period. A special tax period of only one month is allowed where a taxable person feels sure that his 'tax inputs' will exceed his 'tax outputs' in the usual course of events. For example, a small grocer selling zero-rated goods might be entitled to regular refunds of tax from the Customs and Excise. It would be hard on such small businessmen if they had to wait for three months to recover tax paid on inputs.

A typical extract from the return might look like this:

Output tax for period		26 323.10
Tax on imported goods		974.40
Underpaid tax from previous period		196.70
Total tax due		27 494.20
Less		
Input tax for period	23 649.60	
Tax overpaid previously	None	
		23 649.60
Net tax payable		3 844.60

Where the input tax exceeded the output tax the difference between the two figures would be 'Net tax refundable by Customs and Excise' and not 'Net tax payable'.

Accounting Records

The introduction of VAT required the redesign of many business forms and book-keeping rulings, which needed to take account of the new system. These rulings are improved from time to time, and the reader is urged to consult his supplier for appropriate rulings.

15.3 VAT Calculations

In 1979 the Chancellor of the Exchequer raised the rate of VAT to 15 per cent on all goods, and abolished the multiple rates which had been used earlier. This is a relatively easy figure to calculate, but in these days of cheap electronic calculators most businesses use a calculator anyway. For the benefit of students the following sample calculations may be helpful.

(1) *To add 15 per cent VAT to find output prices*
Take the desired selling price, say £12

$$15\% \text{ of } £12 = \frac{15}{100} \times £12 = \frac{£180}{100} = £1.80$$

$$\therefore \text{ Selling price with tax} = £13.80$$

(2) *To reduce a selling price to the net of tax price*
This calculation is used when the businessman knows the total sales including VAT for the day, and wishes to calculate the VAT element and the net of tax sales figure.

Suppose daily takings are £274.50.

This includes 15 per cent VAT, so it is 115 per cent of the net-of-tax takings figure. The VAT element is therefore

$$\frac{15}{115} \times £274.50$$

$$= \frac{3}{23} \times £274.50$$

$$= \frac{£823.50}{23}$$

$$= £35.80$$

$$\therefore \text{ Sales net of tax} = £274.50 - £35.80$$

$$= £238.70$$

Check. To check the correctness of this calculation, take the sales net of tax figure

	£238.70
Add 15% = 15 × 2.387	= 35.80
This gives the 'Daily Takings'	= £274.50

15.4 Rapid Revision

Cover the following page with a sheet of paper and uncover one question at a time.

Answers	Questions
—	1. What is value added tax?
1. It is a tax which replaced purchase tax and selective employment tax.	2. What is the basis of the tax?
2. It is levied on the value added to goods at each stage of manufacture and distribution.	3. Who is liable to pay this tax?
3. The final consumer actually pays, but the tax is collected from any individual or firm which is a 'taxable person' under the regulations.	4. Who is a 'taxable person'?
4. Any individual, partnership or corporation which supplies goods and services worth more than £15000 per year, or who voluntarily registers.	5. What are the duties of a 'taxable person'?
5. (a) To register on form VAT 1. (b) To record his 'outputs' and charge tax on them to his customers. This gives his 'output tax'. (c) To record his 'inputs' and hence calculate his 'input tax'. (d) To render a return each quarter, and remit any tax payable. (e) To keep proper accounting records.	6. When is tax payable?
6. When 'output tax' exceeds 'input tax'.	7. When is tax refundable?
7. When 'input tax' exceeds 'output tax'.	8. What are the rates of tax?
8. (a) Standard rate = 15%. (b) Zero rate = 0%.	9. What fraction must be deducted from 'gross takings' to give the tax charged?
9. 15% Rate = $\frac{15}{115} = \frac{3}{23}$.	10. Go over the page again until you feel sure of the answers.

Exercises Set 15

1. Rule up an invoice similar to the one on page 233. The supplier is R. Montague Ltd, 24 High Road, Sleighton, Suffolk. The customer is R. Jones, 14 Hill Road, Bemfleet, Essex. Use today's date. Terms Net. Enter the following items on the invoice:

    200 large folders @ £1.50 each. VAT rate 15 per cent
    500 small folders @ £0.75 each. VAT rate 15 per cent
    20 books (*How to run a small business*) @ £3.50. VAT rate zero.

2. A shopkeeper's takings (all his goods being charged to consumers with VAT at 15 per cent) were as follows: Monday £289.50, Tuesday £346.50, Wednesday £115.45 Thursday £186.60, Friday £376.70, Saturday £396.45. Calculate: (a) his total takings; (b) his output tax; (c) his net-of-tax takings.

3. A small businessman is supplied with goods valued at £5780 in a given tax period. This figure is increased by 15 per cent VAT. His sales during the same period totalled £11 285, according to his till rolls, and this figure included VAT at 15 per cent charged to customers. Calculate the tax payable to Customs and Excise.

4. A grocer only deals in goods charged at the zero rate, but pays VAT on many items supplied to him. During the tax month of July he pays tax on goods supplied to him worth £4800, net of tax. What sum will pass between the grocer and the Customs and Excise in respect of this transaction and who will pay whom? (VAT 15 per cent.)

5. A professional man is told by the Customs and Excise authorities that his profession is exempt from VAT. What are the likely effects of this upon him? In your answer mention the following matters: (*a*) charges to be made for VAT to his customers; (*b*) registration on form VAT 1; (*c*) charges made to him by his suppliers.

16

THE CASHIER'S DEPARTMENT

16.1 Legal Tender

In every society, except the most primitive, some form of money is in use. In earlier times the majority of goods were bartered; that is, exchanged for one another. Money was reserved for important matters like 'bride price' and 'blood price'. 'Bride price' is self-explanatory. 'Blood price' was paid by a man who had been so unfortunate as to kill another man; otherwise the 'avengers of blood' would pay his family a visit and exact vengeance by killing someone of equal status to the unfortunate deceased. In advanced nations these practices have long since ceased, but prices are fixed every day for countless products and services. To enable these prices to be satisfactorily paid the law-making body designates what is known as 'legal tender'—that is, a method of payment which it is agreed satisfies all debts.

Legal tender in the United Kingdom consists of coins of the realm and Bank of England notes. The denominations are as follows:

The halfpenny	$= \frac{1}{2}$p	The fifty-pence piece	= 50p
The penny	= 1p	The £1 note	= £1.00
The twopenny piece	= 2p	The £5 note	= £5.00
The five-pence piece	= 5p	The £10 note	= £10.00
The ten-pence piece	= 10p	The £20 note	= £20.00
The twenty-pence piece	= 20p	The £50 note	= £50.00
		Other high notes are also issued.	

If a creditor is offered payment in legal coins or notes he must accept them. If he refuses to do so the debtor is not discharged from payment, but he is discharged from having to tender payment. He has offered once and that is enough. The creditor must now come and request payment.

There is a further restriction on legal tender. Imagine a customer who offered to pay a bill for £50.00 in halfpennies. This would be a great imposition on the shopkeeper forced to count so many tiny coins. To prevent this sort of payment a limit is set on each coin's use as legal tender. The limit for bronze coins is 20 pence. A shopkeeper offered more than twenty pennies may refuse to accept them. For decimal silver the limit is £2.00, except for the 50-pence coin. These are legal tender up to £10.00. Notes are legal tender for any amount.

If offered coins or notes within the limits of legal tender the shopkeeper or other creditor must accept them in settlement of the debt owed.

One sometimes hears, at times of financial crisis, of tourists and other visitors being in difficulty because hotel-keepers will not accept their foreign notes in settlement of hotel bills, etc. This is because the rate of exchange is upset by the financial panic. An hotel-keeper hesitates to take foreign currency for fear it declines in value. One does not hear of such difficulties as far as home nationals are concerned— legal tender is always legal tender. Only very rarely, as when an entire nation's currency collapses, does legal tender in that country cease to bo valuable. This happened in Germany at the end of the Second World War, for example.

16.2   Other Means of Settling Indebtedness

Naturally the cashier's department will be very concerned with cash receipts and payments, but there are certain serious inconveniences about 'legal tender', which have reduced cash payments enormously in recent years. The chief one is that cash which is legal tender has the characteristic known as **negotiability**. A £1 note is a negotiable instrument. This means that, when passed on to someone else who takes it in good faith and for value, it gives a perfect 'title' or right of ownership. This perfect right of ownership cannot be destroyed, even by the true owner. An example will illustrate this.

Example

London Bank Ltd send £5000 of soiled banknotes by van to the Bank of England. On the way they are stolen. The thief uses some of the money to buy a car from Sunshine Garages Ltd. He insists on paying in cash, and tenders £1350 in notes. The garage proprietor counts them out and banks them after the thief has driven off. London Bank Ltd are able to prove that the notes are the stolen notes, but can do nothing about it. Sunshine Garages Ltd took the notes in good faith, for value given (the car), without notice of any defect in the thief's title. They therefore receive a good title to the notes, which are now their property. All London Bank Ltd can do is to carry on looking for the thief and have him convicted.

It follows that theft of money is very common, and all too easy in many cases. To prevent it businessmen often pay in other ways, notably by cheque and credit transfer.

A complete list of methods of payment includes the following:

(*a*) *Legal tender* in coins and cash.

(*b*) *Payment by cheques* drawn on one of the commercial banks (see pages 242 and 243).

(*c*) *Payments by credit transfer*. These instruct the bank to transfer sums of money to the bank accounts of named people, without cash being handled at all. These credit transfers are often called **bank giro** today.

(*d*) *Payments by Barclaycard or Access cards.* These are special credit card systems first devised by Barclays Bank, which enable a card holder to sign for goods and services. The embossed plastic card is impressed on the slips which are then signed, and an account to the amount signed for will be rendered to the customer monthly.

(*e*) *Payments by standing order.* These instruct a banker to pay a fixed sum of money at a certain date each month. They are particularly useful for paying mortgages, hire purchase repayments and other regular payments of predetermined amounts.

(*f*) *Direct debit transfers* are another way to pay debts. Instead of the debtor writing out a cheque, or a credit transfer, the creditor requests the bank to deduct the money from the debtor's account. Naturally, this will be agreed to by the debtor only if absolute confidence exists that the creditor will not demand more than is due. It is most useful in situations like the payment of rates to local authorities. The rate varies each year, so that it is difficult to make out a standing order. A ratepayer signs a form agreeing to let the local council debit his account directly for the sum due. Clearly any unfair practice that took place could be corrected later anyway.

(*g*) *Payments through the Post Office, and National Giro:*

(i) Payment for items less than five new pence may be made in stamps.

(ii) *Postal orders* are sold at values ranging from 20 pence to £10. A small charge called 'poundage' is made varying from $12\frac{1}{2}$ pence to 20 pence. The payee's name should be filled in on the order and the name of the Post Office where it is to be cashed. If it is crossed by the sender it cannot be cashed, but must be paid into a bank account. It can still be passed on to another and be banked by that person.

The counterfoil is used: (*a*) to make claims if the postal order is lost, although these will not be honoured if it has already been cashed; (*b*) to enable the purchaser to get his money back—even if the name of a payee has been filled in. To do this he presents both halves.

(iii) *Inland telegraph money orders.* Ordinary money orders are no longer issued but telegraphic money orders may still be despatched. An application form is completed and presented with the money to be transmitted, and the fee, to the counter clerk. The payee will then be sent a telegram telling him to call at a named Post Office, where he will be paid the money. The payee must sign for the money and also name the sender correctly. This is a safety device, since there would be some danger that a third party might attempt to draw the money. Money orders may also be sent to countries overseas, provided they are in the list of countries printed in the *Guide* with which the United Kingdom has reciprocal arrangements.

(iv) *National Girobank*. The United Kingdom National Giro was introduced in 1968, and has now been renamed National Girobank. Many other countries have used Giro systems for many years. The explanation is that Giros are more suitable for countries which lack a sophisticated banking system. In its few years' existence the Giro has not been a major success, despite the advanced computerised organisation. It provides most of the normal banking facilities to the general public, many of whom do not have accounts with one of the commercial banks. Standing order and even overdraft facilities are now available. The Giro system is particularly useful to firms such as mail order houses, whose home agents (mostly housewives from the non-banking sector of the community) are able to pay their weekly payments into their local Post Offices for the credit of the mail order house's account. The in-payments must be in cash and cheques are not accepted. The reader should look at typical Giro forms which are available at Post Offices.

(v) *Cash-on-delivery services*. COD services are a way of securing payment for goods when the consignee is not known well enough to be given credit by the consignor. The consignor fills up a form at the Post Office stating the value of the goods, called the 'trade charge'. This sum of money will be collected by the postman on delivery, and if it is not forthcoming he will retain the packet and return it to the Post Office. The addressee can then collect the parcel from the Post Office on payment of the trade charge, which will be remitted by money order to the consignor. If not collected by the consignee in a reasonable time the packet will be returned to the consignor. There is a uniform charge for the COD service of 50 pence. The limit on trade charges is £100.

(*h*) *Payments overseas*. These are settled in a variety of ways and a detailed discussion of them is not appropriate to this book. Brief descriptions of some of them are given below, but for a fuller account the reader is referred to *Commerce Made Simple*.

Cash with order (CWO). This is safe from the seller's viewpoint but disadvantageous to the buyer as his capital is expended without any return until the goods arrive—possibly three months later.

Documents against payment. Here the goods are sent to their destination but the documents of title are sent to the customer's correspondent bank in the United Kingdom, with instructions that they are not to be released until the buyer pays the 'at sight' Bill of Exchange sent with them. The bank contacts the buyer's banker abroad, and on payment the buyer receives the documents and can claim the goods.

Documents against acceptance. If credit is to be given, the seller will use the same procedure but the documents will be released against the acceptance of a 'term' Bill of Exchange. The customer will write 'accepted' and sign a Bill of Exchange requiring him to pay the bill at some future date. He now has time to sell the goods, before he honours the bill.

(i) *International Reply Coupons.* It often happens that a correspondent wishes, as a matter of courtesy, to send a stamped addressed envelope for a reply. This is not possible where the addressee lives in a foreign country, since a stamped addressed envelope would not have the foreign stamps required. For a small charge reply coupons may be purchased. These will be exchanged in the addressee's country for stamps equivalent to the cheapest surface mail. More than one coupon must be sent for airmail replies. Charges for these coupons are given in the *Postal Rates Overseas Compendium* obtainable at any Post Office.

16.3   Cheques

Cheques are by far the commonest method used for settling indebtedness, and about three million are cleared every working day. A cheque is an order to a banker to pay a sum of money to a named person, or to his order. This means that if the named person orders the banker to pay someone else the banker will pay that person instead. Cheques may be written on any piece of paper, or even on an object like a table-cloth, but bankers prefer them to be on standard-sized pieces of paper which fit their machines. A cheque book is issued free of charge to everyone who opens a current account.

It must be clearly stated who is going to sign cheques, and specimen signatures must be lodged with the bank. This helps to ensure that forgeries do not go undetected. Quite often two signatures are required, thus making it more difficult for employees to embezzle money.

Advantages of Paying by Cheque

(i) It is just as easy to pay £1000 as it is to pay £1. Payment by cheque eliminates the need for counting and checking banknotes—a time-consuming business if a sum of £1000 is paid in £1 notes.

(ii) A cheque can be safeguarded by crossing it. Even if it is stolen it is impossible for a thief to obtain cash.

(iii) The money never leaves the bank, so it is extremely safe.

(iv) In some countries, including the United Kingdom (by the *Cheques Act, 1957*), the cheque acts like a receipt. It is proof, once it has been cleared, that the money has been received.

Cheque Crossings

To safeguard a cheque it must be crossed. A cheque without a crossing is called an **open cheque**, and may be cashed across the counter of a bank. Provided that the cheque is not forged, the banker cannot be held liable if he pays an open cheque in this way. It is much better to cross all cheques when they are made out, and it is common to have all cheques crossed in the printing process.

(i) *General crossings*. These are made by drawing two parallel lines across the cheque. Some people write the words '& Co.' between the lines, but it is not necessary today. The effect of such a crossing is to prevent cash being handed over the counter in exchange for the cheque. It must be cleared into a bank account. However, it does not need to be the account of the person named on the cheque—any account will do. Therefore the cheque is still an 'order' cheque: it may be passed on to a third party or any number of successive parties, and it will still be payable into the account of the last person 'ordered' to receive the money. Other similar crossings not specifically mentioned in the *Bills of Exchange Act, 1882*, occur where a cheque is crossed 'a/c payee', or where the words 'not negotiable' are inserted (see below).

(ii) *Special crossings*. Where a cheque is 'crossed specially' the name of a collecting banker is written in between the lines of the crossing. The payment can be collected only by that banker, for the credit of the payee.

Crossed 'a/c payee'. With this crossing the payer safeguards himself by suggesting that it should be paid only into the account of the payee. If the cheque is paid into any other account the bank is 'put upon enquiry' over the circumstances, i.e. it will be liable to the payer if an unauthorised person should collect the money. The bank must enquire whether the payee has given authority for the cheque to be cleared through the account of the person who has paid it in.

Crossed 'not negotiable'. Where a cheque is marked 'not negotiable' it loses the properties of a negotiable instrument, the chief of which is the ability to transfer a better title of ownership than that of the original giver. Any person receiving a cheque of this sort from a transferor knows that he takes it subject to any defects in title of the transferor. He is therefore put upon his guard to ensure that the transferor really does own the cheque.

Opening a Crossed Cheque

A crossed cheque can be opened by inserting the words 'Please pay cash' and signing the alteration with a full signature. The banks are not keen on this type of alteration which puts them upon enquiry to ensure that the alteration is in fact the action of the customer from whose current account the money is to be withdrawn.

16.4 The Cashier's Functions

The chief cashier is a trusted and responsible employee, whose status lies just below that of the accountant. They will usually work closely together, and may even be in the same department. Besides the chief cashier it is common to have a number of assistant cashiers in a large organisation, each of whom will be responsible for a section of the work. The chief cashier will exercise considerable control over these assistants, chiefly by devising systems of collection appropriate to the business and instituting checks that correct procedures are being followed.

Cash Handling

The handling of cash is one of the most difficult activities to control. The best guarantee of success in cash handling is the absolute honesty of the cashier and assistant cashiers, who should be chosen for their integrity and paid a salary commensurate with their responsibilities. The use of sophisticated cash registers is very advantageous, and enables the class of staff employed at the tills to be reduced, but even the most advanced machines are not proof against a cunning and determined cashier resolved to divert cash or stock into his own pocket. It is estimated that in the United Kingdom alone between £150 million and £300 million is pilfered every year by cashiers in the retail trade. Collusion between cashiers and managers of retail outlets is difficult to detect and when discovered often merely results in dismissal. The thief moves on to take employment elsewhere.

Plate 22 shows a modern cash register and coin dispenser, which displays most of the features which make a modern till so advantageous

Plate 22. An NCR point-of-sale terminal for retail trade (reproduced by courtesy of NCR Ltd).

wherever money is collected. It illustrates a machine which not only calculates the change for the customer, but also dispenses it in a conveniently placed cup. The cashier handles only the amount tendered, and any notes to be given as change. The coins are dispensed automatically and need not be counted out by the cashier.

The features of these tills which contribute to the security of cash are as follows.

(*a*) Every item purchased is registered both on the visible scale as it is 'rung up', on the till receipt which is eventually given to the customer, and on the **audit roll** in the cash register.

(*b*) The total bill is displayed for the customer's benefit and is also printed on the till receipt, and the audit roll.

(*c*) The amount tendered by the customer is recorded.

(*d*) The change due is automatically calculated, printed on the till receipt for the customer's benefit, and, in the case of the coin-dispensing machines, is automatically dispensed as far as coins are concerned.

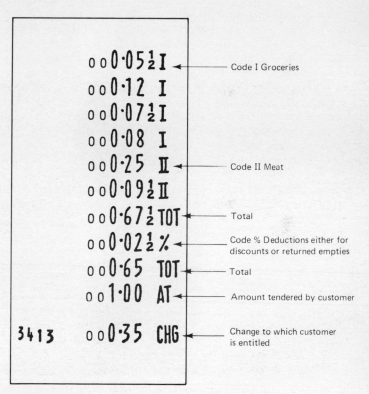

Fig. 16.1. A till receipt.

(*e*) This sequence of events means that what is registered on the keyboard is displayed; what is displayed is printed, both on the till receipt and on the 'audit roll'. This is in a locked compartment and cannot be altered or removed by the cashier. What is printed on the roll is added into a sales total figure, and this figure must be completely accounted for, when the till is cashed up.

(*f*) By a system of coding, usually a number code, the total sales of various departments may be counted up on 'automatic counters' to give the 'customer activity' in each department.

Fig. 16.1 shows such a till receipt with the coding indications printed on it.

16.5 Remittances Inwards

It has already been said (see page 89) that where a firm receives cheques, postal orders or cash in registered letters or ordinary mail a proper system is necessary for recording the arrival of such payments. The mail inwards supervisor should record all such moneys received, and investigate at once any discrepancies between the **remittance advice note** accompanying a payment and the sum of money enclosed. The cashier should be required to certify that all sums of money transferred from the supervisor are correct when taken over.

Remittances inwards are usually recorded in the three-column cash book by the cashier. This is a basic book-keeping record, and its place in the 'double entry' system is shown on page 220. Sometimes the remittances are recorded on special 'cash inwards' sheets, which are like half a three-column cash book, i.e. the debit side only of such a book. These special cash systems are marketed by many of the business systems firms named elsewhere in this book.

Banking Payments Received

A wise cashier banks cash received every day, and busy supermarkets may bank every hour. The sums paid in are recorded in duplicate on

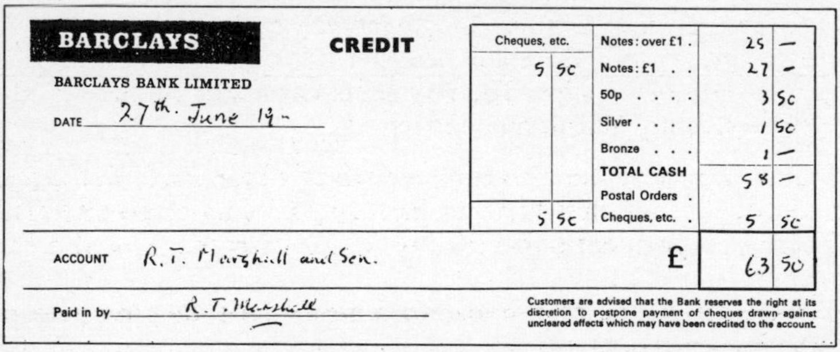

Fig. 16.2. A paying-in slip.

a **paying-in slip**. Cheques are recorded separately from cash, which is divided up into various classes of notes and coins. Fig. 16.2 illustrates this paying-in slip.

Banking Payments Through the Night-safe Services

Current-account customers who wish to bank moneys after closing hours are able to do so through the night-safe system. The basic idea here is that moneys collected after the banks close are put into a leather bag with the paying-in slip in duplicate. The bag is locked and is put into the night safe. The night safe consists of a small opening in the bank wall giving access to a chute which leads down into a strong room or vault. Protective devices inside the locked door prevent anyone possessing a key from getting out what has been put into the safe.

The customer takes his locked bag to the bank, opens the night safe with the key provided, pushes the bag past the safety devices, which are like a one-way valve, and re-locks the door. Next morning the bags are opened and their contents are credited to the appropriate account.

This service is very useful to multiple-shop organisations who require managers to bank their daily takings except for a small float of change for the tills next day. By ensuring that all sums are banked the Head Office achieves day-to-day control of the business, and managers who are too lazy to cash up, or are taking unauthorised time off from work, can be detected.

16.6 Remittances Outwards

When statements are received from suppliers they should first be checked against the creditors' ledger account to confirm that they are correct. They should then be passed to the cashier for payment.

Usually some sort of mechanical or electronic cheque-writing system will be used. The payments cash sheet and the cheque are written simultaneously, the name and amount on the cheque being reproduced onto the cash sheet below it, or copied automatically by the machine. If a credit transfer system is being used instead of a cheque system the procedure will be very similar, but the credit transfer slips will replace the cheques used. Extra copies of the payments sheet are printed and sent to the bank with the credit transfer slips. These are sometimes called the 'bank giro' slips. The payments cash sheet is then used to make the following accounting entries:

(*a*) The entries in the creditors' accounts in the creditors' ledger. These entries record that the firm has settled its indebtedness to the creditors by a 'payment outwards', on which discount may also have been taken.

(*b*) An entry in the cash book, to remove the total sum paid out from the bank account.

(*c*) An entry in the discount received account to record the profit earned by paying promptly. Discount received is a reward for settling debts immediately they fall due.

These three sets of entries ensure that a correct 'double entry' procedure has been followed.

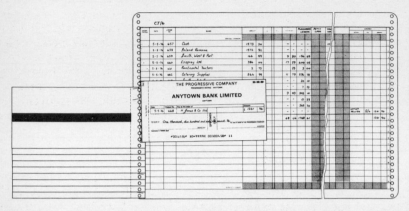

Fig. 16.3. Simultaneous writing and recording of cheques (reproduced by courtesy of Kalamazoo Ltd). The top cheque is written first, with the other nine simply folded back to the left. The first cheque is then torn off and the remainder dealt with similarly.

16.7 A Firm's Relationship with its Bankers

Bankers offer a wide range of services to their customers. A full description of these services may be found in *Commerce Made Simple*. Here it is only necessary to touch upon these services, and the relationship that exists between the bank manager and the chief cashier. Since a firm always needs to anticipate its cash requirements a close link should be established between the banker and the firm. This will simplify the day-to-day arrangements, ensuring courteous attention at all times. It will also enable the banker to know the firm's situation better, and judge its importance in the industry and the local community. Should the firm require financial assistance this will be available more quickly and more willingly since the bank manager is more likely to extend credit to an account he knows from personal experience to be fundamentally sound.

Current Accounts

Banks extend current-account services to anyone whom they regard as reliable. A new customer will be asked for a reference, and if this proves satisfactory the bank will accept an initial deposit which will be entered in a current account. A cheque book will then be issued free of charge.

Once a customer has received a cheque book it may be used to order the banker to pay out sums of money from the current account. The name 'current account' comes from the French word *courant*, which means 'running', and implies that money is being paid into, and paid out of, the account as often as the customer finds convenient. The balance of the account changes from day to day as the various transactions proceed. The usual method of paying money into an account is by means of a **paying-in slip**, while the **cheque** is the usual way of withdrawing money from the account.

Overdrafts are allowed provided they are sanctioned by the branch manager, and loans are sometimes made. An **overdraft** permits the customer to draw out more money than he has paid in. A **loan** actually transfers a sum of money into the current account of the borrower, but a **loan account** is opened to record the debt that arises as a result. Usually a firm which has received a loan is not allowed to overdraw as well. Interest is charged, usually at 2–5 per cent above base rate, on both loans and overdrafts.

Deposit-account Services

Deposit accounts are accounts in which individuals and firms deposit cash resources that are not needed at present. They bear interest at 2 per cent less than the bank's base rate. The bank lends these funds to borrowers at 2–5 per cent more than the base rate, the interest being shared therefore with the depositor. Since the bank is using these moneys it cannot always regain them at short notice, and in theory the bank is supposed to be given seven days' notice before money is withdrawn. In fact the bank usually waives this notice, but charges seven days' interest instead on sums drawn out.

Unlike a current account, a deposit account does not carry the right to use a cheque book. Bank passbooks (paying-in books) are used by the depositor who may pay in cash, postal orders, or cheques.

Bank Statements

Every month at least the cashier will ask the bank for a bank statement. This is a copy of the bank's record of its transactions with the firm. The cashier will compare this record with the record in the threecolumn cash book. Usually they will disagree. The explanations for this failure to agree are as follows:

(*a*) *The bank often takes action without bothering to notify the firm.* For example it deducts **bank charges**, for operating the current account, or **bank interest** on overdrafts when they fall due. It also receives sums of money as credit transfers, or bank giro transfers, without notifying the firm of their arrival. The cashier is expected to sort out these matters when the bank statement is received. This is done by updating the cash book, recording the sums transferred to the firm and deducting those sums taken away for services rendered.

(*b*) *There are delays inevitable in the banking system.* Imagine that a cheque is paid out to a creditor, but he does not go to the bank and present it for several weeks. Clearly, the sum paid away will not in fact have left the bank. The bank will still think its customer has these funds in his possession. Similarly, even when cheques have been presented, some delay arises as they are cleared. A cashier who banks fifty cheques at 9.30 a.m. on the last day of the month, and collects his bank statement at the same time, cannot expect those fifty cheques to appear on the statement. They will appear in due course, when time enables them to be cleared. In order to explain these differences the cashier will draw up a **bank reconciliation statement**.

(*c*) *Mistakes often occur.* These may be made by the cashier or by the bank. If the two records cannot be 'reconciled' every figure must be scrutinised to find the mistake.

Preparation of a Bank Reconciliation Statement

Consider the following information from Mr A. Dealer's cash book and bank statement (shown below).

Readers who are not very knowledgeable about accounts should note that the bank records appear to be the reverse of the records of A. Dealer. Since Dealer has deposited his money in the bank he is a creditor for the sums deposited, although these appear as debits on his own cash book. This is quite logical—Dealer keeps the record according to *his* viewpoint; the bank keeps the record according to *its* viewpoint.

CASH BOOK (BANK COLUMN ONLY)

Dr.							Cr.
19..			£	19..			£
Feb.	1	To Balance	225.00	Feb.	2	By Green	47.60
	10	,, Ambrose	50.75		14	,, Howard	28.50
	17	,, Bloggs	62.62		19	,, Ives	36.70
	18	,, Crayford	73.50				

A rough calculation shows that the balance on this Cash Book is £299.07—a debit balance.

BANK STATEMENT
A. Dealer in account with Barclay's Bank Limited

Date	Details	Dr.	Cr.	Balance
19..				
Feb. 1	Balance Forward		225.00	225.00
2	Green	47.60		177.40
12	Ambrose		50.75	228.15
16	Howard	28.50		199.65
16	Charges	5.25		194.40
17	Bloggs		62.62	257.02
28	Bank of England		12.58	269.60
	(bonds)			

A careful look at these two accounts will show:

(*a*) The balances do not agree: £299.07 according to the cash book, £269.60 according to the bank statement.

(*b*) Both accounts did agree on 1st February, so the problem is quite recent. Sometimes we may find a time lag lasting months, usually because someone has failed to bank a cheque.

(*c*) Ives's cheque sent to him on 19th February has not yet been paid in by Ives. He may be a sole trader who bothers to go to the bank only once a week or so.

(*d*) Crayford's cheque received by 28th February, that is today, has been entered in A. Dealer's cash book and paid into the bank, but it is not recorded on the bank statement. This is another example of a time lag; the bank will probably credit it tomorrow to the account.

(*e*) The bank has charged Dealer £5.25 bank charges. Dealer did not know about this deduction from his funds, but now he has learned of it he should deduct this amount from the bank account in his three-column cash book.

(*f*) The bank has received some interest from the Bank of England for Dealer. This is clearly interest on gilt-edged securities, and Dealer should record the money received on his bank account.

We must now proceed to reconcile the two records.

Procedure for Drawing up a Bank Reconciliation Statement

The procedure is as follows:

(*a*) Compare the two accounts and note all the items of disagreement, as we have done in (*a*) to (*f*) in the last section.

(*b*) Adjust all items that can be put right in the cash book—items which are wrong only because of our lack of knowledge of what our bankers have done.

(*c*) Reconcile the rest in a reasonable statement, starting with one balance and finishing with the other.

Our calculations then look like this:

REVISED CASH BOOK (BANK COLUMNS ONLY)						
Dr.						Cr.
19..		£	19..			£
Feb. 1	To Balance	225.00	Feb. 2	By Green		47.60
10	,, Ambrose	50.75	14	,, Howard		28.50
17	,, Bloggs	62.62	19	,, Ives		36.70
28	,, Crayford	73.50	28	,, Bank Charges		5.25
28	,, Interest		28	,, Balance c/d		306.40
	Received	12.58				
		£424.45				£424.45
Mar. 1	To Balance b/d	306.40				(*cont'd*)

BANK RECONCILIATION STATEMENT
(as at 28th February)

	£
Balance as per Cash Book	306.40
Add back the cheque not yet presented (because the bank has not yet been asked for the money)	36.70
	343.10
Deduct the Crayford cheque not yet cleared (because the bank is not yet crediting us with the money)	73.50
Balance as per Bank Statement	£269.60

Clearly, we have been able to explain the disagreement successfully. Bank reconciliation statements are typed out neatly and filed away for inspection when required.

16.8 Points to Think About and Discuss

(*a*) Thinking in the very widest terms of the security of cash, what measures would you recommend to prevent: (i) the theft of petty cash by persons in the office; (ii) wage snatches by criminal gangs; (iii) burglaries after office hours?

(*b*) A businessman applies to a bank for permission to open a current account and to be issued with a cheque book. What measures do you consider the bank should take to ensure that he is a suitable person to have such an account?

(*c*) A cashier is devising a set of rules to be followed by the Mail Inwards Department whenever letters are found to contain remittances from debtors. The firm has 56 000 mail order accounts and many of these customers send cash, either registered or unregistered. They all send postal orders and cheques, many of which are not crossed. Suggest how these, and other methods of remitting funds, should be dealt with in the rules.

(*d*) The cashier of a supermarket has detected the following matters in recent months:

  (i) Cashiers at tills have placed money received from customers in their own handbags instead of in the tills.
  (ii) Cashiers have deliberately given change for a £5 note to customers related to them, who tendered only £1 for their purchases.
  (iii) Cashiers have left a bag of goods (value 10p) near the till. It has been added onto the bill of every customer and the total for the day has then been taken home in goods off the shelves, half by the cashier and half by the manager.
  (iv) A cashier with a 'sprained ankle' was found to have slipped

twenty-three 10p pieces into the bandage round the 'injured' foot.

How can such thefts be prevented? Is it desirable to prosecute employees in these cases?

16.9 Rapid Revision

Cover the page with a sheet of paper and uncover one question at a time.

Answers	Questions
—	1. What is 'legal tender'?
1. It is a means of payment recognised in law as satisfying debts.	2. What does 'legal tender' consist of?
2. Bank notes of various denominations and coin of the realm.	3. What other ways are often used to pay debts?
3. (a) Postage stamps; (b) postal orders; (c) cheques; (d) bills of exchange; (e) credit transfers; (f) debit transfers.	4. What methods of payment involve the greatest risk of loss?
4. Any system where cash is handled.	5. What safeguards can be devised for cash handling?
5. (a) Employ responsible and well-paid staff. (b) Use a modern cash register which has built-in safeguards. (c) Make cashiers take out 'fidelity bonds' which give insurance cover against defalcations. (d) Institute spot checks by the internal audit department.	6. How may cash takings be disposed of after banking hours?
6. By using the night-safe system.	7. What is a current account?
7. It is a bank account into which money may be paid, and from which money may be withdrawn, without notice.	8. What is a deposit account?
8. It is an account where surplus funds are deposited, at interest, but from which funds can only be obtained on giving seven days' notice.	9. Go over the page again until you feel you are sure of the answers.

Exercises Set 16

1. Why is it usual to appoint a chief cashier as well as an accountant? How do their functions differ?

2. What is 'legal tender'? What are the limits of legal tender for (a) decimal bronze coins; (b) 50p pieces; (c) Bank of England notes?

3. Name four different methods of payment. Describe one method in detail.

4. (*a*) Describe in as much detail as you can the National Girobank system; (*b*) explain the purpose of two documents which are used in connection with Giro transactions.

5. Your firm has just opened a branch in a small town and wishes to open a bank account. (*a*) If you were instructed to do this, what action would you take? (*b*) Draft either a cheque form or a paying-in slip, and make specimen entries.

6. You are employed in the cashier's section of your firm and are responsible for the efficient and safe handling of receipts and payments of cash. (*a*) How would you control the remittances received in the morning's post? (*b*) How would you satisfy the senior cashier that the money he had issued to you for petty cash had been used for the firm's business? (*c*) What method would you use for paying remittances into the bank?

7. You have just received your firm's bank statement made up to 30th April, and you notice that it quotes a credit balance of £970.45 whereas the balance in your firm's cash book was £860.32 on that date. When the previous bank statement (made up to 31st March) was received, the credit balance at the bank was £903.26 as against the firm's cash book balance of £1064.50.

Explain ways in which these two differences could have occurred.

8. (*a*) Why are cheques often used in payment of accounts? (*b*) What effect has a crossing on a cheque? (*c*) Is it customary to send a receipt if an account is paid by cheque? If not, why not? (*d*) What action would you take if a creditor told you he had not received the cheque you sent him a week before?

9. (*a*) Give two instances when uncrossed cheques could be used; (*b*) how would you 'open' a crossed cheque?

10. Bankers offer their customers the use of both current and deposit accounts. Explain each of these services, pointing out their similarities and their differences.

11. What do you understand by the following banking terms? You should answer as fully as possible: (*a*) current account; (*b*) credit transfer; (*c*) crossed cheque; (*d*) foreign exchange; (*e*) overdraft.

12. Name three ways of sending money by post. Say in what circumstances you would choose each of them and explain the procedures necessary.

13. (*a*) What is an open cheque? (*b*) What effect has a crossing on a cheque? (*c*) What is the effect of these particular crossings?

(*d* Give one further example of a crossing and say what is its effect.

14. A businessman has the following accounts to pay: (*a*) one to the Gas Board

for £15.52; (*b*) one to his Trade Association for £10.50 annual subscription; (*c*) several to trade creditors for varying amounts.

Suggest three different methods of paying these accounts (one for each), and describe the procedure which will be necessary in each of the methods you choose.

15. (*a*) When would you consider it appropriate to use the following methods of payment: (i) cash by registered post; (ii) credit transfer; (iii) standing order; (iv) COD?

(*b*) Explain briefly how the National Girobank system differs from the credit transfer system for the payment of money.

16. Describe the operation and advantages of a cash register.

17. (*a*) The morning post contains the following remittances:

Sender	Method of Payment	Amount £
J. Smith Ltd	Cheque	4.52
R. Peters	Cheque	6.50
P. South & Co.	Cheque	7.14
M. Rayner	Postal Order	8.50
R. Jones	Registered Mail (five £1 notes)	5.00
The Albright Co. Ltd	Cheque	4.70
R. Smith	Postal Order	3.85

In addition, the following payments are made in cash at the main office:

Paid by:	Money paid
J. Brown	Three £1 notes, two 10p coins, and one 5p coin
R. Smith	One £5 note, two £1 notes, one 50p coin
S. Wilson	One £5 note, and four 10p coins.

Prepare a paying-in slip for all the above receipts to be paid into the bank. The company for which you work is Western Designs Ltd. Their account number is 1093706.

(*b*) Explain briefly the following bank services and state the circumstances in which they would be used: (i) night safe facilities; (ii) standing orders as a method of payment.

18. The following shows the entries in T. Fitt's cash book in March:

19..		£	19..			£
Mar. 1	To Balance at bank brought forward	115.00	Mar. 5	By	Drawings—self	20.00
			15	„	Noah	80.00
				„	Oliver	25.00
16	„ Brown	25.00	29	„	Rigg	95.00
25	„ Abel	185.00		„	Lee	15.00
31	„ Warner	286.00	31	„	Balance at bank carried forward	376.00
		£611.00				£611.00

Mar. 31	To Balance	376.00

Early in April he received this statement from his bank:

T. FITT: IN ACCOUNT WITH LOANSHIRE BANK LIMITED

Date	Particulars	Debit £	Credit £	Balance £
Mar. 1	Balance forward			115.00
5	Self—T. Fitt	20.00		95.00
17	Sundries		25.00	120.00
18	Oliver	25.00		
18	Noah	80.00		15.00
26	Sundries		185.00	200.00
28	Cheque returned unpaid	25.00		175.00
31	Charges	4.00		171.00
31	Lee	15.00		156.00

Draw up a cash book, starting with the present balance of £376.00 and correct such differences as are caused by a lack of knowledge of the bank's activities. Then reconcile the revised cash balance with the balance at the bank in a bank reconciliation statement.

19. From the following prepare a bank reconciliation statement as at 30th June, after first bringing the cash book up to date if this is required:

J. JONES & CO.

CASH BOOK ON 30TH JUNE, 19..

19..		£	19..		£
June 4	To Bank Loan	500.00	June 1	By Balance	227.10
11	,, R. Gee	3.20	8	,, T. Smith	40.60
30	,, L. Mitre	4.00	15	,, R. Port	4.96
			29	,, B. Lemon	62.10

BANK STATEMENT AS AT 30TH JUNE, 19..

Date	Particulars	Debit £	Credit £	Balance £
June 1			(Red) *Dr.*	227.10
4	Loan		500.00	272.90
8	Sundries	40.60		232.30
11	,,		3.20	235.50
16	Bank of S. Africa Div.		12.40	247.90
29	Sundries	62.10		185.80
30	Charges	0.50		185.30

THE WAGES DEPARTMENT

17.1 The Payment of Wages

No subject is of greater importance to the average employee than the wages or salary that he will earn from his employment. *Wages are the rewards paid to employees for the labour services they have supplied to the enterprise.* The word 'salaries', which today is often associated with higher grade employees, or 'white collar' employees in the clerical and administrative fields, actually has exactly the same meaning as wages. It is from the Latin word *salarium*—meaning 'salt money'—an extra wage paid to soldiers in the North African campaigns for the purchase of salt to replace that lost by perspiration in the African sun.

In small enterprises a single clerk may be concerned with making up the wage packets and their distribution to staff. In large enterprises a pay-roll will be prepared which may require thousands of staff to be paid by credit transfer. Whatever the enterprise, mistakes may occur, and employees should always check their wages and the calculations so that any discrepancy can be adjusted. Many pay-packets are prepared in special envelopes which enable the contents to be counted without opening the pay-packet. An employee who wishes to complain must do so before the packet is opened.

A difference in attitude, which is slowly changing, is found between the payment of wages to manual workers and the payment of salaries to other staff. Traditionally, the manual worker has always been an hourly employee, or at best an employee on a weekly wage. He has therefore been paid strictly by the hour or by the number of specified hours in his week. The hours of salaried staff are unspecified, and it is presumed that the employee will put in whatever extra work is required to complete the activities of the office each day. Neither of these approaches is really satisfactory—the manual worker is turned into a clock-watcher and demands payment for overtime as of right; the office worker may be exploited by being required to work un-rewarded at busy periods. In recent years these traditional attitudes have been modified, and further modifications are probable, and indeed desirable.

17.2 The *Truck Acts*, and the *Payment of Wages Act, 1960*

Many years ago employers often paid workers with 'truck'—that is, 'small goods' of various sorts. Thus a farm worker might be paid in eggs or milk, and a clothing worker in fancy waistcoats. Another system paid the workers in vouchers which could be exchanged at the employer's shop. These shops became known as 'tommy-shops', and some idea of the quality of the goods supplied can be gathered from the slang expression 'a lot of tommy-rot', which is still used to describe anyone who is talking rubbish. Payment, by arrangement with the landlord of the local public house, was often made in premises where alcoholic liquor was on sale, and the money paid out was soon collected in again over the counter. All such practices are now forbidden under the *Truck Acts, 1831* and *1870*. Employees must be paid in 'legal tender', i.e. notes and coins of the realm; but if they agree they may be paid by cheque or credit transfer into a bank account, under the *Payment of Wages Act, 1960*. This Act also specifies that employees absent through sickness or injury may be paid by postal order and may not object to this method of payment. The *Equal Pay Act, 1970*, gave women equal pay with men from December 1975.

An employer is not permitted to make deductions from the wages for any expenses incurred in paying wages in these statutory ways, but neither is he compelled to contribute towards the bank charges of employees.

Certain statutory deductions (that is deductions authorised by Act of Parliament) must be made by employers. The commonest are:

(*a*) Tax deductions under Schedule E, the so-called Pay-As-You-Earn system of taxation. The employer is made the Government's agent for the collection of taxation, and must deduct the tax before making out the pay slip, and remit the money to the Inland Revenue authorities.

(*b*) National Insurance Contributions. Since April 1975 all such contributions are earnings-related and payable on scales laid down by Statute. The *Employer's Guide to National Insurance Contributions* is supplied to the employer by the Department of Health and Social Security. The old insurance card system has been ended and contributions deducted are paid direct to the Inland Revenue authorities.

(*c*) State pension contributions for special employees such as teachers, police, etc., are deductible under a variety of special Acts.

17.3 Calculating Wages

There are many ways of calculating wages, and each has its advantages and disadvantages. The commonest are as follows:

Flat rates. These are rates that do not vary at any time. For example, a maintenance man who may be called out in the middle of the night may agree to accept a flat rate for all his work, irrespective of the awkwardness of the hours worked.

Time rates. The employee is paid a fixed sum per hour, day, week or month. This method rewards all employees equally, the strong and the weak, the industrious and the lazy, the conscientious and the irresponsible. It offers no incentive to the keen worker to turn out more than average output, or to render more scrupulous service. It is mostly used for office workers, or 'service' employees of all types.

Piece rates. Here the employee is paid per unit of product, or per job completed. A careful check must be made of the quality of the work performed—a person who scamps his work must have it returned to him. Records must also be kept of the output of each employee in the workshop or factory using this system.

Bonus rates. These are rates which are based upon the principle that any extra output or effort will be shared fairly between the employer and the employee. A well-known system fixes a standard time for each task to be performed, and if it is performed in less time the employee will be given a bonus of 50 per cent of the time saved. Thus a job expected to take five hours but completed in four hours will earn for the employee four and a half hours' pay; four hours actually worked and a half-hour bonus money.

Commission. Commission is a reward paid to salesmen as a percentage of the sales made. It is an incentive payment, encouraging him to greater efforts in his selling activities.

Voluntary deductions. Besides the compulsory deductions referred to above, there are many voluntary deductions which may be made at the request of the employee. Union contributions, charitable donations, save-as-you-earn contributions and social club contributions are typical voluntary deductions.

17.4 Time Cards

Since many workers are paid on the basis of the time spent at work, many firms operate a time-card system which requires the employee to 'clock on' and 'clock off'. At the entrance gates a rack of card holders is erected on either side of a clock mechanism which will stamp any card inserted into it with the time shown on the clock. On arrival the employee takes his card from the 'Out' rack and clocks in, replacing it in the 'In' rack. As he leaves he takes it from the 'In' rack, clocks off and replaces it in the 'Out' rack. The card bears an accurate record of the time spent on the premises. Usually employees are allowed to be 3 minutes late without penalty—after that they lose a quarter of an hour's wages. Fig. 17.1 shows such a time card.

17.5 The Traditional Wages Book

A traditional wages book is illustrated in Fig. 17.2. A careful study of the columns will show the student how the final sums due to the employee have been calculated, and what other payments must be made to outside bodies like the Commissioners of Inland Revenue and charitable organisations.

NAME R.Thompson							
NO. 172				WEEK ENDING 3rd. June 19··			
DAY		IN	OUT	IN	OUT	IN	OUT	TOTAL

DAY		IN	OUT	IN	OUT	IN	OUT	TOTAL
M	AM	8.00						
	PM		12.30	1.30	5.30			$8\frac{1}{2}$
Tu	AM	8.01						
	PM		12.30	1.30	5.30	6.00	8.00	$10\frac{1}{2}$
W	AM	7.58						
	PM		12.15	1.30	5.30	6.00	9.00	$11\frac{1}{4}$
T	AM	8.02						
	PM		12.30	1.30	6.30			$9\frac{1}{2}$
F	AM	8.00						
	PM		12.00	1.00	5.30			$8\frac{1}{2}$
S	AM	7.30						
	PM		12.15					$4\frac{3}{4}$
Su	AM	9.00						
	PM		1.00					4
						TOTAL HOURS		57

Fig. 17.1. A time card.

17.6 Modern Wages Systems

The systems to be described in this section have been developed in recent years to provide complete records of wages payments without repetition of work.

For a satisfactory wages system three things are essential:

(a) A pay-roll providing the sort of information shown in Fig. 17.2.

(b) An individual record for each employee which can be referred to whenever the employee queries his pay for any reason. It would not be satisfactory to show an employee the wages book itself for he can then see what other people earn; this can be embarrassing and can lead to bad relations between staff.

(c) An advice note to go into the wage packet of the employee; or information which may be written on the packet.

Clearly, it would be a great advantage if these could all be prepared at once, without any rewriting from the wages book to the individual record and the wage packet. There are many such systems, but the one described here is by courtesy of Kalamazoo Ltd (see Figs 17.3 and 17.4).

A flat board giving a good writing surface is supplied to the wages clerk. This board is called the **copy-writer**, and has at the top a series of studs which engage with holes in the paper placed on the board. As the illustrations show, a set of ten advice notes is first laid on the

No	Name of Employee	Earnings				Tax Details to Date						Deductions					Net Pay	Employer's N.I. Contributions
		Basic	Overtime	Other	Gross Pay	Gross to Date	Tax free	Taxable Pay	Tax Due	Tax Paid	Refunds	Tax	National Insurance	Other Ins.	Voluntary	Total Deducts		
1	R. Brown	10.50	8.60	0.40	19.50	138.66	138.66	—	—	—	—	—	1.09	—	0.01	1.10	18.40	1.68
2	T. Jones	10.50	8.60	1.50	20.60	142.40	82.40	60.00	11.70	8.50	—	3.20	1.14	—	0.01	4.35	16.25	1.76
3	V. Smith	17.50	1.50	1.40	20.40	168.20	90.60	77.60	13.25	9.20	—	4.05	1.11	—	0.01	5.17	15.23	1.72
4	M. Stanton	10.50	7.50	0.40	18.40	142.40	142.40	—	—	—	—	—	1.00	—	0.01	1.01	17.39	1.55
5	R. Vickery	10.50	8.60	0.40	19.50	140.50	140.50	—	—	—	—	—	1.09	—	0.01	1.10	18.40	1.68
6	G. White	23.50	—	4.75	28.25	172.60	90.60	82.00	14.10	10.60	—	3.50	1.55	—	0.01	5.06	23.19	2.40
		83.00	34.80	8.85	126.65							10.75	6.98	—	0.06	17.79	108.86	10.79

Figures for management to be used in controlling costs and fixing selling prices

Sums due to Inland Revenue Dept.

Donations to charities

Cash to be collected from bank for wage packets

Cash to Inland Revenue Dept.

Fig. 17.2 The wages book.

copy-writer with the holes punched at the top engaging with the studs to keep the advice notes steady. A sheet of carbon is laid over the advice note and over this is placed the wages book in loose-leaf form. This is called the **pay-roll form**, and in the example shown is written in the opposite way to that of the wages book shown in Fig. 17.2, so that the calculations are vertical instead of horizontal. This vertical system saves 20 per cent of addition and subtraction time because it is the natural way to work. Cross-totting is never as easy as long-totting.

Over the pay-roll sheet is placed a further piece of carbon and the individual record sheet of the employee. These sheets are ruled to give 26 weeks of the employee's records, and are stored in a locked index when not required. Any employee who wishes to query his pay can then be shown his own record without seeing those of other employees.

The clever part of the whole system is the positioning of this individual record sheet on top of the pay-roll sheet and the advice notes. If it is positioned so that the next clean space on the individual record is over the next clean space on the pay-roll and advice sheet, then whatever is written on the individual record sheet will be carbon copied without any further effort onto the pay-roll and advice note below.

We thus have three records printed at once, and a copying error is impossible. The individual record returns to its locked index. The pay-roll is totalled to give the managerial figures required for total wages and cost records.

The advice slips are torn off across the perforations and folded in batches of ten before being separated and used to prepare the wage packets.

This is a good example of the type of improvement that can be made in a book-keeping system by the expert accountant. At present over three million people in Great Britain alone are paid by the Kalamazoo system.

17.7   Wages by Cheque, or Credit Transfer

Many employees agree to be paid by cheque or credit transfer, thus overcoming the problems of wage-snatches and robberies at premises known to pay their employees in cash. More and more people today receive nothing in their wages envelope but an advice note similar to that described in the last section. The money is simply credited to their bank accounts and no actual cash is handled. This is the credit transfer system and it is strongly recommended as the best way to pay wages.

The basic idea is this: the pay-roll is done in the usual way, but instead of going to the bank to draw the pay-roll in cash and notes, from which the wage packets may be prepared, the cashier takes to the bank a list which is a copy of the pay-roll. The bank is also supplied with a credit transfer slip for each employee. Against each name is the sum due to that employee, which the bank will now transfer to the employee's account. The cashier gives the bank an authorisation to

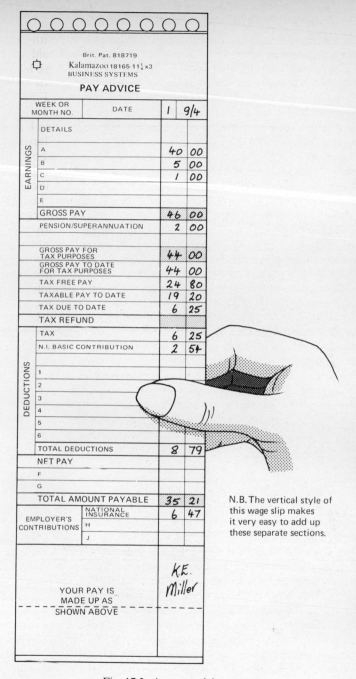

N.B. The vertical style of this wage slip makes it very easy to add up these separate sections.

Fig. 17.3. A wages advice note.

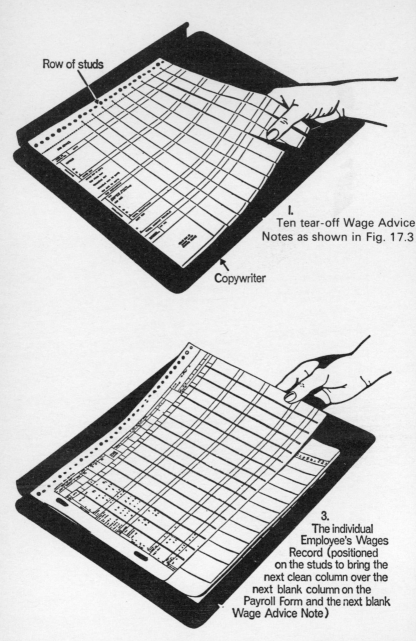

Row of studs

I.
Ten tear-off Wage Advice
Notes as shown in Fig. 17.3

Copywriter

3.
The individual
Employee's Wages
Record (positioned
on the studs to bring the
next clean column over the
next blank column on the
Payroll Form and the next blank
Wage Advice Note)

Fig. 17.4. A modern

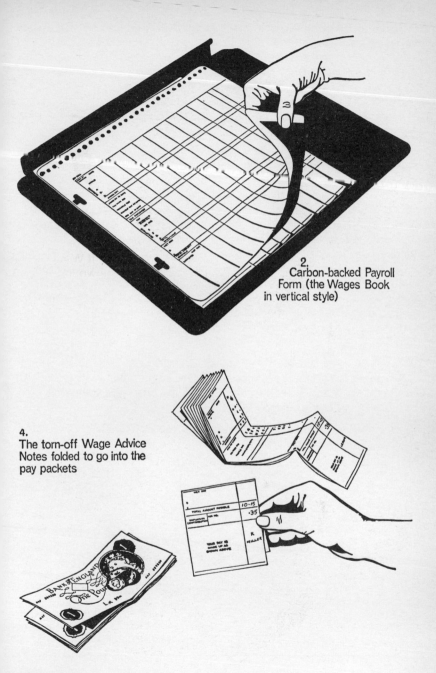

2.
Carbon-backed Payroll
Form (the Wages Book
in vertical style)

4.
The torn-off Wage Advice
Notes folded to go into the
pay packets

wages system.

debit the firm's account with the total pay-roll. The firm has thus paid the wages in a very safe and economical way. No security guards are needed; there is no tedious counting of notes or handling of coins. For the employee, there is no queuing up to collect his pay packet, and no chance of spending it before he gets home.

17.8 Cash Wages and Wage Packets

Where wages are still paid in cash the pay-roll totals, together with a **coin summary**, are sent to the cashier. He obtains the necessary money from the bank, using a security company if necessary. It is usual to pay the wages in wage envelopes which have special features. First, the front cover of the envelope may show in detail how the wage is calculated. If a wages advice slip is enclosed in the envelope with the money the front cover of the envelope will at least show the amount enclosed. This is to enable the employee to check the money before he opens the packet. To assist him the envelope has perforated holes cut in the back to enable the employee to see the money through the holes. The notes are bigger than the envelope, and are folded over with the envelope flap in such a way that they stick out and can be counted. An employee who has opened his envelope is deemed to have agreed that the contents are correct.

17.9 Wages and the Control of Cash

Whenever large amounts of cash are being handled care is needed at all stages. When drawing money from the bank the following precautions may be adopted:

(*a*) Employ a specialist security organisation. The charges payable are not excessive, and as these companies guarantee the safety of all sums handled there are effectively no losses.

(*b*) If a special organisation is not employed vary the route taken from week to week to ensure that movements are erratic and unpredictable by outsiders planning a wage-snatch.

(*c*) Security cases for money are available. One type has pockets containing power-operated telescopic antennae. When snatched from an authorised holder the antennae shoot out in all directions forming an object too large to go into a car door for a quick getaway, while a siren attracts attention to the snatch-thief.

(*d*) Check the character of all employees concerned in the transfer of money, who should in any case be active employees, not persons nearing retirement age.

Having ensured the safe arrival of the money it must then be equally carefully protected within the firm itself. Practices like the preparation of wage packets for 'ghost' employees are common. Supervision at actual payout points, checking the pay-roll against personnel records, and paying by credit transfer to employees' bank accounts discover or deter the dishonest cashier.

Careful investigation of all discrepancies on the making up of pay-packets will also reveal dishonesty or incompetence in the handling of money. All wage clerks should be carefully selected, references should be taken up and their status and pay should be appropriate to their responsibilities.

17.10 Pay-As-You-Earn (PAYE)

In earlier times income tax affected only the very rich, and it was charged at a low rate. Those who paid income tax could usually pay the small sums required without difficulty. Today about 38 per cent of all income is taxed away for Government purposes, and the tax burden falls on people of quite small income. To enable such people to pay taxation without difficulty the 'pay-as-you-earn' taxation system was devised. A knowledge of PAYE is essential for all wages' clerks.

The PAYE system operates on the following lines:

(a) *The employee's code number*. This is a number allocated to the employee by the Inspector of Taxes for his area. It is calculated by taking account of all the coding allowances to which he is entitled. These include the following:

Personal allowances—for the support of the taxpayer (and a wife, or husband, if appropriate).
Children's allowances· (in certain circumstances) if appropriate. The system of children's allowances for all children has been discontinued.
Dependent relative, housekeeper and other allowances.
Expense allowances for certain trades where heavy-duty clothing, etc., has to be provided out of income.

Every employee is sent a form P2 (Notice of Coding) about February each year, giving the calculation of this personal coding. It is possible to raise objections to the coding given, but ultimately it becomes the code number from which the tax payments will be calculated. Fig. 17.5 shows a typical Notice of Coding form.

Emergency Code Numbers. Where an employee for some reason has no code number—perhaps because of a change of employment made without obtaining a P45 (see below) from the previous employer—the tax is deducted temporarily under an emergency card, a P13. The tax payable on an emergency card is higher than on most code numbers.

(b) *The employer's guide to pay-as-you-earn*. This is sent free to all employers before the start of the tax year on 6th April.

(c) *Tax tables A and B*. These tax tables, a page for every week in the year, are sent to the employer and show, already calculated, how much tax is payable.

Table A for any given week shows the total tax-free pay allowed for every code number by that week in the year. For example, the employee whose code number is 215 might be allowed £581.70 tax-free pay by the fourteenth week of the year. If the employee is not earning a large salary, so that by the date in question only £420.00 has been earned, then all the pay is tax free and no deduction will be made. If the employee has earned more than £581.70—say £800—then the taxable pay is £800 – £581.70, which is £218.30. Reference to Table B (see page 270) shows as follows:

Tax due on £218.30 = £55.90

By looking at the employee's records the wages clerk can see that the total tax deducted up to last week was:

Tax deducted to Week 13 = £53.60

Clearly the tax due to be deducted in Week 14 is £55.90 – £53.60,

The notes refer to forms P3(1978)(PAYE Coding Guide) and P3(CB)(1977) enclosed or sent with a previous notice of coding.

See note	**CODING ALLOWANCES**	£
11	Expenses, etc.	
13	Building Society interest payable ...	
13	Loan, etc., interest	
14	Personal	
14	Age (estimated total income £..............)	
14	Wife's earned income	
14	Additional personal	
14	Children including reduced allowance £..............	
14	Dependent relatives	
15	Life insurance	
	....	
	....	
	TOTAL ALLOWANCES DUE	
	Less	
16	**Allowances given against other income** £	
	Untaxed interest	
	National Insurance Benefits ...	
	Occupational pensions	
	....	
	....	
	NET ALLOWANCES	
	Less	
17	**Tax unpaid for earlier years**	
	19 – £ *equivalent to a deduction of*	
	1977 – 78 £ *(estimated) equivalent to a deduction of ... ...*	
18-20	**Other adjustments**	
	ALLOWANCES GIVEN AGAINST PAY	

SPECIMEN

Your code for 1978-79 is ▶

HPB 52-1224/1A

Fig. 17.5. A P2 (Personal Coding) form (reproduced by permission of the Controller of Her Majesty's Stationery Office).

which comes to £2.30. When this amount is deducted from the employee's wage packet the correct amount of tax (£55.90) has been deducted for the 14-week period.

The system is very flexible. Suppose that Mr *A* has married during the week and is now entitled to the married man's allowance. This will raise his code number as soon as he notifies the Tax Office. The revised code number may mean that his tax-free pay is raised very considerably,

WEEK 14
July 6 to 12

TABLE A—FREE PAY

Code	Total free pay to date	Code	Total free pay to date	Code	Total free pay to date	Code	Total free pay to date	Code	Total free pay to date	Code	Total free pay to date	Code	Total free pay to date	Code	Total free pay to date
	£		£		£		£		£		£		£		£
0	NIL														
1	5·60	51	140·00	101	274·40	151	409·50	201	543·90	251	678·30	301	813·40	351	947·80
2	8·40	52	142·80	102	277·20	152	412·30	202	546·70	252	681·10	302	815·50	352	950·60
3	10·50	53	145·60	103	280·00	153	414·40	203	549·50	253	683·90	303	818·30	353	953·40
4	13·30	54	148·40	104	282·80	154	417·20	204	552·30	254	686·70	304	821·10	354	955·50
5	16·10	55	150·50	105	285·60	155	420·00	205	554·40	255	689·50	305	823·90	355	958·30
6	18·90	56	153·30	106	288·40	156	422·80	206	557·20	256	692·30	306	826·70	356	961·10
7	21·70	57	156·10	107	290·50	157	425·60	207	560·00	257	694·40	307	829·50	357	963·90
8	24·50	58	158·90	108	293·30	158	428·40	208	562·80	258	697·20	308	832·30	358	966·70
9	27·30	59	161·70	109	296·10	159	430·50	209	565·60	259	700·00	309	834·40	359	969·50
10	29·40	60	164·50	110	298·90	160	433·30	210	568·40	260	702·80	310	837·20	360	972·30
11	32·20	61	167·30	111	301·70	161	436·10	211	570·50	261	705·60	311	840·00		
12	35·00	62	169·40	112	304·50	162	438·90	212	573·30	262	708·40	312	842·80		
13	37·80	63	172·20	113	307·30	163	441·70	213	576·10	263	710·50	313	845·60		
14	40·60	64	175·00	114	309·40	164	444·50	214	578·90	264	713·30	314	848·40		
15	43·40	65	177·80	115	312·20	165	447·30	215	581·70	265	716·10	315	850·50		
16	45·50	66	180·60	116	315·00	166	449·40	216	584·50	266	718·90	316	853·30		
17	48·30	67	183·40	117	317·80	167	452·20	217	587·30	267	721·70	317	856·10		
18	51·10	68	185·50	118	320·60	168	455·00	218	589·40	268	724·50	318	858·90		
19	53·90	69	188·30	119	323·40	169	457·80	219	592·20	269	727·30	319	861·70		
20	56·70	70	191·10	120	325·50	170	460·60	220	595·00	270	729·40	320	864·50		
21	59·50	71	193·90	121	328·30	171	463·40	221	597·80	271	732·20	321	867·30		
22	62·30	72	196·70	122	331·10	172	465·50	222	600·60	272	735·00	322	869·40		
23	64·40	73	199·50	123	333·90	173	468·30	223	603·40	273	737·80	323	872·20		
24	67·20	74	202·30	124	336·70	174	471·10	224	605·50	274	740·60	324	875·00		
25	70·00	75	204·40	125	339·50	175	473·90	225	608·30	275	743·40	325	877·80		
26	72·80	76	207·20	126	342·30	176	476·70	226	611·10	276	745·50	326	880·60		
27	75·60	77	210·00	127	344·40	177	479·50	227	613·90	277	748·30	327	883·40		
28	78·40	78	212·80	128	347·20	178	482·30	228	616·70	278	751·10	328	885·50		
29	80·50	79	215·60	129	350·00	179	484·40	229	619·50	279	753·90	329	888·30		
30	83·30	80	218·40	130	352·80	180	487·20	230	622·30	280	756·70	330	891·10		
31	86·10	81	220·50	131	355·60	181	490·00	231	624·40	281	759·50	331	893·90		
32	88·90	82	223·30	132	358·40	182	492·80	232	627·20	282	762·30	332	896·70		
33	91·70	83	226·10	133	360·50	183	495·60	233	630·00	283	764·40	333	899·50		
34	94·50	84	228·90	134	363·30	184	498·40	234	632·80	284	767·20	334	902·30		
35	97·30	85	231·70	135	366·10	185	500·50	235	635·60	285	770·00	335	904·40		
36	99·40	86	234·50	136	368·90	186	503·30	236	638·40	286	772·80	336	907·20		
37	102·20	87	237·30	137	371·70	187	506·10	237	640·50	287	775·60	337	910·00		
38	105·00	88	239·40	138	374·50	188	508·90	238	643·30	288	778·40	338	912·80		
39	107·80	89	242·20	139	377·30	189	511·70	239	646·10	289	780·50	339	915·60		
40	110·60	90	245·00	140	379·40	190	514·50	240	648·90	290	783·30	340	918·40		
41	113·40	91	247·80	141	382·20	191	517·30	241	651·70	291	786·10	341	920·50		
42	115·50	92	250·60	142	385·00	192	519·40	242	654·50	292	788·90	342	923·30		
43	118·30	93	253·40	143	387·80	193	522·20	243	657·30	293	791·70	343	926·10		
44	121·10	94	255·50	144	390·60	194	525·00	244	659·40	294	794·50	344	928·90		
45	123·90	95	258·30	145	393·40	195	527·80	245	662·20	295	797·30	345	931·70		
46	126·70	96	261·10	146	395·50	196	530·60	246	665·00	296	799·40	346	934·50		
47	129·50	97	263·90	147	398·30	197	533·40	247	667·80	297	802·20	347	937·30		
48	132·30	98	266·70	148	401·10	198	535·50	248	670·60	298	805·00	348	939·40		
49	134·40	99	269·50	149	403·90	199	538·30	249	673·40	299	807·80	349	942·20		
50	137·20	100	272·30	150	406·70	200	541·10	250	675·50	300	810·60	350	945·00		

Fig. 17.6. An extract from Table A (reproduced by permission of the Controller of Her Majesty's Stationery Office).

and as a result he will have overpaid tax. Suppose his total tax deducted to last week was £136.50 but now, due to the new code number, his total tax due is only £104.20. This means he is due for a refund of £32.30, and the money will be repaid in the packet at once. The young

WEEK 14
(July 6 to July 12)

TABLE B

TAX DUE ON TAXABLE PAY UP TO £360

Total TAXABLE PAY to date	Total TAX DUE to date	Total TAXABLE PAY to date	Total TAX DUE to date	Total TAXABLE PAY to date	Total TAX DUE to date	Total TAXABLE PAY to date	Total TAX DUE to date	Total TAXABLE PAY to date	Total TAX DUE to date	Total TAXABLE PAY to date	Total TAX DUE to date
£	£	£	£	£	£	£	£	£	£	£	£
1	0·25	61	15·25	121	30·25	181	45·25	241	63·75	301	84·15
2	0·50	62	15·50	122	30·50	182	45·50	242	64·10	302	84·50
3	0·75	63	15·75	123	30·75	183	45·75	243	64·40	303	84·80
4	1·00	64	16·00	124	31·00	184	46·00	244	64·75	304	85·15
5	1·25	65	16·25	125	31·25	185	46·25	245	65·10	305	85·50
6	1·50	66	16·50	126	31·50	186	46·50	246	65·45	306	85·85
7	1·75	67	16·75	127	31·75	187	46·75	247	65·80	307	86·20
8	2·00	68	17·00	128	32·00	188	47·00	248	66·10	308	86·50
9	2·25	69	17·25	129	32·25	189	47·25	249	66·45	309	86·85
10	2·50	70	17·50	130	32·50	190	47·50	250	66·80	310	87·20
11	2·75	71	17·75	131	32·75	191	47·75	251	67·15	311	87·55
12	3·00	72	18·00	132	33·00	192	48·00	252	67·50	312	87·90
13	3·25	73	18·25	133	33·25	193	48·25	253	67·80	313	88·20
14	3·50	74	18·50	134	33·50	194	48·50	254	68·15	314	88·55
15	3·75	75	18·75	135	33·75	195	48·75	255	68·50	315	88·90
16	4·00	76	19·00	136	34·00	196	49·00	256	68·85	316	89·25
17	4·25	77	19·25	137	34·25	197	49·25	257	69·20	317	89·60
18	4·50	78	19·50	138	34·50	198	49·50	258	69·50	318	89·90
19	4·75	79	19·75	139	34·75	199	49·75	259	69·85	319	90·25
20	5·00	80	20·00	140	35·00	200	50·00	260	70·20	320	90·60
21	5·25	81	20·25	141	35·25	201	50·25	261	70·55	321	90·95
22	5·50	82	20·50	142	35·50	202	50·50	262	70·90	322	91·30
23	5·75	83	20·75	143	35·75	203	50·80	263	71·20	323	91·60
24	6·00	84	21·00	144	36·00	204	51·15	264	71·55	324	91·95
25	6·25	85	21·25	145	36·25	205	51·50	265	71·90	325	92·30
26	6·50	86	21·50	146	36·50	206	51·85	266	72·25	326	92·65
27	6·75	87	21·75	147	36·75	207	52·20	267	72·60	327	93·00
28	7·00	88	22·00	148	37·00	208	52·50	268	72·90	328	93·30
29	7·25	89	22·25	149	37·25	209	52·85	269	73·25	329	93·65
30	7·50	90	22·50	150	37·50	210	53·20	270	73·60	330	94·00
31	7·75	91	22·75	151	37·75	211	53·55	271	73·95	331	94·35
32	8·00	92	23·00	152	38·00	212	53·90	272	74·30	332	94·70
33	8·25	93	23·25	153	38·25	213	54·20	273	74·60	333	95·00
34	8·50	94	23·50	154	38·50	214	54·55	274	74·95	334	95·35
35	8·75	95	23·75	155	38·75	215	54·90	275	75·30	335	95·70
36	9·00	96	24·00	156	39·00	216	55·25	276	75·65	336	96·05
37	9·25	97	24·25	157	39·25	217	55·60	277	76·00	337	96·40
38	9·50	98	24·50	158	39·50	218	55·90	278	76·30	338	96·70
39	9·75	99	24·75	159	39·75	219	56·25	279	76·65	339	97·05
40	10·00	100	25·00	160	40·00	220	56·60	280	77·00	340	97·40
41	10·25	101	25·25	161	40·25	221	56·95	281	77·35	341	97·75
42	10·50	102	25·50	162	40·50	222	57·30	282	77·70	342	98·10
43	10·75	103	25·75	163	40·75	223	57·60	283	78·00	343	98·40
44	11·00	104	26·00	164	41·00	224	57·95	284	78·35	344	98·75
45	11·25	105	26·25	165	41·25	225	58·30	285	78·70	345	99·10
46	11·50	106	26·50	166	41·50	226	58·65	286	79·05	346	99·45
47	11·75	107	26·75	167	41·75	227	59·00	287	79·40	347	99·80
48	12·00	108	27·00	168	42·00	228	59·30	288	79·70	348	100·10
49	12·25	109	27·25	169	42·25	229	59·65	289	80·05	349	100·45
50	12·50	110	27·50	170	42·50	230	60·00	290	80·40	350	100·80
51	12·75	111	27·75	171	42·75	231	60·35	291	80·75	351	101·15
52	13·00	112	28·00	172	43·00	232	60·70	292	81·10	352	101·50
53	13·25	113	28·25	173	43·25	233	61·00	293	81·40	353	101·80
54	13·50	114	28·50	174	43·50	234	61·35	294	81·75	354	102·15
55	13·75	115	28·75	175	43·75	235	61·70	295	82·10	355	102·50
56	14·00	116	29·00	176	44·00	236	62·05	296	82·45	356	102·85
57	14·25	117	29·25	177	44·25	237	62·40	297	82·80	357	103·20
58	14·50	118	29·50	178	44·50	238	62·70	298	83·10	358	103·50
59	14·75	119	29·75	179	44·75	239	63·05	299	83·45	359	103·85
60	15·00	120	30·00	180	45·00	240	63·40	300	83·80	360	104·20

Fig. 17.7. An extract from Table B (reproduced by permission of the Controller of Her Majesty's Stationery Office).

INCOME TAX

PARTICULARS OF EMPLOYEE LEAVING

PART 1

		District number	Reference number
1.	Employer's PAYE reference		

2.	Employee's National Insurance number *(copy from Deduction Card)*		

		Mr. Mrs. Miss etc.
3.	Employee's surname *(Enter in BLOCK letters)*	
	Employee's first two forenames *(Enter in BLOCK letters)*	

		Day	Month	Year
4.	Date of leaving *(Enter in figures)*			19

		Code	Wk. 1 (or Month 1)
5.	Code at date of leaving If on Week 1 (Month 1) basis also enter "X" in box marked "Wk. 1 (or Month 1"		

			Week	Month
6.	Last entries on Deduction Card *If Week 1 (Month 1) basis applies complete item 7 instead*	Week or Month No.		
		Total pay to date	£	p
		Total tax to date	£	p

7.	Week 1 (Month 1) basis applies	Total pay in this employment	£	p
		Total tax deducted in this employment	£	p

8.	Works Number	9. Branch, Department, Contract, etc.	

10. Employee's private address

11. I certify that the particulars entered at items 1 to 9 above are correct.

Employer

Address

Date

INSTRUCTIONS TO EMPLOYER
1. Complete this form (including the shaded boxes) if a code (other than NI) is in use when an employee leaves. Take care that the carbon entries on Parts 2 and 3 are legible.
2. Enter the code (number and letter) at item 5.
3. If the employee was engaged after 6 April last include in item 6 the pay and tax notified to you in respect of previous employments.
4. Detach PART 1 and send it to your Tax Office IMMEDIATELY.
5. Hand PARTS 2 AND 3 (unseparated) to the employee WHEN HE LEAVES.
6. If the employee has died, please enter "D" in this box ▶ and send ALL THREE PARTS of this form (unseparated) immediately to your Tax Office.

For Tax District use

For Centre use		
Amended	M/E	P

P45   HPB 1166 7/77

Fig. 17.8. A form P45 (reproduced by permission of the controller of Her Majesty's Stationery Office).

couple will be able to meet some of the requirements of setting up a home together with the tax refunds set free by the PAYE system. Figs 17.6 and 17.7 illustrate Tables A and B.

(*d*) *Remittance advice cards.* These are supplied to the employer to enable him to account to the Inland Revenue each month for the tax deducted.

(*e*) *The Form P45—for employees who change employment.* Where an employee changes employment the new employer will need to know what tax the old employer has deducted, so that deductions can resume at the same point. To make this easy the employee is supplied with a form P45 before leaving. This form has three copies, of which the top copy is sent to the Inland Revenue authorities by the old employer as a signal that the employee has ceased employment. The other two copies are taken by the employee to the new employer who uses one to prepare a tax deduction card and sends the other to the local Inspector of Taxes as a signal that the employee has commenced employment. Fig. 17.8 shows a form P45.

(*f*) *The Form P60—the annual certificate of tax deducted.* At the end of the year an employer prepares two documents, a P60 and a P35. The P60 is given to the employee and shows the gross wages paid during the year, the gross tax deducted and the net wages paid after deductions of tax. This form P60 should not be destroyed by the employee, but should be retained as it will be needed when preparing the personal tax return for the tax office at the start of the new tax year. The form P35 is used by the employer to account in full for all the tax deducted from all the employees during the year. Fig. 17.9 shows a typical form P60.

17.11 Other Tax Schedules

Other types of income—for example, income from business activities, income from rent, income from interests and dividends, etc.—is taxable under other schedules than Schedule E, which is the PAYE schedule. The study of these schedules is rather specialised and is a matter for the accountant rather than one of office practice.

17.12 The National Insurance Scheme

Besides the deductions for taxation the employer is also required to deduct contributions payable under the National Insurance scheme. This scheme provides a range of benefits to citizens, the funds being largely derived from contributions made by deduction from salary. These contributions have, since April 1975, been earnings-related. This means that the employee earning a low wage pays only a small contribution, while the employee on a high salary pays larger contributions. The actual tables of contributions are printed in a special *Employer's Guide to National Insurance Contributions.* For some employees—those over the age of 65, for example—there are no contributions, but the

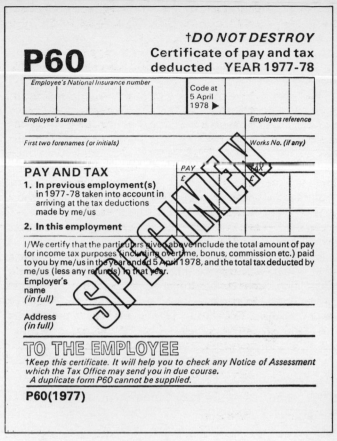

Fig. 17.9. A form P60 (reproduced by permission of the Controller of Her Majesty's Stationery Office).

employer still pays a considerable sum which may be as high as £6 per week. For married women the employee's contribution is only a few pence, but the employer pays a larger contribution. For ordinary employees the contribution averages about £3.50 per week, with the employer paying about twice as much as well.

The benefits received include old age pensions, which are now earnings-related, sickness benefit, unemployment benefit, workmen's compensation, maternity benefits and death benefits.

Employers now pay the funds over to the Inland Revenue Department each month. Formerly a system of 'stamping' cards was used, a tedious process which has now yielded to computerisation.

17.13 Pension Contributions

Traditionally State pensions under the National Insurance scheme have been small, and many firms ran extra pension schemes for their staff. Where such schemes are approved by the Inland Revenue authorities, any contributions deducted from the employee's salary are deducted from the taxable income so that tax is not paid on the contributions (see Fig. 17.3, page 263). April 1978 saw the start of an enlarged National Scheme which gives everyone in employment two pensions: the basic Old Age Pension and a higher Earnings-related Pension. Firms with excellent schemes have been allowed to contract out of the official earnings-related scheme, but the new scheme means that almost all employees will retire with reasonable pensions.

17.14 Sickness Benefit Deductions from Wages

An employee who is absent from work through sickness may get no pay and be solely dependent upon sickness benefit. Some firms pay their workers during genuine sickness, but since the employees will receive sickness benefit as well it would mean that they were better off when absent from work than when working. To avoid this, many firms who pay wages during sickness deduct the sickness benefit from the wage or salary payable. This would be shown on the pay-roll under the heading 'Other deductions'.

17.15 Points to Think About and Discuss

(*a*) A new employee is told by her firm that she must agree to open a bank account if she is to take employment, so that her wages may be paid monthly into her account. Reluctantly she does so, and then finds that her superior, who has worked for the firm for many years, insists upon being paid in cash. Discuss whether the firm is treating her unfairly, or illegally.

(*b*) Most office workers are paid on a time basis, attendance for a specified number of hours being required. Discuss whether this is a very good method. What are its advantages and disadvantages? What modifications could be devised to improve it?

17.16 Rapid Revision

Cover the page with a sheet of paper and uncover one question at a time.

Answers	Questions
—	1. What were the *Truck Acts*?
1. Acts of Parliament which controlled the way in which workers were paid.	2. What Act controls the payment of wages today?

Answers	Questions
2. The *Payment of Wages Act, 1960*.	3. How may wages be paid?
3. In legal tender, or (if the employee agrees) by cheque, or credit transfer.	4. How may wages be paid to a sick employee?
4. By postal order.	5. What are statutory deductions from pay?
5. Deductions authorised by Act of Parliament. The commonest types are: (a) tax deductions; (b) National Insurance contributions; (c) special pension contributions (teachers, etc.).	6. What are voluntary deductions from pay?
6. Deductions which the employee has requested. The most usual are: (a) SAYE (save as you earn contributions); (b) charitable donations.	7. What is a coin summary?
7. It is a list of coins required in order to pay wages.	8. What is a form P2?
8. A 'Notice of Coding' under the PAYE tax system.	9. What is a P13?
9. An emergency card for tax purposes where a new employee has failed to furnish correct information about his tax position.	10. What is a P45?
10. It is a form used when an employee changes jobs to notify his new employer of his tax position.	11. What is a P60?
11. It is a form sent to all employees at the end of the year telling each what his total earnings and tax for the year amounted to.	12. Go over the page again until you feel you are sure of the answers.

Exercises Set 17

1. Rule up a Wages Book similar to the Wages Book shown in Fig. 17.2 and enter the following details:

R. Lawrence Gross pay 27.62. Deductions: Tax 7.30; National Insurance 1.80; Union 1.62; Charities 0.16.

T. Gold Gross pay 25.88. Deductions: Tax 6.32; National Insurance 1.71; Union 1.62; Charities 0.23.

M. Silva Gross pay 42.75. Deductions: Tax 11.15; National Insurance 2.78; Union 1.62; Charities 0.25

A. Copper Gross pay 28.34. Deductions: Tax 7.55; National Insurance 5.23; Union 1.62; Charities 0.16.

Calculate the net pay and total the important columns.

2. Rule up a Wages Book similar to the one in Fig. 17.2 and enter the following details.

R. Burton	Gross pay 45.65. Deductions: Tax—nil; National Insurance 2.97; Union 0.33; Refund of Tax 4.27.
E. Taylor	Gross pay 47.25. Deductions: Tax 2.35; National Insurance 3.07; Union 0.33.
R. Rogers	Gross pay 47.35. Deductions: Tax 3.25; National Insurance 3.07; Union 0.33.
P. Lucas	Gross pay 46.85. Deductions: Tax 1.85; National Insurance 3.04; Union 0.33.

Calculate the net pay and total the important columns.

3. Give three methods of payment for wages. Explain fully the procedure in each case, mentioning the advantages and disadvantages.

4. Name two compulsory and two optional deductions from wages. Write fully about two of them.

5. Several methods are used for determining the weekly wage of employees, including: (i) time rates; (ii) piece rates; (iii) commission.

(*a*) Describe each of the above three methods and, in each case, indicate the type(s) of worker for whom the method would normally be used; (*b*) mention the advantages of each method; (*c*) what records must be kept under each separate method in order to provide information from which the wages can be calculated?

6. The clock-card of an employee, J. Ayres, is shown below. He is paid at the rate of £1.50 per hour for a 40-hour week and time-and-a-quarter for the next six hours. After that he is paid time-and-a-half for work on week-days and double-time for work on Sundays. Note: The official starting time (Monday to Friday) is 8.00 a.m. The employees are allowed 3 minutes grace without deduction.

NAME
NO.   WEEK ENDING 3rd May, 19..

DAY		IN	OUT	IN	OUT	IN	OUT	TOTAL
M	AM	8.00						
	PM		12.30	1.30	5.30	6.00	8.30	
T	AM	8.01						
	PM		12.30	1.30	5.30	6.00	8.00	
W	AM	7.58						
	PM		12.15	1.30	5.30	6.00	9.00	
T	AM	8.02						
	PM		12.30	1.30	6.30			
F	AM	8.00						
	PM		12.00	1.00	5.30	5.45	9.45	
S	AM	7.30						
	PM		12.15					
S	AM	9.00						
	PM		1.00					

TOTAL HOURS

(*a*) Complete the card down to and including the figure for total hours; (*b*) calculate the total gross wages for the week; (*c*) what compulsory deductions will be made by the employer?

7. (*a*) Describe the purpose of: (i) a pay-roll; (ii) a pay advice (for the employee); (iii) an employee's individual pay record.

(*b*) A small firm intends to use a copy-writer system for the preparation of wages documents. Give a brief explanation of this method.

8. A new employee has just joined your firm. What information will you require in order to make up his wages? Where will you obtain this information and to whom should you apply for clarification on any point about which you feel doubtful?

9. You are responsible for the preparation of wages for piece-rate workers: (*a*) list the items of information required for the calculation of wages; (*b*) outline a suitable procedure for obtaining, making up and paying out the wages for these employees.

10. Salaried staff are paid monthly by credit transfer in your firm. What details would be required before you could arrange to include a new member of the salaried staff on the pay-roll?

11. Distinguish between flat rates, piece rates, bonus rates and hourly rates of wages. Which classes of employee would be paid by each of these methods?

12. Outline controls you would institute to ensure that wages clerks were honest and reliable on taking up employment, and remained so over the years.

13. What does the *Payment of Wages Act, 1960*, say about: (*a*) payment by cheque or credit transfer; (*b*) payment of employees who are absent through sickness or injury?

14. Write a brief account of the PAYE system of personal taxation. Mention in your account the use of tax tables, code numbers and forms P45 and P60.

15. A new employee arrives to commence employment with XYZ Limited. What documents should he present to his new employer, and what actions should the employer take to ensure he receives his correct wages in due course?

16. In what ways may an employer satisfy the requirements of the *National Insurance Acts* as far as deductions from the salaries of his employees are concerned? What benefits do employees derive from these National Insurance schemes?

17. What are the differences between PAYE deductions and National Insurance deductions from salary? What benefits are achieved from these payments?

18. Distinguish between 'free pay' and 'taxable pay'. Distinguish between 'gross pay' and 'net pay'.

19. What are earnings-related insurance contributions and by whom are they paid?

20. When is a P45 used? What happens to it once it has been issued by the employer? Why is it so important to the working of the PAYE system?

21. Explain the meaning of: (i) PAYE; (ii) P45; (iii) P60; (iv) P13; (v) free pay.

22. State briefly what benefits you might obtain from paying: (*a*) National Insurance contributions; (*b*) income tax; (*c*) a voluntary donation to the Royal National Life-boat Institution?

23. The following is taken from a company's wages book. It gives details of wages for the week ended 30th June.

	Week ending 30th June						
		Deductions					Employer's contrib.
Name	Gross wages	I tax	Nat. Ins.	TU	SAYE	Net wages	Nat. Ins.
	£	£	£ ·	£	£	£	£
Black, W.	74.50	5.20	4.86	1.25	5.00	58.19	8.97
Green, S.	48.40	3.80	3.14	1.00	—	40.46	5.79
Grey, R.	36.50	2.25	2.39	0.50	5.00	26.36	4.41
Brown, T.	82.80	4.50	5.38	1.25	—	71.67	9.87
White, J.	65.60	—	4.27	1.25	—	60.08	7.89
	307.80	15.75	20.04	5.25	10.00	256.76	36.93

(*a*) State the amount to be drawn from the bank to pay the wages and draw up an analysis showing the numbers and denominations of notes and coins you will need to provide for the wage packets.

(*b*) How was the amount of income tax payable by each person decided?

(*c*) What will the company do with the amounts of money it has deducted?

(*d*) What is the total cost for the week to the employer of employing these five people? (RSA—Adapted)

24. (*a*) You are working in the wages department of your company and you are told to complete a P45 for an employee leaving. (i) What information will you enter on it? (ii) Where will you get this information? (iii) What happens to the three parts of this form?

(*b*) You are also told to start an Emergency Card P13 for a new employee. (i) Why is this necessary? (ii) What effect is this likely to have on the amount of tax the employee will have to pay? (RSA)

25. (*a*) What is a P13 used for? (*b*) What is a P60 form? (*c*) When a person is given a wage increase, what difference does this make to the statutory deductions from his/her pay? (*d*) What amounts of overtime pay will be added to an employee's basic pay if he works six hours overtime at time-and-a-half, and his basic rate of pay is £1.80 per hour? (RSA)

26. Name two *compulsory* deductions from wages. Explain briefly for what purposes these deductions are made. (RSA)

18

THE PERSONNEL OFFICE

18.1 Introduction

Nothing is of greater importance to a firm than the qualities and abilities of the staff it employs. Wages and salaries take about 76 per cent of the entire national wealth, so that this expense alone is of enormous importance to every firm. In return for the sums earned employees must be able and willing to give good value for money by performing competently and quickly the services for which they are paid. Good industrial relations are essential, and the personnel office will be largely instrumental in achieving them, if the personnel officer and personnel staff perform their functions properly.

18.2 Functions of the Personnel Office

The following functions are performed by the personnel office:

(*a*) The recruitment of staff.
(*b*) Their training and development.
(*c*) The description of jobs, and the devising of methods of payment and promotion from grade to grade.
(*d*) The provision of welfare facilities and the devising of pension schemes.
(*e*) The preparation of contracts of employment, and the drawing up of redundancy schemes where appropriate.
(*f*) The dismissal of employees.

Many firms will be too small to employ a specialist personnel officer and the owner will perform the majority of these functions. Larger firms may appoint a senior member of the staff to supervise these activities. The company secretary, the administration officer or heads of departments are suitable people to perform these functions. In the largest organisations a central personnel office, keeping adequate centralised staff records, will handle these activities.

18.3 The Personnel Officer

The personnel officer may be a professionally qualified member of the Institute of Personnel Management. The officer must secure for the firm personnel of the right quality and experience, in a wide range of employment situations. Since internal promotions are naturally favoured by staff, whose contentment in their present situations is often related directly to their future prospects, the personnel officer must devise adequate methods for selecting and re-training staff and for notifying all personnel of vacancies in fields that may interest them. It is necessary to consider genuine cases of dissatisfaction, and act sympathetically where domestic or other difficulties are being faced by employees. Reports of incompetence, negligent staff behaviour, unpunctuality or poor attendance must be firmly dealt with.

18.4 Job Grading

Before staff are recruited it is essential to have a picture of the types of persons required, the qualities they should have, the skills they should display, the salary payable, etc. These ideas will crystallise out if careful job descriptions of all posts are prepared. Jobs may be graded into five main grades. These are:

(a) Routine tasks under close supervision.
(b) Routine tasks, less closely supervised and with some measure of responsibility.
(c) Supervisory roles over routine activities.
(d) Posts requiring initiative, and giving opportunities to acquire special skills and experience.
(e) Supervisory and management posts requiring skill, experience, initiative and judgement.

Within these grades there is usually a need to subdivide into two, or perhaps even three grades. For example, an employee of limited ability never likely to reach supervisory level may still look forward to some recognition of his/her ability if the grading is such that a number of years' experience in a particular field merits an upgrading to a higher level of pay. At the very top levels, where staff of excellent ability have to be attracted and motivated, a number of grades reflecting increasing experience and widening horizons will reduce staff turnover.

18.5 Personnel Records

Personal files. Whenever staff are employed records at once begin to accumulate. The original application form for employment, the record of any interview held, or preliminary test conducted, and a medical report usually start the collection. Subsequently, training records, merit ratings, proficiency tests, absence records, etc., are added. The personal files of staff are confidential, and should never be left where other staff can read them.

Visible records. Where large numbers of staff are employed, a visible record system is desirable, and many firms which market business systems offer simple folders and binders which can be used for displaying records quickly and easily. As many as 28 records per page are visible at once in the Kalamazoo binder for the cards illustrated in

Fig. 18.1. The visible edge of the card contains room for the names of the member of staff and may be decorated with visible marker 'flashes' which pin-point particular information. Thus various qualifications could be 'flashed' by different coloured signals: supervisors in red, pensionable workers in yellow, registered disabled personnel in green, etc. A file of such cards is easily carried to a meeting with the managing director or the union negotiating panel, or the staff association annual general meeting.

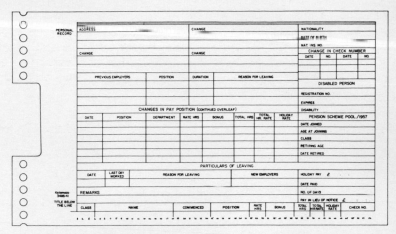

Fig. 18.1. A visible index personnel record form (reproduced by courtesy of Kalamazoo Ltd).

Strip-index Records

These are useful for giving a visual display of the staff in departments, or staff with special qualifications (see Fig. 18.2). They can be used to assist in devising staff duty rotas, holiday rotas, etc.

Developments in the employment sector in recent years have called for a more systematic record of the employer–employee relationship. Not only is it essential to give employees a written statement of their terms of employment but employees claiming compensation for wrongful dismissal in industrial tribunals make it necessary to establish before

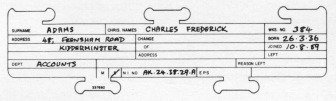

Fig. 18.2. A card strip index for personnel (reproduced by courtesy of Kalamazoo Ltd).

the tribunal that proper records have been kept of all aspects of the employee's training, attendance, conduct, etc. For this reason **employee data folders**, containing records of the original application, induction period, training and promotion, attendance, accidents, etc., are desirable. A typical data folder is reproduced in Fig. 18.3.

Note the confidential nature of some of the information, and the consequent need to maintain good security on personnel records, so that they are not available for general scrutiny.

18.6 Recruitment of Staff

There are many different ways of obtaining staff. Some write in, asking for employment. Others may be attracted by advertising in the press, on the cinema screen, or on television. Some firms rely on employment agencies to select suitable staff for them, and for the very highest posts management selection agencies screen the applicants and submit short lists of suitable candidates for posts.

Preparatory Work

The preparation of a number of forms is usually helpful in the selection procedures. These are:

(*a*) An application form, listing the candidate's name, address, telephone number, qualifications, experience, previous employment, referees, etc. Such forms may be very detailed.
(*b*) A job description, outlining the type of service the applicant would be expected to perform.
(*c*) An information sheet about the firm or institution requiring staff, describing its activities, products or services, and describing the area, housing and other facilities available, etc.

Short-listing

From the forms returned the most suitable applicants will be selected for a short-list. They will then be called for interview, and requested to bring with them such documents as are necessary to prove their qualifications listed in the application form, and the original copies of any testimonials sent. References should be taken up—preferably before the candidates are invited for interview—and a summary of the chief points for and against a candidate should be drawn up for the benefit of the interviewing panel.

Interviewing

The purpose of an interview is to assess the personal qualities of the applicants, to assess their character and test their knowledge of the field of activity they are intending to carry out. A more detailed description of the work involved will be given to the applicants at the interview and any reservations they have about the post can be heard and

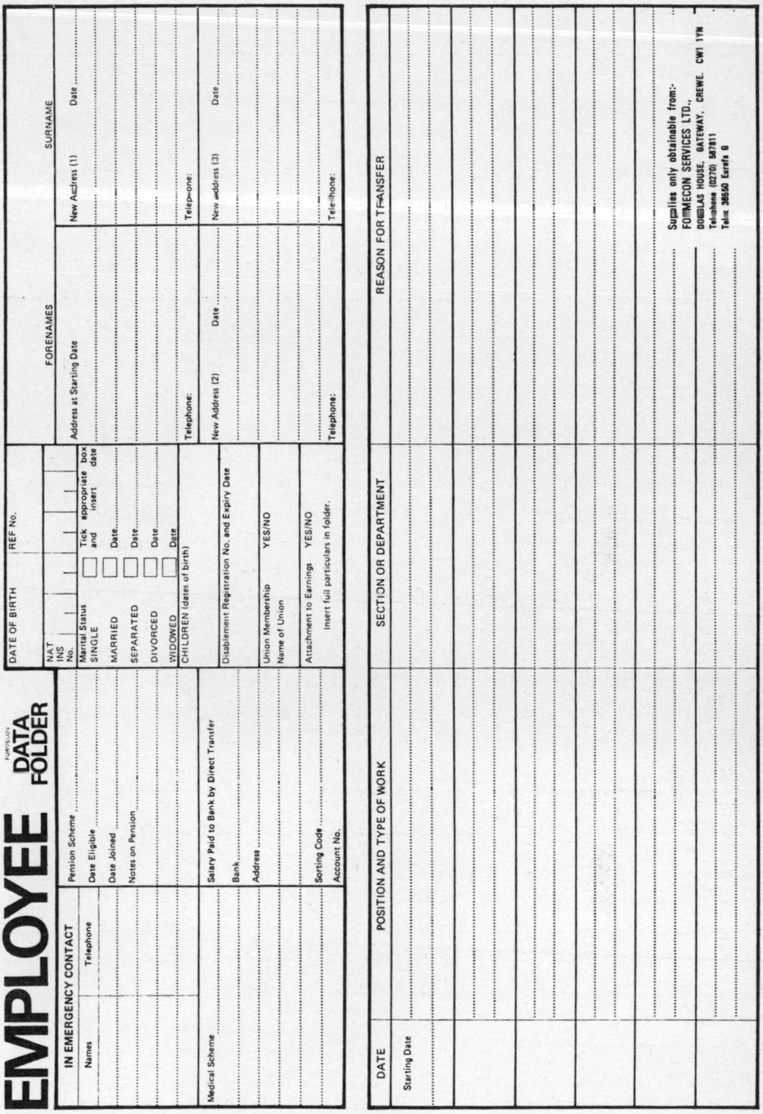

EMPLOYEE DATA FOLDER

DATE OF BIRTH   REF No.

FORENAMES   SURNAME

IN EMERGENCY CONTACT

Names	Telephone

Pension Scheme

Date Eligible

Date Joined

Notes on Pension

NAT INS No.

Marital Status — Tick appropriate box and insert date

SINGLE

MARRIED   Date

SEPARATED Date

DIVORCED   Date

WIDOWED   Date

CHILDREN (dates of birth)

Address at Starting Date

New Address (1)   Date

Medical Scheme

Salary Paid to Bank by Direct Transfer

Bank

Address

Sorting Code

Account No.

Disablement Registration No. and Expiry Date

Union Membership   YES/NO

Name of Union

Attachment to Earnings   YES/NO
Insert full particulars in folder.

Telephone:

New Address (2)   Date

Telephone:

New address (3)   Date

Telephone:

DATE	POSITION AND TYPE OF WORK	SECTION OR DEPARTMENT	REASON FOR TRANSFER
Starting Date			

Supplies only obtainable from:-
FORMECON SERVICES LTD.,
DOUGLAS HOUSE, GATEWAY, CREWE. CW1 1YN
Telephone (0270) 587811
Telex 36650 Eurefc G

Fig. 18.3. An employee data folder.

answered. Finally, the candidate selected may be offered the post, and upon acceptance will be bound by the contract of employment.

Induction

On the first day of the new employment the employee should bring along (i) the P45 which enables tax records to be established and continued without overcharging and (ii) the letter of appointment.

The new employee should then be 'inducted' by the personnel officer and others so that the firm and its products, its aims and organisation are fully explained. Some idea of the range of topics that need to be covered in the induction period is given by the induction checklist reproduced in Fig. 18.4. Note that in signing the document the new employee recognises that an adequate induction programme has been followed.

18.7 The *Employment Protection (Consolidation) Act, 1978*

This Act of Parliament consolidated all previous legislation on employment, though it has also been slightly amended by the *Employment Act, 1980*. These acts reduced the insecurity experienced by some workers whose terms of employment permitted their employers to dismiss them virtually without notice. The Act requires a statement in writing to be given to the employee within 13 weeks of taking up employment, stating the date of commencement of employment, the rate of remuneration and method of its calculation and the intervals at which it is to be paid. The terms of unemployment with regard to holidays, sickness and sick-pay, pension and length of notice must also be stated. The minimum length of notice is one week for an employee who has been employed for at least 4 weeks, rising to two weeks after two years and then one week for each year of employment up to a maximum of 12 weeks' notice after 12 years' service.

18.8 Staff Training

Staff training may be divided into four main sections:

(*a*) *Induction training.* This enables the new employee to know about the firm, its products, its organisation and his/her place within that organisation.
(*b*) *Job training.* This will teach apprentices and other new employees the particular skills they require and the routines and business systems used.
(*c*) *Long-term craft training, or professional education.* Over a period of years young employees will be assisted to master their own trades and professions, often by day-release courses at local technical colleges.
(*d*) *Supervisory and management training.* This is designed to prepare the experienced worker for employment at higher levels.

INDUCTION CHECKLIST

NEW EMPLOYEE FULL NAME		
DEPARTMENT & JOB		DATE STARTED

The object of good induction training is to obtain the best performance from the new employee and to relieve anxiety. Try to complete this form on the first day. Put a tick in each box when each point is understood by the new employee.

On completion hand second copy to new employee and return top copy to...

GENERAL INFORMATION		RULES, HEALTH AND SAFETY	
1. COMPLETE EMPLOYEE DATA FOLDER		31. COMPANY RULES (HAND COPY TO EMPLOYEE)	
2. OBTAIN P45 FORM (IF AVAILABLE)		32. DISCIPLINARY PROCEDURE AND APPEALS	
3. PROVIDE WRITTEN OR VERBAL JOB DESCRIPTION		33. INFORM WHERE FACTORIES/OFFICES ACT DISPLAYED	
4. EXPLAIN RATES OF PAY (a) BASIC		34. TIME KEEPING AND RECORDING	
5. (b) OVERTIME		35. LATENESS – EFFECT ON PAY	
6. (c) BONUS/COMM.		36. ILLNESS – SICK NOTE REQUIREMENTS	
7. (d) HOLIDAY PAY		37. ILLNESS – EFFECT ON PAY	
8. HOW, WHEN & WHERE PAID		38. ACCEPTABLE REASONS FOR TIME OFF OR ABSENCE	
9. HOURS OF WORK (OR SHIFTS IF ANY)		39. ABSENCE – EFFECT ON PAY AND COMPANY	
10. BREAKS		40. AFTER ABSENCE REPORT TO...............................	
11. OVERTIME AVAILABILITY AND ARRANGEMENTS		41. PROCEDURE FOR ARRANGING TIME OFF	
12. DEDUCTIONS (a) SAVINGS		42. SMOKING REGULATIONS	
13. (b) CHARITABLE		43. FIRE DRILL (a) WHAT TO DO	
14. (c) TRADE UNION (VIA COMPANY)		44. (b) EMERGENCY EXITS	
15. (d) OTHER (e.g. social club)		45. (c) WHERE TO ASSEMBLE	
16. EXPLAIN PAY SLIP FORMAT		46. (d) WHO TO REPORT TO	
17. CONFIRM COMPANY HOLIDAY ARRANGEMENTS		47. (e) LOCATION OF FIRE FIGHTING EQUIP.	
18. EXPLAIN HOLIDAY QUALIFICATIONS		48. SPECIAL SAFETY PRECAUTIONS/HEALTH HAZARDS	
19. CHECK CONFLICTING HOLIDAY COMMITMENTS		49. SAFETY REGS. AND POLICY STATEMENT (Show copy)	
20. PENSION SCHEMES AND/OR STATE SCHEME		50. YOUR SAFETY OFFICER/REP. IS................................	
21. CANTEEN FACILITIES		51. SAFETY CLOTHING/SHOES/GLOVES/ETC.	
22. SOCIAL AND RECREATIONAL FACILITIES		52. EAR/EYE PROTECTORS/HELMETS/BARRIER CREAMS ETC	
23. TRANSPORT AND PARKING		53. SAFETY CLOTHING/PROTECTORS Obtain from...............	
24. PERSONAL PROBLEMS CONSULT..........................		54. LIFTING AND HANDLING INSTRUCTIONS	
25. TRADE UNION MEMBERSHIP AND THE COMPANY		55. ENCOURAGE TIDINESS TO REDUCE ACCIDENTS	
26. COMPANY/GROUP PRODUCTS OR SERVICES		56. ACCIDENTS/Dangerous Occurences report to...............	
27. COMPANY HISTORY		57. ACCIDENT BOOK/Gen. Register held by.......................	
28. COMPANY ORGANISATION AND COMMITTEES		58. FIRST AID BOX/ROOM IS SITED AT............................	
29. EDUCATION TRAINING PROMOTION AND TRANSFER		59. FIRST AID OFFICER IS..	
30. SUGGESTION SCHEME (give booklet if available)		60. EMPLOYEE COMPLAINTS are dealt with by...................	

61. TOUR OF PREMISES:– *Introduce to other members of department and ensure that they will help the newcomer to settle down. Explain each persons job. Point out location of toilets, washroom, lockers, cloakroom, fire exits and equipment, first aid box/room, canteen, special hazards and prohibited areas etc.*	I have received the above induction training:-	New employee signature
	Induction Supervised by:–	Signature on behalf of employer
62. OTHER INFORMATION:	Notes	

This form should not be reproduced in whole or part without the written consent of Formecon Services Ltd. Gateway, Crewe, CW1 1YN.

FS.51   Telephone: 0270 587811 Telex: 36550 Eurofs G   © Copyright 1979

Fig. 18.4. An induction check-list.

18.9   The Welfare of Employees

Most firms feel some sense of obligation to employees, and assist those who get into difficulties, especially if it is through no fault of the employee. Certain basic welfare facilities are provided in offices by law—for example, First Aid facilities and canteen facilities. Many firms exceed their strict legal obligations—for example, by paying employees while they are sick and absent from work because of accidental injuries. Many provide insurance policies to cover their employees against death, so that some basic sum will be available to dependants. Many provide recreational facilities, sports grounds or entertainment for children at festival times.

This type of welfare provision is not motivated solely by generosity. Such facilities reduce labour turnover, and therefore save money in securing new staff and training them until they are competent. They encourage staff loyalty, so that extra effort will be forthcoming at peak periods of activity. Industrial unrest is reduced, sickness and absenteeism may decline when such services are provided, and the employee will consequently be more productive. The personnel officer will play a considerable part in this type of activity, often acting as management representative on canteen, recreational, or staff association committees.

18.10   The Dismissal of Employees

Inevitably, occasions arise when dismissal of an employee is necessary. The circumstances may arise because of dishonesty, or scurrilous behaviour of other sorts. It may be that the employee is incompetent, or uncooperative to such a degree that he interferes with the smooth running of the organisation. Redundancy can also be the cause of the dismissal. Under the *Trade Union and Labour Relations Act, 1974*, an employee who claims he has been unfairly dismissed can appeal to an industrial tribunal.

An employer may always dismiss an employee who admits dishonesty, without notice. He may refuse to give a reference, and if he does give one he may give the true reasons for the dismissal without fear of an action for defamation. Bad behaviour of other sorts may also justify instant dismissal. Incompetence in that particular work would not usually justify dismissal without notice.

A reference is given by an employer as a gesture of kindness to an employee. An employee cannot demand a reference as a right; no legal obligation exists to give a reference. Where an employer is dissatisfied with the work of an employee he is entitled to say so, and so long as he does not show malice the statements made or written are not defamatory. Malice is an improper motive. It would be malicious to make a false statement out of a wish to harm the employee and this would entitle the employee to sue for defamation.

Personnel officers are naturally very careful to avoid statements which defame ex-employees. On the other hand, they have a duty to other employers to disclose circumstances such as dishonesty or scurrilous behaviour. There is some danger that they will be held to be negligent in the courts if they give glowing references when they know of some reason why that person should not be employed. A common practice is to insert a disclaimer in references. This disclaims responsibility for losses suffered by anyone placing reliance on the statements made.

18.11   Points to Think About and Discuss

(a) Charles Brown is starting work today straight from school. What types of training might be necessary: (i) immediately; (ii) in the first few years of employment; (iii) in later years (say ten years or more after joining the firm)?

(b) Two members of staff are being considered for dismissal. Tom Smith is unsatisfactory in most ways, has a poor attendance and punctuality record, watches the clock and is off home as soon as his hours of work are over. Bill Jones is a union enthusiast who has brought sections of the work force out on strike several times recently.

What should be the correct management approach in these cases?

(c) A proposal that a staff swimming pool should be provided has been made by the staff association. Consider the suggestion, and suggest arguments for, and against, proceeding with the project.

18.12   Rapid Revision

Cover the page with a sheet of paper and uncover one question at a time.

Answers	*Questions*
—	1. List the functions of the personnel office.
1. (a) To recruit staff; (b) to train and develop staff; (c) to devise adequate job descriptions, and a ladder of promotion; (d) to devise and operate welfare schemes; (e) to prepare contracts of employment; (f) to prepare redundancy schemes; (g) to dismiss employees; (h) to give references and testimonials.	2. What professional body is active in the field of personnel?
2. The Institute of Personnel Management.	3. What is job grading?
3. Job grading is a system of classifying jobs to define the skills needed, the qualities required by the employee, and the promotion prospects.	4. What forms should be sent to a person enquiring about a particular post?
4. (a) An application form; (b) a job description; (c) an information sheet about the firm, its products and the locality.	5. What documents should a new employee take along on the first day of employment?

Answers	Questions
5. (*a*) A letter of appointment; (*b*) a P45.	6. What is an induction programme?
6. It is a programme, usually drawn up by personnel department, to introduce new employees to the firm and help them to understand their position in the organisation.	7. What Act of Parliament controls the employment of staff today?
7. The *Employment Protection (Consolidation) Act, 1978.*	8. What notice is an employee entitled to?
8. (*a*) Employees who have worked for at least 4 weeks—1 week's notice; (*b*) after two years' employment—1 week's notice for each year of employment; (*c*) not less than 12 weeks' notice if employed for 12 years or more.	9. Go over the page again until you feel you are sure of the answers.

Exercises Set 18

1. The company for which you work wishes to adopt a standard form of application which could be used by all applicants for employment in its offices. Draft a suitable application form.

2. The personnel officer wishes to notify all departments of the firm that Monday, the 21st June, will be the occasion of a day's outing to Stratford-on-Avon in celebration of the firm's centenary.

Draft an internal memorandum from the personnel officer notifying all departments of the outing and the fact that the factory will be closed on that day.

3. In connection with staff appointments, write brief notes on: (*a*) application forms; (*b*) testimonials; (*c*) referees; (*d*) P45.

4. Discuss the ways in which an organisation may provide for the safety, health and welfare of its office employees.

5. Design a visible record card suitable for student records in a college office. Information is required concerning a student's address (including the local authority in whose area he resides), date of birth, course, department, examinations passed, name and address of employer, together with other relevant personal data. Your illustration should also indicate (*a*) the information conveyed on the visible edge; (*b*) the use of a signalling device.

6. When a person leaves the service of one employer to begin with another employer, what documents is he expected to provide and what information do they contain?

7. A firm employs the following personnel:

There is a managing director to whom the general manager and two senior executives are accountable. Each of the senior executives has a secretary. There are three managers:

Personnel, with a shorthand-typist and two clerks.
Production, with a staff of one shorthand-typist and two clerks.

Company secretary, with a staff of three filing clerks, three copy-typists, three shorthand-typists and two wages clerks.

The personnel manager reports to one senior executive.

The production manager reports to the other senior executive.

The company secretary reports to the general manager.

Make out an organisation chart, showing clearly the lines of authority.

8. You are a member of the personnel department of a large industrial organisation. What information would you want the head of another department to give when asking you to find a new employee?

9. One of your duties as a clerk in the personnel department of a large business organisation is to keep records of all applications for employment. Draft a ruling for this record, with appropriate headings, and make three specimen entries.

10. Your company has decided to keep its personnel records on cards. (a) Design a suitable card having in mind the sort of information to be recorded; (b) state any advantages that ensue from introducing signalling devices.

11. You are employed in the personnel department of a firm. One of your friends, who is about to take up duties in a similar department, writes and asks you to explain what such a department does and how it fits into the company organisation generally.

Write your letter in reply.

12. (a) Design a record card for use in a personnel department, with provision for the following information:

Employee's name   Date left
Employee's address   Date of birth
Department   Education and qualifications
Date joined   Job title
                                   Salary

Fill in the relevant information as for a junior clerk.

(b) What means can you suggest for quick recognition of cards of a particular department?

13. What do you regard as the main personal qualities and abilities necessary for: (i) a receptionist; (ii) a copy typist; (iii) a filing and records clerk?

14. (a) What documents should employees produce when changing employment? (b) What information about them should the new employer record at that time and during their employment: (i) for the purpose of preparing wages, (ii) for inclusion in general personnel records?

15. Make a list of four qualities which an audio-typist should possess.

16. (a) Explain the business and personal attributes you would expect office staff to possess. (b) What training and qualifications should clerical staff have when they are engaged in general office duties (not shorthand and typewriting)?

17. You are employed in the personnel department of a large concern.

(a) Draft an advertisement to appear in the press for a vacancy which exists for a telephonist.

(*b*) What qualities, knowledge and skill do you consider the successful applicant should possess?

(*c*) Why is it important for an organisation to have a competent telephonist?

18. (*a*) What action is necessary by both employers in connection with PAYE when an employee changes employment?

(*b*) What action should be taken by an employee in relation to sickness benefit if absent from the office through illness?

19. You are asked to draw up a holiday rota (two weeks' holiday each) for the ten members of your staff covering the months of July, August and September. They are as follows:

Yourself	Manager in charge
Mr A	Your deputy
Miss B	Telephonist
Miss C	Typist-telephonist
Mrs E	General clerk (with past wages experience)
Mr D	General clerk
Mr F	Wages clerk and book-keeper
Miss G	Typist
Miss H	Personal secretary
Mr J	Junior accountant.

Miss B is to be married on Saturday 1st July and will be on honeymoon for the next two weeks. Mr J's wife is a nurse and has had to book her holiday from 5th August to 19th August. Mr F prefers a September vacation.

20. The four chief aspects of your department's work are: (*a*) staff recruitment (*b*) staff training; (*c*) staff records; (*d*) wages.

Topman and Deputy supervise staff recruitment and also assist with training. Training is carried out chiefly by Knowall, Knowhow and Adviser. Records are kept by Loggitt and wages are prepared by Cashman. Adviser at one time was in charge of records and Knowall was at one time wages clerk. In the five-week period commencing on 4th April all seven of these staff have to attend a one-week course on computer appreciation at the staff training college. Devise a rota which will ensure that all aspects of the department's activities are kept going during this period.

THE PURCHASING OFFICE

19.1 Purchases

Three main kinds of purchases are made by firms. They are:

(i) *Purchases of assets*, like plant, machinery, motor vehicles, office equipment or fixtures and fittings. These items are purchased for long-term use in the business and are sold only when they have depreciated over many years in the service of the firm.

(ii) *Purchases of consumable items*, such as solvents and lubricants used in manufacture, petrol and oil for motor vehicles, stationery for office use and postage stamps. These items are consumed more rapidly than assets, and become losses of the business during the year in which they were purchased.

(iii) *Purchase of goods for re-sale, or of raw materials for manufacture into goods for sale.* These items are passed on to the eventual customer at a profit, and are the source of the profits of all trading firms. Firms who offer services only do not handle this class of purchases, since they do not deal in *goods*.

19.2 Centralised Buying

In small enterprises the proprietor may be solely responsible for buying the goods required. In larger firms a central buying department will usually handle all purchases. The head of this department may be a member of the Institute of Purchasing and Supply.

There are certain advantages in centralised buying. These may be listed as follows:

(*a*) The buying department has the time and the organisation to evaluate various products on the market and to pick the most appropriate for the firm's purposes. Cheapest is not necessarily best, and delivery dates may be more important than uniform quality.

A purchasing officer will discover the names of suitable suppliers: (i) from past records maintained in the purchasing department; (ii) from trade journals, published weekly or monthly; (iii) from an appropriate trade organisation, which is prepared to supply lists of members who offer particular products or services.

Difficulty is sometimes experienced if suppliers do not fulfil orders on time, or demand payment at once because their own financial organisation is weak and they are short of working capital. The purchasing department may consult the records at Companies House to attempt an evaluation of such firms, or may require clauses about **liquidated damages** to be inserted into the contract. Such a clause attempts to estimate the loss late delivery will cause, and requires the supplier to pay compensation if he fails to keep his bargain.

(*b*) A system of records built up in the purchasing office enables supplies to be ordered as they are required. Calculations are made to discover the minimum stock levels necessary to keep production going until further supplies arrive, and as these minimum stock levels are reached orders will be passed to suppliers to replenish stocks. Catalogues and price lists will be collected and filed for future reference. A catalogue gives a detailed description of goods, reference numbers, etc. It is usually expensive to produce and cannot be reprinted too frequently. For this reason firms publish price lists separately, which can be reprinted at regular intervals to take account of price changes.

(*c*) Centralised buying results in the placing of larger orders, which therefore qualify for **quantity discounts**. For example, if stationery supplies are ordered by departmental heads they will each place small orders. A centralised buying department buying for the whole firm achieves very great economies by demanding 'quantity' discounts. In times of shortage they may also receive more favourable treatment than competitors because the supplier is anxious to preserve the goodwill of larger customers.

(*d*) Budgetary control is easily achieved where a single purchasing officer supervises the activities of a number of buyers. Calculations can be made which reveal the limits to which each buyer may go in purchasing items for his department, and an **'open to buy'** figure will tell him how much he is entitled to spend in the week or month ahead.

19.3 The Index of Suppliers

The work of the purchasing department will result in a list of approved suppliers, whose products are of the type sanctioned by the purchasing officer, and whose terms and conditions of sale are acceptable. A succession of orders will then be placed over the years with these firms, and should result in the establishment of sound links with these suppliers. Naturally such firms would hesitate to offend a valued customer, and will abide by the agreements made over the years.

An index of suppliers should be created which lists all the details of the firms dealt with. Such an index would include the names, addresses and telephone numbers of suppliers, the personal contact within the firm, the type, quantities and quality of goods usually ordered, the terms agreed for delivery and payment, etc. Such an index saves time, and also disappointment which may be caused if there is no clear policy on such matters and buyers approach untried firms of doubtful integrity.

19.4 Purchasing Routines

The procedure adopted for any order may be something like the following:

(*a*) A requisition form is raised by the department concerned. Usually this will be handwritten, and most probably it will not be in the correct terminology. For example, translucent paper might be incorrectly described as 'transparent'. The purchasing department will amend the requisition, and produce an 'Order master', for a spirit, dye-line or ink duplicator.

(*b*) This master will be used to prepare several copies of a tender-quotation form. This form will invite **quotations** from suppliers. A quotation is an offer to supply at a firm price, and if accepted it will become a binding contract on the supplier. These are sent out to suitable suppliers.

(*c*) On the closing date for receipt of quotation the tenders received will be considered and the best quotation will be accepted. The master will be used to prepare an official 'Order form'—which will be sent to the supplier—and several copies, including two for the goods inwards department. They will thus know that an order is expected.

(*d*) Upon receipt of the goods the goods inwards department will observe the rules laid down by the purchasing officer.

Typical rules might be as follows:

(i) No delivery note is to be signed unless the goods it refers to have been personally checked by the clerk signing.

(ii) A 'clean' delivery, i.e. a signature without comment of any sort, must not be given if there is any sign of damage to cartons, or cases. Damage, discoloration or dampness is to be recorded on the sheet where the signature is given.

(iii) Deliveries made at lunch-time are to be signed for by the duty clerk. No delivery is to be refused because the duty clerk is not available.

(iv) Once the goods have been accepted complete one copy of the order form, which becomes a goods received note, will be passed to the purchasing department. This proof of receipt will be kept in the purchasing department until the statement requesting payment is received by the accountant. He will seek the purchasing department's acknowledgement that the goods have arrived, and they will confirm that this is indeed the case. Approval will be given to the accountant to pay the statement and it will be included in the next batch of remittances. Fig. 19.1 shows a typical order form.

19.5 The Order Form

As will be seen in Fig. 19.1, the order form should have certain information on it. The chief matters given are:

(*a*) The name and address of both parties to the contract. Orders are offers to buy, or they may be acceptances of quotations. Whichever they are, they are vital elements in a contract. A contract consists of an offer, validly accepted. Usually the supplier will be asked to acknowledge the order, and a tear-off portion may be provided for this purpose.

(*b*) A clear description of the goods or services required, giving price, colour, discount and carriage terms as quoted.

(*c*) The date, and a reference number.

(*d*) Clear instructions with regard to time and place of delivery.

(*e*) A warning that no goods are accepted unless supplied against a signed order.

The top copy of the order, sent to the supplier, will bear the signature of the purchasing officer.

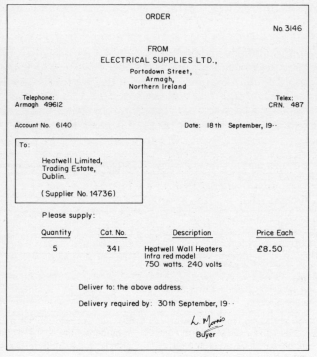

Fig. 19.1. An order.

19.6 Some Purchasing Terms

(*a*) *Ex works.* This means that the price quoted is the price at the time the goods leave the supplier. Carriage charges will be additional to the price quoted.

(b) *Carriage paid*. This means that the price quoted includes delivery to the customer's door.

(c) *Carriage forward*. This means that the carriage will be payable by the purchaser to the carrier. The latter will usually insist on payment before delivery.

(d) *Terms net*. This means that no cash discount or settlement discount is allowed.

(e) *Trade discount* is a reduction in the catalogue price of an article to enable the retailer to make a profit. Thus, a suite of furniture advertised to the public at £300.00 might be sold to a retailer at 40 per cent trade discount, i.e. at £180.00.

(f) *Shortage*. A shortage arises when an order is only partially filled by a delivery. The discrepancy between the quantity ordered and the quantity supplied may be due to theft, accidental loss or deliberate short delivery by the supplier. He may acknowledge this by some phrase like 'Balance to follow' on the advice note.

19.7 Rapid Revision

Cover the page with a sheet of paper and uncover one question at a time.

Answers	Questions
—	1. What are the three classes of items purchased by firms?
1. (a) Assets like plant, machinery, etc; (b) consumable items used up in the manufacturing or office procedure; (c) goods for re-sale.	2. What are the advantages of centralised buying?
2. (a) The specialist buyers have time to evaluate products and equipment; (b) they establish links with accredited suppliers so that many purchases become routine; (c) better terms are negotiated in return for bulk orders; (d) a system of budgetary control supervises the expenditure of departments.	3. What is an index of suppliers?
3. A list of approved suppliers whose goods conform to agreed standards and who can be relied upon to meet the terms and conditions usually required by the firm.	4. List the forms or documents used in a modern purchasing department, in ordering and authorising payment for goods.
4. (a) A requisition; (b) a quotation; (c) an order; (d) a 'goods received' note; (e) a statement; (f) a remittance advice note.	5. What is the meaning of 'ex works', when being quoted prices by suppliers?
5. It is the price of the article when it leaves the supplier's premises, without any carriage or other charges.	6. Go over the page again until you feel you are sure of the answers.

Exercises Set 19

1. (a) Describe the office routine necessary for purchasing goods from the time that the buyer learns that goods are needed until the goods are received from the supplier and the invoice checked and passed for payment.

(b) Explain the relationship of the purchasing department to the other departments of a medium-sized manufacturing concern.

(c) Prepare an order form, setting out all the essential information.

2. A buyer is offered goods by one supplier at *15 per cent trade discount, ready delivery, cash one month net, carriage paid.* Another supplier offers goods at the same price with *25 per cent trade discount, 2 months delivery, carriage forward and 5 per cent cash discount within 10 days from date of invoice.*

What factors will the buyer have to take into account in deciding which of the quotations to accept? In your answer show that you understand the terms in italics used above.

3. (a) State how the purchasing officer of a manufacturing business might obtain the names of suppliers of the commodities he needs. (b) Presuming that for a particular commodity you have found six possible suppliers, draft a letter of enquiry, which can be sent to all six, setting out your requirements, and requesting quotations.

4. You are about to place an order for £200 worth of goods with Unreliable Ltd. You have not done business with this company before and know nothing of its financial circumstances. What action do you recommend before sending the order?

5. A purchasing officer wishes to lay down a set of rules to be followed when goods inwards are received. Draw up a set of rules mentioning in particular what to do about damaged cases.

6. What considerations should be borne in mind before an order is placed with a new supplier?

7. The purchasing department of a firm wishes to order a large quantity of a new item which it has not obtained previously. Describe the office procedure which will be followed and the documents which will be involved up to the stage when the firm pays for the items obtained.

8. A buyer receives quotations from three suppliers, as follows:

	Trade discount	Delivery	Terms of payment
A:	$12\frac{1}{2}\%$	Ready	One month net
B:	20%	3 months	$2\frac{1}{2}\%$ cash discount
C:	15%	14 days	CWO

By referring to the above quotations, state the factors which the buyer should take into account before he decides which supplier's offer to accept.

9. Prepare and complete an order form, setting out all the essential information for a gross of loose-leaf folders (Catalogue No. A412) as quoted by Super Stationery Ltd, 146 Paramound Road, Silvertown, at 25p each, less 10 per cent trade discount.

(RSA)

10. What is the difference between a catalogue and a price-list? Some manufacturers issue price-lists separately from their catalogues, and at more frequent intervals. Why do they do this? Do the purchasers derive any advantage from this practice?

11. You are employed as a typist in the order department of a large manufacturing concern. Much of your work consists in typing orders. Explain what is involved in this work and give a brief account of the working of the department.

12. Write brief notes on three of the following in connection with the buying of goods or services: (*a*) quotation; (*b*) tender; (*c*) trade discount; (*d*) goods received note; (*e*) 'to follow'.

20

THE FACTORY OFFICE

20.1 Production

For many firms, manufacturing is the chief activity. Their output may be purchased by large-scale wholesalers who undertake the transport, warehousing and marketing activities. Other firms turn out such sophisticated products that it is essential to supervise the marketing as well as the manufacture, but the marketing activity is less involved and time-consuming than the technological work they must perform.

Production is the process in which raw materials, obtained by the purchasing department, are transformed into finished products by the factory workers using methods devised by the design staff. These methods usually involve the use of special tools and equipment. The control of production is achieved by the passing of data and instructions on materials, methods and machines from the **production office** to the workshop supervisors, who allocate the work to individual craftsmen or groups of semi-skilled employees. These instructions and data are most easily passed in written form, as **job cards** for each operation, so that a considerable number of documents are necessary to control the activities in a workshop with a large work-force. The chief activities to be controlled are as follows:

(*a*) *The routing of components* during manufacture as successive processes are performed.

(*b*) *The loading of machines*, to ensure that they are as fully occupied as possible, and not idle waiting for work. Cards called machine-loading tickets are produced which are fitted into racks representing the available machines. When the machine becomes idle the next job card is taken from the rack and the machine is set up.

(*c*) *The issue of jigs and tools*. These are special pieces of equipment, manufactured by the tool-making shop, which enable a piece of equipment to be held firmly during the manufacturing process (a jig) or to be cut, drilled, smoothed or polished.

(*d*) *Progress-chasing*. It is sometimes necessary to speed up production of a vital part, so that a production line is not delayed. If this part is not obviously available someone must discover where it is and ensure that those craftsmen working on it realise that their deadline for completion is approaching. The progress made has to be reported regularly, so that decisions to accelerate the work if necessary can be implemented.

(*e*) *Inspection and quality control.* This involves the random selection of units of production and their testing, measuring and analysis to ensure that the product is of high quality.

(*f*) *Stock control.* This involves reordering where necessary and the issue of and accounting for supplies required on the shop floor. All these activities require documentation, writing, typing and checking to ensure that all activities proceed correctly. The use of automated preparation of such documents by machines like line-selection spirit duplicators (see page 147) reduce these routine activities.

20.2   The Documentation of Production

Production consists of the assembly of a large number of components on some basic framework which has itself to be manufactured at the start. All the components take different times to produce, and those which are easy to make would quickly run ahead of the slower items if all were turned out continuously. It follows that 'batch production' is used for all those items which can be produced more quickly than the main components. If a car factory can produce 6000 bodies a day, but a certain component like a light switch can be made at a speed of 3000 per hour, then a day's requirement of switches can be made in two hours. It will be best to turn out, say, a month's requirements, which will take about three days (working 20 hours a day), and then turn these employees over to some other component which is also easy to produce.

The **planning department** will issue the **planning master** to the production office, and they will use it to prepare the documents needed. The 'master' document carries the following information:

(*a*)   The name of the part—to identify it.
(*b*)   The material required and its location.
(*c*)   The machines to be used.
(*d*)   The methods of work and the labour to be employed.
(*e*)   The time allowed. This will be the result of work study carried out, and subsequent negotiation with the union representatives.
(*f*)   The special jigs and other equipment to be drawn from stores.

The **stock control section** in the production office will now raise a second 'master' document called the **batch heading master** which gives instructions about the number of units which are to be made in this particular batch.

These two masters will now be used to run off copies of the following documents:

(*a*)   *A cost card.* This is a full copy, with spaces against each activity where the costs can be inserted. Thus the line 'draw 3 mm steel rod from store' would have the cost of the rod inserted as the steel was issued.

(*b*) *A progress record card.* This is again a full copy, where the times of commencing and finishing each operation are noted down. Thus the instruction 'Pass to machine shop' would have recorded against it the time the batch was passed, and the time it was cleared by the machine shop.

(*c*) *A route card.* This shows the sequence of operations, and is usually used as a label to identify the parts and to record inspections carried out at various stages of the activities.

(*d*) *A material requisition.* This shows the batch heading and materials data only. When the material is drawn from store the details are filled in and the card is sent to the costing department and stock control department. Sometimes it is an actual punched card and can simply be fed into an electronic data processing system.

(*e*) *A machine-loading ticket.* One of these will be produced for each operation, and will be used by the machine shop supervisors to allocate work to a machine. Details of the time taken will be entered on it, or punched into it if it is a punched card, and this will be fed back to the costing department.

(*f*) *An operation job card.* Once again this may be a punched card. It carries instructions to the operator, and is used to supply information to the wages department and the costing department. An example is shown in Fig. 20.1.

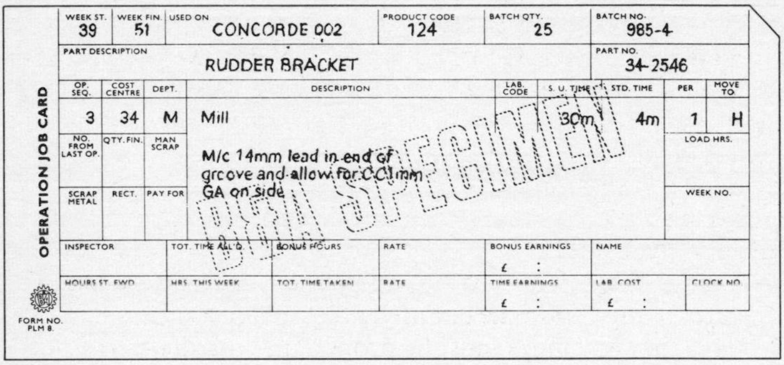

Fig. 20.1. An operation job card (reproduced by courtesy of Ozalid (UK) Ltd).

(*g*) *A progress advice and move note.* This tells the transport department or some internal distribution organisation to move the batch to another department or depot. The return of the note to the progress department informs them when the move has taken place.

(*h*) *A finished parts stores receipt.* This is used to instruct the stores that they are receiving a certain quantity of a certain part. The batch will then be stored and issued as required to the main assembly shop.

After this group of documents has been produced the master will be returned to the stock control section for filing until required again.

20.3 Functions of the Factory Office

The factory office performs many activities besides the documentation of production described above. Some of these activities must now be described.

(*a*) *Delivery queries*. There will be many occasions when goods for some reason are not ready for delivery on time. It will be a major interest of the factory office to reduce these occasions as much as possible, and where some delay is inevitable to notify customers accordingly with a suitable explanation. Possibly a special clerk will act as 'delivery date' progress chaser, and give particular attention to the completion of orders. All delivery queries should be routed to this clerk, who is in a position to answer queries. He will work in close liaison with shop supervisors and the despatch and transport departments.

(*b*) *Records*. A series of planning boards and wall charts is usually kept to enable the fullest use to be made of staff and machines. These show the allocation of work to particular production departments or 'cost centres', and to particular machines and operators. As work progresses to other parts of the shop new jobs can be allocated to the cost centre left idle and the tool setters and other skilled men can be made available to set up the machines for the new activity. On completion of particular jobs the machine running times and number of units produced are entered on the job cards by supervisors, and recorded in the office by the cost clerk and the progress record clerk.

(*c*) *Staff records*. The factory office will send to the wages department and personnel department information about hours worked, rates of pay, piece-work figures, absenteeism and many other matters. It will arrange duty rosters and holiday rosters; report on training progress; prepare accident reports and submit recommendations on many welfare proposals such as pension queries, compensation claims and recreational facilities.

(*d*) *Legal requirements—a safe system of work*. The *Factories Act, 1961*, places a duty upon the employer to provide a safe system of work. This means that machines must be properly guarded; cranes, hoists and lifts must be regularly inspected; gangways and fire escapes must be kept unobstructed, etc. The general supervision of such matters will lie within the field of the **works manager's** responsibilities, and the regular review of arrangements to secure a safe system of work will be one of the duties of a factory office, possibly in liaison with a works safety committee representing all parties. As already explained (see page 48), the *Health and Safety at Work, etc., Act, 1974*, set up a Health and Safety Executive which will supervise the adoption by all employers of the codes of practice introduced under the Act.

20.4 Rapid Revision

Cover the page with a sheet of paper and uncover one question at a time.

Answers	Questions
—	1. What is the factory office for?
1. To organise the production processes so that maximum efficiency is achieved.	2. What particular activities must it control?
2. (a) The loading of machines; (b) the routing of components during manufacture; (c) the issue of specialised jigs and tools; (d) the issue of stocks and their replenishment from time to time; (e) quality control.	3. What is a progress chaser?
3. A member of staff who ensures that components or materials required urgently are made available as necessary.	4. Which type of machine is most helpful in documenting production?
4. A line selection machine, which uses a 'planning master' to prepare a variety of documents needed to control the production processes.	5. Name typical production documents.
5. (a) A cost card; (b) a route card; (c) a progress record card; (d) a material requisition; (e) a machine-loading ticket; (f) an operation job card; (g) a finished part stores receipt.	6. What Acts of Parliament control the work of a production department?
6. The *Factories Act, 1961*, and the *Health and Safety at Work Act, 1974*.	7. Which aspects require closest attention?
7. The requirements to provide a safe system of work.	8. Go over the page again until you feel you are sure of the answers.

Exercises Set 20

1. What functions does the factory office perform? In your answer refer particularly to the part it plays in organising the work carried out in workshops and on assembly lines.

2. What is meant by 'machine loading'? Why is it important to keep machines fully employed?

3. Explain the functions of: (a) a progress chaser; (b) a rate fixer. State in which department of a manufacturing firm each would be employed.

4. What is a 'planning master' document? What is a 'batch heading' master document? Illustrate your answer by referring to the production of a batch of 20 000 volume controls for television sets. The volume control has eight different parts, each of which is made by a separate operation. The assembly of these eight parts then requires three different activities.

5. List the office processes which would be needed in a factory office to authorise the issue of steel rod from stores for a particular process, record the issue when made, and allocate its cost to the product into which it is manufactured.

6. What is a delivery query? How might such queries be handled in a production office employing a total of 45 people, each having a special job to perform?

7. 'I am responsible for all staff records except wages records, in the three workshops on this site,' declared Mrs A. What records might she keep and what purpose would they serve?

8. List five points of safety that should be carefully supervised by a works' manager.

9. What part does the office play in factory work?

10. If a business is to produce competitively it must have an efficient factory. This requires good preparatory work in the factory office. Explain.

21

STOCK RECORDS

21.1 The Importance of Stocks

Purchases and production both result in 'stock', which may be described as reserves of goods of various sorts. Some stocks are of **finished goods**, which have been manufactured for re-sale. Others are **stock-in-trade**, which means goods purchased for re-sale. Then there are **raw material stocks** and **components**, waiting to be manufactured; **spare parts** purchased in anticipation of the breakdown of plant, machinery and motor vehicles; and **consumable stocks** of such items as stationery, to be used in the course of business. All these items require supervision, for if stocks are exhausted the activities which depend upon them will come to a halt. Thus the factory must not be deprived of raw materials or components needed for manufacture or assembly, shop counters must be refilled with stock as soon as the customers empty them, lorries must not be kept idle for lack of spare parts and packs of invoices and other documents must be ready for office staff to complete their day-to-day activities.

21.2 The Importance of Stock Records

Stocks represent a part of the owner's capital. This capital has been used to make available the types of stock described above. Stocks are clearly of great value, and represent money in a different form. They are therefore attractive to thieves, and may be stolen or misappropriated at any time. Some types of stock are more attractive than others—for example, spare tyres for motor vehicles are more easily disposed of than bulk sulphur. Plain notepaper commands a ready market, but printed letter-heading paper is of little use to a thief. For reasons of security alone, stock records are essential.

Stock records are also necessary to ensure that supplies do not run out. Minimum stock levels are calculated and as soon as this level is approached a requisition is raised and passed to the purchasing department. Some firms actually 'bag up' the minimum stock of small components. For example, the last twenty taps in a builders' merchant's stock might be placed in a canvas bag and tied up with a label saying 'Not to be opened until a requisition for further supplies has been sent to the purchasing department'. The storekeeper, seeing that he is approaching the point where the minimum stock will need to be broken into, cuts the label from the bag. He raises a requisition, copying the part number and other details from the label, and sends it to the purchasing department, which will then order a further supply.

Minimum Stock Levels

A number of considerations enter into the calculation of minimum stock levels. The chief of these are:

(a) The normal delivery period, i.e. the time gap between the ordering of the goods and their supply by the manufacturer or wholesaler.

(b) The quantity used per day, or week.

Suppose that delivery takes three weeks, and that a particular component is used at the rate of 2000 units per week. Clearly, the minimum stock must be 6000 units, and urgent reordering is necessary when stock levels fall to this point. However, it may be that this component is used more frequently at certain times of the year, so that seasonal considerations enter into the size of the stocks to be held. A wholesaler who runs out of umbrellas just as the rainy season starts is missing business opportunities which will not recur for a further year. The likelihood of future shortages, or of transport or postal disruption by strikes, may make it prudent to order further supplies at once even though the minimum level has not yet been reached. By contrast overcautious attitudes on stock replacement (i.e. overprovisions of stocks) are undesirable. All stocks represent capital in an unproductive form. When stocks are too large for the needs of a business the **rate of stock turnover** is lowered and total profit is reduced. There is also the chance that perishable stocks will deteriorate, or that the large stocks available will represent a special attraction to thieves.

Optimum Order Size

When the point has come for stocks to be replenished, the question of how much to order engages the attention of the purchasing staff. The minimum stock level described above might be all that is necessary, since a further order could be despatched as soon as the present order is filled. Often, however, it is more favourable to buy quantities, since **quantity discounts** can then be obtained. In times of shortage extra supplies might be ordered, and in times of industrial unrest it might be desirable to build up stocks in order to obtain reserves to carry the firm through a difficult period. Thus the **optimum order**, i.e. the best possible size of order, may be greater than the minimum stock figure.

The Location of Stocks

Stocks are kept in places which are convenient for the staff requiring them, often in special stores with a qualified storekeeper in charge. The chief purpose of stock records is to show at a glance how much is in stock and how the stocks that have been passed through the stores have been disposed of. Since the stocks are specialised, and often heavy, it is most sensible to locate them close to the point where they are required. A mechanic, needing a special spanner, must be able to obtain it in as short a time as possible. The invoice typist needing further packs of continuous stationery must have a supply close at hand. Thus, the stationery supplies will be in the charge of a named individual in each office, and the raw materials and components needed for manufacture will be kept in the workshop stores built as an integral part of the machine shops or assembly plants they serve.

21.3 Modern Methods of Recording Stock
Running Stock Balances

In former times stock records were kept in bound books. These are very inconvenient for most stores, since the book is necessarily heavy and several storekeepers may need access to it at the same time. Today stock records are usually kept on a card index system, preferably a visible index system like the one shown in Fig. 12.7 on page 184. Sometimes it is more convenient to have the stock card actually kept in the container used to store the parts of which it is a record. For example, small components are often kept in bins, and the 'bin card' is either kept with the parts or used as a label for the bin, in a small mounting on the outside. When a part is required for use its removal from the bin is recorded on the bin card. A typical stock card is shown in Fig. 21.1. The reader will note that a running balance total at the edge of the card keeps an up-to-date record of the stock in hand. 'Spot' checks held by the internal audit department will reveal whether any stock is missing from the bin or compartment where it is usually stored.

STATIONERY STOCK CARD

Item A 4 bank paper   Maximum Stock: 50 reams   Minimum Stock: 20 reams

Date	Receipts Quantity Received	Invoice No.	Supplier	Issues Quantity Issued	Requisition No.	Department	Balance in Stock
1st Feb 19-							38
4th " "				10	1724	Sales	28
11th " "				12	1836	Advert.	16
19th " "				5	1924	Admin.	11
20th " "	30	17,065	Dick & Co.				41

Fig. 21.1 A stock record card.

The Importance of Running Balances

These are important for the following reasons:

(*a*) They check the actual stock available at any time and thus assist in detecting theft and fraud.

(*b*) They confirm the delivery of supplies from the supplier and the issues made for production or use.

(*c*) They provide a framework which permits the **perpetual inventory** method to be used (see below).

21.4 Methods of Taking Stock

Stocktaking at the End of the Financial Year

The process of valuing stock can be an arduous one, for it involves the physical checking of the stock, pricing it at cost price, current selling price or at some other valuation, multiplying the price by the number of units in stock, and adding the totals.

To reduce the work as much as possible, it is usual in some businesses to hold a stocktaking sale. This has a dual purpose. First, it reduces the physical number of items to be counted and, second, it gives the proprietor or manager an opportunity to appraise the stock. An astute businessman will notice many significant things about his stocks at sale-time. Certain lines will be found to have sold badly—the shop is cluttered up with huge supplies of slow-moving items. This is almost certainly the fault of the buyer concerned. The elimination of these slow-moving lines, clearing the shelves for newer, more saleable items, will help the business in future years.

If stock is taken annually, the work is an unusual activity and has to be treated as a special operation. Staff will need to be briefed on their duties, and clear guiding lines will have to be laid down by the accountant who is supervising the stocktaking. This preparation can put the accounts department under pressure at a time when many other activities associated with the end of the financial year are also requiring close attention. In any case annual stocktakings are really too infrequent to keep an adequate check either on the possibilities of fraud and misappropriation or on the type of bad buying described above.

Perpetual Inventory Stocktaking

The perpetual inventory or 'continuous stocktaking' method of taking stock overcomes these difficulties. A team of specialist stock-takers, under the control of the internal audit staff or the accountant, check stock all the year round, by random sample methods. This means that they select items to check at random, without any warning to staff. There is no chance for a fraudulent storekeeper to cover up the disparity between his actual stock and his 'book' stock, as sometimes happens at the annual stocktaking. This team is engaged in stocktaking activity full time. They are specialists, not casual stocktakers, and become used to the work. They may notice discrepancies that would escape the attention of an inexperienced stocktaker. This regular checking detects bad buying and slow-moving items sooner than the annual method. The pressure at the annual stocktaking is released, and the annual stock figures are obtained merely by adding the balances shown on the stock record cards, after turning them into valuations using the method prescribed by the accountant.

21.5 Stock Valuation

The valuation of stock at the close of a financial year is very important to the company accountant, because stocks affect two of the three sets of figures which he is required by law to publish for the information of the shareholders. These are the turnover, the profit and loss account and the balance sheet of the business. Turnover is the total sales of the business. From this total sales figure the profits of the business can be ascertained in a trading and profit and loss account, but only if the figure for stocks is accurately known. The stock valuation therefore is essential to a correct profit figure. Similarly, since stocks form part of the assets of the business, accurate stock figures are necessary if a correct balance sheet is to be presented to the shareholders.

Methods of valuing stock. Several different methods of stock valuation are used. These are:

(*a*) Cost price.
(*b*) Current selling price.
(*c*) Average cost price.
(*d*) Last price in (the FIFO method).
(*e*) Selling price less gross margin.

A short explanation of each of these is given below. The rule for valuing stock is laid down in *Statements of Standard Accounting Practice No. 9* and in the *Companies Act, 1981*. It says:

Stock should be valued at cost price, or net realisable value, whichever is the lower.

This basis is recognised by the professional accountancy bodies and is recommended as part of a cautious business policy. It values stock at the lower price out of two relatively easy prices to arrive at. It has the advantage that the businessman does not take any profit if stocks increase in value, since he ignores the increase by valuing stock at the cost price. If stocks decline in value, and will now realise less than they cost, he values them at the realisable value and so takes the loss in value into account. The prudent businessman never accepts a profit until he has actually made it, and always accepts a loss that he has suffered, even though prices might just possibly recover again.

Explanations of the different valuations

(*a*) *Cost price.* Goods are valued at the invoice price charged for them when they were purchased from the supplier.

(*b*) *Current selling price.* Goods are valued at the price the merchant would realise for them if he sold them on the date of the stocktaking at competitive prices. This is sometimes called **current valuation**. For example, shop-soiled goods might be valued at a low figure.

(*c*) *Average cost price.* Where goods in stock were bought on a number of different occasions it is sometimes convenient to calculate their value not at the individual prices but at an average price for the various consignments.

(*d*) *Last price in* (the FIFO method). This method assumes that stock will be sold in the order in which it is received, i.e. the oldest stock will be disposed of first. This means that any remaining stock will be valued at the last price in for equivalent quantities. This is really very similar to the cost-price method.

(*e*) *Selling price less gross margin.* Many branches of multiple-shops and supermarkets do not know what the stock cost them, because Head Office prefers to keep such information private. All the goods supplied to branches are supplied at selling prices, and when stocktaking is carried out the stock is valued at these selling prices. Head Office will, however, deduct the *gross margin*, i.e. the profit margin that has been added, to give the stock value for accounting purposes.

21.6 Rapid Revision

Cover the page with a sheet of paper and uncover one question at a time.

Answers	Questions
—	1. What is stock?
1. Reserves of goods of various sorts.	2. How is stock obtained?
2. By purchasing or manufacturing the items.	3. What problems arise whenever stocks are held?
3. (*a*) Security problems—most stocks are pilferable, and attractive to thieves; (*b*) storage problems—stocks may be perishable, or liable to deteriorate under the influence of temperature, humidity, insect pests, microbes, etc.; (*c*) financial problems; stocks represent capital tied up unproductively.	4. What is a maximum stock?
4. The largest stock that may be held of a particular item. It sets the upper limit for any orders.	5. What is a minimum stock?

Answers	Questions
5. It is the lowest level to which stock must be allowed to fall before re-ordering.	6. What determines the minimum stock level?
6. (a) The time for delivery, between ordering and receiving the goods; (b) the average consumption of that item in the delivery period.	7. What is the 'optimum order size'?
7. It is the best size of order to place, so that the best quantity discount possible is obtained, without tying up excessive capital.	8. What is stocktaking?
8. It is a process of checking stock, and valuing it. It is essential to take stock before profits can be calculated.	9. What is a perpetual inventory?
9. It is a process for continually checking stock on a random sample basis, using a team of specialist stocktakers.	10. Go over the page again until you feel you are sure of the answers.

Exercises Set 21

1. Why is it important to control stock? In what ways are stock records maintained in a busy workshop stores?

2. You are responsible for the ordering and issuing of stationery in your department. What precautions would you take to ensure: (a) that you do not keep too large a stock; (b) that the stock does not run out? Give a sample of a ruling for the Stationery Stock Book.

3. What is meant by: (a) minimum stock level; (b) maximum stock level; (c) reorder point; (d) optimum order size?

4. Draft a stock sheet and enter three items as examples.

5. Design a stock record card and explain its use.

6. (a) Rule up a stationery stock record card for A4 typewriting paper and make the following entries:

   Maximum stock: 50 reams   *Minimum stock:* 20 reams
  1.3.19.. Balance in stock: 45 reams
  8.3.19.. Issued 10 reams to sales department
10.3.19.. Issued 12 reams to typing pool
22.3.19.. Bought 25 reams from L. P. Stevens & Co. Ltd
  1.4.19.. Issued 8 reams to purchases department
12.4.19.. Issued 10 reams to typing pool
23.4.19.. Issued 10 reams to works department

When restocking this item on 30th April, what quantity would you order?
   (b) Explain the importance of the maximum and minimum figures in connection with stocktaking. (c) What do you understand by: (i) a ream: (ii) A4?

7. You work for a small business which uses a bound book for keeping its stock records. There is a suggestion that a card system would be more appropriate. You are required: (*a*) to set out, in the form of a simple report, the advantages and disadvantages of bound books and cards for stock record purposes: (*b*) to draft a card you think might be suitable.

8. (*a*) (i) What is meant by FIFO? (ii) What is the purpose of annual stock-taking? (iii) What is the 'continuous stocktaking' system? (iv) What is a requisition note?
   (*b*) A firm uses the visible card index system for maintaining its stock records. Draw up a stock record card for pink A4 bank paper and make four entries relating to the movement of the stock. (BEC General)

9. On 1st April, 19. ., the central stores of G. Smith & Co. Ltd, High Street, Welbridge, had 48 reams of A4 lined paper in stock. During the month of April the following issues were made.

5th April	Sales department	10 reams
7th April	Planning department	6 reams
9th April	Publicity department	8 reams
15th April	Accounts department	10 reams
26th April	General office	8 reams

The maximum stock level is 100 reams and the minimum stock level is 25 reams. On the appropriate date an order for a further supply was placed with G. Roberts Ltd, 15 Low Road, Welbridge, and this supply was received five days later.

(*a*) Enter all the above details in a stationery stock record card ruled up for the purpose, invent your own document numbers inserting them in the appropriate columns, and complete the balance in stock column.

(*b*) Using a form of your own design, make out the order for the further supply of stationery mentioned above.

(*c*) What is the purpose of stocktaking? (RSA)

10. You are asked to value your company's stocks on 31st July, 19. ... A new employee has been told to assist you and he tells you that he knows that stock can be valued at: (i) cost price; (ii) selling price; (iii) average cost price; (iv) last price in; (v) selling price less gross profit. He asks you to explain how these different methods work and how you will make your choice of method. Answer him as briefly and accurately as you can.

11. What is a perpetual inventory?

12. A new employee in the stores department tells you that he cannot see why the firm goes to the trouble to take stock—it only wastes the time of the people busy enough already. State how you would explain: (*a*) the reasons for taking stock; (*b*) the ways in which stock is valued for stocktaking purposes.
   Suggest any means of making the stocktaking burden easier.

13. (*a*) It is customary for a business to value its stock in monetary terms at least once every year. Why is this done? (*b*) Some companies value their stocks more frequently—as often perhaps as once a week. Why do you think they find this necessary? (*c*) Mention two methods of valuing stock and say what kind of businesses might use them. (BEC General)

14. (*a*) Explain the statement that 'for the purpose of stocktaking stock should be valued at the lower of cost price or net realisable value'. (*b*) At stocktaking, 320 of a certain article are found in stock, the current selling price of which is £0.60 each. 200 of these articles were bought on 1st January for £0.45 each and 300 on 1st March for £0.48. State with reasons at what price you would value these 320 articles for stocktaking purposes.

22

THE SALES DEPARTMENT

22.1 Wholesale Selling

In a free enterprise economy goods flow to the consumer through a variety of channels. Each channel has developed over the course of the years as a particular solution to the problems facing producers and consumers, and with every product there are least two or three ways in which the product is transferred from the producer to the eventual user. The two routes for the sale of fish outlined below will illustrate the differences.

Route one

1. Caught by local fishermen. 2. Auctioned on the quay to local housewives, or hoteliers.

Route two

1. Caught by a trawler. 2. Frozen in the ship's factory. 3. Stored in the refrigerated warehouse of a frozen food company. 4. Transported in a refrigerated container to a warehouse operated by a supermarket chain. 5. Delivered to branches of the company in a refrigerated van. 6. Sold to housewives from refrigerated counters.

In route one a single selling activity was sufficient. In route two the goods changed hands three times. At each point where they change hands goods are said to be 'sold' by one party to another for a consideration called the 'price'. The goods then become the property of the purchaser who has given value for them, and it is immaterial whether he pays at once (a cash sale) or pays later (a credit sale).

The two major divisions of selling are **wholesale selling** and **retail selling**. Retail selling is the final link in the distribution network, where goods are sold in small quantities to the final consumer. Wholesale selling is bulk selling, in which a large quantity of goods is sold to a middleman, or wholesaler. The wholesaler then sells them to several retailers, who eventually market them to the final consumer.

The practices followed in these two branches of selling are rather different and require different documentation. First we shall consider wholesale selling, by a typical sales department of a manufacturing company.

22.2   The Functions of the Sales Department

The sales department has the following functions:

(*a*) To prepare or commission attractive brochures and publicity material for the company's products.

(*b*) To obtain and train a sales force of **representatives**, or **commercial travellers**, who are knowledgeable about the company's products and will find customers for them.

(*c*) To devise, in consultation with Organisation and Methods staff where necessary, a system of documentation and controls which will keep selling expenses as low as possible and inform top management about developments.

(*d*) To stage demonstrations of the company's products at appropriate times and places, and to participate in exhibitions organised by trade associations and similar bodies.

(*e*) To explain the complaints of customers to the production department with a view to improving the product.

(*f*) To rebut the complaints of customers on behalf of the firm if the complaints are unjustified and result from the customer's failure to follow the recommendations given in the company's literature.

(*g*) To take responsibility for all those obligations which exist between the organisation and its customers and clients. These may include liaison with the production department to maintain product quality, so that customers are pleased with their purchases; the observance of contractual terms so that, for example, if a warranty is offered which guarantees free servicing or maintenance it is carried out; delivery at the time required, at the place required, in the way agreed, etc.

These activities may be only regional or national in character but in recent years it has become more and more necessary to market a product on a world-wide basis and set up overseas agencies, or branches, to sell products internationally. Sales forces of this size require careful control if they are to fulfil their functions properly and yet still contribute to the profits of the company.

Advertising and the Sales Department

Advertising is a necessary adjunct to selling. The old proverb 'Good wine needs no bush' (a vine hung up at the door was the sign for a wine shop in days before people could read) is not true today. A product cannot achieve any reputation unless it is widely advertised in the competitive world of modern commerce. One advertising consultant uses the slogan 'If you don't advertise you certainly know what you're doing —but you're the only one who does'. The enormous costs of laying down a production line, which may have cost millions of pounds, can be recovered only if the product sells, and the best way to achieve sales is to advertise. The advertising department may be a part of the sales department. If not, the two departments will work in close liaison with one another, and the return from particular promotions will be rigorously investigated to determine which method of advertising gives the best results.

22.3   The Sales Force

The **sales director** of a large company will control the operations of a sales force of representatives and agents throughout the country, and possibly the world. He is usually a strong personality, and may be a director of the company. He represents his selling organisation at the board meetings helping to formulate company policy and objectives in the selling field. He then has the task of implementing this policy, conveying it to his area managers and agents, briefing salesmen about the targets set by top management in the months ahead and adapting procedures and organisation to achieve them.

He will examine reports of sales achieved and problems that have arisen, pinpoint weaknesses and investigate staff activities where it seems that the potential sales are not being realised.

Sales representatives will be assigned to a particular territory, where they establish a personal link with the company's customers. They demonstrate and explain products, arrange for the service of equipment, update customers on the latest development and methods, and listen to the customer's particular needs. Some system of reporting back on all calls made will ensure that the sales director is informed about the needs of the customers, the success or otherwise of the calls made and the time spent on the enquiry. Sometimes a traveller may make considerable efforts on the customer's behalf and then not be rewarded with an order. At other times a very large order may follow from a simple phone call or the provision of an illustrated brochure. Fig. 12.8 on page 185 illustrates a useful visible record system which is small enough to put into a traveller's pocket, and which when that particular set of enquiries has been dealt with can be posted back to Head Office to inform it of the results achieved, and the necessary action required in each case.

The representative's itinerary is important, since correspondence and messages must be able to reach him daily. His programme will be drawn up in consultation with his area manager, who will operate from a central point in the group of territories he controls. Procedures will be laid down to enable the area manager to be kept fully informed, with reports being written up in the car before driving away from a call, and arrangements prescribed for ringing in at agreed times to acquaint the area manager with his position. To enable these calls to be controlled he will usually have a credit card which connects him by telephone at the expense of Head Office.

22.4   Attracting Customers

In order to attract customers it is necessary to keep one's products constantly before the public, by a succession of presentations, demonstrations and advertising campaigns. It greatly assists such campaigns if continual revision of the appearance and design of the product takes place, so that there is some refinement to discuss or some new model to introduce. It could be argued that some of this innovation is wasteful or socially unnecessary, but as far as the particular firm is concerned it is justified by the increased sales which result.

The following ways of attracting customers are regularly used:

(*a*) *Exhibitions and Trade Fairs.* Here the firm, in conjunction with other firms in the industry, participates in a national or international demonstration of its products. Such shows as the Motor Show, the Farnborough Air Display and the International Business Show attract buyers from all over the world.

(*b*) *Wholesalers' displays.* Many wholesalers put on demonstrations and displays of the products they handle at regular intervals. Retailers who live in their particular areas visit the showrooms to hear accounts from representatives of the variety and purpose of the equipment their firms supply. These events are usually held on the 'early closing' day of shops in the area. Often sales managers will appear personally to demonstrate the products and discuss their features, assisted by the representative who travels in the area.

(*c*) *Illustrated brochures, leaflets and price lists.* A good supply of brochures should always be available for despatch to customers who enquire by post or telephone. This is at once convenient to the sales department, since special letters are not required, and satisfactory to the potential customer. The immediate despatch of the material required gives an impression of efficiency, and keeps interest in the product alive. The provision of **business reply cards**, asking for a demonstration or a visit by a representative, will again assist the sales department to follow up the enquiry.

(*d*) *Magazine and press advertising.* This type of advertising is not cheap but it is selective to some extent and therefore effective in directing the advertisement towards a particular section of the population. There are several hundred specialist magazines which cater for the interests of groups, from archaeologists to zoologists. Some of these groups are enormous—teenagers, for example. Others are less numerous, like brass-rubbing enthusiasts. Particular products which interest these groups will sell well if featured in this type of magazine. Even the national press, while less varied than the magazine industry, has a variety of appeal which leads sales managers and advertising departments to choose one paper, rather than another, to feature a particular product.

(*e*) *Television advertising.* The greatest impact on the general public can undoubtedly be made on the television screen. By entering the homes of practically everyone in the land a television advertisement can create an enormous demand for a firm's products. It does not follow that all such campaigns are inevitably successful, but where a product meets a popular need and is competitively priced the television advertisement more than repays its extra cost.

(*f*) *Special campaigns.* These may take the form of a special mailing to interested parties, using address lists purchased for the purpose. Thus local authorities sell the electoral register, which may be used to prepare a mailing to a particular town or rural locality. Many professional bodies issue membership lists, and the yellow pages of telephone directories give classified lists of retailers in a particular field. Representatives may also be enlisted in special campaigns to enlarge trade in their areas, often with special prizes for the best salesman.

Free samples and coupons are popular ways to encourage the sale of goods in such special campaigns. The retailer who supplies goods in exchange for the free coupon is compensated by the firm for the value of the coupon.

Such campaigns need considerable planning and often require that stage or screen personalities who are to assist with the campaign are booked up in advance. Special publicity material must be prepared, supplies be made available in the shops and the general organisation in the proposed sales area be improved to ensure full coverage during the actual campaign.

22.5 Documentation of Sales

The sale of goods is the chief activity of a trading concern, and every aspect of a sale must be adequately documented. The sequence of operations is as follows:

(*a*) *The enquiry.* An enquiry may arrive by post, telegram or telephone. It should be forwarded at once to the sales manager who will take appropriate action to follow it up. Brochures and price lists may be sent, with a personal letter. It may be desirable to phone the enquirer immediately to give information about the product, or to arrange for the local representative to call on the enquirer.

(*b*) *The quotation.* Where necessary the enquirer will be given a quotation. This is an offer to supply, at a stated price, goods in the quantity and of the quality described, on the terms and conditions described in the quotation. If accepted within the time limit stated, or within a reasonable time if no time limit is given, it becomes a legally binding contract between the parties.

(*c*) *The order.* This document has already been described (see page 293–4). It must be carefully scrutinised to ensure that it is correct in every detail and if defective in any way a phone call should be made to clarify the detail. If it is a telephone order it should be confirmed in writing.

It may be necessary to acquaint the accounts department with the details if the order is from a new customer who is asking for credit. They will then institute the necessary enquiries for references before sanctioning credit.

(*d*) *The invoice.* An invoice is a business document which is made out whenever one person sells goods to another. It is made out by the person selling the goods, and in large businesses it may have as many as eight copies, of different colours.

Fig. 22.1 shows the usual form of invoice in use in large firms. It includes the VAT details required on tax invoices (see Chapter 15). It will usually have the following information: (i) names and addresses of both the interested parties to the sale; (ii) the date of the sale; (iii) an exact description of the goods, with quantity and unit price, and details of the trade discount (if any) given; (iv) VAT details; (v) the terms on which the goods are sold, i.e. the discount that may be taken and the credit period allowed. 'Terms Net' means no discount is allowed.

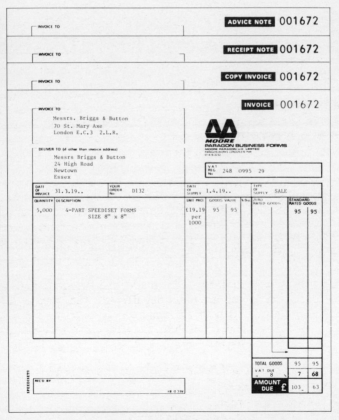

Fig. 22.1. A four-copy invoice set.

The words 'Prompt Settlement' mean no credit period is allowed.

Lastly, many firms write 'E & OE' on the bottom of the invoice. These letters mean 'Errors and Omissions Excepted'. If an error or omission has been made, the firm selling the goods may put it right.

The four copies of the invoice shown are processed as follows:

Top copy. This is sent by post or by hand to the person buying the goods, who uses it to record the purchase in the Purchases Day Book.

Second copy. This is usually the Sales Day Book copy, which is kept by the seller, entered in the Sales Day Book, and then filed to be kept as a copy of the contract of sale.

Third and fourth copies. These are sent together to the stores department of the seller, where the storekeeper takes the goods out of the store. The third copy, often called the **delivery note**, is given to the carman to take with him in cases where goods are being delivered to the buyer's warehouse. He presents it with the parcel of goods and gets a signature on it to prove that the goods arrived safely. This copy is then taken back by the carman to the storekeeper and is filed in the stores department after being entered in the Stores Record Book. The fourth copy is wrapped up in the parcel before it is given to the carman. It is often called the **advice note** and it enables the buyer's storekeeper to check the contents of the parcel and record in the Stores Record Book the stores that have just arrived.

Other copies. Where a set of invoices has more than four copies they will usually include: (*a*) a representative's copy which is sent to the traveller handling the order; (*b*) a traffic planning copy for the transport department; (*c*) a consignee's copy for the actual consignee, as distinct from the head office of the buyer's firm.

Pro-forma Invoices

Sometimes goods are sent 'on approval'. As they have not been sold an invoice cannot be made out, but an exactly similar document called a **pro-forma invoice** is sent instead. If the customer approves the goods he will notify the seller and the pro-forma invoice will then become an invoice, which will in due course be paid by the customer.

From the moment that delivery is made, and the second copy of the invoice is passed to the accounts department, the sales department ceases to be concerned with the transaction directly. The accounts department will in due course render a statement of account (see page 225) and receive the payment for the order.

Some Abbreviations Used in the Documentation of Sales

COD: Cash on delivery.
CWO: Cash with order.
E & OE: Errors and omissions excepted.

22.6   Retail Selling

Retail sales are usually cash sales, though a variety of other methods of payment have been devised. A full description of the types of retail outlet is not appropriate to this volume, but is given in a companion volume, *Commerce Made Simple*.

The chief office activities required in cash-selling are those described in Chapter 16: the recording and banking of cash takings. Where retail sales are not cash sales, but credit sales, there is a need to record and control the credit granted to customers.

The chief types of non-cash-selling carried on in retail trade are hire purchase selling and selling on 'budget accounts' or 'credit accounts'.

Hire Purchase Selling

Hire purchase is the purchase of goods under an agreement called a hire purchase agreement. This permits the buyer to pay only a small part of the purchase price, called the **deposit**, at once. The rest is payable over a period of time by regular **instalments**.

The essence of a hire purchase agreement is that the property in the goods does not pass until the final instalment is paid. This means that the vendor owns the goods right up until the last moment of payment. The *Consumer Credit Act, 1974*, now controls hire purchase, but as yet new procedures are still under discussion. Until the necessary Orders are made, the *Hire Purchase Act, 1965*, is the effective Act of Parliament. Full details of the arrangement made between the hirer and the owner of the goods are listed in the Memorandum of Agreement. Under the *Hire Purchase Act, 1965*, the memorandum is very important, for a hire purchase agreement is enforceable only if a note or memorandum is available in writing. This must contain the following matters:

(i) A statement of the cash price, the total HP price, the number, due dates and amount of each instalment.

(ii) A list of the goods sufficient to identify them.

(iii) The provisions for layout, legibility, and wording prescribed by the Board of Trade. This includes in particular a clearly marked box like that shown below.

This document contains the terms of a hire purchase agreement. Sign it only if you want to be legally bound by them.
Signature of Hirer ....
The goods will not become your property until you have made all the payments. You must not sell them before then.

(iv) A statutory notice of the hirer's rights under the Act.

The memorandum must be signed by the hirer or buyer in person, and by the owner or his agent. A wife cannot sign for her husband, even if she has her husband's authority.

Frequently the retailer is not rich enough to finance hire purchase schemes, and merely completes the memorandum as agent for a **finance company** which pays the retailer the balance of the purchase price and arranges to collect the instalments from the customer.

Budget Accounts

Many retailers allow customers to run a budget account. This entitles the customer to buy goods up to eight times the value of a monthly budget figure, or up to thirty times the value of a weekly budget figure, which the customer is prepared to pay regularly. Thus a customer who can afford to pay £5 per month would be permitted to buy up to £40 worth of goods. At any time the customer who has partly extinguished his debts may purchase a further supply of goods provided he does not exceed the total of £40.

Credit Accounts

Here the retailer permits the customer to buy on credit, but renders a monthly account in the usual way. Credit control is essential and has been fully discussed already (see page 226).

22.7 Rapid Revision

Cover the page with a sheet of paper and uncover one question at a time.

Answers	Questions
—	1. What are the two chief aspects of selling?
1. Wholesale and retail.	2. Which of these do we usually associate with a sales department?
2. Wholesale selling	3. What are the functions of a sales department?
3. (a) To prepare and commission brochures, posters and other advertising material about the firm's products; (b) to train a staff of representatives or commercial travellers; (c) to stage demonstrations of the firm's products at appropriate places and times; (d) to control expenses; (e) to keep top management informed.	4. What are the functions of advertising?
4. (a) To inform the public about the firm's products, and explain their uses and attributes; (b) to persuade the public to buy the product, especially where it is in competition with other brands; (c) to keep the firm's name constantly before the public.	5. What problems arise in dealing with a sales force?

Answers	Questions
5. (*a*) The sales representatives must be knowledgeable about the product. This involves training courses, and seminars to update their information; (*b*) the sales territory must be defined and arrangements made to contact the representative; (*c*) an adequate scheme of remuneration must be devised.	6. What means may be used to bring the firm's products to the notice of the public?
6. (*a*) National press and television; (*b*) magazine advertising; (*c*) local press, and local campaigns aimed at doorstep sales; (*d*) special mailings and free sample offers; (*e*) wholesalers' demonstrations; (*f*) exhibitions and fairs.	7. Go over the page again until you feel you are sure of the answers.

Exercises Set 22

1. Your employer, who has recently arrived from overseas, asks you to explain the Business Reply Service and explain how it might be useful. Write a memorandum setting out clearly the essential features of the Business Reply Service.

2. (*a*) A firm receives an order from a customer who has no credit account with that firm and does not enclose any payment with its order. What action should be taken by the firm?

(*b*) What records about customers would you expect a firm's credit control department to keep? What would the firm do if one of its customers had not yet settled an account which was several months overdue?

3. (*a*) You are employed as a sales clerk with responsibility for credit control and you receive an order to the value of £500 from a firm with whom you have had no previous dealings. The representative who was successful in securing the order asks you to consider giving the purchaser one month's credit. What action would you take before executing the order?

(*b*) What information about customers would you require on your sales record cards?

4. You are employed in the sales department of your firm and are responsible for recording visible card records of potential customers who write to the firm in response to advertisements in the press and television. If an order is not received within 14 days of sending the catalogues a letter following up the enquiry is sent.

(*a*) Design a visible record card suitable for potential customers, setting out all the relevant information required in the sales department and include the name, address and follow-up date on the visible edge.

(*b*) Explain how you would use the visible edge and a signalling device to maintain a follow-up system, and, in this particular instance, to pinpoint the date on which the letter should be sent.

5. You have been asked to make yourself responsible for orders received. Some

orders come by telephone; some through a personal visit from the customer when notes are made of the visitor's requirements; some by letters; and some on your firm's own order form.

Suggest a simple procedure for recording the orders and mention any documents you would use.

6. Explain the form and use of: (a) a quotation; (b) an order; (c) a price list; (d) a pro-forma invoice.

7. A parcel of goods is sold by a wholesaler to a departmental store. Outline the office work involved in the seller's office from the time the order has been placed to the time the cheque in payment has been received.

8. (a) Describe a suitable office routine for selling goods on credit, from the time that the goods are advertised to the time when payment is made by the customer.

(b) State the documents handled and the filing systems used in a sales department which includes sections for home sales, export sales, advertising and transport.

9. (a) One of your firm's representatives has obtained an order worth £100 from a new customer and wishes you to grant two months' credit. What steps might the firm take to determine whether or not to allow this credit?

(b) List other terms of payment which might be arranged for the settlement of accounts generally.

10. (a) State how the sales department of a business might attract customers.

(b) What essential information would the sales department need to include in its quotations or estimates?

11. Your company wishes to sell goods in the following ways: (a) on credit; (b) by COD; (c) against cash with order. Outline three suitable office routines—one for each of the above methods—from the time when an order is received until the times when goods are despatched and payment is made.

12. (a) What is the difference between trade discount and cash discount? (b) Give the meaning of three of the following terms and abbreviations: E & OE, CWO, net, poundage, insured, deposit, instalment, HP.

13. Describe the advantages that a firm may derive from giving credit to its customers. State the dangers in this practice and show what action can be taken to minimise such dangers.

14. Explain the meaning of trade discount and cash discount.

A business sells goods to R. Martin for £600 on 1st January subject to trade discount of 40 per cent and $2\frac{1}{2}$ per cent cash discount within one month. What would be the amount that Martin would pay if he settled his account on 17th January? What must he pay if he settles the account on 20th February?

15. Explain the hire purchase method of selling. What are its advantages and disadvantages?

16. (a) List *four* ways in which a supplier may draw his products to the attention of customers. (b) Explain one of the methods in reasonable detail.

17. Your firm has received an order from a Mr W. Robinson for £100 worth

of goods on credit. You have had no previous dealings with this man and know nothing about him. What steps would you take before executing the order?

18. The manufacturing company for which you work employs about 100 sales representatives. Each is provided with a car, and between them they cover the whole of Great Britain and Ireland. It is decided to start a system recording details of the cars used by the representatives, the mileage each covers, repairs and maintenance, and other relevant details.

(*a*) Explain what types of equipment might be used for such records and say which you consider to be the most appropriate. Give reasons for your choice.

(*b*) How might you ensure that all relevant information was obtained for entering in the records?

23

THE EXPORT DEPARTMENT

23.1 Introduction

Every country has to import some goods and services from other countries. To pay for these goods and services she must export her own products and skills. In this way a country earns sufficient foreign exchange to be able to pay for the imported raw materials, finished goods and services. This type of international trade enriches the countries who take part in it, because it increases the variety of foods and manufactured products which their peoples can enjoy.

23.2 Problems Faced by the Exporter

(a) *Language*. When we enter an export market we must expect to translate the packaging, informative literature, and technical handouts into the language of the country concerned. We must have salesmen who are able to speak the language fluently and qualified to sell the product in that language.

(b) *Standardised units*. There are a great many technological problems arising from the use in different countries of different units of length, weight, capacity, voltage, screw threads, etc.

In North America and many Middle Eastern countries the domestic electricity supply is 110–120 volts only, and the frequency is 60 Hz; in Britain it is 240 volts and 50 Hz. This means that special motors, transformers and other equipment are needed if a British firm is to succeed in these export fields. One of the reasons that Britain is changing over to metric units is to enable us to adopt the same threads and the same units of length, weight and capacity as our competitors abroad.

(c) *Currency*. Clearly, prices of goods sold abroad have to be converted into the currency units of the country where they are to be sold. Since rates of exchange fluctuate, particularly in some politically unstable countries, the prices decided upon may prove to be insufficient to yield a profit if the rate of exchange alters. An exporter who contracts to supply goods at a fixed price may find that this contract price is no longer satisfactory.

(d) *Licences and other documentation*. There are a host of regulations to fulfil in most branches of the export trade. Not only may a licence be required before goods can enter a foreign country, one may even be needed from this country before they proceed overseas.

(*e*) *Risks of the export trade.* These are numerous. We have the sheer physical hazards of crossing oceans by sea or air, the corrosion that comes to iron and steel products from the salt air spray, the chance that goods will be damaged in rough weather or even jettisoned to save the vessel. There are the risks of theft at the docks, or in transit; the risks of non-payment by the buyer or refusal by his government to release foreign exchange. Even where these risks can be assumed by insurers or *del credere* agents, the premiums paid or the commission given eat into profit margins and make export trade less attractive than home trade.

Against this formidable list of problems can be set the very great rewards to be won by successful overseas trade where sound arrangements can be made with foreign buyers.

23.3 Functions of the Export Department

The export department has to overcome the problems outlined in section 23.2 above. Some of the staff must be fluent in the foreign languages required. The firm must appoint agents overseas who will sell the firm's products. If foreign branches are opened they will usually be supervised by the export manager. Foreign staff may be brought in to attend training sessions or 'familiarisation seminars' to enable them to know more about the products they are selling. They may assist in the preparation of sales literature, brochures, posters and other advertising material in their own languages while they are in this country. Listed briefly, the functions of the export department are:

(*a*) *To ensure that the product conforms with the technical requirements of the country of destination.* This may mean modifying the product in consultation with the production department to fit electric motors and other equipment appropriate to the country concerned.

(*b*) *To arrange adequate documentation.* Documentation must comply with the requirements of: (i) the country of destination, which may require special documents for its import department, customs, central bank, etc.; (ii) the international conventions on road, rail, sea and air transport. In particular the TIR regulations, which allow loaded road haulage vehicles to go through customs without being inspected, are very strictly controlled. The **TIR carnets**, or books of documents, are purchased from the controlling offices in Switzerland. For EEC countries **T Forms** fulfil a similar function.

(*c*) *To communicate with overseas agents and branches.* This may be by air mail, or sea mail, but more often communication is achieved through the **telex system** or **Intelpost systems**.

(*d*) *To arrange packaging and despatch.* This may involve special considerations with regard to packing; times of departure of vessels and aircraft; compliance with insurance requirements and possibly with legal controls if goods are dangerous.

(e) *To ensure that financial safeguards over payment are arranged.* There are several different methods of arranging payment, of which the commonest are:

(i) Irrevocable credits confirmed by a London bank. When made available by the foreign customer these enable the London bank to pay the exporter, or accept a Bill of Exchange for him, which he can then discount on the London Discount Market.

(ii) Irrevocable credits with a foreign bank. These are similar to confirmed credits, but the London bank operates only as a correspondent and forwards the documents abroad for payment or acceptance by the foreign banker.

A full description of export trade is given in *Commerce Made Simple* and *Export Made Simple*.

23.4 Documents Used in the Export Office

Overseas trade has to be particularly well documented since Government controls on both goods and finance are usually strict. Traditionally, merchants have devised their own documents to suit their own needs. In the last few years it has become increasingly obvious that much routine clerical time was being wasted in completing forms that carried the same information, but differently placed on each form. Some years ago the Board of Trade set up a Joint Liaison Committee to investigate the whole problem of export documentation, with a view to preparing an **aligned series**, i.e. a complete set of documents of standard size with the same information in the same position. Modern duplicator techniques permit all the documents to be run off from a 'master document', and where certain details are not required on a particular form a mask is fitted over the 'master' which obliterates the details not required. This work is now carried out by the **SITPRO Board** (the Simplification of International Trade Procedures Board). This body has now aligned some 50 forms, all of which can be run off either completely or partially from a SITPRO master document. The latest version of this document is reproduced in Fig. 23.1. From this it is possible to reproduce all the main export documents. These are: (*a*) the export invoice; (*b*) the bill of lading, or the short-form bill of lading or the sea waybill; (*c*) the customs entry form; (*d*) the national standard shipping note; (*e*) the insurance certificate; (*f*) the export consignment note; (*g*) the export cargo shipping instructions; (*h*) the certificate of origin; and (*i*) the European T forms (for transits through customs points).

With so many documents to prepare the advantages of SITPRO aligned documents are obvious. They enable documents to be run off in a reprographic department by a spirit duplicator, offset duplicator, plain paper copier or similar system. One of the best systems is the

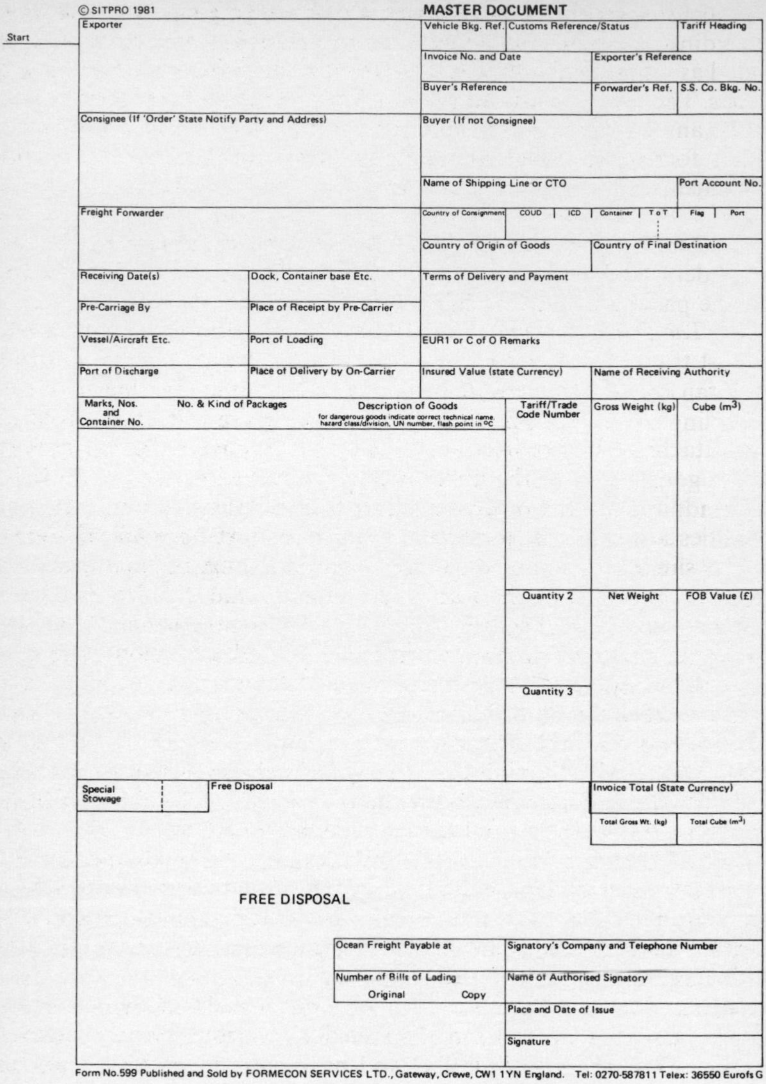

© SITPRO 1981   **MASTER DOCUMENT**

Start

Exporter		Vehicle Bkg. Ref.	Customs Reference/Status		Tariff Heading
		Invoice No. and Date	Exporter's Reference		
		Buyer's Reference	Forwarder's Ref.		S.S. Co. Bkg. No.
Consignee (If 'Order' State Notify Party and Address)		Buyer (If not Consignee)			
		Name of Shipping Line or CTO			Port Account No.
Freight Forwarder		Country of Consignment	COUD	ICD	Container	T o T	Flag	Port
		Country of Origin of Goods	Country of Final Destination		
Receiving Date(s)	Dock, Container base Etc.	Terms of Delivery and Payment			
Pre-Carriage By	Place of Receipt by Pre-Carrier				
Vessel/Aircraft Etc.	Port of Loading	EUR1 or C of O Remarks			
Port of Discharge	Place of Delivery by On-Carrier	Insured Value (state Currency)	Name of Receiving Authority		

Marks, Nos. and Container No.	No. & Kind of Packages	Description of Goods (for dangerous goods indicate correct technical name, hazard class/division, UN number, flash point in °C)	Tariff/Trade Code Number	Gross Weight (kg)	Cube (m³)
			Quantity 2	Net Weight	FOB Value (£)
			Quantity 3		

Special Stowage	Free Disposal		Invoice Total (State Currency)	
			Total Gross Wt. (kg)	Total Cube (m³)

FREE DISPOSAL

	Ocean Freight Payable at	Signatory's Company and Telephone Number
	Number of Bills of Lading Original Copy	Name of Authorised Signatory
		Place and Date of Issue
		Signature

Form No.599 Published and Sold by FORMECON SERVICES LTD., Gateway, Crewe, CW1 1YN England.   Tel: 0270-587811 Telex: 36550 Eurofs G

Fig. 23.1. A master document from an aligned series.

Rank Xerox Automatic Overlay Device. Secretaries working in export departments should draw the attention of their departmental heads to this system, which can prepare five ranges of export documents automatically on ordinary plain paper. The process is controlled from a pegboard panel in the Xerox copier which controls an overlay web to position the framework of the required form over the copy paper. Only those parts of a master copy which actually need to appear on a particular form are reproduced. Instead of having stocks of invoices, bills of lading, consignment notes, etc., the different documents are prepared as required in only one second, from the same pack of plain copy paper. The saving in inventory costs is obvious, and the machine cannot make any copying errors from one form to another as often happens when forms are typed manually. A few words about the various documents may be helpful at this point.

(*a*) *The Export Invoice.* This is similar to an ordinary invoice but contains details of the vessel carrying the goods, the shipping marks used on the packages and the charges made.

(*b*) *The Bill of Lading.* This is the most important document in the export trade, because it represents the goods while they are in transit, and can be sold to transfer their ownership. Since the buyer of a bill of lading might run some risk if the goods were lost at sea, it always has attached to it the insurance policy which covers the consignment. If the goods are lost the buyer claims from the insurers.

In addition to the ordinary bill of lading described above two new varieties are available in recent years. The **short-form bill of lading** is a very simple version of the original bill of lading, because it does not carry on the back of the form the very long and detailed contract of carriage between the shipowner and the consignor. Instead it refers in a box on the front to the standard terms and conditions offered by the shipowner to all those whose goods he carries. The other version is called the **sea waybill**. This is non-negotiable, which means the cargo cannot be transferred from one owner to another while it is on the high seas. This type of waybill is perfectly satisfactory when, for example, a multinational company sends goods to one of its subsidiaries overseas, and does not intend to sell the cargo to anyone else.

(*c*) *The Customs Entry, C 273.* This is required mainly for statistical purposes, to provide monthly export figures, etc. Special declarations are used when claiming 'process-inwards relief'. This relief is given to exporters whose goods are made from imported raw materials which have paid duty on entry to the country.

(*d*) *The National Standard Shipping Note.* This is intended to replace all the shipping notes formerly issued by various ports around the country. Designed by SITPRO and now reproduced from their new master document, it may be submitted to any Port Authority which is taking over goods for shipment. It tells them what goods are being handed over to their care, which ship they are to be loaded on, etc.

(*e*) *The Insurance Certificate.* A certificate proving that a policy has been taken out either with Lloyd's or with an insurance company to cover the goods while in transit.

(*f*) *The Export Consignment Note.* This is a delivery note given to the road haulier who is taking goods to the docks to instruct him when and where to deliver the goods, and to secure a signature for them from the port authority or other warehouseman.

(*g*) *The Export Cargo Shipping Instructions*. When goods are sent to a freight forwarder to be packed for export and shipped by him, he has to be instructed on the nature of the goods, destination, etc. This form gives him all the details that he needs to know.

(*h*) *The Air Waybill*. Under the *Carriage by Air and Road Act, 1979*, which revises the rules of the Warsaw Convention in 1929, every consignment of goods by air must be covered by an air waybill in three parts. Part One is marked 'for the Carrier' and signed by the consignor. Part Two is marked 'for the Consignee' and travels with the goods. It is signed by both the carrier and the consignor. Part Three is signed by the carrier and returned to the consignor. We thus have each of the parties receiving a copy of the waybill signed by the other parties to the transaction.

(*i*) *The Port Rates Schedule*. When goods are handled the Port Authority charges rates payable by the shipper. These schedules must be completed in duplicate; one will be returned stamped as proof of payment.

(*j*) *European T Forms and Movement Certificates*. These serve two purposes. Movement certificates indicate the nature of goods being moved, so that customs authorities know what duty to charge. T forms indicate that the goods in a vehicle are merely passing through a country and will not be unloaded. In this case they are passed quickly into the country and out again without wasting time on Customs inspection other than to ensure that the Customs seals put on when they started the journey are still unbroken.

(*k*) *The Certificate of Origin*. Certificates of origin are needed only where a free-trade area is afraid that its tariffs to non-members will be avoided by circuitous routings. For instance, if India allows British goods in duty-free, but charges German goods a tariff, a German firm might seek to evade the tariff by sending the goods to Britain first and having them re-exported to India. A certificate of origin is usually issued by the Chamber of Commerce to certify that goods have been either entirely, or largely, manufactured in the country stated.

23.5 Standard Terms and Conditions

Goods are sold on certain standard terms, the meanings of which are understood by businessmen all over the world. They are published in a booklet produced by the International Chamber of Commerce, called *Incoterms 1980*. At present there are 14 incoterms with three-letter symbols to identify them. They are:

EXW (Ex works). The seller's duty is to make the goods available at his premises. The buyer must move the goods from the works and pay all charges for transport, insurance, etc.

FRC (Free carrier-named point). The seller's duty is to deliver the goods to the carrier at a named point. The buyer must pay all charges and assume all responsibilities from that named point.

FOR/FOT (Free on rail or truck). The seller's duty is to deliver the goods to the railway (the word 'truck' refers to a railway waggon). The buyer must pay all charges and assume all responsibilities from that moment onwards.

FOA (Free on board at airport). This is the same as FOB (see below) except that it applies to airports and aircraft.

FAS (Free alongside ship). The seller's obligations are fulfilled when the goods arrive alongside the ship. The foreign importer must then pay for loading, freight and insurance charges.

FOB (Free on board). This means that the price quoted covers all charges up to the time the goods cross the ship's rail; after that the foreign importer becomes liable. The export office must notify the foreign buyer so that he can arrange insurance.

CFR (Cost and freight). Here the seller pays all charges up to the arrival of goods on board ship and the freight to the port of destination. The risk passes to the buyer as the goods cross the ship's rail, and insurance cover must be arranged by the buyer from that point.

CIF (Cost, insurance and freight). Here the final price on the invoice includes the cost of the goods, the insurance charges and the freight charges as far as the foreign port.

DCP (Carriage paid to: note that the D in the code stands for Delivered, but is not used in the verbal description). This is similar to CFR in that the seller pays the charges for carriage to the named destination, but the risk passes to the buyer as soon as goods are handed over to the first carrier, and not as they cross the ship's rail.

CIP (Carriage and insurance paid to). This is the same as OCP except that the seller must also arrange and pay for insurance of the goods to the named destination.

EXS (Ex ship). The seller must make the goods available to the seller on board the ship at destination. The buyer must then unload and clear the goods from the port area.

EXQ (Ex quay). There are two types of contract: 'ex quay duty paid' and 'ex quay—duties on buyer's account'. The seller must deliver the goods on the quayside at destination, either duty paid or duty unpaid. The seller bears all charges from that point, including customs duties if the second alternative applies.

DAF (Delivered at frontier). The buyer delivers the goods at the frontier, but before they go through the customs point of the country of arrival. The seller must pay any customs duties on entry.

DDP (Delivered duty paid). This is the term with the maximum burden for the seller. Goods must be delivered to the buyer's premises, duty paid—but terms like 'DDP exclusive of VAT and/or taxes may be agreed. (Note the term *franco domicile* is now obsolete.)

23.6　The Despatch of Goods

Clearly exports need special attention as far as packaging and despatch are concerned. These matters are dealt with in Chapter 24.

23.7　Post Office Services for the Exporter

The Post Office offers a wide range of services to exporters. Some of the services mentioned are also available in the United Kingdom, for internal trade.

The important feature of postal services is that as members of the Universal Postal Union the Post Office has a unique system for delivering goods to destination. Secure relationships exist with 210 countries, but a few countries at any time may—for reasons of war or civil unrest—be temporarily out of touch. There is access to a reasonably efficient system in most countries, and customs procedures have been considerably simplified. The chief services are:

(*a*) *Correspondence services*. Letter services are still important for the transmission of documents, payments, etc. Both surface and airmail services are offered, though fewer and fewer ships are available these days, and consequently airmail is becoming more common. There is an **advice of delivery** service, to assure the exporter that his letter has arrived; a **registration** service; a **Swiftair** service for express delivery of letters to Europe, and letters and printed papers to some countries outside Europe. **International reply coupons** enable an exporter to send the equivalent of stamps for a reply to his letter. Bulk postings of **direct mail advertising** (DMA) are accepted at special rates for countries outside Europe, and travel by **accelerated surface post**. With accelerated surface post the letters travel by air on the long-haul routes between continents but are treated as surface mail while in the country of departure and the country of destination. With Europe direct mail advertising uses the **bulk airmail** service.

(*b*) *Movement of goods*. Goods may be moved as **letters** (up to 2 kg) or as **small packets** or parcels. They can travel by air, surface or accelerated surface post. It is essential to meet customs regulations, either by the affixing of gummed labels or by the handing in, with the packet or parcel, of a set of customs documents. As usual with such documents, there are several forms to fill up, and enormous labour can be saved if an aligned set of documents is used. These are provided by specialist printers. Fig. 23.2 shows the Postabroad Documentation Set supplied by one company in this field.

(*c*) *Datapost*. The Datapost service is for the rapid transmission of urgent documents, computer printout or any other items such as spare parts or samples for exhibitions. There is a weight limit of 10 kg. There is a 'Datapost on demand' service at all Post Office counters, but for firms sending regularly by this service it is usual to make a door-to-door

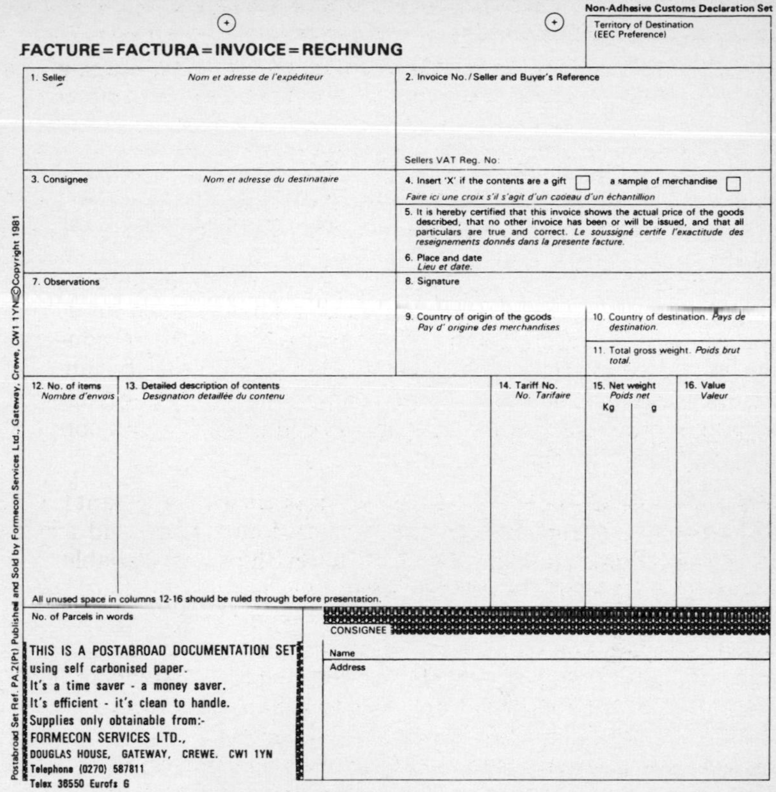
Non-Adhesive Customs Declaration Set

Territory of Destination (EEC Preference)

FACTURE = FACTURA = INVOICE = RECHNUNG

1. Seller *Nom et adresse de l'expéditeur*

2. Invoice No./Seller and Buyer's Reference

Sellers VAT Reg. No:

3. Consignee *Nom et adresse du destinataire*

4. Insert 'X' if the contents are a gift ☐ a sample of merchandise ☐
Faire ici une croix s'il s'agit d'un cadeau d'un échantillon

5. It is hereby certified that this invoice shows the actual price of the goods described, that no other invoice has been or will be issued, and that all particulars are true and correct. *Le soussigné certifie l'exactitude des reseignements donnés dans la presente facture.*

6. Place and date *Lieu et date.*

7. Observations

8. Signature

9. Country of origin of the goods *Pay d' origine des merchandises*

10. Country of destination. *Pays de destination.*

11. Total gross weight. *Poids brut total.*

12. No. of items *Nombre d'envois*	13. Detailed description of contents *Designation detaillée du contenu*	14. Tariff No. *No. Tarifaire*	15. Net weight *Poids net* Kg g	16. Value *Valeur*

All unused space in columns 12-16 should be ruled through before presentation.

No. of Parcels in words

CONSIGNEE
Name
Address

THIS IS A POSTABROAD DOCUMENTATION SET
using self carbonised paper.
It's a time saver - a money saver.
It's efficient - it's clean to handle.
Supplies only obtainable from:-
FORMECON SERVICES LTD.,
DOUGLAS HOUSE, GATEWAY, CREWE. CW1 1YN
Telephone (0270) 587811
Telex 38550 Eurofs G

Postabroad Set Ref. PA.2(Pt) Published and Sold by Formecon Services Ltd., Gateway, Crewe, CW1 1YN © Copyright 1981

Fig. 23.2. A 'Postabroad' non-adhesive customs documentation set.

arrangement. Up to 17 countries are concerned, and the service is expanding.

(*d*) *Intelpost*. Intelpost is a satellite service for facsimile copying of documents to major countries around the world. The document is scanned by an electric eye in the facsimile copying machine. What the eye sees is then sent by satellite to a receiving machine in the country of destination. The scanning takes four minutes, and the resulting copy is acceptable to banks, customs authorities, etc., as a true copy.

(*e*) *Telex*. The telex system is a system of printed communication between firms, a copy of all messages sent being produced on teleprinters at both the receiving and transmitting installations. Teleprinters are hired to firms by the Post Office Corporation at nominal charges of a few pounds per week. The subscriber is given a telex number similar to a telephone number and business associates around the world can obtain access to his teleprinter 24 hours per day. The time gap between countries in different time zones therefore makes no difference to the effectiveness of the telex system. A London firm calling the number of an Australian subscriber whose offices are closed because it is night time, will automatically switch on the teleprinter and the message will be passed. On arrival next morning the Australian telex operator will pass the messages to the department concerned. A reply can be prepared and sent, although the London offices are now closed in their turn.

Charges for actual calls are low; for example, at the time of writing about 16p per minute to Belgium, and £0.98 per minute to Australia from the United Kingdom. Telex has revolutionised communication between firms. One bank in London advertises that it can make money available anywhere in the world in five minutes, an impressive display of the ease of modern communication.

23.8 Rapid Revision

Cover the page with a sheet of paper and uncover one question at a time.

Answers	*Questions*
—	1. Why are exports important?
1. Because the only way to pay for the goods we need to import from abroad is to earn foreign exchange by selling to other countries.	2. What particular problems face the exporter?
2. (*a*) Language problems; (*b*) currency problems; (*c*) licensing regulations; (*d*) problems of documentation; (*e*) controls over quality, safety, packaging, etc., vary from country to country; (*f*) marine and aviation risks; (*g*) risks that debtors will prove to be bad.	3. What documents are met with in the export trade?
3. (*a*) Export invoices; (*b*) bills of lading; (*c*) sea waybills; (*d*) customs entries; (*e*) shipping notes; (*f*) insurance certificates; (*g*) export consignment notes; (*h*) export cargo shipping instructions; (*i*) air waybills; (*j*) port rates schedules; (*k*) certificates of origin.	4. What is the meaning of FAS?
4. Free alongside ship.	5. And of FOB?
5. Free on board.	6. And of CIF?
6. Cost, insurance, freight.	7. What is the significance of these different abbreviations?
7. There are 14 of them altogether. They are called Incoterms. Each one tells the point to which the exporter will cover the goods. With FAS he sees them to the ship's side. With FOB he pays all charges until the ship's rail is crossed. With CIF he covers the property until it reaches the foreign port.	8. What is the telex system?

Answers	Questions
8. A system of communications which sends messages direct from one office to another subscriber's office anywhere in the world.	9. What services does the Post Office supply to exporters?
9. (*a*) Letter post; (*b*) small packet post; (*c*) parcel post; (*d*) accelerated surface post; (*e*) bulk air mail; (*f*) Datapost; (*g*) Intelpost; (*h*) telex.	10. Go over the page again until you feel sure of all the answers.

Exercises Set 23

1. What problems face the exporter of goods? Describe the special features of an export department, designed to overcome these problems.

2. What documents are met in the export trade which are not necessary in the home trade? How may such documents be prepared economically?

3. Explain briefly the difference between the export of goods on FAS terms and export on CIF terms.

4. Two identical consignments of goods are being exported to Japan. One consignment is on FOB terms, the other on CIF terms. Which will have the larger invoice price, and why?

5. An insurance agent is drawing up a 'statement of risk' slip for an exporter, with a view to obtaining insurance cover for him. The cargo consists of 20 crates of furs to be shipped from Leningrad to London. List the risks that should be considered in such a consignment, so that the exporter will be adequately covered.

6. Consider how an export department should communicate with an overseas agent on the following matters: (*a*) a request for details of the invoice number of a consignment of goods already arrived at their destination in the agent's country and which he is waiting to have released from customs; (*b*) a request for 50 000 brochures to be sent in time for the local motor show in four months' time; (*c*) an order for an urgent spare part weighing half a kilogram; (*d*) best wishes from the management to the staff of the overseas agency on the occasion of the local 'New Year' festival.

7. What is a Bill of Lading? What is its importance in the export trade?

8. An export house is arranging the purchase of textile machinery for a Hong Kong mill. What chain of events will lead to the eventual arrival of the machinery in Hong Kong?

9. 'Export documentation is more expensive that home documentation.' List the documents likely to be necessary in: (*a*) a home sale of 5 pieces of machinery, delivered by road and paid for COD; (*b*) an export sale of 5 pieces of machinery, air freighted to Australia and paid for by irrevocable letter of credit.

10. Your firm is considering setting up a branch in a foreign country. List some of the considerations that should be borne in mind when considering such a project. From the list select two problems that you feel are the most essential and describe them in detail.

24

THE DESPATCH AND TRANSPORT DEPARTMENTS

24.1 The Distribution of Goods

At one time efficiency of business was chiefly thought of in terms of production, and mass production methods were devised to reduce costs in the manufacturing field. These methods themselves produced a crisis in distribution, for the endless streams of products pouring from the production lines had to be cleared into warehouses or refrigerated stores, and passed on to the retailer and the eventual consumer. This led to large-scale wholesaling, with huge depots located in convenient spots, where they could serve dense populations. At the same time the use of large-scale handling methods, or unit-loads, increased. The best known is the **container**, a large steel-framed sealed box in which large quantities of goods can be transported easily and safely. A similar method is the **palletised load**, in which a large number of small boxes are loaded onto a single pallet, or baseplate, which can be lifted by a forklift truck or by slings from a crane.

24.2 Packaging

Packaging protects goods going long distances from damage in transit. It is a specialist activity to pack goods properly, and the packaging industry provides many aids which will assist in the safe transit of goods. While packaging is essential, much of it is thrown away after use, so that packaging materials should always be kept as cheap as possible.

The following points are of interest:

(a) *Safety*. The goods must be properly protected. The chief causes of damage are: knocks and shocks received in loading and unloading; the shifting of cargo; pressure from above when goods are piled on top of one another; damage by weather, particularly water, but also cold and heat. Dangerous goods may need special packaging and must be notified to the shipowner or other interested party.

(b) *Economy*. Goods packed in wooden or metal cases are safe, but packing costs are high. This may be reduced if the containers can be returned, but as such containers occupy as great a space on the return journey as they do on the outward journey the cost of return will be great, especially if it is paid by volume rather than weight. One firm has specialised in collapsible containers, which fold down into a small size for the return journey. Cardboard containers are cheaper, and not worth returning, but they will not withstand pressure from above like a solid case of metal or wood.

(*c*) *Markings and identification.* Labels may be torn off, water may damage handwritten labels, and insects even eat away the paste or glue used to attach labels. To identify packages properly it is best to use stencilled marks in large clear lettering, preferably on all sides of the case. However packed, the marks are then visible. This will assist the identification, distribution and prompt handling of goods, which are often assembled with the goods of other merchants in loading points on wharfs and quays.

24.3   The Sequence of Despatch Activities

The despatch of goods is authorised by the copy invoices already shown (see page 318), the delivery note and advice note. These are sent to the despatch department by the invoice clerk, and authorise the appropriation of goods to the order. A list of the activities in despatch might be as follows:

(*a*) Arrival of the documents from the invoice clerk, usually with labels.

(*b*) Allocation of goods from stock to the contract. The appropriate items are assembled from their store places, records being made of the removal of goods on bin cards, etc.

(*c*) Packaging of the goods in the most appropriate way. This may involve the use of corrugated packing material, shredded paper waste or straw, expanded polystyrene shapes especially designed for particular goods, etc. It may be necessary to make wooden cases and reinforce them with metal or nylon strip material.

(*d*) The advice note will either be packed with the contents, or secured in a special envelope to the goods in transit. This may be in an envelope which also acts as a tie-on label.

(*e*) Suitably secure labels, either gummed, nailed or stapled to the boxes, will be attached, or the marks will be stencilled onto the crates about to be despatched.

(*f*) The delivery note, or consignment notes covering a number of deliveries, will be prepared for the driver or carrier who is delivering the goods. For export orders the consignment note may be accompanied by customs entry forms, TIR carnets, certificates of origin and export licences, as well as instructions regarding the issue of bills of lading. Air consignments will require an air waybill.

24.4   The Transport Department

The transport department is a very important department of many firms. It employs not only drivers and drivers' mates for the actual vehicles but also many staff involved in the essential work of planning and controlling vehicle movements. Parliament in the United Kingdom, and other governments elsewhere, have prescribed many rules on the construction and use of vehicles. For the public safety these rules are strictly enforced, and firms who are found to be breaking them may even lose their licences to operate vehicles.

Office procedures in transport vary enormously, but a typical procedure for road transport might be as follows:

(*a*) *The transport programme is drawn up.* This is a list of journeys to be made to meet customer requirements. It involves drawing up schedules of regular customers, the days on which deliveries are to be made, the size of the order, the address for delivery, etc.

(*b*) *The allocation of the programme to vehicles.* Only some of the vehicles of a firm will be available on any given day. Others will be at depots overnight in other parts of the country, or undergoing maintenance in vehicle servicing workshops. The planning clerks have to allocate the deliveries to the vehicles available in accordance with agreed working practices. Thus some drivers may be entitled to refuse loads which will exceed their statutory or agreed duties.

Suppose a heavy goods vehicle averaging 35 mph is driven by a driver working an 8-hour day. This represents a 140-mile journey each way. A long-distance journey may therefore be effected by one driver taking it down 140 miles to a change-over depot, where he hands it on to another driver who has in turn brought a lorry up 140 miles to that point. By returning in the other vehicle each driver gets back to his base depot in the 8 hours, with goods that have travelled 280 miles.

(*c*) *Destination sheets.* These are drawn up, to show in detail the programme of deliveries for the next day. They list such headings as: (i) Vehicle no.; (ii) Trailer no.; (iii) Driver's name; (iv) Mate's name; (v) Collect from; (vi) Deliver to; (vii) Contents of load; (viii) Mileage, etc. The destination sheets are used by the foreman of the transport yard whose duty it is to ensure that the loads actually go.

(*d*) *Delivery notes are then made out.* These may be merely the delivery note sent down by the invoicing clerk, but in many cases are more involved, with as many as eight copies. These include a copy for the transport department, for the customer, a signed receipt note, a Pass Out (which releases the vehicle through the gates of the factory or plant) and a computer copy. Fig. 24.1 illustrates a typical delivery note.

(*e*) *Other aspects of control.* Many other aspects require control, particularly the **costing of journeys**, **vehicle location** (since vehicles which are not kept track of are easily stolen, or may miss journeys for which they have been programmed), and **returned loads**. A vehicle unable to deliver its load which returns full has to be checked to ensure that the contents are still intact and have not been partially off-loaded. Pilferage is a major problem, and joint inspection by two members of staff is usual to ensure accurate records.

TRANSPORT COPY ⭕			BULK TANKER DELIVERY GENERAL REFINERIES LIMITED LION HOUSE, HIGH STREET, RAINHAM, ESSEX					Nọ 7364 DATE 27/3/19··		
Tare or Gross	DAY	MONTH		Weigh Code	GRADE OF SUGAR	VEHICLE No.	Tons	Grams	CONTRACT No.	
32	27	MARCH		17	FINE	XZY 123	28	200	7/17854	GROSS
										TARE
							28	200		NET

BAR 511

BUYER   DELIVERY NO.   CONSIGNEE

N.T. SHELDRAKE

QUALITY CONFECTIONERY LTD.,
HIGH ROAD,
PARKSTONE QUAY,
ESSEX,

PLEASE RECEIVE ONE BULK TANKER CONTAINING APPROXIMATELY   28   TONS SUGAR

EX ESSEX REFINERY/MILESTONE WHARF
PER REFINERIES TRANSPORT LTD.
Tanker Control   01—881 18827

SPECIAL INSTRUCTIONS

Deliver earliest possible

G/W Weigher................................

Tare Weigher................................

Fig. 24.1. A tanker delivery note.

Drivers' hours records and **vehicle maintenance records** must be kept, and may be required for inspection purposes. Regular testing of vehicles at official **Vehicle Testing Stations** must be arranged, and supervision of axle loadings be maintained to ensure that vehicles are loaded only to the limits laid down in the **plating regulations**. These require vehicles to carry a 'plate' bearing the official axle loadings and total loadings permitted, so that 'spot' checks by police controls may be made when a vehicle is suspected of overloading.

A particularly clever device which is at present being introduced is the **tachograph**. This is a device which incorporates marker pens which record every movement the vehicle makes. A clockwork mechanism rotates the device throughout the 24 hours and a new card is fitted each day. A completed card shows when the vehicle moved off, how fast it went, when it stopped and when it re-started. Although some lorry drivers object to this device, and call it a 'spy in the cab', it does substantiate the behaviour of a driver who is operating his vehicle in a proper way.

Movements of goods by rail entails rather similar procedures. The loss of personal supervision inevitable when goods are sent by rail is counterbalanced by the more economic operations achieved on long-haul routes. The containerisation of goods and their despatch on liner trains ensures rapid delivery and minimum losses by pilfering. Goods are usually sent either at **'owner's risk'** or at **'company risk'**—the charges being higher where the risk is borne by the railway company.

Sea transport and air transport procedures would require the extra documentation procedures mentioned on pages 327–30.

24.5 Rapid Revision

Cover the page with a sheet of paper and uncover one question at a time.

Answers	Questions
—	1. What are the functions of the despatch and transport departments?
1. (*a*) To assemble goods for despatch according to the invoices; (*b*) to pack, label and mark all crates, cartons or packets; (*c*) to select the best method for transporting the goods to the consignee.	2. What is a container?
2. It is a strong metal box used for transporting goods as a unit load.	3. What is a pallet?
3. It is a wooden or fibre-board platform on which many small packages can be moved as a unit load.	4. What do the words 'unit load' mean?
4. They mean a single load, one large unit being moved instead of many small ones.	5. Why is documentation very important?
5. Because delays in transit are very often caused by poor documentation. Customs posts will often not clear goods from the port or airport area unless documentation is correct.	6. What documents are commonly met with?
6. (*a*) Invoices; (*b*) advice notes; (*c*) delivery notes; (*d*) consignment notes; (*e*) air waybills; (*f*) TIR carnets; (*g*) EEC T forms.	7. What do TIR carnets and EEC T forms do?
7. Enable lorries to go through customs posts without examination so long as the customs seal is unbroken.	8. What is a tachograph?
8. A 'spy in the cab' device which tells the operator the time of departure, the speed at every part of the journey, the waiting time, etc.	9. Go over the page again until you feel you are sure of the answers.

Exercises Set 24

1. You work in the despatch department of a large manufacturing company. Describe the office routine involved in the despatch of goods for the home market, for delivery by the company's fleet of vehicles.

2. What considerations enter into: (*a*) packaging and (*b*) documentation of goods for delivery by road?

3. (a) Describe a typical office procedure necessary for transporting goods by one of the following methods: (i) road; (ii) rail; (iii) air.

(b) Give the meaning of the following abbreviations used in connection with transport: (i) B/L; (ii) CIF; (iii) FOB.

4. Write short notes on: (a) a delivery sheet; (b) a consignment note; (c) 'Owner's risk' and 'Company risk'.

5. Goods may be conveyed by rail at 'Company risk' or 'Owner's risk'. (a) What do these terms mean? (b) In what circumstances might each be used? (c) What risks are involved in the transportation of goods?

6. Discuss three ways of transporting goods. What documents would you use when sending goods by one of these methods?

7. You wish to send a consignment of goods to one of your branches 30 miles away. Mention three methods of conveyance which could be used and describe the procedure and documents likely to be needed for any two of these methods.

8. Choosing *two* of the following methods of transport, describe the procedures and documents involved when despatching goods: (a) by hired road transport; (b) by British Rail; (c) by air; (d) by sea.

9. What is a tachograph? How does it help in controlling road vehicles?

10. Draw up a simple log to record the quantities of petrol or diesel oil supplied daily to a firm's own vehicles. Make *five* specimen entries, including commercial vehicles and travellers' cars.

11. A growing retail business is considering the purchase of a delivery van to make deliveries to customers within a ten-mile radius. What documents will be needed and what system must be adopted to see that this part of the business is efficiently conducted?

12. The methods of inland transport are: road, rail, canal and air. These methods are not equally suitable for all kinds of goods. Mention a few of the advantages and disadvantages of each method giving an example of goods that could suitable be carried in each case.

25

SOURCES OF INFORMATION

25.1 Introduction

One cannot possibly know all the information that is needed to carry out even the simpler jobs in a modern office. It is necessary at times to turn to a reference book, and the range of books that will be helpful is very great. Many are specialist books, serving a particular aspect of the work of an office. A good example is the *Post Office Guide*, an indispensable aid for the post department. Others are general works of reference, such as *Pears Cyclopaedia*, offering information on a large range of matters which may arise over the course of the year. The most useful person in an office is often not the person who professes to know everything but the person who is surrounded by a selection of suitable reference books. The quick use of such books comes only with practice, and the reader is urged to build up a selection of such books for personal use in the office.

On a point of good office discipline, it is desirable that junior staff should be encouraged to use reference books rather than ask unnecessary questions. Although modern offices are less strict than in former times about staff talking in working hours it is a great nuisance if a junior member of staff interrupts the train of thought of senior personnel to ask routine questions which can be answered by reference to the calendar, a dictionary or a *Pears Cyclopaedia*.

An office that is poorly supplied with reference books will be a less satisfactory place to work in for that reason. Suggestions of necessary reference books are usually welcome, and senior staff should regularly review, update and improve the supply available.

Reference books may be conveniently divided up as shown in section 25.2 below.

25.2 A List of Reference Books

(*a*) *Correspondence and the use of the English language*
  (i) A good dictionary—for example, the *Concise Oxford Dictionary* or *Chambers's Twentieth Century Dictionary*.
 (ii) *Fowler's Modern English Usage*.
(iii) *Roget's Thesaurus of English Words and Phrases*.
 (iv) *The Typist's Desk Book*, by M. Berry.
  (v) *Black's Titles and Forms of Address*.

(vi) *The Pitman Dictionary of English and Shorthand.*
(vii) *The Dictionary of Typewriting*, by M. Crooks and F. Dawson.

(b) Post Office services

(i) *Post Office Guide.*
(ii) *Post Offices in the United Kingdom.*
(iii) Telephone directories.
(iv) *STD Dialling Instructions and Call Charges.*
(v) *UK Telex Directory.*

(c) People

(i) *Who's Who.*
(ii) *Debrett's Peerage* or *Burke's Peerage.*
(iii) Professional lists, according to the needs of the office—for example, *Medical Register* or *Medical Directory Law List, Crockford's Clerical Directory.*
(iv) Service lists: *Army List, Navy List*, and *Air Force List.*
(v) A local street directory or electoral roll, where appropriate.
(vi) *Vacher's Parliamentary Companion* (pronounced *Vasher's*).
(vii) *Vacher's European Companion* (pronounced *Vasher's*).

(d) Trade and industry

(i) *UK Kompass.*
(ii) *Kelly's Manufacturers and Merchants Directory.*
(iii) *Kelly's Post Office* (*London*). (NB Kelly's local directories other than London have been discontinued.)
(iv) *Yellow Pages* as appropriate.
(v) *Stock Exchange Official Year-Book.*
(vi) *Directory of Directors.*
(vii) Individual specialist directories as required—for example, *Benn's Hardware Directory, Food Trades Directory, Sell's Building Index.*

(e) Travel

(i) *ABC Rail Guide.*
(ii) *ABC World Airways Guide* or *Airport Times.*
(iii) *AA* or *RAC Handbook.*
(iv) A good world atlas and gazetteer.
(v) An atlas and gazetteer of London and/or the local area, as appropriate.
(vi) *Hotels and Restaurants in Great Britain.*
(vii) *Good Food Guide.*

(f) General and current information

(i) *Whitaker's Almanack.*
(ii) *Pears Cyclopaedia.*

   (iii) *Annual Abstract of Statistics* and the *Monthly Digest of Statistics.*

   (iv) *Britain: an Official Handbook.*

   (v) *Keesing's Contemporary Archives.*

(g) Miscellaneous

   (i) A decimal ready reckoner

   (ii) *Willing's Press Guide.*

   (iii) *Municipal Year Book.*

Finally, since an enormous range of reference works is available, most libraries have a copy of *British Sources of Reference and Information,* edited by T. Besterman, which is a major reference book about reference books.

25.3 A Brief Description of Some of the More Important Reference Books

Dictionaries. While many dictionaries offer roughly the same information the *Concise Oxford Dictionary* is a particularly reliable reference work. It tells you the following things:

   (i) How to spell the word.

   (ii) How to pronounce the word.

   (iii) What part of speech it is (i.e. noun, verb, adjective, etc.).

   (iv) What the word means.

   (v) The derivation of the word (i.e. where it originated, from Latin, Greek or a foreign language).

   (vi) Derivatives of the word (what other words have been formed from it).

   (vii) Cross-references to other words that are related.

   (viii) How to form the plural of the word.

Chambers's Twentieth Century Dictionary is very comprehensive and has several useful appendices.

According to the work of the office a secretary might also need translating dictionaries and specialist dictionaries—for example, *Chambers's Dictionary of Science and Technology.*

Fowler's Modern English Usage. A guide to the normally accepted 'correct' use of the English Language. It includes points of grammar, punctuation, idioms, etc.—for example, the difference between *i*nquiry and *e*nquiry.

Roget's Thesaurus. The word 'Thesaurus' comes from the Greek for 'treasury'. This book is a treasury of English words and phrases, listing all words of similar meaning, or related meaning. The clerk or executive who is 'stuck for the best word' to explain his meaning will always find it in the thousands of words classified in the *Thesaurus.* For example, under the heading 'probity' or 'honesty', appear 24 groups of words, totalling altogether over 500 words or phrases about upright behaviour.

The Typist's Desk Book. A handy little book which, besides giving typing hints, includes forms of address, abbreviations, words with unusual spellings, foreign phrases, etc.

The Dictionary of Typewriting, by M. Crooks and F. Dawson, has for long been the standard reference book on typewriting. Since it first appeared over 50 years ago it has presented an alphabetical reference on all typing difficulties. There are many useful articles on clerical activities such as duplicating, filing, etc., and many useful references to professional and official bodies.

Post Offices in the United Kingdom. This is a useful book for checking the correct form of postal addresses.

Telephone directories. These are issued free to all subscribers for their own locality and give names and addresses of most of the people who are on the telephone. A few people who, perhaps because they are particularly famous, or for some other reason, prefer not to have their telephone number widely known have what are called 'ex-directory' numbers. Such subscribers can be contacted by telephone only if they give their ex-directory number to personal friends. Telephone directories for other areas may be purchased by subscribers for a modest charge.

Classified trade lists are also issued, in what are called the 'yellow-page' directories. This idea proved to be such good business for the telephone service that 'yellow pages' have been bound into many ordinary alphabetical directories as a separate section at the end. This enables housewives or businessmen who want a particular service—say, the plumber—to find a list of all the plumbers in the area. A quick run down the list will enable the housewife to find a plumber near her home, whom she can phone for assistance in any emergency.

Now that STD services (subscriber trunk dialling) have spread to all areas, so that it is even possible to dial a subscriber as far away as New Zealand without assistance from the operator, it is essential to have a *Dialling Instructions and Call Charges* booklet, which is issued free by the Post Office to all subscribers.

A *Telex Directory* is also available which gives details of telex subscribers throughout the world (see page 333 for a description of the telex system).

The ABC Railway Guide. This is published monthly and lists all railway services to and from London, alphabetically, according to the destination from London, as well as the major provincial Inter-City services. It gives details about towns such as the early closing day, the population and the name of the chief hotels. It can also indicate how to travel to places without a direct rail connection by showing bus connections to the nearest rail service. In some offices regional and Continental railway guides may also be useful.

The ABC World Airways Guide. This is a similar volume, on a world-wide scale, giving details of scheduled air services throughout the world, fares, freight rates, principal travel agents and details of visa and health requirements. *Airport Times* is an inexpensive publication, appearing monthly, with sufficient detail about flight schedules for most offices.

The AA Handbook and RAC Handbook. These handbooks are available to members of these motoring organisations. Many motorists have back copies which they are prepared to give away. The maps and gazetteer section are very useful for planning convenient routes from place to place, and there is much useful information on hotels, garage facilities and apartments in every town in the country.

An Atlas. This is a volume of maps showing the world, continents and countries. Generally speaking each map is repeated twice; once to show the political features, i.e. which areas are under different governments, and the second time to show the physical features—the mountain systems, river systems, low-lying areas, etc. The index is helpful to locate towns and cities which you wish to check up on. A rather similar book, called a 'gazetteer', is a geographical dictionary which gives details of countries and towns, their populations, chief products, national incomes, etc. This can be a very useful reference book, especially to a secretary asked to provide an executive with a mass of background information on a country or place which is to be visited shortly.

Hotels and Restaurants in Great Britain. This includes a useful section on London's specialist restaurants such as Chinese, Greek and seafood restaurants.

The Good Food Guide. Published by the Consumers' Association, this book aims to provide unbiased reports on restaurants.

A–Z maps. These maps are prepared by the Geographers' Map Co. Ltd, of Sevenoaks in Kent. Based on the official Ordnance Survey Maps they include, besides a detailed street map of major towns, an index to all street names and references to places of public interest and entertainment. By showing the house numbering along the streets they enable you to judge where to leave public transport services for easiest access to the address you wish to reach.

Whitaker's Almanack. This is an annual publication which contains a vast collection of information on the countries of the world, their rulers, political organisation, population, production, etc. Originally an almanack was a list of months and days, astronomical facts for the year, tidal information, etc. This is still to be found in Whitaker's, but sections on the Monarchy, the Houses of Parliament, the Law Courts, societies and associations and many other topics make it an invaluable reference work on all aspects of British life.

Who's Who. This provides information on prominent people in this country—for example, MPs, people with titles, honours and sporting and entertainment personalities. A biographical dictionary, or the various volumes of *Who Was Who*, will give information on people no longer living. There are also Who's Who publications for specialist fields, such as *The Authors' and Writers' Who's Who*.

The Medical Register. This is the official list of qualified doctors. There is also a *Dentists' Register* and similar lists for opticians, chiropodists, etc. The *Medical Directory* also lists medical practitioners, but in slightly more detail. Information on hospitals and their medical staff is included as well. Similar directories are issued in most other professional fields; for example, *Crockford's Clerical Directory* is the official guide to clergy of the Church of England.

Vacher's Parliamentary and *European Companions*. These books are updated every three months and give the names and departments of all Parliamentary and Governmental personalities in the United Kingdom and Europe. They enable office staff to pinpoint officials with responsibilities in particular fields, and enable them to address correspondence to the person most interested in it.

UK Kompass. A guide to the manufacturers of a detailed list of goods. A second volume provides information on the companies included.

Kelly's Manufacturers and Merchants Directory. Both a classified guide and an alphabetical listing of manufacturers and merchants.

Kelly's Post Office (London) covers the postal districts of London. As well as a street directory, indicating commercial premises but not listing private individuals, there is a classified trade section. Lists of official personnel, local government offices, churches, etc., are provided.

Stock Exchange Official Year-Book. This gives financial information on firms, and is also a useful source for general information on companies.

The Directory of Directors. An alphabetical list of directors indicating the various companies with which they are associated, as well as a little biographical information.

Pears Cyclopaedia. This is a useful small encyclopaedia with many references about the world, everyday information and home and personal matters. It is inexpensive and covers many of the points an office junior may need to look up.

Annual Abstract of Statistics and *Monthly Digest of Statistics*. Official statistics for Britain in the past year, covering trade, population, weather, crime, etc.

Britain—An Official Handbook. A general description of Britain and its institutions, with some facts and figures.

Keesing's Contemporary Archives. These volumes are compiled from weekly supplements providing a digest of world affairs. The information is gathered from newspapers, parliamentary proceedings and other official publications.

Ready reckoners. These are volumes of calculations already worked out to save time and trouble. Suppose that your firm produces an article at $52\frac{1}{2}$ pence each, and that you are continually required to check invoices for sales of this item. To work out what a hundred or a thousand cost will be a matter of mental arithmetic—but 144 of them may be more troublesome. A ready reckoner will tell you whether the typist has made a slip or not.

Willing's Press Guide. A guide to newspapers, national and provincial, and magazines published in Britain. Some overseas newspapers and magazines are also indicated.

The Municipal Year Book. The guide to local councils and their services.

Business Equipment Digest. This is a controlled-circulation monthly magazine distributed free to office managers responsible for the purchase of office equipment and supplies. By regularly reviewing each field of office activity and evaluating new equipment, systems, etc., it helps keep senior staff up to date and alert to developments in every field.

25.4 Other Sources of Information

While reference books are the most useful source of information, other sources are available. The following are of interest:

(*a*) The **time** can be discovered by telephoning the talking clock, on the code number given in every *Dialling Instructions and Call Charges* booklet.

(*b*) The **weather** in any area may be discovered by telephoning an appropriate 'weather' telephone number. This is often very useful to travellers wishing to arrive suitably clad for functions.

(*c*) *Trade Associations.* Nearly all the trades have a trade association or professional body which acts as a source of valuable information for its members. Membership is usually relatively cheap, and a great deal of useful information is provided in the handbook produced for members each year. More specialised enquiries will usually be dealt with by a research department, whose staff are available to answer telephone enquiries, or to assist callers.

(*d*) *Research and Information Bureaux.* Many private firms operate in this field, supplying information and data for a fee. They keep comprehensive files on many subjects, with cross-referencing. Some systems are based on optical methods which depend upon 'optical coincidence' cards. These cards have as many as 20 000 reference squares, through which tiny holes can be drilled with a very accurate, optical drill. Articles, books and records stored in the retrieval system can be pinpointed by optical measures. Thus the entire collection of references to—say—moulded aluminium, can be pinpointed by the light showing through the holes in the cards. One manufacturer of such systems is George Anson & Co. Ltd.

(*e*) *Press Cuttings Agencies.* These agencies supply cuttings on particular topics to those interested. The fees are reasonable, and the coverage of local, national and international papers is much wider than an ordinary firm could obtain from its own efforts without setting up a special organisation.

26

PASSING AN EXAMINATION IN OFFICE PRACTICE

26.1 Passing Examinations

It has been said: 'An examination is very much like real life. You are given certain facts and a given set of circumstances. You then do the best you can with them, solving the problems involved in the most satisfactory way.' Whether examinations can ever be perfectly fair is debatable. The odd candidate may fail unjustifiably because of ill-health on a particular day. What is quite certain is that they are fair in this respect: *the candidate who is well prepared, has worked hard and has no special difficulties will almost certainly pass.* In 'special difficulties' we must include candidates who suffer from physical disabilities, and foreign candidates who sit examinations in a language not their own.

To assist the reader who has been using this book as preparation for an examination in office practice or clerical duties, the checklist given below has been prepared. Check over the items separately during the revision period, using the index to refer to the particular section of the book where that topic is discussed. Do written work, if possible on every topic, by selecting a suitable question from the chapter concerned. The reader will then find, when the examination question papers are distributed, that they present no embarrassment. The only problem will be which questions to answer, since they are all equally attractive, and present no difficulties.

26.2 Checklist of Examination Topics

  (i) *The Organisation of Business*
     The office as an organisation centre
     Organisation charts
     Types of offices
     Statutory control of offices
     The location of offices
     Office layout

 (ii) *Trading Activities*
    (*a*) *Purchasing*

Requisitions	Orders
Quotations and tenders	Taking delivery of goods inwards

    (*b*) *Manufacturing*

Production	Job cards

Production control   Records of finished goods

(c) *Warehousing*

Stock records	Maximum stock
Goods inwards book	Stocktaking
Stock controls	Stock valuation
Minimum stock	Requisition forms

(d) *Selling*

Enquiries	Home and export sales
Sales promotion	Terms of sale: cash, CWO, etc.
The sales force	Mail order
Advertising	Budget accounts
	Credit control

(e) *Distributing*

Despatch	Transport
Packaging	Documentation

(iii) *Administrative Activities*

(a) *General administration*

Mail inwards; sorting; security of remittances; distribution to departments.

Mail outwards; collection, stamping and franking; recording and registering.

Communications; telephones, internal and external; telex, typing and secretarial services; reception and messenger services; maintenance, cleaning and canteen services.

(b) *Personnel*

Personnel records	Contracts of employment
Recruitment and training	Wages and salaries
	Promotion
Welfare and First Aid	Confidential nature of personnel work
Terms of employment	

(c) *Accounts and payments*

Receipts and payments	Wages systems
Double-entry bookkeeping	Pay-As-You-Earn
	National Health Insurance
Simultaneous records	Graduated contributions
Petty cash (imprest system)	Cash discounts
	Trade discounts
Cash registers	Quantity discounts
Cash dispensers	Credit control
Budgetary control	Costing
Cheques	Postal payments
Credit transfers	Giro payments
Debit transfers	
Bankers' services	

(*d*) *Centralised filing*

Vertical filing	Index tabs and signals
Horizontal filing	Concertina files
Lateral filing	Manilla files and wallets
Indexing	Box files
Visible indexes	Lever-arch files
Visible strip indexes	File folders
	Filing rules

(*e*) *Reprography*

Carbon copies	Offset duplicating
NCR paper	Photocopying
Spirit duplicating	Thermal copying
Dyeline duplicating	Xerography
Stencil duplicating	Plain-paper copying

(iv) *Other Aspects of Office Practice*

(*a*) *Documents*

Enquiries	Requisitions
Quotations	Bin cards
Invoices	Stock record cards
Delivery notes	Cheques
Advice notes	Postal orders
Consignment notes	Telegraphic monetary orders
Receipts	Credit transfers
Bills of lading	Paying-in slips
Air waybills	Standing orders
Continuous stationery	Giro forms
PAYE, P2, P11, P13,	Petty cash vouchers
P45, P60	Remittance advice notes
Clock cards	Credit notes

(*b*) *Sources of information*

Dictionary	Classified telephone directories
Atlas	The *Post Office Guide*
Ready reckoner	Telex directory
Whitaker's Almanack	Kelly's street guides
Pears Cyclopaedia	*Who's Who*
ABC *Rail Guide*	Crockford's *Clerical Directory*
ABC *Air Guide*	Army, Navy and Air Force lists
AA and RAC hand-books	*Law List*
A–Z maps	
The Stock Exchange Official Year-Book	
Telephone directories	

(*c*) *Office equipment*

Mail-opening machine	Collators

Date stamps and time stamps
Ambidex sorter
Franking machines
Addressing machine
Manual typewriters
Electric typewriters
Electronic typewriters
Word processors
Copyholders
Stencil tools
Communication trays
Cash registers
Cash dispensers
Filing cabinets
Flexiform cabinets
Punches
Sorters

Shredders
Envelope sealer
Staplers
Guillotines
Add-listing machines
Electronic calculators
Electronic-printing calculators
Computers:
  Central processor
  Punched card reader
  Paper-tape reader
  Line printer
  Console communicator
  Key-edit device
  Visual display unit
  Minicomputers
  Microcomputers
  Floppy discs

APPENDIX 1

OFFICE PRACTICE ASSIGNMENTS

Most Office Practice syllabuses include a requirement that students should carry out a series of practical assignments. As much as 30 per cent of the marks may be awarded for this practical work, which is assessed by the course tutor as the course proceeds. The practical work is collected together in an 'Assignment Folder', a lightweight folder with some simple means of securing papers.

A list of equipment, materials, etc., required in the model office for students to carry out these assignments is given on pages 374–5.

Each assignment is intended to represent one hour's work by the student, though this may be exceeded if instruction in the use of equipment, etc., is required, or if discussion with other members of the group is necessary. All students should perform Assignment No. 25.

Assignment No. 1: The Spirit Duplicator (*Office Machinery*)
1. Read pages 144–7 in the textbook about spirit duplication.
2. Look at Plates 9 and 10.
3. Collect together the materials necessary to make a spirit master. These are (*a*) a sheet of master paper, (*b*) a sheet of hecto transfer paper, (*c*) a ballpoint pen (but you may type any text if you prefer to do so).
4. Using a piece of scrap paper prepare the wording of a notice to be duplicated. It should announce a Discothèque to be held in the near future. Check your wording to ensure that you have included all the necessary details of date, time, place, etc.
5. Now make your spirit master. It is to have two items on it: (*a*) the disco notice which you have prepared (display it attractively to occupy half the page); (*b*) a telephone message form, as illustrated on page 77 of this book.
6. Use your master copy to run off four copies. You may need to be instructed in the use of the machine by your teacher, or perhaps the head of the reprographics section in your college or school.
7. On a sheet of A4 paper write a short account of the use of the spirit duplicator beginning 'First check that the spirit duplicator has plenty of spirit in the reservoir bottle'.
8. Assemble your project for assessment. It should include your written answer, and two of the copies you produced. One should be complete, the other divided into its separate pieces.

Assignment No. 2: The Telephone (*Communication*)
1. Read pages 71–7 in this textbook—sections 6.4 and 6.5.
2. Take a sheet of A4 paper and head it with your name, group and the heading of this assigment. Without looking at any telephone directory write on the paper a list of twelve place names. Six of these should be the names of villages or districts near your home town: six should be large towns in other parts of the

country. Using a copy of the 'STD Dialling Instructions' booklet for your area, find the correct dialling codes for the 12 places and write them down on your paper.

3. Using your *local* telephone directory find one person who is on the telephone in each of the six villages near your home. Record their names, addresses, STD codes and phone numbers as shown below:

Martin, K. E., 25 Whitebriar Lane, Cottingley, Cambs. 0038–172659

4. Using the spirit duplicator run off a supply of the telephone message forms illustrated on page 77 of this book. You will find it most economical to do the form twice on an A4 sheet of paper, so that each copy you print can then be cut in half to make two forms for use in the model office during Office Practice lessons.

5. Now use one of these forms to record the details of the following telephone call, which you are supposed to receive at 12.30 today.

'Hallo, is that Mr Farmer's secretary? Oh good! This is Aviation Components Ltd here. My name is Curtis. I know that Mr Farmer is away at your refresher course until tomorrow, but this message is extremely urgent. Would you make sure he receives it as soon as he returns. It's about the drilled assemblies he is costing for us for the new C235 airbus. We've received a new specification from the Ministry and it means that the assemblies have to be made in thicker material than before. Instead of 1 millimetre it has to be 2 millimetres for the main assembly and $1\frac{1}{2}$ millimetres for the others. Would you ask him to take this into account in the costings, and also check on the availability of supplies of these materials. You will make quite sure that he gets this message, won't you? These things have to be right for the aeronautics industry; I'm sure you understand. Richard Curtis, of Aviation Components Ltd.'

6. Assemble your assignment for marking. It should consist of your headed sheet of A4 paper, one print of the telephone message forms as run off on the spirit duplicator, and a completed form conveying the message given above.

Assignment No. 3: Invoices (Office Procedures)

1. In this assignment you are required to make out a set of invoices and answer some simple questions about them. To begin with, produce a set of four invoices by using the spirit duplicator and drawing up a master similar to the invoice shown on page 318 of this book. If these are already available—someone else in the class having produced useful samples—you may use them from stock. You also need carbon paper to interleave so that you can produce a four-copy set.

2. The details to be entered on the invoice either in ballpoint pen or typewritten are as follows:

Your firm is named T. Wotherspoon Ltd, of 44 Brook St, Ditchley, Worcs. DI5 7TU.

Your customer is Mr R. Medhurst, 19 The Glades, Somertown, South Yorkshire SO5 2BR.

The order is for the following:

    5 Cassna electronic calculators @ £7.36 each

    6 Marvel tape cassettes @ £1.45 each

The VAT on these items is 15% in each case.

Your VAT Registration No. is 1785926A. The tax point is today's date. The Order No. is 7529, the date is yesterday's date and the invoice date is today's date. The type of supply is a SALE.

The goods are to be delivered to 19 The Glades, Somertown.

Use an adding-listing machine or electronic calculator to assist you with the calculations and to determine the VAT to be charged. Preserve the adding-list, or a piece of paper showing your rough calculations.

3. Having produced the invoices remove the carbon paper and write 'Top Copy', 'Second Copy', 'Third Copy' and 'Fourth Copy' on them. Take a sheet of A4 paper, divide it into four pieces and on each piece write a short account of the use of that copy, beginning 'First Copy: this copy is ...' etc. Clip these explanations to the appropriate copies with a stapling machine.

4. Present your completed assignment to the teacher or lecturer in charge for assessment. It should consist of four invoices with explanations attached, your calculations and a sheet of A4 paper headed with your name and class details, on which your grade can be recorded.

Assignment No. 4: The Post Office Guide (*Reference Books*)

1. In this assignment you are asked to use the *Post Office Guide* to settle a number of different points, which you are to imagine have been raised in the office where you are employed. Use a sheet of A4 bond paper, headed with your name and class or group, to record your final answers. Rough work should be carried out on sheets of paper which should be preserved for inclusion in your folder.

2. The office proposes to mail a leaflet to 3600 doctors about a new drug which is to be marketed. The leaflets cost £2.80 per 100, and weigh 50 grams when inserted in an envelope. They are to be sent by first-class mail. You are asked to discover the total cost of this mailing, bearing in mind that the envelopes are 35 pence per 100, all the doctors live in the United Kingdom and the labour cost is estimated at £8.50.

3. A further 400 doctors are ship's surgeons and are to be reached through their shipping offices abroad: 100 are in Australian waters, 100 in Singapore, 100 can be reached via Hong Kong and 100 via New York offices. You are asked to cost this Merchant Navy mailing using the overseas postal rates for the countries concerned.

4. Rule up an envelope with a suitable address as shown in the *Post Office Guide* for one of the ship's surgeons mentioned in (3) above.

5. Write a short account of the 'datapost' service, as explained in the guide.

6. Your office wishes to send a diagram of a piece of chemical apparatus by the Intelpost service to Dallas, USA. Discover whether this is possible and what the Intelpost service is.

Assignment No. 5: Making up a Wage Packet (*Wages and Salaries*)

(Schools and Colleges wishing to obtain supplies of Kalamazoo wages material may do so from the suppliers, Kalamazoo Ltd, Birmingham B31 2RW)

In this assignment you are required to draw up wages slips similar to the ones illustrated on pages 263 and 264–5. You are then required to do a notes and coin summary for the cashier to enable the money to be obtained for the wages envelopes.

1. Read carefully the pages on 'Modern Wages Systems', pages 260–2.
2. Study Fig. 17.3 (page 263) and Fig. 17.4 (pages 264–5), making quite sure you understand the 'earnings' and 'deductions' sections.
3. Take three wages slips of the sort illustrated on page 263 and head them with the week of the year (week 14) and the date (July 12th). Put the names of the three employees shown below at the bottom of the slips.
4. The following details relate to three employees in your firm. Tom Bellinger is a driver, William Brown is a salesman and Yvonne Murray is a secretary. The week is week 14 and the date July 12th. The notes below will help you.

	T. Bellinger	W. Brown	Y. Murray
Earnings	£	£	£
Basic pay	56.00	35.00	54.00
Overtime	12.60	—	—
Commission	—	17.00	—
Pension contributions	—	1.80	2.40
Gross pay to last week for tax purposes	920.00	550.00	696.00
Tax-free pay (see page 269)	Code 251	Code 155	Code 161
Taxable pay to date	See note (*e*) below		
Tax due to date (see page 270)	See note (*f*)		
Tax	See note (*g*) and next line down		
Tax paid up to last week	78.50	39.00	84.00
National Insurance Contribution	See note (*h*)		
Employer's Pension Contribution	See note (*i*)		

You should now be able to complete the pay-slips, including the 'Total amount payable'.

Notes
(*a*) You will need to work out the gross pay for the week from the figures given.
(*b*) Pension contributions are deducted from gross pay to give gross pay for tax purposes.
(*c*) Gross pay to date for tax purposes is found by adding this week's gross pay for tax purposes to last week's total 'gross pay to last week for tax purposes'.
(*d*) Tax-free pay can be looked up on page 269 against the code numbers shown.
(*e*) This is found by deducting 'tax-free pay' from 'gross pay to date for tax purposes'.
(*f*) Tax due is shown in the table on page 270.
(*g*) The tax that is actually to be deducted this week has to be worked out by taking away last week's tax due from the 'tax due to date' you have just found from Table B on page 270. In a real office this would be found on the employee's Wages Record Card. To help you do this assignment it is given on the next line of figures below 'Tax'.
(*h*) This has to be found from the *Employer's Guide to National Insurance Contributions.* A copy of this may be obtained free of charge for use in your

college or school from your local Department of Health and Social Security. This will give both the employee's and the employer's contribution.

(*i*) Pension contributions by the employer vary with the scheme accepted by the firm. In this case we will imagine that the employer pays £5 per week for staff who are not required to contribute (Mr Bellinger) and three times the employee's contribution for those who do pay contributions (Mr Brown and Miss Murray). These entries will go in line H of the 'employer's contributions' section.

5. Take the three sets of figures for wages actually payable and make out a 'notes and coins' summary from them so that the correct amounts can be drawn from the bank. Your summary should be made out as follows:

	£10	£5	£1	50p	10p	2p	1p
Mr Bellinger							
Mr Brown							
Miss Murray							
Total needed							

Assignment No. 6: An Alphabetical Index (Storage and Information)

In this assignment you are asked to prepare 20 address 'cards' for a card index, in the way explained below. You will then put them into correct alphabetical order.

1. First take 3 sheets of A4 bond paper. Fold them in half, then in half again and then in half again. Each page is now divided into 8 pieces making 24 pieces altogether. Cut these up.

2. Now take any magazine or newspaper. Working through carefully select those advertisers who give names and addresses. Copy out the name, address and, if possible, telephone number of each advertiser on to one of your slips of paper. You will find that local advertisers in local magazines and papers give names and addresses more frequently than the national advertisers in the national press. Write the names and addresses fairly low down on the 'page', leaving the top margin free. Repeat this until you have 20 names and addresses. Four pieces will then be left as spares.

3. Looking at your pack decide on each name which is the correct first-indexing unit (see pages 190–1) of the name appearing on each card. Underline this first-indexing unit in each case. Present them to your lecturer or teacher and ask for confirmation that you have selected the correct first indexing unit in each case.

4. Now print the name recorded on each card in correct style along the top margin of the card. Thus a card with the address

The Oscar Lightfoot Trading Co. Ltd
24 Deansway
Holchester
Kent
(Holchester 612)

would be printed along the index as follows.

Lightfoot Trading Co. Ltd, The Oscar

5. Now consider whether any of your cards could be looked up in any other way, so that a person might look them up differently. In the example given above, some people might look up the firm under 'Oscar'. If so, use one of your spare papers to make a cross-reference card. Just print this card along the margin only, e.g.

Oscar Lightfoot Trading Co. Ltd, The
(See Lightfoot Trading Co.)

6. Now arrange the cards in alphabetical order, including any cross-reference cards in their correct place. Secure them with a paper clip.
7. Now make an 'out' card which will stick up above the other cards to show where a card has been removed. For this you need a piece of coloured thin card. You can make one from any piece of scrap card. It needs to be the same width as your other pieces of paper, but slightly deeper. Cut the top of the card so that it sticks up above the other cards with a tab which says 'out' (see page 186, Fig. 12.9).
8. Present your set of 'cards' and 'out' marker for assessment by your teacher. Keep them in your assignments folder in an envelope bearing your name, class or course group, and the heading as shown at the start of this assignment. Date the envelope with today's date.

Assignment No. 7: Registered Letters and Postal Orders (*Methods of Payment*)
In this assignment you are asked to answer a range of questions on registered letters and postal orders. Please number the answers you give in the same way as the questions are numbered. You need *not* copy out the questions. You will need to refer to a current edition of the *Post Office Guide*.

1. Take a sheet of A4 paper, and head it with your full name, class or group, and today's date. Then write the assignment heading, shown above. Now answer this question: 'What is a registered letter service? Explain how the system works.'
2. A registered parcel has been wrapped in strong brown paper, and then tied with string. The knots of the string have been sealed with sealing wax. No gummed paper or cellulose tape has been used before the string was tied round. Is the parcel acceptable for registration? Give your reasons.
3. What sizes of registered letter are sold by the Post Office? Give the code letter of each envelope and its measurements.
4. What are the regulations about banknotes sent by registered post as far as compensation is concerned?
5. What is meant by the term 'advice of delivery' as far as registered post is concerned?
6. What values of postal orders are issued by the Post Office, and what poundage fee is charged?
7. You are about to pay a small account through the post by a postal order. What should you do to (*a*) the order and (*b*) the counterfoil before you send the payment off?
8. Give in the sheet or sheets with your answers to these questions for assessment.

Assignment No. 8: The Reception of Visitors (*Communication*)
In this assignment you are asked to answer certain questions about the reception of visitors. The end of the assignment consists of an imaginary series of incidents

in a reception office. These can be acted out by members of your class in a role-playing manner with the receptionist answering in any way he/she likes where this is indicated by the line of dots. The rest of the class, and the teacher, will assess the performance and suggest improvements.

1. Take a sheet of A4 paper and head it with the details of this assignment and with your own name and class group. Date the page with today's date.

2. A girl of 16 applies to your office for a post as receptionist. She says in her letter that she has no experience in business and has been doing a Home Economics option at her school. Suggest reasons why she would not prove suitable for such a post at this stage of her career.

3. Receptionists usually perform other work as well as their reception duties. What types of work might a receptionist undertake in the intervals between the arrival of visitors?

4. Rule up a suitable page for a reception register. Record on it the names of three visitors; the firms they are employed by (if applicable); who they came to see in your building and any other details you consider necessary.

5. Write the phrase 'Assessment of role-playing situation' on your paper and hand it to your lecturer or teacher while the class or group acts out the following series of visits to an imaginary reception office. Study the text for a few moments and decide what your answers will be:

Visitor No. 1: Good morning. My name is Larch. I believe you are expecting me. I am a little early though.

Receptionist: Oh yes. You are to see Mr Turner, our chief buyer. Just one moment while I telephone his secretary. (Lifting telephone): Is that you, Mary. Mr Turner's visitor has arrived. He is a little early. — — — — — Yes, all right. If you'll come down to collect Mr Larch I'll ask him to wait in the small reception room.

Receptionist: ....

(and she shows him into the small reception room)

Visitor No. 2: I say, Miss, can you help? There's one of your drivers collapsed in the yard. A couple of chaps are picking him up but he looks pretty bad.

Receptionist: ....

Visitor No. 3: Good morning. I am Detective Sergeant Brown, CID. I've called to see your security officer, Mr Peters is the name, I believe.

Receptionist: Yes, that is correct. Have you some identification on you? (He shows his warrant card.) Thank you. Is Mr Peters expecting you?

Visitor No. 3: No, it's an urgent matter. If he's not available I'd better see his deputy.

Receptionist: ....

Assignment No. 9: The Ink Stencil Duplicator (Office Machinery)

1. Read pages 147–55, which deal with ink stencil duplicators. Look at Figs 11.4–11.8 in particular.

2. Obtain and inspect closely an unused stencil for the ink stencil duplicator. Notice the quality of the surface, the method for fixing it to the duplicator, the carbon paper interleaved with the stencil and which way round it is fitted.

3. If permitted to do so you may use the stencil for preparing an actual piece of reprographic work. If you are a typist you may be able to obtain a commission for a piece of work, from a teacher or lecturer, or from the Students' Society

or some other organisation. If you are not a typist it may be possible to use the stencil to rule up a couple of useful forms for use in office practice lessons— for example, a blank invoice and a blank circulation slip similar to those shown on pages 318 and 90.

4. Test read the stencil and correct any errors on it. This is a most important practical point. If a stencil has an error on it, the error can be corrected quite easily. If it is used to print 300 copies each copy will need correcting for every error on it; three errors means 900 corrections. Never hurry over a stencil—a perfect stencil means perfect copies.

If it is not possible to make up a stencil of your own, use a stored stencil from some previous piece of work. (*Lecturers and teachers should accumulate a stock of these for use with this assignment. Most reprographic departments will retain suitable stencils which are no longer required and make them available.*)

5. Obtain instruction in the use of the ink stencil duplicator, particularly with regard to correct positioning of the stencil on the machine. Test run a copy to see how the text is positioned on the copy paper, and adjust if necessary.

6. Run off a suitable batch of copies so that you appreciate possible difficulties, such as copies failing to separate from the stencil.

7. Obtain instruction in replenishing the ink supply, and make sure you understand how the ink circulates so that it finally forces its way through the holes in the stencil paper to produce a copy. Write a short account of this for your assignment, entitled 'How the Ink Stencil Duplicator Works'.

8. Your final assignment should consist of:

(*a*) A short written passage: How the Ink Stencil Duplicator Works.

(*b*) The best copy you produced, with any errors which you allowed to pass through by careless checking corrected in red.

(*c*) The worst copy produced, with an explanation at the foot of the page explaining what caused the poor copy quality.

Assignment No. 10: Telex Messages (*Communications*)

1. Read pages 333–4 about the telex system and page 345 about the telex directory.

2. The telex message shown in Fig. A.1 (overleaf) came in overnight. Study it to make sure you understand the various parts of the message. Head a sheet of A4 paper with your name, group and the heading of this assignment. Then write a short explanation of what you would do with this message which is still attached to the telex machine.

3. You are concerned about the safe arrival at destination of two parcels sent to the Yamamota Corporation, Asahikawa, Hokkaido, Japan. Make up a telex message to your Tokyo agent asking him to trace the parcels (Invoice No. 7278) shipped by ss *Tokyo Maru*, which docked in Tokyo three weeks ago. Ask him to contact Yamamota Corporation on Extension 299 to tell their purchasing officer D. Otemachi the exact position. Stress the essential nature of the consignment and insist that he expedites delivery, by air if necessary, to Hokkaido. Your Tokyo agent's code is 21790 Japco J and yours is 81539 CBTSBG. Use today's date and it is the 32nd message today (SRL32). Your personal contact at the agents is T. Kyowa. Use your own first name and surname as a signature. Copy this message out, preferably on a special telex message pad if one is available in your model office. If not, use a separate piece of paper. Give in this message form with the A4 title sheet, for assessment.

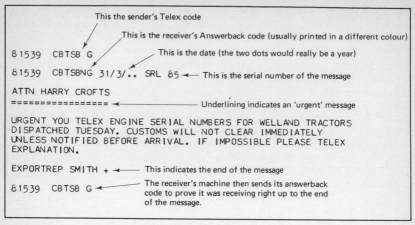

Fig. A.1. A telex message.

Assignment No. 11: Terms Used in Commercial Transactions (Office Procedures)

1. Read the list of terms given at the end of this assignment in the passage headed 'Terms in Common Use in Offices'.
2. Using a sheet of scrap paper arrange them in alphabetical order.
3. By referring to this textbook, and any other reference books you may need, find out the exact meaning of each term and write a short explanation of it —between three lines and eight lines long for each term.
4. Write out, or type out, in alphabetical order, the list of terms with the definitions and explanations you have discovered.

Terms in Common Use in Offices: 1. Imprest system. 2. Computer print-out. 3. Cash discount. 4. Aligned documentation. 5. Chronological order. 6. DDP. 7. Direct debit. 8. Goodwill. 9. Justified right-hand margin. 10. Terms net, prompt settlement.

Assignment No. 12: The Credit Transfer System (Methods of Payment)

1. In this assignment you have to make sure you understand the credit transfer system, and can prepare a set of credit transfer slips, etc., for processing by the bank.
2. Read the relevant parts of pages 239–40 and 262 in this textbook.
3. Study Fig. A.2 which illustrates a typical credit transfer slip.
4. You work for Lewis Electrics Ltd and their main Pay-Roll Headings are as follows: Name of Employee, Employee's Branch and Code No., Employee's Account, Employee's Account No., and Amount Payable.
5. Draw up a pay-roll sheet on A4 paper with the headings given above. Enter the following five sets of details on the pay-roll, and add up the grand total:

T. and J. Wright — Midland Chesterton 40–16–07
G. Brown — Barclays Chesterton 20–17–35
M. Pearson — Lloyds Chesterton 30–91–95
R. and S. Patel — Nat-West Cambridge 52–10–45
V. and W. Greenslade — Midland Cambridge 40–16–08

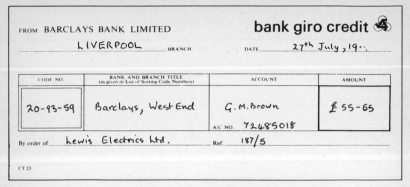

Fig. A.2. A credit transfer slip.

(details continued)

T. and J. Wright	51872094	£394.27
G. Brown	31627876	£136.45
M. Pearson	81592728	£162.95
R. and S. Patel	41357260	£428.67
V. and W. Greenslade	47982466	£513.85

6. You now need five credit transfer slips. If you have a supply available in your school or college model office you may take these from stock. If stocks are not available draw up five slips of paper as shown in Fig. A.2 and fill them in with the details given above, so that a slip can be sent to each bank which needs to be informed.

7. Check your total again by adding up the five slips, preferably using an adding-listing machine or an electronic printing calculator.

8. Now write a model cheque for the total amount. You may do this on a blank cheque from your model office if a supply is available; if not draw one up similar to the one shown on page 248. Make the cheque payable to Barclays Bank Ltd for the full value of the wages to be paid, using today's date.

9. Your final assignment should consist of a pay-roll sheet, five credit transfer slips and a cheque. Write your name and class at the foot of the pay-roll sheet for identification purposes. Clip the assignment together with a stapling machine.

Assignment No. 13: The Requisitioning of Stock (Materials and Stationery—their Use and Control)

1. Your office supervisor has decided to appoint you as the stationery clerk, starting from next week. She has stated that the chief aim is to develop a more satisfactory system than the existing one, in which the petty cashier has the keys to the stationery store and gives out stationery as and when required. She proposes that you should replace this by a system which gives out the majority of stationery required on Monday afternoons (**requisitions** must be put in by 12 noon on Mondays). To cover possible emergency requirements an **emergency requisition** may be put in before 9.30 any day, and you will give out the stationery before 10.30.

2. To enable the system to start at once she asks you to draw up two forms, headed 'Stationery Requisition' and 'Emergency Stationery Requisition'. The details to be included are as follows:

(*a*) The heading.
(*b*) Simple instructions asking staff to give them in before the times mentioned in (1) above.
(*c*) A special note on the Emergency Form asking people to keep its use to an absolute minimum and think ahead when ordering stationery.
(*d*) A subheading at the top of 12 ruled lines reading 'Please supply the following stationery:'.
(*e*) 12 ruled lines headed

Item   No. Required   Ref. No. if known   Any other details

(*f*) A section to make sure you know who wants it and where they are. It should contain the following information:

Requested by ...... Room ...... Building ...... Telephone. ...... Date requested ......
Signature of person requesting ...... Date supplied ......

3. Your supervisor also states that she wishes you to be able to tell how much stationery has been supplied to each member of staff, with a view to detecting any excessive use of stationery. Consider how this could be achieved and write a short report of about ten to fifteen lines on the matter for your supervisor, Thelma Wright.

Assignment No. 14: Preparing an Index for a Publication (*Storage of Information*)

1. You work for a publishing house as the secretary to an editor of educational books. An author has recently supplied a small textbook entitled 'International Trade'. It is the author's duty to supply an index for the book, but he is taken seriously ill and the editor asks if you would be prepared to draw up an index instead. The agreed fee is to be £40. The task is made easier for you, because it is the firm's policy to underline all important new topics with a thick line when they are first mentioned in the text and these words form the basis for the index. This has already been done.
2. The index is in the following style.

Index
   A
   American regulations,
      dangerous goods,
      inter-state,
      marine,
   Annual shipments,

First each section of the index is headed with a capital letter, *A*, *B*, etc. Each word or phrase then begins with a capital letter, but small letters are used for any subdivisions under the main word. There is a comma after every phrase, where the page numbers will appear, but these are not known at present as the type has not been set.
3. The words underlined are given in a list at the end of this assignment. You will find it best to do a rough copy first (by putting down all the letters of

the alphabet on a large sheet of paper and fitting the words in under the letters as best you can, in the correct order).
4. Then write out a list in two columns, like the Index in this textbook. You may type this final list if you prefer.
5. Give in your assignment with a cover page bearing your name and the title of this assignment. Clip the index on to it.
The word list is as follows:

Balance of payments, account sales, general agreement on tariffs and trade, CIM consignment note, frustration of contract, lien of carrier, necessity, consequential loss insurance, floating currency, loading broker, perils, bareboat charter, indemnity, pilfering, average adjuster, London acceptance credit, customs duty, imports, Lloyd's A1, European Community. T. forms, Hague–Visby rules, letter of hypothecation, quotation, utmost good faith, irrevocable credits, subrogation, transit form, clauses: AR, clauses: change of voyage, J policy, options, insurance, Queen's enemies, documentary letters of credit, underwriters, air waybill, with average policies, visible trade, Incoterms 1980, double indemnity, European Community: EUR forms, groupage, bills of exchange, York–Antwerp rules, break-points, complaints, free alongside ship, inherent vice, ex gratia payments, red line clauses.

Assignment No. 15: Vacher's Parliamentary Companion (*Reference Books*)
1. Your firm, Antarctic Water Co. Ltd of Milford Haven, Dyfed, Wales, has developed a revolutionary method of preserving icebergs by spraying them with plastic foam. This reduces the rate at which they thaw, and makes it possible to tow them to places short of water. You wish to give a demonstration at the port of Milford Haven to show this idea to interested MPs and representatives of the Ministry of Overseas Development. To do this you propose to tow over an Arctic iceberg (it would be too far to tow an Antarctic one).
2. Obtain a copy of *Vacher's Parliamentary Companion* from the library or Model Office. From this Companion, find the names and addresses of the following, who are either known to be interested or are invited as a matter of courtesy.

(*a*) The Prime Minister.
(*b*) The MPs for Pembroke and Carmarthen.
(*c*) The MP for Bristol South-East.
(*d*) The Heads of five Departments or Divisions of the Ministry for Overseas Development which would in your opinion be most likely to be interested in water supplies for developing countries. Make a note against their names of the posts they hold which lead you to conclude that they would be interested.
(*f*) Finally draft a letter to be sent to all these people inviting them to the demonstration. The group will meet at the Lord Nelson Hotel, for lunch at 12.30, and will be taken from there to the port and by sea to the place where the iceberg is to be anchored. Warn them that they will be landing on the iceberg, and protective clothing will be supplied. Overnight accommodation will be provided at the hotel. Make up your own date (two months ahead) as it is necessary to catch the iceberg first.

(3) Your assignment will therefore consist of a list of names, addresses and positions held, and a neatly written (or typed) draft of the letter you propose to send.

Assignment No. 16: The P45 Wages Form (Wages and Salaries)

1. In this assignment you have to concentrate your attention upon the P45 Wages Form, but it is not possible to obtain copies of the form for use in schools and colleges as it is an important tax document which can only be reproduced with the permission of the Controller of HM Stationery Office.
2. First read the section about the P45 form on page 272 of this textbook.
3. Now look carefully at the illustration of the form on page 271, studying each box carefully.
4. Take a sheet of A4 paper and write your name and class or group upon it. Head the page with the title of this assignment and then answer the following questions, beginning a new line for each question. You do not need to copy the question out, just put the number and the answer. As full an answer as possible is advisable for this consignment.

Questionnaire on the P45 form

(i) When is a P45 made out?
(ii) Who makes the P45 out?
(iii) Where does the top copy go?
(iv) If the employee is still alive what happens to copy number 2 and 3?
(v) If the employee has died what happens to copies 2 and 3?
(vi) What is the purpose of a P45 in the tax system? (This may take two or three sentences to explain.)
(vii) Why do you think the employer is required to 'certify' that the information given on the form in parts 1–9 is correct?
(viii) Why do the Tax Office need to be informed when an employee has died?

5. Give in your answer sheet for assessment.

Assignment No. 17: Adding-Listing Machines (Office Machinery)

1. Read pages 202–3 about adding machines and calculators.
2. Look at Plates 16 and 17 (page 204).
3. In this assignment you have to prepare a set of 10 invoices, and 'batch them up' for accounting purposes into a batch of invoices with adding-list total attached. If they are available, you may use blank invoices from the model office store made available by your teacher or lecturer. If blank invoices are not available take five sheets of A4 paper, cut them in half to give 10 pieces of A5 paper, and use these 10 pieces to draw a blank invoice, of a very simple type, using page 318 as a guide.
4. From any telephone directory select the names and addresses of 10 firms. Write (or type if you prefer) these names and addresses on the 10 invoice blanks you have prepared. On each invoice write *one* of the lines given below, so that each invoice has some details of goods supplied, and the VAT on them. The ten entries are as follows:

	No.	Description	Net value	VAT	Total
(a)		1 Typewriter	£256.00	£20.48	£276.48
(b)		2 Copies *The War at Sea* (£5.50)	£11.00	—	£11.00
(c)		1 Gas cooker	£145.00	£11.60	£156.60

No.		Description	Net value	VAT	Total
(d)	20	Reams A4 Bond paper (£1.55)	£31.00	£2.48	£33.48
(e)	4	Floating mowers (£14.60)	£58.40	£4.67	£63.07
(f)	3	Electric irons (£9.40)	£28.20	£3.53	£31.73
(g)	1	Photocopier	£169.50	£13.56	£183.06
(h)	1	Rubber stamp tidy	£3.58	£0.29	£3.87
(i)	10	Packs staples (£0.85)	£8.50	£0.68	£9.18
(j)	500	Jiffy bags (3p each)	£15.00	£1.20	£16.20

5. Using either an adding-listing machine or an electronic printing calculator, and using the invoices and not this textbook, check that the net value on each invoice when added to the VAT gives the total figure shown on the invoice. Tick each invoice in the bottom right-hand corner when you have found it to be correct.

6. Now use the add-lister or the printing calculator to add up the ten 'Net values' (turning the invoices over in turn as you record the figure shown). Repeat this with the ten 'VAT' amounts, and do the same with the ten 'Total' figures. You now have three lists, giving three grand totals.

7. Check that the grand total of 'Net values' + the grand total of 'VAT' = the grand total of 'Totals'.

8. Write your name, course, etc., on a sheet of A4 paper and staple to it the three lists from the adding machine, so that each is clearly visible. Place this name sheet on top of the batch of invoices and staple all of them together in the top left-hand corner. Now give your assignment in for assessment.

Assignment No. 18: Switchboard Assistant (Communications)

This assignment is not an easy one to carry out, since it involves the cooperation of the school or college switchboard staff. It may also involve missing some of your office practice lessons, and this is not always a good thing. If your teacher or lecturer can make the necessary arrangements it is a useful assignment. The idea is that you spend at least one hour, and preferably longer, assisting the switchboard operator. This involves being a general 'Man Friday' or 'Girl Friday'. Man Friday was, of course, Robinson Crusoe's native companion on the island where he was shipwrecked. In modern terms the name is used for a person who is generally helpful whatever is going on. Since receptionists often do many other things besides answering the telephone—particularly running messages, duplicating, stuffing envelopes and routine work of this type —it is very useful for them to have a 'Friday-person' to help them. Never disparage such activities or regard them as lowly activities. They are essential to the success of the firm and every top executive has done them at some time. A managing director who is able to say to the telephonist 'All right, I'll mind the switchboard—you cut off and see the cashier about your holiday-money, but get back as quick as you can' will gain respect, not lose it. Another point is that the switchboard is the focal point of modern offices. You will learn more about how a school or college is run in the reception office than anywhere else in the building.

1. The assignment consists in assisting the switchboard operator or receptionist. If the receptionist is not too busy you may be able to learn how to use the

switchboard and to listen in to the conversations between the receptionist and the extensions. If this is not possible because the time you are there is particularly busy you will still learn a great deal.

2. To earn a grading for this assignment write a short account of the things you did during the time you were in the reception office or switchboard room. Include any messages you ran, or other help you gave to the receptionist. Explain what type of switchboard was in use, and how it worked. You may find pages 69–82 helpful here.

Assignment No. 19: Export Documentation (*Office Procedures*)

1. An export consignment of heavy motor vehicles destined for the Australian Land Survey Bureau, Australian National University, Canberra, Australia, is to be shipped to Australia by British Leyland. The goods will be carried by Great Container Lines, and have to be fully documented.

2. Draw up a list of documents you consider will be necessary, to cover the following points:

(a) The sale of the motor vehicles to ANU.

(b) Their delivery to the ship's side at Liverpool.

(c) Notification to the port of their movement to the ship.

(d) Their passage through Customs at Liverpool.

(e) Their insurance on the sea voyage.

(f) Their acceptance on board ship by the master of the vessel.

(g) Their proof to the Australian authorities that the goods are British made.

(h) Their release to the Survey Bureau in Australia on 'documents against acceptance' terms.

3. Write a short explanation of each of these documents, showing the part it plays in ensuring that everyone concerned is fully informed about the consignment.

4. Explain how SITPRO documentation would help in such an involved transaction.

Assignment No. 20: Banker's Standing Orders (*Methods of Payment*)

1. For this assignment you require four copies of a Banker's Standing Order Form like the one shown in Fig. A.3. If these are available from your model office stock you may use them from stock. If not, make a supply using either the spirit duplicator, the ink stencil duplicator or some other reprographic method.

2. Your firm pays two sums of money by standing order through the Cambridge Branch of Midland Bank Ltd. The details are given below. You are asked to complete two blank forms with the details supplied, keeping a carbon copy of each for your own records.

3. Since your firm pursues a policy of requiring cheques and other payment orders to be signed by two people, you are asked to sign in the capacity of cashier, on both the top copy and the carbon copy of each order. Ask your lecturer or teacher to sign as 'Director'.

4. Since your firm has a sophisticated 'cash flow' analysis which will be affected by these payments you are also to write a memo to the Accountant notifying him of the two payments, the dates on which the first payment will be made and the intervals at which the standing orders are payable. You may use a memo form from stock if a supply is available.

BANKER'S ORDER FORM

Standing Order

To   <u>Midland Bank Ltd.</u>

Monthly ☐   Quarterly ☐

Annually ☐

(Please tick as required)

Branch _____

Date _____

Please make payments and debit my/our account in accordance with the details below

Bank _____

Branch _____

Sorting code number _____

For Account of _____

Account number _____

Amount payable (in figures) _____

Amount payable (in words) _____

_____

First Payment to be made on _____ and at intervals as shown above

Last payment to be made on _____ (if no final payment date write 'indefinitely')

Please complete if appropriate:

This order cancels our existing order for_____ per_____

(Signed)   (1)_____(Cashier)

(2)_____(Director)

Fig. A.3. A banker's order form.

5. After completing the assignment give it in clipped together with a sheet of A4 paper, headed with your name, class or group, and the title of this assignment. It will therefore consist of the title sheet, two Banker's Orders with duplicate copies, and a memo for the Accountant.

6. The details of the orders are as follows:

(*a*) A. S. Kerswill and Co. Ltd, Leeder House, Erskine Rd, London, NW3. They bank with Midland Bank Ltd at the Queen Victoria St branch whose sorting code number is 40:05:34. A. S. Kerswill's bank account is number 60498521 and the payment is for £9.25 which covers the subscription rate for *Vacher's Parliamentary Companion* (£4.00) and *Vacher's European Companion* (£5.25). It is to be paid annually, indefinitely, and the first payment is to be next Monday. No previous order exists for these reference books.

(*b*) United Camside Finance Co. Ltd, 24 Union St, Cambridge. They bank with Barclays Bank Ltd, Chesterton Branch, and the sorting code is 20:17:35. Their account number is 19254866 and the amount payable is £42.50 (payable monthly). First payment is to be made on the first day of next month and the last payment on the first day of this month, five years from now. No previous order has existed.

Assignment No. 21: The Control of Equipment (Materials and Stationery)

1. In this assignment you have to draw up an inventory sheet for the room in which you learn your office practice. An inventory is a list of items in the room. It can be used to control the equipment and record any additions or reductions, and explain what caused them to be written off. The usual thing is to have a sheet of paper or thin card in a loose-leaf folder or file, ruled with suitable headings, such as the following:

Item of equipment (with reference nos if necessary)	No. of items in stock on -------	Additions	Reductions (with reason)	No. of items in stock on -------

Suppose that a lecturer or teacher takes over the classroom in September this year. He/she would check the inventory and record the items of equipment available, including reference numbers of such items as typewriters, etc. Any new equipment supplied by the Education Committee during the term would be noted on its arrival, and any equipment transferred to the care of other staff, or removed because of breakages, etc., would similarly be noted down on the day it was removed. Usually breakages must be reported to the managers or governors who take official note of the losses or damage suffered.

2. Draw up such a list, with the appropriate headings, and enter on it all the equipment in the room: desks, chairs, tables, typewriters (if any), pictures, reference books, office equipment, etc. Record the reference numbers of items likely to be stolen, since these can often assist police with their enquiries.

3. At the end of the year, the list will be checked again, and any shortages must be reported. If the inventory is satisfactory it will be filed away until the next session begins. However, when this new session begins there should be no major changes in the inventory since the end of the previous session and it would be time-wasting to draw up the list all over again. It is usual therefore to use a narrow half-page, which is inserted in the loose-leaf file so that the new session's records only carry on from the previous year. Such a page would be headed:

No. of items in stock on -------	Additions	Reductions (with reason)	No. of items in stock on -------

4. Prepare four such half-pages to fit over your main inventory sheet. Place them on top of the inventory and punch holes in the collection with a two-hole punch. Use treasury tags to secure them together. Write your name and group on the top sheet of these half-sheet pages, and give the inventory in for assessment.

Assignment No. 22: A Tickler System (Storage of Information)
1. Read pages 179–80 about the Tickler system. Study Fig. 12.6.
2. Now obtain a small cardboard box, such as a shoebox, and enough thin card to make 31 daily cards and 12 monthly cards. This may take some time to collect, but such waste packets as cereal packets, sweet boxes, etc., can quite easily provide adequate material for a tickler system.
3. The series of activities listed below are to be performed at certain times in the month, and at certain times in the year. Record these on the appropriate cards and you will soon see how the system works.
4. *Activities performed at monthly intervals. (Record on the daily cards on the date shown.)*
On 7th of each month review stationery supplies.
On 10th of each month pay accounts payable.
On 15th of each month review representatives' expenses and send cheques.
On 20th of each month review sales activity in each department and consider any adjustments.
On 28th of each month do monthly salaries.
On last day of each month send off PAYE Inland Revenue cheque for PAYE deducted.
5. *Activities performed at longer intervals. (Record on the monthly cards, on the month shown.)*
(*a*) On March 24th, June 24th, September 24th and December 20th do VAT returns up to the end of the previous month.
(*b*) In April do Inland Revenue returns for financial year ending on March 31st.
(*c*) In January and June review wages paid and give merit rises, promotions, etc.
(*d*) In February and August review insurance policies and adequacy of cover.
(*e*) In first week of July, October and January do quarter's final accounts and compare with results of same quarter in previous five-year period. Update statistics with the present results.
(*f*) On March 15th, June 15th, September 15th and December 15th do cash-flow budgets for six-month period ahead, and consider whether there is room for any 'cash-flow' smoothing activities.
6. The assignment is to be graded on the basis of its efficiency as a system. Present your tray of cards, fully marked up with the item shown and a short written account of the system which begins 'To use the tickler system I start on January 1st with the 12 monthly cards and the 31 daily cards in correct order.' (Then explain how the system is used.)

Assignment No. 23: The Education Authorities Directory *(Reference Books)*
1. You have been asked to conduct a sample survey about one of your firm's products, which is a piece of educational equipment. The enquiry is to be conducted at various levels. United Kingdom students are advised to proceed as

follows, using the *Education Authorities Directory*. Overseas students should adapt the assignment to fit their own national system.

2. The enquiry is to be conducted with a selected group of education authorities, which will be picked at random from the following groups:

(*a*) One Greater London education authority (there are 21 to choose from, including Inner London).

(*b*) One Greater Manchester authority (there are 10).

(*c*) One authority from the other major metropolitan areas (there are 26 in the areas of Merseyside, South Yorkshire, Tyne and Wear, West Midlands and West Yorkshire).

(*d*) Three English County Council Authorities (there are 43).

(*e*) One Welsh County Council (there are eight).

(*f*) One Regional Council from Scotland (there are 12, counting the three 'Island' authorities).

(*g*) One Northern Ireland authority.

Select your authorities as explained in 3 below.

3. To select the authorities at random start with group (*a*). Write the 21 names of the authorities (you will find them in the Directory) on small pieces of paper, all of the same size, one name on each. Put these in a hat, shake it up and ask a friend to draw one name out of the hat. This will be the Greater London Authority to be consulted. Repeat this with each of the groups (*b*) to (*g*).

4. Now find the name of the Chief Education Officer of the authorities selected, and the address of the Education Offices. Make sure to note his/her title, degrees, etc.

5. Now find the name of the Principal Supplies Officer, who will be chiefly interested in the product you propose to market. His name appears somewhere in the list of officials serving the authority.

6. Present your assignment in the following form:

(*a*) A list of the authorities selected, either typed or handwritten. This list should carry your own name and group for identification purposes.

(*b*) A second list, which carries not only the names of the authorities but under each authority the names of the two officers to whom letters are to be sent and the address of the authority.

Assignment No. 24: Post Office Postal Services (Communication)

1. In this assignment you need to use the *Post Office Guide*, and the *Inland Compendium on Postal Rates* which is issued with the Guide. You should also look at a Supplement to the Guide. These are issued free to those who buy a Guide and complete the post card (supplement request form) included in it.

2. Your school or college office is about to send out some examination certificates to former students who were successful in their examinations in the previous academic year. It is a policy to send these Recorded Delivery by first-class post, and also to complete an Advice of Delivery form which is obtainable at any Post Office. Read up about Recorded Delivery and Advice of Delivery in your copy of the Guide.

3. Where a student has to be sent only one certificate the weight of the letter is found to be 72 grams. Where there are two certificates the weight is 112 grams and three certificates weigh 152 grams. There are 72 single certificates,

13 double certificates and three students have to be sent three certificates. You are asked to work out from the inland postal rates compendium how much in stamps must be put on each of these envelopes, including the Recorded Delivery charge.
4. Now find the total postage involved to post all the letters, the amount to be put on each Advice of Delivery form and the total cost altogether for both the letters and the Advice of Delivery forms.
5. If you have a supply of imitation Recorded Delivery slips and Advice of Delivery forms complete one of each addressed to an imaginary address in your local area.
6. Look at a supplement to the *Post Office Guide*. Notice that the supplement is printed on one side of the paper only. What do you think is the reason for this? Write a short explanation.
7. Give in your assignment, which should consist of your list of calculations for parts 3 and 4 above, your completed Recorded Delivery and Advice of Delivery slips, and an explanation about the supplement.

Assignment No. 25: Arranging Your Assignment Folder for Assessment (Storage and Information)

As your course draws to a close you will be asked to arrange your Assignment Folder in good order ready for assessment by your local examiner. A small proportion of the folders will also be called for by the examinations board so that they can ensure that the standard achieved is a fair one. It is therefore important to submit your assignment folder in good order. This last assignment will help you do that.

1. Your assignment folder should be a simple, lightweight folder which provides some means of securing papers. Heavy-duty lever-arch files or ring binders should not be used. They are too expensive to post and too bulky to carry about, since examiners may have several hundred to attend to.
2. No other work but assignment work should be included in the folder. All course work, homework, etc., should be kept quite separate in a course folder or heavy-duty files, and no material of this sort should be sent in when assignment folders are called for by examining boards.
3. Assignments have to be collected into a suitable order based on a specific filing system. You have no doubt studied several such systems during the last year. The most obvious methods are as follows:

(*a*) *Chronological order*. Here you would arrange the assignments in date order, according to when you did them.
(*b*) *Syllabus order*. Here you would arrange them in the order that they are given in the syllabus. Most syllabuses have the assignment topics listed in numerical order, and you are expected to do an assignment on one of the aspects of the work included in each of these numbered groups. This syllabus order might therefore also appear to be a numerical order.
(*c*) *Subject order*. You will have covered several different subjects in these assignments. For example, you may have done an assignment on Spirit Duplicating or Xerography. You could arrange your assignments in alphabetical order of subjects.

4. Whichever order you decide to use you must write a short account of the method of filing you have chosen and why you chose this particular method.

5. You are also expected to include cross-reference pages—for example, an assignment on Typewriters comes in the Office Machinery section of the syllabus. If you file the assignment under T for Typewriters you might like to have a cross-reference page headed 'Office Machinery—see Typewriters'.
6. You should also note that in most examinations you have to score at least half marks on the assignment section to pass. If you give your folder in for assessment and it scores less than half marks you cannot have another try and re-submit it under the rules. This means you should make a really splendid effort first time. Your class-mates may criticise it for you and suggest ways of improving it before you submit it, but of course the work done to improve it must be yours alone.

Model Office Requirements

If pupils or students are to perform these assignments with a minimum of teacher/lecturer guidance the following items should be available in the model office.

Documents
    Credit transfer slips (see page 363)
    Telephone message forms (see page 77)
    Invoices (see page 318)
    Pay-roll sheets headed as suggested in Assignment 12 (4)
    Blank cheques
    Recorded delivery slips (see page 104)
    Parcel proof of posting slips (see *Post Office Guide*)
    Banker's order forms (see page 369)
    Memo slips (see page 35)
    Kalamazoo wages materials (see page 263)
    Telex message pads (obtainable from the Post Office—see Telex Directory)

Equipment
    Spirit duplicator (hand model or electric model)
    Model telephone set
    Adding-listing machine or electronic printing calculator
    Stapling machine. Ink stencil storage box

Reference Books
    The *Post Office Guide*, including the *Inland Postal Rates Compendium*, the *Overseas Postal Rates Compendium* and at least one *Supplement*
    Commerce Made Simple
    Vacher's Parliamentary Companion
    The *Education Authorities Directory*
    The *Employer's Guide to National Insurance Contributions*
    The STD code book for the area
    The local telephone directory
    The Telex Directory (the Post Office will give away out-of-date copies which are adequate for training purposes)
    Tax Tables (obtainable from the Inland Revenue local office)

Materials

Carbon paper, spirit duplicator master paper, hecto transfer paper, spirit run-off paper, ink duplicator stencils, correcting fluid.

Note

Even imitation documents—such as blank cheques—can be misused at times. It is essential for staff to draw the attention of students and trainees to the need for honesty and integrity at all times where documents are concerned. The dire consequences, both in law and from the career point of view, should be emphasised.

Index

384

Index